PERSONAL TAXATION

Finance Act 2013

ATT

Study Text

In this edition

- Plenty of **exam focus points** to ensure you focus on the exams you will be facing in 2014

- A **question and answer bank** including preparatory and exam standard short and long form questions and pilot paper questions for this paper. Marking schemes have been added to some of the answers so that you can gauge how well you are doing

- A **general index**

- **Thorough** and **reliable** updating for **Finance Act 2013** with changes highlighted in the text

FOR EXAMS IN MAY AND NOVEMBER 2014

BPP
LEARNING MEDIA

Third edition September 2013
printed text ISBN 9781 4453 6773 6
e text ISBN 9781 4453 6811 5

British Library Cataloguing-in-Publication Data

A catalogue record for this book
is available from the British Library

Published by

BPP Learning Media Ltd
BPP House, Aldine Place
London W12 8AA

www.bpp.com/learningmedia

Printed in the United Kingdom by Ricoh
Ricoh House
Ullswater Crescent
Coulsdon
CR5 2HR

Your learning materials, published by BPP Learning
Media Ltd, are printed on paper obtained from
traceable, sustainable sources.

Every effort has been made to contact the copyright
holders of any material reproduced within this
publication. If any have been inadvertently overlooked,
BPP Learning Media will be pleased to make the
appropriate credits in any subsequent reprints or
editions.

We are grateful to the Association of Taxation
Technicians for permission to reproduce past
examination questions and model solutions.

Contents

Introduction

Chapters

Question and Answer bank

Index

Review form

A note about copyright

BPP LEARNING MEDIA

Using your ATT texts

The ATT texts aim to ensure your success in the 2014 exams.

Key features of this text include:

- **Exam focus points** to help ensure you focus your efforts on the exams you will be facing in 2014.

- Changes introduced by the **Finance Act 2013** highlighted throughout the text. This enables you to identify material that may have changed since your previous studies.

- **Relevant legislative references** provided throughout the text. As you are permitted to take your legislation into the examination room, it is important that you develop the habit of looking up references in the legislation as you study. Publications taken into the examination must be bound copies. They can be **underlined, sidelined and highlighted. Annotating, use of 'post-its' and tagging is NOT allowed.**

- **Worked examples** throughout the text.

- **Chapter roundups** at the end of each chapter summarising the key points covered in the chapter.

- **Quizzes** at the end of each chapter designed to test your grasp of the principles explained. Solutions to the quiz follow immediately.

- **A separate short form and long form Question and Answer section**. At the end of the chapters there are short form and often also long form questions that you should attempt. Some of the long form questions are preparatory questions and others are exam standard. Some of the answers contain marking schemes which will help you gauge how well you are doing.

- A **general** index is included at the back of the text.

The examination papers

Overview of the examination structure

The examination

The ATT examination offers a choice from six free-standing Certificates of Competency in a modular structure. It is possible to take an examination in one topic only. This will lead to the award of a Certificate of Competency in that topic.

The certificate papers are:

1   Personal Taxation
2   Business Taxation & Accounting Principles
3   Business Compliance
4   Corporate Taxation
5   IHT, Trusts & Estates
6   VAT

Relevant tax administration and accounting issues are examinable in each paper.

The papers may be sat on a modular basis, ie they may be sat as and when the candidate decides.

There are also two E-Assessments: one in Professional Responsibilities & Ethics and one in Law. However, certain law and ethical issues may be also examined in the main papers where appropriate.

Certificates of Competency

A certificate will be valid for a three-year period but will be renewable for any number of further three-year periods.

Ethics and Law E-Assessments

Students must sit ATT E-Assessments in Professional Responsibilities & Ethics and in Law. Each E-Assessment lasts for one hour and is made up of 60 multiple choice questions, where the correct response must be identified from a choice of four, or multiple response questions, where several correct responses must be identified from a choice of up to six.

All questions have the same value towards the overall mark. Each E-Assessment is preceded by a short non-timed, non-scored tutorial for candidates to familiarise themselves with the computer testing environment.

Certificates of Competency are not available for success in the E-Assessments.

Professional Responsibilities & Ethics E-Assessment questions are set from the ATT and CIOT joint ethics manual, Professional Responsibilities and Ethics for Tax Practitioners, which is available for purchase directly from the ATT's website at www.att.org.uk.

The law questions are set from the ATT and CIOT joint law manual, Essential Law for Tax Practitioners, which is available for purchase directly from the ATT's website at www.att.org.uk.

Questions in the ATT's E-Assessments are drawn from the same question bank as the CIOT's E-Assessments. The questions for ATT and CIOT are of the same standard. There is no difference in terms of level or difficulty. Consequently, a pass in the ATT's Professional Responsibilities & Ethics E-Assessment qualifies for a credit for the Chartered Institute of Taxation (CIOT) E-Assessment in Professional Responsibilities & Ethics. A pass in the ATT's Law E-Assessment qualifies for a credit for the CIOT's E-Assessment in Law.

Examination pass mark

To pass a Certificate paper a candidate must achieve 50% of the total marks available.

To pass an E-Assessment a candidate must correctly answer 40 out of the 60 questions set.

Those who fail a paper will be permitted to re-sit any subsequent examination, provided that they submit an examination entry form and fee at each attempt and are registered as a student at the time of re-sitting.

Reference works and calculators for the examination

Pocket calculators (except those with an alpha-numeric keyboard) may be brought into the examination. Candidates are also allowed to bring into the examination room:

- Tolley's Yellow Tax Handbook and Orange Tax Handbook, or
- CCH Editions Ltd Tax Statutes and Instruments including the Index Volume, or
- HMSO copies of taxing statutes.

Publications brought into the examination must be bound copies. They can be underlined, sidelined and highlighted. Annotating, use of 'post its' and tagging is **not** allowed.

No other written material or calculation aid will be permitted.

Candidates will be provided with a sheet giving the tax rates and tables required for the examination.

Members

Membership can be applied for by those who:

- Hold, or are entitled to hold, three valid Certificates of Competency from Papers 1 to 6 (including the two compulsory papers – Personal Taxation and Business Taxation & Accounting Principles), **and**

- Have passed the separate ATT E-Assessments in Professional Responsibilities & Ethics and Law (or hold, or are entitled to hold, a valid Certificate of Competency from the old Practice Administration & Ethics paper), **and**

- Can demonstrate at least two years' acceptable current practical experience in UK taxation.

Format and syllabus of Certificate papers

Each Certificate paper is 3¼ hours in length. The first 15 minutes is designated as reading time. During this time you may read the question paper and legislation and annotate the question paper. You are not permitted to write in the answer folders or use a calculator. The Presiding Officer will inform you when you can start writing.

We recommend that you spend the reading time focusing on the long form questions to ensure that you have understood the requirements and which topics each question is testing. If relevant you could use some of the reading time to locate the legislation you feel you may need to refer to later when answering a particular question.

Questions will not be set which require knowledge of:

- Any statute receiving Royal Assent or any statutory instrument made less than five months before the examination date,

- With the exception of Inheritance Tax, any legislation repealed or suspended more than five months before the examination date,

- Any case reported less than three months before the examination date.

Questions may be set:

- On prospective legislation passed more than five months before the examination date even if it is not in force,

- On matters which are not specifically listed in the syllabus but which are related to topics within the syllabus (for example, accountancy principles for the computations of business income),

- On matters which require a knowledge of taxes which are not specifically within the syllabus of a particular paper but are within the syllabus as a whole.

Both the May and November 2014 examinations will be based on Finance Act 2013.

Certificate papers are a mixture of computational and written questions and no question choice. The short form questions carry marks of between two and four marks each and in total account for 40% of the available marks. There are therefore between 10 and 20 such questions in each paper. The remaining available marks are accounted for by between three and five longer questions carrying from 10 to 20 marks each. Law, ethics and accounting topics may be examined in the Certificate papers.

Law

The degree of law tested on each paper is determined by its relevance to that paper. You will need to purchase the latest edition of the ATT's manual 'Essential Law for Tax Practitioners' as this contains all of the law examinable in both the Certificate papers and the Law E-Assessment. The law topics examinable in each of the Certificate papers are included in the ATT's detailed syllabus.

Accounting

If you are sitting Papers 2, 3, 4 or 6 you will also need to purchase the latest edition of the ATT's manual 'Essential Accounting for Tax Practitioners' as this contains all of the accounting topics examinable in those Certificate papers. The accounting topics examinable in each of the Certificate papers are included in the ATT's detailed syllabus.

Ethics

You may also be examined on professional ethics in the Certificate papers. You will need to purchase the latest edition of the ATT's manual 'Professional Responsibilities and Ethics for Tax Practitioners' as this contains the examinable topics. In addition you must refer to the following document, which is available from the ATT's website:

- Continuing Professional Development Regulations and Guidance 2011

You can find a detailed syllabus on the ATT's website (www.att.org.uk). Click on the 'Students' tab at the top, click 'Current students' in the left hand navigation bar, and then click the 'ATT Prospectus and Syllabus' link which contains the detailed syllabus. Please make sure that you are looking at the syllabus for the **2014 examinations**.

The overall objectives and learning outcomes of each of the papers are as follows.

Paper 1: Personal Taxation

Overall objectives

Successful completion of this paper will involve you being able to calculate an individual's income tax and capital gains tax liabilities and to demonstrate a sound understanding of how these liabilities are affected by an individual's residence and domicile status. You should also have a sound understanding of when these liabilities must be reported and paid and the implications of failing to meet these obligations. You should be aware of the legal and ethical issues connected with the taxation of individuals.

Learning outcomes

You should be able to demonstrate that you

- Are able to calculate the income tax payable by an individual

- Are able to calculate the capital gains tax payable by an individual

- Understand how an individual's residence and domicile status affects their personal tax liabilities

- Understand an individual's compliance obligations regarding their personal tax liability

- Understand the relevant professional ethics and legal issues when dealing with the tax affairs of individuals

- Are able to communicate with clients and colleagues in a professional manner in written correspondence

Paper 2: Business Taxation & Accounting Principles

Overall objectives

Successful completion of this paper will involve you being able to calculate the profits and gains assessable in respect of both incorporated and unincorporated businesses, and the corporation tax payable by incorporated businesses. You should also have a sound understanding of the compliance obligations affecting businesses, including those relating to VAT and national insurance, and be able to record transactions in financial statements. You should be aware of the legal and ethical issues connected with the taxation of businesses.

Learning outcomes

You should be able to demonstrate that you

- Are able to calculate the profits assessable in respect of a business

- Are able to calculate the chargeable gains incurred by, or in respect of, a business after taking account of any available reliefs

- Are able to calculate the corporation tax payable by an incorporated business

- Understand the compliance obligations affecting businesses, including those relating to VAT and national insurance

- Are able to record transactions in financial statements

- Understand the relevant professional ethics and legal issues when dealing with the tax affairs of businesses

- Are able to communicate with clients and colleagues in a professional manner in written correspondence

Paper 3: Business Compliance

Overall objectives

Successful completion of this paper will involve you being able to demonstrate a sound knowledge of, and be able to calculate, employment income, national insurance and VAT in respect of a business and its employees. You should also have a sound understanding of a business's obligations regarding payroll administration, VAT compliance and the construction industry scheme, and the implications of failing to meet those obligations. You should be aware of the legal and ethical issues connected with business compliance.

Learning outcomes

You should be able to demonstrate that you

- Are able to calculate the employment income assessable on a business's employee

- Are able to calculate the national insurance payable by employees and employers

- Are able to calculate the amount of VAT payable by a business to HM Revenue & Customs

- Understand the compliance obligations for a business regarding payroll administration

- Understand the compliance obligations imposed by the construction industry scheme

- Understand the VAT compliance obligations for a business

- Understand the implications of a business failing to meet its compliance obligations regarding payroll, construction industry or VAT administration

- Understand how to record transactions in financial statements

- Understand the relevant professional ethics and legal issues when dealing with business compliance

- Are able to communicate with clients and colleagues in a professional manner in written correspondence

Paper 4: Corporate Taxation

Overall objectives

Successful completion of this paper will involve you being able to calculate a company's corporation tax liability. You should have a sound understanding of the tax issues relating to different types of corporate structures throughout their business lifecycle, including incorporation, extraction of funds, operating as a group or overseas, and on their eventual disposal. You should also have a sound understanding of when a corporate business's tax liability must be reported and paid. You should be aware of the legal and ethical issues connected with corporate taxation.

Learning outcomes

You should be able to demonstrate that you

- Are able to calculate a company's corporation tax liability

- Understand the tax implications of incorporating a company

- Understand the tax implications of extracting profits from a company

- Understand the tax implications of disposing of a business or a share of a business

- Understand the tax implications of corporate group structures

- Understand the corporation tax implications of trading abroad

- Understand the tax implications of different types of companies and corporate structures

- Understand the compliance obligations affecting a corporate business

- Understand the relevant professional ethics and legal issues when dealing with corporate taxation

- Are able to communicate with clients and colleagues in a professional manner in written correspondence

Paper 5: Inheritance Tax, Trusts & Estates

Overall objectives

Successful completion of this paper will involve you having a sound understanding of how an individual's inheritance tax liability is calculated and how this is affected by an individual's domicile status. You should understand the legal and tax implications of using trusts. You should understand how to calculate the tax liability incurred by the executors in respect of the administration of an estate and the law relating to wills and intestacy. You should also understand the compliance obligations relating to inheritance tax, trusts and estates. You should be aware of the legal and ethical issues connected with inheritance tax, trusts and estates.

Learning outcomes

You should be able to demonstrate that you

- Are able to calculate the inheritance tax payable by an individual
- Understand how an individual's domicile affects their inheritance tax liability
- Are able to calculate the tax payable in respect of a trust
- Are able to calculate the tax liability incurred by the executors in respect of the administration of an estate
- Understand the compliance obligations relating to inheritance tax, trusts and estates
- Understand the relevant professional ethics and legal issues when dealing with inheritance tax, trusts and estates
- Are able to communicate with clients and colleagues in a professional manner in written correspondence

Paper 6: Value Added Tax

Overall objectives

Successful completion of this paper will involve you being able to calculate a trader's VAT liability. You should understand the VAT implications of supplying or purchasing land and buildings or construction services and should also have a sound understanding of a trader's VAT compliance obligations. You should be aware of the legal and ethical issues connected with VAT.

Learning outcomes

You should be able to demonstrate that you

- Are able to calculate the amount of VAT payable by a trader
- Understand the VAT implications of a trader supplying or purchasing land and buildings or construction services
- Understand a trader's VAT compliance obligations
- Understand the relevant professional ethics and legal issues when dealing with VAT
- Are able to communicate with clients and colleagues in a professional manner in written correspondence

HOME STUDY PLANNER

1 Introduction

This BPP Learning Media Home Study Planner will guide you through this 2013 edition of the BPP Learning Media Study Text. This Home Study planner is intended for use by students who are studying on their own. If you are attending a taught course, your course provider may provide you with a different programme of studies.

2 Using the Home Study Planner

This Home Study Planner is made up of 22 **Study Periods**.

The technical content in each Study Period should take about 3 hours.

In addition to the tax topics you must also ensure that you are familiar with the law and ethics topics which are examinable on each paper. The final Study Period provides guidance on how to study these topics.

Exams

If you are a home study student you will have three course exams.

To gain the greatest benefit from the exams, you must set aside a period of three hours and fifteen minutes during which you will have no interruptions.

By sitting these exams, you will substantially increase your chances of passing the real exams.

Please note, these exams are available only as part of the home study package. If you are attending a taught course, your provider may provide you with other exams to sit at different times during your studies.

3 Getting ready to study

To get off to the best possible start to your study, you should take time to read the following guidance.

Before you begin your studies, you may want to spend some time thinking about how to approach them. Consider the following.

(a)   **The study environment.** Studying while working is very different from studying full time. Time management is crucial.

(b)   **Types of subject.** You need to think about the form the exam will take and the skills it will draw on. For example, does it test knowledge, numerical skills, application of knowledge or application of theory?

(c)   **What is your learning style?** Your learning preferences should affect the way you approach this study material.

(d)   You need to think about **how to work through the text**, how to take notes and how to do examples.

(e)   How will you approach your **revision**?

(f)   You need a technique for dealing with **common types of question**.

(g)   You must approach the exam in a **methodical manner**.

Approaching Personal Taxation

This guidance describes what the paper seeks to achieve, the skills you are expected to demonstrate and how you can improve your chances of passing the paper.

Paper 1, Personal Taxation, seeks to test the liability of individuals to:

* Income tax
* National Insurance Contributions, and
* Capital gains tax.

Because you are not expected to have any previous knowledge of these subjects, we will be introducing them to you from first principles. If you have any previous knowledge, perhaps as a result of work experience, or as a result of having studied for other papers within the ATT syllabus you can modify the amounts of time you spend on each topic, to take account of your knowledge.

The exam may also contain questions on certain legal topics and ethical considerations of being in practice.

The examination

The examination is made up of two parts:

Part I – which is made up of a number of short form questions (SFQs), with mark allocations ranging from 2 to 4 marks. There are 40 marks available in Part I of the exam. As you work through the Study Text you will encounter SFQs in the Question and Answer Bank and in the course exams. By practising this kind of question you can help prepare for the real exam as you go along. SFQs can be on any syllabus area and Part I of the exam typically includes a cross section of questions taken from all areas of the syllabus.

Topics covered in the last five past papers are set out below:

	May 2011	November 2011	May 2012	November 2012	May 2013
1	IT: Property income	IT: Beneficial loan	IT: Taxable income	IT: Benefits – beneficial loan	CGT: Chattels rules
2	Admin: Self assessment filing date	IT: Share Incentive Plan (SIP)	IT: ISA limits	IT: Property income	IT & CGT: SEIS reliefs
3	Admin: Appeals	IT: Benefits– mileage allowance and mobile phones	CGT: Compensation	Admin: POAs & late income tax payment interest	IT: Overseas aspects – residence
4	IT: Benefits – beneficial loan	CGT: Share matching rules	Admin: CGT payment date & late payment interest	IT: Overseas aspects – domicile	CGT: PPR eligible periods
5	IT: Overseas aspects – Remittance basis charge	IT: Bond chargeable event gain	IT: Accrued income scheme	IT: Overseas aspects – residence	IT: Older taxpayer IT liability
6	IT: EIS – relief withdrawal	Admin: Filing and claim deadlines	Admin: Late payment penalties	IT: Anti-avoidance – POAT	Admin: Tax return deadlines
7	IT: Social Security benefits	Admin: Short return	IT: Pension annual allowance charge	IT: REIT income and IT liability	Admin: Late filing and payment penalties
8	CGT: Insurance proceeds	IT: Termination payments	CGT: PPR relief	IT: Tax credits	IT: Overseas aspects – DTR
9	CGT: Quoted shares	CGT: Small part disposal of land	Admin: HMRC enquiries	CGT: Inter-spouse transfer	NIC: Annual maxima
10	CGT: Gift relief	CGT: Chattels rules and capital losses	IT: Qualifying care relief	CGT: QCBs	CGT: Part disposal & chattels loss
11	CGT: Overseas aspects – residence	Law: Employees' common law duties	CGT: Chattels rules	CGT: Taxable gain and identifying chargeable assets	CGT: Valuation and deemed disposal
12	Ethics: Relevant communications	Law: Legal estates in land	NIC: Classes of NIC	Admin: CGT instalments	IT: Accrued income scheme
13	Law: Title over land		CGT: Separation & divorce		
14			Ethics: Conflicts of interest		
15			Law: Employment statement		

BPP LEARNING MEDIA

Part II of the exam is made up of between three to five long form questions with a total of 60 marks. The marks are shared between the questions, but ATT have indicated that they may not be allocated evenly. On past papers the marks have been allocated as follows:

	May 2011	November 2011	May 2012	November 2012	May 2013
Question 1	12 marks	20 marks	15 marks	20 marks	20 marks
Question 2	18 marks	10 marks	20 marks	10 marks	10 marks
Question 3	18 marks	10 marks	10 marks	10 marks	20 marks
Question 4	12 marks	20 marks	15 marks	20 marks	10 marks

You must be prepared to answer long form questions as you cannot pass the exam from the short form questions alone, and practising the questions at the end of each Study Period and in the Course Exams will help with this.

Make sure you consider how long a question is supposed to take. Where a question has a mark allocation this will be an indication of the time it is expected to take. As an estimate, you have 3 hours writing time to answer the questions, so each mark should take, on average, 1.8 minutes of your time. Therefore a 20 mark question should take around 36 minutes to answer. This is only a rough guide, but it helps you to allocate your time in the exam, so that you do not spend more time on a question than it requires to gain the available marks, as this might make your answers to later questions weaker.

Topics covered in the last five actual past papers are set out below:

	May 2011	November 2011	May 2012	November 2012	May 2013
Q1	IT payable on employment benefits NIC on benefits Law: Employment written statement	CGT on gift and on company takeover Capital loss arising on loan to a trader Definition of a debt on a security	IT payable on employment benefits Maternity pay	FHL conditions IT payable on employment income and benefits, and property income	IT payable on employment income and benefits, termination and investment income Law: Statutory redundancy pay
Q2	IT & CGT payable calculation, investment income, chattels Tax credits calculation	Income tax on IIP and discretionary trust Ethics: Engagement letter	CGT calculation Small part disposal of land rules Disposals to connected persons Lease Law: Charges over land	CGT valuation Negligible value claim CGT calculation Use of loss on unquoted trading company shares	Shares from employment: SIP conditions and calculations
Q3	Admin: Penalties for late return and late tax Ethics: Disclosure	CGT on disposal of EIS shares IT & CGT reliefs for VCT and EIS share acquisitions	CGT on takeover involving loan notes, shares and cash QCBs vs non-QCBs Earn out	IT treatment of termination payments NIC position for termination payments Law: Unfair dismissal & fair dismissal	CGT on share transactions Connected person loss Overseas aspects: CGT on becoming non-resident
Q4	Share schemes: EMI	IT payable calculation on restricted shares, investment income, property income POAT tax charge Law: Legal interests in land	Share schemes: Savings related option plan Company Share option plan	CGT: Defining terms, chargeable & exempt assets Admin: Reporting gains & paying tax Overseas aspects: Disposal of overseas assets	IT & CGT: Lease assignment and grant

Detailed Home Study Planner

Use this planner and your exam timetable to plan the dates on which you will complete each Study Period.

Study Period	Guidance through Study text	Attempt Questions
1 **Calculating income tax**	You must thoroughly understand how the basic income tax computation works. Subsequent Study Periods will deal with the calculation of the different types of income subject to income tax. This Study Period introduces the basic knowledge of how an income tax computation is put together and how income tax is calculated. This knowledge will be tested throughout the exam. The last ten exams have included an income tax computation as part of a long form question.	SFQ 1.1 – 1.18 LFQ 1.1 – 1.4
Examined: May 2007 November 2007 May 2008 November 2008 May 2009 November 2009 May 2010 November 2010 May 2011 November 2011 May 2012 November 2012 May 2013	Please read Chapter 1 after reading the guidance here. This essential Study Period is likely to take longer than 3 hours, so you may wish to split the period into two: Sections 1 – 6 and then Sections 7 – 10. Read through Section 1 to gain background knowledge about the UK tax system. This is not usually examined but will help your understanding. Read through Section 2 to familiarise yourself with who pays income tax in the UK. You will return to the overseas aspects of income tax in a later Chapter. Read through Sections 3 to 9 in detail, making notes and working the examples. Take note of the step by step approach to building up an income tax computation in the right order in Section 3. Work through the Illustrations and Examples carefully to understand the rates of tax. Ensure you understand the order in which income is taxed. Learn the format of the income tax computation. Remember all income must be included **gross** in the income tax computation. You must be able to identify the types of exempt income in Section 10.	

2 Investment income	You are likely to be asked to calculate income tax for individuals in both the short form and the long form questions.	SFQ 2.1 – 2.18 LFQ 2.1 – 2.3
	The rates of tax you will use differ depending on whether the income being taxed is non savings, savings or dividend income. You will be expected to be able to identify the different types of income and calculate tax at the appropriate rate.	
	You may also be expected to deal with the more complex tax treatment of certain investments, such as the accrued income scheme for securities and the taxation of life assurance policies.	
Examined: Sample Paper May 2007 November 2007 May 2008 November 2008 May 2009 November 2009 May 2010 November 2010 May 2011 November 2011 May 2012 May 2013	Please read Chapter 2 after reading the guidance below:	
	Read through Section 1 to understand the meaning of what is included as savings income, ie interest. Note that interest can be received either gross (ie with no tax deducted before it is paid to the investor) or net (of 20% tax). Attempt Example 1.	
	Next read Section 2. Make sure you understand that dividends are **always** received net (of 10% tax) and are usually taxed after all other income. Try Example 2.	
	Read through Section 3 on tax-free investments. Could you spot them in the exam? Try Example 3.	
	Now work through Section 4. The EIS and VCT schemes are very popular with the examiner. Both were examined in the November 2010 and 2011 exams while the EIS scheme was examined in May 2011. The Seed Enterprise Investment Scheme (SEIS) was introduced from 6 April 2012. Work the examples carefully and follow through Illustrations 1 & 2 on the SEIS scheme and dividends from VCTs. You should use your legislation to highlight the conditions for the schemes.	
	Next move on to 'Other income' in Section 5. Note the way that income from trusts (try Example 6) and estates (work through Illustration 4) is taxed, and the associated tax credits available to the recipient of the income. Note the 'catch all' category of miscellaneous income (we return to property income in a later period).	
	Read through Section 6 on the anti-avoidance rules. Work quickly through pre-owned assets, attempting Examples 7 and 8, then take time to understand how the accrued income scheme works as this has been a popular topic over the last few papers. Work through the Illustrations then try Example 11. Lastly try Example 12 which tests life assurance policies.	
	Finally, take note of the key income tax planning idea in Section 7 for jointly owned investments, which was examined in a long question in May 2010.	
	Refer to the rates and allowances in the Tax Tables included at the front of the Study Text as you go along so that you know what information you will be given in the exam.	

3 **Tax credits and social security benefits**	This Study Period deals with social tax credits and social security benefits. It also covers Qualifying Care Relief. Tax credits and social security benefits are examinable at the computational level. You will only be required to identify which benefits are taxable and correctly include them in an income tax computation.	SFQ 3.1 – 3.3 LFQ 3.1 – 3.3
Examined: Sample Paper May 2007 November 2007 November 2008 May 2010 November 2010 May 2011 May 2012 November 2012	Read through Chapter 3 after reading the guidance below: Read through Section 1 as background information on child and working tax credits. Note that tax credits are non-taxable benefits. Next, look at the social security benefits in Section 2. Some of the rates are given in the tax tables, so make sure you know which ones. Note the new high income child benefit charge (Section 2.5.2) which was introduced towards the end of the 2012/13 tax year. 2013/14 is the first full year to which it has applied, so make sure you know how to deal with it. Qualifying care relief is relatively new to the syllabus (Section 2.5.3) so work carefully through Example 2 to ensure you can apply the rules.	
4 **Property income**	This Study Period considers how to calculate the amount of income arising from UK property. In the exam, property income calculations can come up in both the short form and the long form questions. You may also be asked factual questions, such as the conditions for rent a room relief to apply. Questions may combine the income tax and capital gains tax aspects of owning and disposing of land and buildings (capital gains tax will be covered in later Study Periods).	SFQ 4.1 – 4.7 LFQ 4.1 & 4.3
Examined: Sample Paper May 2007 November 2007 November 2008 May 2009 November 2009 May 2010 November 2010 May 2011 November 2011 November 2012	Please read through Chapter 4 of the Study text, after reading the guidance here. Read through Sections 1 – 8 which deal with how to compute property income. You need to be able to calculate: • Property income net of allowable expenses (and capital allowances) (please try Example 1) • Property losses • The portion of a lease premium received on a short lease that is taxable on the landlord (please try Examples 2 and 3). You need to be able to state: • How to set off property losses. • The conditions for, and the tax implications of, a property being treated as a furnished holiday letting. The conditions changed from 6 April 2012, and are still high priority for your studies. • The conditions for rent a room relief to apply and the tax implications of this relief applying. • How a landlord of a UK property, who is not resident in the UK, is taxed on the property income received. • The tax implications of receiving rental income from a Real Estate Investment Trust, which were recently examined in the November 2012 exam.	

BPP LEARNING MEDIA

5 **Employment income**	This Study Period deals with the calculation of the employment income figure that an employed earner must include in his income tax computation.	SFQ 5.1 – 5.23 LFQ 5.1 - 5.6
	Questions have appeared in every examination sitting so far and can focus on many different aspects of the employed earner. For example, understanding the basis of assessment for employment income, identifying and calculating taxable employment income, including the tax value of benefits received and identifying tax free benefits.	
	You may also be required to show your understanding of the taxation of termination payments received when leaving employment. This came up as an entire long form question in the November 2012 sitting.	
Examined: Sample Paper May 2007 November 2007 May 2008 November 2008 May 2009 November 2009 May 2010 November 2010 May 2011 November 2011 May 2012 November 2012 May 2013	Please read Chapter 5 of the Study text, after reading the guidance below: • Read through Section 1 to understand the types of income that makes up employment income. Make sure that you can explain how the receipts basis, which determines the tax year that employment income is taxed, applies. Work through Example 1. • Then work through Section 2, making notes on how to calculate the taxable value of the benefits that are taxable on all employees, regardless of their income level. Try Examples 2, 3 and 4. • Next, read through Section 3 and make notes on how to calculate the taxable value of benefits only taxable on directors and employees earning £8,500 pa or more. The benefits of a company car and private fuel are an examiner's favourite. Work carefully through the Illustrations and try Examples 5 to 10. • Read through Section 4 and make sure you can identify the benefits that can be received tax free. • Read through Section 5 and ensure you understand when expenses can be deducted from employment income. The 'wholly, exclusively and necessarily' test is key. Try Example 11. • Finally, read through Section 6, making notes on how the different categories of termination payment are taxed. Make sure you can identify which payments are fully taxable, those that are completely exempt and those that are partially exempt from tax. Try Example 12. Also try to understand the effect of foreign service on termination payments.	

6 Employer share schemes	You need to be able to calculate the amount that must be included as part of an employee's taxable employment income in respect of shares they receive from their employer. In particular you must understand:	SFQ 6.1 – 6.43 LFQ 6.1
	• The rules applying to the different share schemes, especially the approved schemes.	
	• The difference in treatment for unapproved share awards and options.	
	This is a very popular topic so you must be able to apply these rules and determine what figure should be included as employment income.	
Examined: Sample Paper May 2007 November 2007 May 2008 November 2008 May 2009 November 2009 May 2010 November 2010 May 2011 November 2011 May 2012 May 2013	Read through Chapter 6 after reading the guidance below:	
	Read Section 1 to obtain a general understanding of the difference between:	
	• An employer giving free or cheap shares directly to an employee, and	
	• The employer granting an option to an employee to buy shares in the future, usually at a favourable, low price.	
	Read Section 2 which deals with shares given directly to employees by their employer. There is an income tax charge if the shares are completely free or the employee pays less than the market value for them. Other tax charges apply if there are any restrictions on the shares. Note the new category of employment' 'employee shareholder status' which provides beneficial tax treatment for shares given to employees in exchange for giving up certain employment rights. Work carefully through the Illustrations and try Example 1.	
	Then read Section 3 on the tax implications of an employer granting an option under an unapproved share option scheme. Try Example 2.	
	Section 4 covers the four approved share schemes. An approved scheme is one where, to obtain favourable tax treatment, certain conditions must be satisfied. Make notes, comparing how each scheme works, the tax implications of each scheme and what profit is charged when the employee sells the shares. Try Examples 3, 4 and 5.	
	Next briefly read through Section 5 on Restricted shares. This is less important than the other topics inthis chapter.	
	You also need to be aware of the National Insurance Contribution (NIC) aspects of share schemes in Section 6. You should return to this section once you have covered NIC in the next chapter.	

| 7
National insurance contributions

Examined:
May 2010
November 2010
May 2011
May 2012
November 2012
May 2013 | In this Study Period we look at National Insurance Contributions (NIC). You need to be able to identify the different classes of NIC payable by employers and employees and also those paid by the self employed.

Read through Chapter 7 on National Insurance Contributions. Make notes on the different classes of NIC payable by employers and employees and make sure you are aware of how the NIC contributions are calculated in both cases (Sections 1 to 5).

You are also expected to have an awareness of the NICs payable by self employed individuals, which is covered in the overview in Section 1.

Work through the Examples, although remember that this topic is examinable at the principles level so an awareness of the topic is all that is required. However, if you do need to make a simple NIC calculation in the exam, the rates are provided in the ATT's Tax Tables.

Pay particular attention to what is included in 'earnings' for NIC purposes in Section 2.2 and note that it includes not just cash payments, such as salary and bonuses, but may also include the employment income figure you calculated in the previous chapter for share schemes if the shares are readily convertible assets (usually quoted shares). You should also be aware that lower NIC contributions are paid by individuals who 'contract out' of the State second pension.

Finally, read quickly through Section 6 which covers the annual maximum amount of NICs payable by someone with more than one employment (the 'annual maxima').

This should be a relatively short Study Period, so take this opportunity to return to the Employer share schemes chapter and revise how NIC applies to taxable amounts from the various share schemes. Also, review any other topics that you have covered so far that you have found challenging or difficult. | SFQ 7.1 – 7.3
LFQ 7.1 |

8 **Pensions**	You may be asked to: • Calculate the amount of pension contributions that an individual can make to either an occupational or a personal pension scheme and obtain tax relief. • Explain the tax implications of making contributions to a scheme, the timing of the contributions and on drawing the pension once the individual retires.	SFQ 8.1 – 8.6 LFQ 8.1 – 8.3
Examined: Sample Paper May 2007 November 2008 May 2009 November 2009 May 2010 May 2012 November 2012	Read through Chapter 8 of the Study text after reading the following guidance: Read through section 1 of the Chapter to gain background knowledge and understand the distinction between occupational and personal pension schemes. Make sure you understand that a pension is (like an ISA) a tax free wrapper around investments, so there is no income tax or capital gains tax on investments within a pension. However, the downside is that an individual cannot take the investment out of the pension until they retire. Read through Section 2 on contributions. Note that the annual allowance rules changed from 6 April 2011 and continue to be highly examinable. Try Examples 1, 2 and 3. Make notes on the following aspects for both occupational and personal pension schemes, as they differ considerably: • Whether payments are made net or gross of tax. • How tax relief is given for pension contributions. In particular make sure you understand how this affects the income tax computation you studied in Study Periods 1 and 2. Try Example 4. Read through Section 3 so that you understand how pension income is taxed on retirement.	

| 9
Overseas aspects of income tax | So far all the individuals we have considered have been UK resident. You may also be examined on:

• Definitions and explanations of terminology used for discussing overseas matters (May 2009 SFQ 7 & 12, November 2012 SFQ 4)

• Determining the status of an individual, to decide if they are liable to UK income tax (November 2007 LFQ 3)

• Understanding the tax implications of individuals coming to and leaving the UK (Pilot Paper SFQ 13, May 2007 SFQ 11, November 2012 SFQ 5)

• Deciding when income is taxable on non-resident and non-UK domiciled individuals (May 2009 SFQ 2, November 2010 SFQ 7, May 2013 SFQ 3)

• The remittance basis (November 2009 LFQ 1, May 2011 SFQ 5)

• Calculating the amount of double tax relief available on foreign income (November 2010 SFQ 3; May 2013 SFQ 8).

The introduction of the statutory residence test from 6 April 2013 makes this a highly examinable topic. | SFQ 9.1 – 9.5
LFQ 9.1 – 9.2 |
| Examined:
Sample Paper
May 2007
November 2007
May 2009
November 2009
November 2010
May 2011
November 2012
May 2013 | Read through Chapter 9 of the Study text after reading the following guidance:

Refer back to Section 2.4 of Chapter 1 to get a feel for the UK tax implications of residence and domicile status.

Now read Section 1 of Chapter 9 and make notes on the meaning of residence and domicile for UK tax purposes. Make sure you understand the three steps approach of the new statutory residence test. Work through the Illustrations and Examples.

Read Section 2 which covers how UK and overseas income is taxed depending on the taxpayer's residence and domicile status, paying particular attention to overseas dividend income and overseas employment income (which was only introduced to the syllabus in 2012). Also, note the temporary non-residents rules for individuals who are only outside the UK for a short period of time. Try Examples 3 and 4.

Then read Section 3 which deals with the remittance basis of taxation, which allows the overseas income of a non-UK domiciled taxpayer to be taxed only when it is brought into the UK. Can you determine whether it applies automatically or if the taxpayer has to make a claim for it to apply? When does a taxpayer have to pay the remittance basis charge? Try Example 5.

Read Section 4 quickly, noting which non-UK residents are entitled to personal allowances and how the allowances of non-UK domiciled individuals are affected by a remittance basis claim.

Finally, read Section 5 on double taxation relief (DTR) and make notes on how relief is given against the UK income tax liability on foreign source income for tax paid overseas. You may be asked to calculate double tax relief in the exam. Try Examples 6 and 7 to check whether you have understood this section. | |

10 **Administration of income tax**	Once we have calculated an individual's income tax liability we need to know: • Self assessment reporting requirements and due dates • Due dates for tax payments. These are easy to learn and easy marks in the exam, so learn them! • Penalties and interest for non-compliance with the rules • HMRC's powers and taxpayer appeals. These topics have been examined as SFQs or as part (or the whole) of a longer question.	SFQ 16.1 – 16.2 & 16.4 LFQ 16.1 – 16.2
Examined Sample Paper May 2007 November 2007 May 2008 November 2008 May 2009 November 2009 May 2010 November 2010 May 2011 November 2011 May 2012 November 2012 May 2013	Read Chapter 16 of the Study text, after reading the following guidance: Chapter 16 considers the tax administration aspects of both income and capital gains tax (CGT). As you have not studied CGT yet, we will focus on the income tax aspects only at this stage and will return to the administration of capital gains tax in a later Study Period. For each section in this chapter, highlight any deadlines or due dates. You may find it useful to locate the rules in your legislation. You already have so much to learn for the exam, you should use your legislation for this topic as much as possible. Remember you can highlight the text, so do that as you follow through with the Text. Concentrate on highlighting key words and figures, not whole paragraphs. Read Section 2 and note the deadline for notifying HMRC of your liability to income tax and the penalties for doing this late. Then read Sections 3 and 4 and note the different deadlines for submitting paper and electronic self assessment tax returns and who can use the short tax return. You must also be able to state the penalties for submitting a tax return late. Section 5 is an essential section as it deals with the payment of income tax. Note the payment dates and identify how payments on account are calculated (try Example 1) and reduced, where applicable. You do not need to read Section 5.3.2 at this stage. From Section 5.4 identify the situations when late payment penalties and interest are charged by HMRC and when the taxpayer can receive interest on a repayment of overpaid tax. Try Examples 3 and 4. Read Section 6 on incorrect returns. Note the deadlines for amending returns for both the taxpayer and HMRC and the penalties for submitting an incorrect return Read Section 7 and note the time period for which records must be kept and the penalties for failing to keep records. Read Section 8 on taxpayer's claims for relief and recovery of overpaid tax. Finally, read through Sections 9 and 10 which deal with HMRC's powers and how the taxpayer can appeal against an HMRC assessment or decision.	
11 **Course Exam**	Once you have completed the above study periods you are ready to sit Course Exam 1 on Income tax and NIC. To gain the most from this exam, set aside 3 hours and 15 minutes to complete it.	Course Exam 1 (Income tax and NIC)

BPP LEARNING MEDIA

12 **CGT basics**	Questions testing capital gains tax (CGT) may require a candidate to: • Determine whether CGT applies or not to a particular disposal • Calculate the CGT liability for a tax year. The areas covered in this study period are essential to your knowledge of CGT and whilst they are unlikely to be examined in their own right, apart from the overseas aspects (for example in LFQ4 in November 2012), they are essential to any question involving CGT.	SFQ 10.1 – 10.5 LFQ 10.1 – 10.2
Examined: Sample Paper May 2008 November 2008 May 2009 November 2009 May 2010 November 2010 May 2011 November 2011 May 2012 November 2012 May 2013	Read through Chapter 10 after reading the following guidance: Read Sections 1 and 2 of the Chapter, which form essential background knowledge to CGT, and make notes making sure you can identify: • Who pays CGT. • The rates of tax applicable to individuals. • Chargeable and exempt persons, disposals and assets. Try Example 1. Section 3 is very brief. Note the date of payment of CGT – the administration of CGT is dealt with in more detail in Study Period 18. Read Section 4 on the overseas aspects of CGT, a key topic, making sure you understand: • The impact of residence and domicile status on the chargeability of an individual to UK CGT on the disposal of UK and overseas assets. • The impact of the remittance basis. • The rules for temporary non-residents. • When double tax relief will be available and how it is calculated (try Example 2). • How the location of assets (UK or overseas) is determined.	

13 **Computing gains and losses**	You may be expected to calculate capital gains tax on a number of different disposals. You must be able to calculate gains/losses quickly and efficiently, as this is the basis of most questions on CGT.	SFQ 11.1 – 11.12 LFQ 11.1 – 11.2
	The following topics have previously been examined:	
	• The basic gain computation.	
	• The use of capital losses	
	• Deductible capital expenditure	
	• Gains on transfers between connected persons, or between husband and wife or civil partners	
	• Valuation of quoted shares	
	• Gains on part disposals	
	• CGT treatment of debts and loans.	
Examined Sample Paper May 2007 November 2008 May 2009 November 2009 May 2010 November 2010 May 2011 November 2011 May 2012 November 2012 May 2013	Read through Chapter 11 of the Study text after taking account of the following guidance:	
	Section 1 is essential. It shows the basic computation of a capital gain. Attempt Example 1.	
	Section 2 shows how to calculate and use a capital loss, and how the use differs depending on whether it is a current year loss or a loss brought forward from an earlier year. Try Examples 2 to 5. Work through Example 6 on the use of losses on death. Then carefully read through the details on share loss relief for losses arising on disposals of shares in EIS type companies, and work through Example 7 on the rules for losses of non-UK domiciled individuals.	
	Next, carefully work through the valuation rules in Section 3 and attempt Examples 8 and 9.	
	Sections 4 and 5 set out the rules for dealing with disposals between connected persons and married couples/ civil partners, particularly the rules for jointly owned property. Try Example 10.	
	Section 6 deals with the fundamental topic of part disposals. You must understand how the cost is split if an asset is disposed of in more than one disposal (Examples 11 and 12). Read the Exam Focus Point after Example 12 and then try Example 13 to revise the chapter so far.	
	Section 7 then stands alone as it explains the CGT implications of the disposal of a debt or a loan. This is a lower priority area than the rest of this study period.	

14 **Shares and securities**	You may be examined on the special rules for calculating gains on the sale of shares and securities. You need to be able to:	SFQ 12.1 – 12.3 LFQ 12.1 – 12.4
	• Apply the matching rules and be able to identify which shares should be included in the share pool	
	• Deal with bonus issues and rights issues of shares	
	• Deal with capital distributions, reorganisations and takeovers	
	• You must also be able to deal with the CGT implications of selling shares received under an employer's approved or unapproved share scheme, so now would be a good time to revisit the Employer share schemes chapter	
	Share disposal questions often involve a lot of facts. Take your time reading through the information given.	
Examined: Sample Paper May 2007 November 2007 November 2008 May 2009 November 2009 May 2010 November 2010 November 2011 May 2012 November 2012 May 2013	Read through Chapter 12 of the Study text after reading the following guidance: Section 1 explains why we need special rules for disposals of shares and securities. Read quickly for background knowledge. Read through Sections 2 and 3 carefully, attempting Examples 1 and 2. At the end of these sections you will be able to deal with calculating a capital gain on the sale of shares. This computation will form the basis of all questions on the disposal of shares. It is important to make sure you understand this part of the chapter well before you progress to the other sections of the chapter. Once you are happy with the basic computation on the sale of shares, you can then look at how we add to the basic rules in certain circumstances. In Section 4 you will learn about: • Bonus issues (Example 3) • Rights issues (Example 4) • Capital distributions (Example 5) • Reorganisations & takeovers (Examples 6 to 8). Make sure you understand and can identify each of these situations. Finally, read Section 5. This deals with the CGT on a disposal of gilts (ie Treasury Stock) and QCBs. Try Example 9.	

15 **Chattels and wasting assets**	This chapter also deals with special rules, this time for the disposal of special assets known as chattels and wasting assets (which includes leases).	SFQ 13.1 – 13.7 LFQ 13.1 – 13.3
	The types of calculation involved make these calculations easy to examine as both a SFQ and also as part of a long question, including many different capital disposals.	
Examined: Sample Paper May 2007 November 2007 May 2008 November 2008 May 2009 November 2009 May 2010 November 2010 May 2011 November 2011 May 2012 May 2013	Read through Chapter 13 after taking note of the following guidance: Read through Section 1 and make sure you can identify a chattel in the exam: it is simply an item of personal property. Understand that wasting chattels are exempt and also how the basic gain computation is affected if there is a sale of a chattel. Quickly note the general treatment of wasting assets (that are not chattels) from Section 2, as background knowledge. This is less likely to appear as a separate question but try Example 4 to test your understanding. Now read through Section 3 very carefully. You must understand the difference between 'assigning' (ie selling) a lease and granting a lease and what makes a lease a 'short' lease. Work through each of the five different situations and try Examples 5 to 8. Try and summarise in your own words how the normal CGT calculation is affected in each situation (eg What cost is used? What proceeds?) Don't waste too much time here – just note down the difference between the different types of computations. You will have time to practise these calculations later, which is the best way to learn and revise them.	

BPP LEARNING MEDIA

16 **Principal private residence relief**	Having calculated a gain on disposal, you may then be tested on the occasions when those gains may either be exempted from tax completely or deferred (ie delayed) by the operation of a CGT relief. The only relief that exempts the gain is Principal Private Residence Relief (although there is also an exemption for employee shareholder status shares and certain reinvestments in SEIS shares). Questions are unlikely to focus on a property that is entirely exempt from tax. It is more likely that you will need to consider situations where a property may be partially exempt, perhaps where there has been a period of absence from the property, during which time the property may have been rented out, or where more than one residence was held at once.	SFQ 14.1 – 14.3 LFQ 14.1 – 14.3
Examined: Sample Paper May 2007 November 2007 November 2008 May 2009 November 2009 November 2010 May 2012 May 2013	Read through Chapter 14 of the Study text after reading the following guidance: Section 1.1 establishes the basic principle of when the relief applies. It is fundamental to your understanding of the rest of the chapter. Understand which periods are deemed to be occupation of the property for CGT purposes – find the rules in your legislation. Try Example 1. Read quickly through Section 2 and be aware of the rules where the taxpayer owns more than one residence. Next, read carefully through Section 3 and make sure you know when letting relief is available, how this relief fits into the calculation and the maximum relief given. Try Example 2 to make sure you have understood the principles. Finally, read quickly through Section 4 and try Example 3 to ensure you know how a period of business impacts the exemption.	

17 **Other CGT reliefs**	The reliefs in this Study Period allow the taxpayer to either defer (or delay) paying their CGT, or exempt the gain. A deferred gain will become chargeable at some point in the future.	SFQ 15.1 – 15.9 LFQ 15.1 – 15.7
	These reliefs can be tested in either a SFQ or as part of a long form question.	
Examined: Sample Paper May 2007 November 2007 May 2008 May 2009 November 2009 May 2010 May 2011 November 2011 May 2012 May 2013	Read through Chapter 15 from the Study Text, after reading through the following guidance:	
	Read quickly through Section 1 to understand which reliefs exempt the gain and what we mean by 'deferral' reliefs.	
	Read through Sections 2.1 to 2.3, which deal with the basic gift relief rules. This is an important area so make sure you understand the fundamentals of how CGT is deferred using the relief. Try Examples 1 and 2 to test your understanding so far.	
	Then move on to Sections 2.4 to 2.7. These are additional rules for certain circumstances that build on the basics you have already learned. Pay particular attention to Section 2.5, sales at an undervalue, where the taxpayer sells an asset for less than it is worth – this is only partly a gift so the rules are modified slightly to deal with this. Try Examples 3 and 4.	
	Read through Section 3 on EIS CGT relief. You have already seen EIS relief from an income tax perspective – and the examiner likes to test both sets of rules together – so you may find it useful to refresh your memory at this point by returning to the relevant income tax chapter. For CGT, concentrate on the amount of deferral relief available, the qualifying conditions for the deferral relief to apply (which are not as strict as for income tax relief) and the occasions when the deferred gain crystallises (ie becomes chargeable again).	
	The new Seed Enterprise Investment Scheme CGT reliefs are covered in Section 4 and the disposal relief for sales of VCT shares is in Section 5.	
	Read Section 6 and note the exemption available on the disposal of employee shareholder statuts shares valued at up to £50,000 on acquisition.	
	Finally, read through Section 7 which deals with the treatment of insurance proceeds (or 'compensation') received when an asset is damaged or destroyed. This is historically a less popular exam topic but has been examined in both SFQs, most recently in May 2012, and in a number of LFQs. Try Examples 7 and 8 to make sure you have understood the basic rules.	

18 **Administration of CGT**	Once CGT has been calculated for an individual we need to know : • Self assessment reporting requirements and due dates. • The due date for payment of CGT. • Penalties and interest for non-compliance with the rules. • HMRC's powers and taxpayer appeals. These could be examined as a SFQ or as part of a longer question.	SFQ 16.3
Examined: May 2007 November 2009 November 2010 May 2011 May 2012 November 2012	Read Chapter 16 of the Study text, after reading the following guidance: You have already studied the administration of income tax in Study Period 10 and in most cases the rules are identical. Read Sections 2 to 4 for revision. Read Section 5 to revise the payment dates for income tax and capital gains tax and understand how payments on account are calculated where there is both income tax and capital gains tax due (try Example 1). Most importantly, note when CGT may be paid by instalments in Section 5.3.2. Now identify from Sections 5.4 and 5.5 the situations when interest is charged on overdue tax and note the penalties that may be due. You could also take this opportunity to revise the HMRC's powers and the rights of the taxpayer to appeal against an HMRC assessment or other decision in Sections 9 and 10.	

19 Other aspects of the syllabus	Certain key law and ethics topics are also examinable on this paper. Examples of questions set on these areas are: May 2007: SFQs 12 & 15, LFQs 2 & 4 November 2007: SFQs 3 & 12, LFQ 4 May 2008: SFQ 12, LFQ 1 November 2008: SFQs 12 & 13, LFQs 1 & 2 May 2009: SFQ 14, LFQs 1 & 2 November 2009: SFQ 13, LFQs 2 & 3 May 2010: SFQ 13, LFQs 1, 2 & 3 November 2010: SFQ 13 & 14, LFQs 2 & 3 May 2011: SFQs 12 & 13, LFQs 1 & 3 November 2011: SFQ 11 & 12, LFQs 2 & 4 May 2012: SFQs 14 & 15, LFQ 2 November 2012: LFQ3 May 2013: LFQ1	SFQ 17.1 – 17.16 LFQs 4.2, 5.5, 14.1 & 15.3
Examined: Pilot Paper May 2007 November 2007 May 2008 November 2008 May 2009 November 2009 May 2010 November 2010 May 2011 November 2011 May 2012 November 2012 May 2013	Read through Chapter 17 of the Study Text. Read Section 1.2. Read through the relevant chapters in the ATT's manual 'Essential Law for Tax Practitioners' that you have not studied or that you need to revisit. Note the type of topics that have been recently examined. Read Section 1.3. Review the examinable documents listed in this chapter, ensuring that you are referring to the correct version of the Professional Indemnity Guidance and Rules. Examples of recent popular exam topics are given in the chapter.	
20, 21, 22 Revision	If you are a home study student attempt Course Exam 2 in Study Period 20. Use the exam to help identify areas where you are weak. Then spend the next session and any remaining time you have revising your weak areas. Just before you are about to start the 'revision phase' of your studies you should sit Course Exam 3. This exam is a good indicator of whether you are ready to move on.	Course exams

BPP
LEARNING MEDIA

Revision Phase

BPP Learning Media provide you with the following material to assist with your revision phase:

Passcards

BPP Learning Media's Passcards will be published in early 2014. BPP Learning Media's Passcards follow the overall structure of the BPP Learning Media Study Texts, but they are not just a condensed book, each card has been separately designed for clear presentation. Topics are self contained and can be grasped visually. **They are the perfect aid to your revision.**

i-pass CD Rom

BPP Learning Media's i-Pass CD-Rom will also be published in early 2014. This is a useful tool which is designed to test the knowledge which is fundamental to your exam. It enables you to attempt tests, making it an ideal revision tool.

i-Pass has two modes. The first one is 'Test as you learn'. This allows you to test yourself on the areas that you are studying at the time or a combination of different areas. Use the sliders to choose the number of questions to do to fit the time you have available.

The second mode provides exam practice by creating an exam containing questions selected at random from those within 'Test as you learn' for you to answer.

Each mode gives you **comprehensive feedback on the questions and your performance**.

Revision Kit

BPP Learning Media's Revision Kit is packed full of past examination questions and answers for you to practise. Plenty of question practice is the key to passing this exam. Many of the answers to questions in the Revision Kit have annotated marking schemes attached. This means that you can see where the easy marks are likely to be awarded on your examination and thus learn how to maximise your chances of passing. There are also a number of recap questions covering key areas of the syllabus.

ATT EXAMINATIONS
MAY AND NOVEMBER 2014
TAX TABLES

Association of Taxation Technicians
Practical Tax People

INCOME TAX — 2013/14

Rates
	%
Starting rate for savings income only	10
Basic rate for non savings and savings income only	20
Basic rate for dividends	10
Higher rate for non-savings and savings income only	40
Higher rate for dividends	32.5
Additional and trust rate for non-savings and savings income only	45
Additional and trust rate for dividends	37.5

Thresholds
	£
Savings income starting rate band	1 – 2,790
Basic rate band	1 – 32,010
Higher rate band	32,011 – 150,000
Standard rate band for trusts	1,000

Reliefs
	£
Personal allowance if born after 5 April 1948[1]	9,440
Personal allowance if born between 6 April 1938 and 5 April 1948[1]	10,500
Personal allowance if born before 6 April 1938[1]	10,660
– Maximum income before abatement of relief – £1 for £2[2]	26,100
Married couple's allowance[3]	7,915
– Minimum allowance	3,040
Blind person's allowance	2,160
'Rent-a-room' limit	4,250
Enterprise investment scheme relief limit[4]	1,000,000
Venture capital trust relief limit[4]	200,000
Seed enterprise investment scheme relief limit[5]	100,000
Employer supported childcare – basic rate taxpayer[6]	£55 per week

Notes

(1) The personal allowance of any individual with adjusted net income above £100,000 is reduced by £1 for every £2 of adjusted net income above the £100,000 limit.

(2) This is the income limit for abatement of the age related personal allowance and then the married couple's allowance.

(3) Only available where at least one partner was born before 6 April 1935. Relief restricted to 10%.

(4) Relief at 30%.

(5) Relief at 50%.

(6) For schemes joined on or after 6 April 2011 the exempt childcare amounts for higher and additional rate taxpayers (based on the employer's earning assessment only) are £28 and £25 respectively.

Income tax – Pension contributions

	Annual allowance £	Lifetime allowance £	Minimum pension age
2013/14[1]	50,000	1,500,000	55

Basic amount qualifying for tax relief £3,600

Notes (1) The £50,000 annual allowance is increased by any unused relief from the previous three years. When considering unused relief, the annual allowance for all years before 2011/12 is deemed to be £50,000.

ISA limits

	Maximum holding £	Maximum holding in cash £
'Adult' ISAs	11,520	5,760
Junior ISAs	3,720	

Notes (1) The Junior ISA can be any combination of cash and stocks and shares.

ITEPA Mileage Rates

Vehicles		2013/14
Car or van[(1)]	First 10,000 business miles	45p
	Additional business miles	25p
Motorcycles		24p
Bicycles		20p
Passenger payments		5p

Note (1) For NIC purposes, a rate of 45p applies irrespective of mileage.

Company cars and fuel – 2013/14

Emissions	Car benefit %[(1)(2)(3)]	
0g/km	0%	
1 – 75g/km	5%	
76 – 94g/km	10%	
95g/km or more	11%	+ 1% for every additional whole 5g/km above 95g/km
Over 215g/km	35%	

Fuel benefit base figure[(2)]   £21,100

Notes
(1) Apply the car benefit percentage to list price of vehicle.
(2) Apply the same car benefit percentage to the fuel benefit base figure to calculate the fuel benefit.
(3) 3% supplement for diesel cars.

Taxable benefits for vans – 2013/14	£
Van benefit – No CO2 emissions	0
Van benefit – CO2 emissions > 0g/km	3,000
Fuel benefit	564

2013/14 Official rate of interest   4.0%

STUDENT LOAN RECOVERY

Employee earnings threshold at which repayment of student loans begin is £1,363.75 per month.

Rate of student loan deductions is 9% of earnings above the threshold rounded down to the nearest whole pound.

STATUTORY SICK PAY

		Weekly rate
Year to 5 April 2014		£
Average weekly gross earnings	£109.00 or more	86.70

STATUTORY MATERNITY PAY

Period	First 6 weeks	Remaining weeks
From 6 April 2013	90% average weekly earnings	Lower of 90% of weekly earnings & £136.78

QUALIFYING CARE RELIEF	Flat rate	Placement < 11	Placement ≥ 11
Year to 5 April 2014	£10,000 per year	£200 per week	£250 per week

CHILD BENEFIT – Year to 5 April 2014

Rates	Weekly rate (£)
First child	20.30
Each subsequent child	13.40

Child Benefit Charge	Withdrawal rate
Adjusted net income >£50,000	1% of benefit per £100 of income between £50,000 and £60,000
Adjusted net income >£60,000	Full child benefit amount assessable in that tax year

ATT EXAMINATIONS
MAY AND NOVEMBER 2014
TAX TABLES

att

Association
of Taxation
Technicians

Practical Tax People

NATIONAL INSURANCE CONTRIBUTIONS

Class 1 Limits

	Annual	2013/14 Monthly	Weekly
Lower earnings limit (LEL)	£5,668	£473	£109
Primary earnings threshold (PT)	£7,755	£646	£149
Secondary earnings threshold (ST)	£7,696	£641	£148
Upper accruals point (UAP)	£40,040	£3,337	£770
Upper earnings limit (UEL)	£41,450	£3,454	£797

Class 1 primary contribution rates

2013/14

Not contracted out[1]

Earnings between PT and UEL	12%
Earnings above UEL	2%

Contracted out to salary related occupational pension scheme[2]

Earnings between PT and UAP	10.6%
Earnings between UAP and UEL	12%
Earnings above UEL	2%
Rebate on earnings between LEL and PT	1.4%

Class 1 secondary contribution rates

2013/14

Not contracted out[1]

Earnings above ST	13.8%

Contracted out to salary related occupational pension scheme[2]

Earnings between ST and UAP	10.4%
Earnings above UAP	13.8%
Rebate on earnings between LEL and ST	3.4%

Other contribution limits and rates

2013/14

Class 1A contributions	13.8%
Class 1B contributions	13.8%
Class 2 contributions	
Normal rate	£2.70 pw
Small earnings exception	£5,725 pa
Class 3 contributions	£13.55 pw
Class 4 contributions	
Annual lower profits limit (LPL)	£7,755
Annual upper profits limit (UPL)	£41,450
Percentage rate between LPL and UPL	9%
Percentage rate above UPL	2%

HARMONISED INTEREST REGIME – HMRC INTEREST RATES

Late payment	3.0%
Underpaid corporation tax instalments	1.5%
Repayment	0.5%

FLAT RATE EXPENSES FOR UNINCORPORATED BUSINESSES

			2013/14
Business use of home	25 – 50 hours use		£10 per month
	51 – 100 hours use		£18 per month
	101+ hours use		£26 per month
Private use of business premises	No of persons living there:	1	£350 per month
		2	£500 per month
		3+	£650 per month

BPP
LEARNING MEDIA

CAPITAL ALLOWANCES

	6.4.13 – 5.4.14[1]	6.4.12 – 5.4.13[1]
Annual investment allowance (AIA)[2]	100%	100%
WDA on plant and machinery in main pool[3]	18%	18%
WDA on plant and machinery in special rate pool[4]	8%	8%

Notes
   (1) Dates for companies are 1 April – 31 March.

   (2) 100% on the first £250,000 (£25,000 from April 2012 to December 2012) of investment in plant and machinery (except cars).

   (3) The main pool rate applies to cars with CO_2 emissions of not more than 130 g/km (160 g/km in 2012/13) acquired on or after 6 April 2009 (1 April for companies).

   (4) The special pool rate applies to cars with CO_2 emissions greater than 130 g/km (160 g/km in 2012/13) acquired on or after 6 April 2009 (1 April for companies).

   (5) Cars acquired before 6 April 2009 (1 April for companies) continue to be written down based on cost rather than emissions with a maximum annual written down allowance of £3,000.

100% First year allowances available to all businesses

1) New energy saving plant and machinery, and water efficient plant and machinery.

2) Capital expenditure incurred by a person on research and development.

3) New zero-emission goods vehicles (between April 2010 and April 2015).

4) New cars registered between 16 April 2002 and 31 March 2015 if the car either emits not more than 95 g/km (110 g/km before April 2013) of CO_2 or it is electrically propelled.

CORPORATION TAX

Financial year	2013	2012
Patent box	10%	-
Main rate	23%	24%
Small profits rate	20%	20%
Augmented profits limit for small profits rate	£300,000	£300,000
Augmented profits limit for marginal relief	£1,500,000	£1,500,000
Standard fraction	$\frac{3}{400}$	$\frac{1}{100}$
Marginal rate	23.75%	25%

Research and development expenditure

	2013	2012
SMEs[1]	225%	225%
Large companies	130%	130%
Above the line credit	10%	-

Note
   (1) Small and medium sized enterprises (SMEs) must have < 500 employees and *either* turnover ≤ €100m or assets ≤ €86m.

VALUE ADDED TAX

	From 4.1.11
Standard rate	20%
VAT fraction	1/6

Limits	From 1.4.13
Annual registration limit	£79,000
De-registration limit	£77,000

Thresholds	Cash accounting	Annual accounting
Turnover threshold to join scheme	£1,350,000	£1,350,000
Turnover threshold to leave scheme	£1,600,000	£1,600,000

INHERITANCE TAX

Death rate	40%[1]	**Lifetime rate**	20%

Note (1) A lower rate of IHT of 36% applies where 10% of more of the deceased person's net estate is left to charity.

Nil rate bands

6 April 1996 – 5 April 1997	up to £200,000	6 April 2003 – 5 April 2004	up to £255,000
6 April 1997 – 5 April 1998	up to £215,000	6 April 2004 – 5 April 2005	up to £263,000
6 April 1998 – 5 April 1999	up to £223,000	6 April 2005 – 5 April 2006	up to £275,000
6 April 1999 – 5 April 2000	up to £231,000	6 April 2006 – 5 April 2007	up to £285,000
6 April 2000 – 5 April 2001	up to £234,000	6 April 2007 – 5 April 2008	up to £300,000
6 April 2001 – 5 April 2002	up to £242,000	6 April 2008 – 5 April 2009	up to £312,000
6 April 2002 – 5 April 2003	up to £250,000	6 April 2009 – 5 April 2018	up to £325,000

Taper relief

Death within 3 years of gift	Nil%
Between 3 and 4 years	20%
Between 4 and 5 years	40%
Between 5 and 6 years	60%
Between 6 and 7 years	80%

Quick Succession relief

Period between transfers less than one year	100%
Between 1 and 2 years	80%
Between 2 and 3 years	60%
Between 3 and 4 years	40%
Between 4 and 5 years	20%

Lifetime exemptions

Annual exemption		£3,000
Small gifts		£250
Wedding gifts	– Child	£5,000
	– Grandchild or remoter issue or other party to marriage	£2,500
	– Other	£1,000

CAPITAL GAINS TAX

2013/14

Annual exempt amount	£10,900

CGT rates for individuals[1],[2]

Gains qualifying for entrepreneurs' relief	10%
Gains falling within remaining basic rate band[3]	18%
Gains exceeding basic rate band	28%

CGT rates for trusts & individuals paying the remittance basis charge

Gains qualifying for entrepreneurs' relief	10%
Other gains	28%

CGT rate for PRs

All gains	28%

Entrepreneurs' relief

Relevant gains (lifetime maximum)	£10 million

Notes (1) For individuals, gains are taxed as if they are the top slice of income.

(2) Capital losses and the annual exempt amount may be offset in the most beneficial manner, ie against gains not qualifying for entrepreneurs' relief first.

(3) The remaining basic rate band is calculated as £32,010 (2013/14) less taxable income less any gains on which entrepreneurs' relief has been claimed.

Association
of Taxation
Technicians
Practical Tax People

Lease percentage table

Years	Percentage	Years	Percentage	Years	Percentage
50 or more	100.000	33	90.280	16	64.116
49	99.657	32	89.354	15	61.617
48	99.289	31	88.371	14	58.971
47	98.902	30	87.330	13	56.167
46	98.490	29	86.226	12	53.191
45	98.059	28	85.053	11	50.038
44	97.595	27	83.816	10	46.695
43	97.107	26	82.496	9	43.154
42	96.593	25	81.100	8	39.399
41	96.041	24	79.622	7	35.414
40	95.457	23	78.055	6	31.195
39	94.842	22	76.399	5	26.722
38	94.189	21	74.635	4	21.983
37	93.497	20	72.770	3	16.959
36	92.761	19	70.791	2	11.629
35	91.981	18	68.697	1	5.983
34	91.156	17	66.470	0	0.000

Retail Prices Index

Where Retail Price Indices are required, it should be assumed that they are as follows.

	Jan	Feb	Mar	Apr	May	Jun	Jul	Aug	Sep	Oct	Nov	Dec
1982	–	–	79.44	81.04	81.62	81.85	81.88	81.90	81.85	82.26	82.66	82.51
1983	82.61	82.97	83.12	84.28	84.64	84.84	85.30	85.68	86.06	86.36	86.67	86.89
1984	86.84	87.20	87.48	88.64	88.97	89.20	89.10	89.94	90.11	90.67	90.95	90.87
1985	91.20	91.94	92.80	94.78	95.21	95.41	95.23	95.49	95.44	95.59	95.92	96.05
1986	96.25	96.60	96.73	97.67	97.85	97.79	97.52	97.82	98.30	98.45	99.29	99.62
1987	100.0	100.4	100.6	101.8	101.9	101.9	101.8	102.1	102.4	102.9	103.4	103.3
1988	103.3	103.7	104.1	105.8	106.2	106.6	106.7	107.9	108.4	109.5	110.0	110.3
1989	111.0	111.8	112.3	114.3	115.0	115.4	115.5	115.8	116.6	117.5	118.5	118.8
1990	119.5	120.2	121.4	125.1	126.2	126.7	126.8	128.1	129.3	130.3	130.0	129.9
1991	130.2	130.9	131.4	133.1	133.5	134.1	133.8	134.1	134.6	135.1	135.6	135.7
1992	135.6	136.3	136.7	138.8	139.3	139.3	138.8	138.9	139.4	139.9	139.7	139.2
1993	137.9	138.8	139.3	140.6	141.1	141.0	140.7	141.3	141.9	141.8	141.6	141.9
1994	141.3	142.1	142.5	144.2	144.7	144.7	144.0	144.7	145.0	145.2	145.3	146.0
1995	146.0	146.9	147.5	149.0	149.6	149.8	149.1	149.9	150.6	149.8	149.8	150.7
1996	150.2	150.9	151.5	152.6	152.9	153.0	152.4	153.1	153.8	153.8	153.9	154.4
1997	154.4	155.0	155.4	156.3	156.9	157.5	157.5	158.5	159.3	159.5	159.6	160.0
1998	159.5	160.3	160.8	162.6	163.5	163.4	163.0	163.7	164.4	164.5	164.4	164.4
1999	163.4	163.7	164.1	165.2	165.6	165.6	165.1	165.5	166.2	166.5	166.7	167.3
2000	166.6	167.5	168.4	170.1	170.7	171.1	170.5	170.5	171.7	171.6	172.1	172.2
2001	171.1	172.0	172.2	173.1	174.2	174.4	173.3	174.0	174.6	174.3	173.6	173.4
2002	173.3	173.8	174.5	175.7	176.2	176.2	175.9	176.4	177.6	177.9	178.2	178.5
2003	178.4	179.3	179.9	181.2	181.5	181.3	181.3	181.6	182.5	182.6	182.7	183.5
2004	183.1	183.8	184.6	185.7	186.5	186.8	186.8	187.4	188.1	188.6	189.0	189.9
2005	188.9	189.6	190.5	191.6	192.0	192.2	192.2	192.6	193.1	193.3	193.6	194.1
2006	193.4	194.2	195.0	196.5	197.7	198.5	198.5	199.2	200.1	200.4	201.1	202.7
2007	201.6	203.1	204.4	205.4	206.2	207.3	206.1	207.3	208.0	208.9	209.7	210.9
2008	209.8	211.4	212.1	214.0	215.1	216.8	216.5	217.2	218.4	217.7	216.0	212.9
2009	210.1	211.4	211.3	211.5	212.8	213.4	213.4	214.4	215.3	216.0	216.6	218.0
2010	217.9	219.2	220.7	222.8	223.6	224.1	223.6	224.5	225.3	225.8	226.8	228.4
2011	229.0	231.3	232.5	234.4	235.2	235.2	234.7	236.1	237.9	238.0	238.5	239.4
2012	238.0	239.9	240.8	242.5	242.4	241.8	242.1	243.0	244.2	245.6	245.6	246.8
2013	245.8	247.6	248.7	250.0*	249.9*	249.3*	249.6*	250.5*	251.8*	253.2*	253.2*	254.4*
2014*	253.4	255.3	255.9	257.7	257.6	257.0	257.3	258.2	260.0	261.0	261.0	262.3

* = assumed

Personal Taxation

Part A:
Personal Income Tax

1

1

Calculating income tax

- identify the UK's main taxes and sources of tax law
- identify who pays income tax
- follow the seven steps to calculating income tax
- identify the components of total income
- identify which payments are deductible from total income
- identify the allowances available to reduce net income
- understand the taxation of non-savings, savings and dividend income
- explain how tax relief is obtained for charitable donations
- identify and calculate the tax reductions available
- identify the various categories of exempt income

References: ITA 2007 unless otherwise stated

1 Introduction

Exam focus point

Read through the introduction to gain background knowledge.

1.1 Taxes in the UK

The following are examples of the main UK taxes:

(a) Income tax
(b) National insurance
(c) Corporation tax
(d) Capital gains tax
(e) Inheritance tax
(f) Stamp taxes
(g) Value added tax
(h) Customs duty, tobacco, petrol and other expenditure taxes

Items (a) to (f) are known as **direct taxes**. Items (g) and (h) are **indirect taxes**. For direct taxes, Her Majesty's Revenue and Customs (HMRC) collects directly (we count the PAYE system as a form of direct collection) from the taxpayer, whereas for indirect taxes HMRC collects from an intermediary, who attempts to pass on the cost to the final consumer.

There are other classifications which may be helpful. Items (a) (b) and (c) are, in general, **taxes on income** whereas those under (d), (e) and (f) are known as **capital taxes**. The indirect taxes in (g) and (h) are often called **expenditure taxes**.

1.2 Sources of tax law

Tax law is made by statute – although it is interpreted and amplified by case law. The main taxes and their sources are set out below.

Tax	Suffered by	Source
Income tax	Individuals Partnerships Trustees	Income Tax Act 2007 (ITA 2007) Income Tax (Trading and Other Income) Act 2005 (ITTOIA 2005) Income Tax (Earnings and Pensions) Act 2003 (ITEPA 2003) Taxation (International and Other Provisions) Act 2010 (TIOPA 2010) Capital Allowances Act 2001 (CAA 2001)
Corporation tax	Companies	Corporation Tax Act 2009 (CTA 2009) Corporation Tax Act 2010 (CTA 2010) Taxation (International and Other Provisions) Act 2010 (TIOPA 2010) Capital Allowances Act 2001 (CAA 2001)
Capital gains tax	Individuals Companies (which pay corporation tax on capital gains)	Taxation of Chargeable Gains Act 1992 (TCGA 1992)
Value added tax	Businesses, both incorporated and unincorporated	Value Added Tax Act 1994 (VATA 1994)
Inheritance tax	Individuals	Inheritance Tax Act (IHTA 1984)

1.3 The legislative process

The **tax year** runs from 6 April to 5 April following. **So, the 2013/14 tax year runs from 6 April 2013 to 5 April 2014.**

Finance Acts make changes which apply mainly to the tax year ahead but increasingly also make changes which apply to subsequent tax years.

Usually there is only one Finance Act each year, for example, the Finance Act 2013 is mainly concerned with the 2013/14 tax year for income tax purposes. However, due to the General Election taking place part way through 2010, there were three Finance Acts in 2010.

The annual Budget process begins with the **Autumn Statement usually in late November/ early December**, updating MPs on the Government's plans based on the latest forecasts for the UK economy from the Office for Budget Responsibility. This is followed by the **Budget speech in March/April**, announcing, amongst other things, the tax changes proposed for the coming tax year. A Finance Bill is printed and, after Parliamentary debate and various amendments, passes into law (by receiving Royal Assent to become a Finance Act) usually at the end of July.

The **Taxes Management Act 1970 (TMA 1970)** provides the authority and the framework for administering the income tax system. Other provisions are found in subsequent Finance Acts, particularly the 2007, 2008 and 2009 Finance Acts.

Statutory Instruments (SIs) are used by the government as a convenient way of introducing detailed legislation. They are numbered on a calendar year basis (eg SI 1989/469 is SI No. 469 issued in 1989).

2 Who pays income tax

2.1 General

The following are liable to income tax:

(a)   **Adults**
(b)   **Children**, however young, and
(c)   Each **partner** carrying on a business in the form of a partnership.

2.2 Husband and wife and civil partners

Married men and women, and same sex couples in a civil partnership, are taxable persons in their own right, each with their own allowances and bands of tax (see below).

If the husband, wife or civil partner was born before 6 April 1935, a married couple's allowance (MCA), is available to reduce the tax of usually whichever spouse or partner has the higher income (see below).

2.3 Children

A child is a taxpayer in his own right.

There is an **important exception** to this rule where **investment income of a minor (under 18), unmarried child** arises from a **gift made by his parent** (eg the parent sets up a bank account for their child). This **income is treated as the parent's income if, in the year, it exceeds £100 (gross)**.

2.4 Residence and domicile

A taxpayer may be:

(a)   **UK resident**, and/or
(b)   **UK domiciled**.

If he was born in the UK of UK domiciled parents and has never left the UK for any length of time he is likely to be both. Any combination is possible (ie UK resident but not UK domiciled, non-resident but UK domiciled, or both non-resident and not UK domiciled) and **depends on whether the individual satisfies the statutory residence test and the facts of each case** (see later in this Text).

Generally, a UK resident person is liable to UK income tax on his UK *and* foreign income whereas a non-resident is liable to UK income tax only on income *arising* in the UK. If non-residents were treated identically to UK residents HMRC would, for example, try to collect income tax from French residents on their French income. You can imagine the reaction.

A UK resident who is not domiciled in the UK may be able to use the *remittance* basis for his foreign income, ie it will only be liable to UK tax to the extent that such **income is brought to the UK**, possibly subject to paying a **minimum annual tax charge** on the unremitted income in certain circumstances (see later in this Text).

2.5 Exempt persons

A number of persons or bodies are **exempt from paying UK income tax**. These include:

(a)   Registered **pension** funds
(b)   UK registered **charities**, and
(c)   Representatives of foreign countries.

3 Calculating income tax

Exam focus point

Sections 3 – 9 explain how to prepare an income tax computation. There is usually one long question in the Personal Tax examination testing this, so this is a high priority area.

There are **seven steps** to calculating an individual's income tax liability. [s.23]

Step 1   Identify the amounts of income on which the taxpayer is charged to income tax for the tax year. The sum of those amounts is '**total income**'.

Step 2   Subtract allowable deductible payments and available losses from total income to arrive at '**net income**'.

Step 3   Deduct the **personal allowance** (and blind person's allowance where relevant) to arrive at '**taxable income**'.

Step 4   **Calculate** tax at each applicable rate on the amount of taxable income left after Step 3.

Step 5   Add together the amounts of tax calculated at Step 4.

Step 6   Deduct from the amount of tax calculated at Step 5 any **tax reductions** to which the taxpayer is entitled for the tax year.

Step 7   Add to the amount of tax left after Step 6 specific **tax charges** (mainly related to pension schemes). The result is the **taxpayer's liability** to income tax for the tax year. Any tax already suffered by deduction at source is deducted from the tax liability to arrive at **tax payable**.

Below we look at each of these steps in further detail.

4 Step 1: Calculating total income

4.1 'Components' of total income

The most common types of income are:

Non savings income:	
Employment income	Income earned from employment including salaries, bonuses and benefits
Pension income	Pensions, annuities and other income received from pension funds
Trade profits	Profits earned from a trade, profession or vocation
Property income	Rent etc, from all types of land and buildings
Discretionary trust income	Income from a discretionary trust
Savings income:	
Interest income	Interest received either 'net' or 'gross'
Dividend income:	
Dividend income	Dividends received

Each of these types (or 'components') **of income, is added together to arrive at 'total income'.**

BPP LEARNING MEDIA

4.2 Categorising income

4.2.1 Non savings, savings and dividend income

A distinction is made between non savings, savings and dividend income as different tax rates apply to each.

Employment income, rental income and discretionary trust income are types of **non savings income**.

Savings income is essentially interest, including interest from banks, building societies, gilts, debentures and the National Savings & Investments (NS&I) Bank.

Dividend income is kept separate from all other income.

4.2.2 Gross and net income

The total income for a tax year (6 April to 5 April) is the *gross* amount **(that is, including any tax deducted at source)** and is in most cases the income received in that year.

Some income is received in full ('gross'), with no tax deducted at source, such as property income.

Other income is received after deduction of tax ('net'), such as employment income, where tax is deducted by the employer under the Pay As You Earn (PAYE) system.

Exam focus point

The salary figure in the exam will always be the **gross** amount and you will be given the amount of tax deducted under PAYE separately.

Other income received net includes:

(a)   **Bank interest, which is received net of 20% tax, so must be grossed up by** $^{100}/_{80}$ to include the gross amount in the income tax computation.

(b)   **UK dividend income, which is received net of a 10% tax credit so must be grossed up by** $^{100}/_{90}$ before including it in the computation.

(c)   **Income from a discretionary trust, which is received net of 45% tax (regardless of its source) and must be grossed up by** $^{100}/_{55}$ to calculate the gross income (see later in this Text).

(d)   **All of the income arising in an interest in possession trust is taxed on the beneficiary,** regardless of whether it is paid to him or not (see later in this Text). He receives the income net of 10% tax if it is dividend income or 20% tax if it is non savings or savings income.

(e)   **Income from the estate of a deceased person (an 'estate in administration')** (see later in this Text) **is also received net** of 10% tax if it is dividend income or 20% if it is non savings or savings income.

Exam focus point

In the exam you may be given either the net or the gross amount of income: read the question carefully.

If you are given the **net** amount, gross up the figure at the appropriate rate. For example, if Jack receives net building society interest of £160 it is equivalent to gross income of £200 (£160 × 100/80) with tax deducted at source of £40 (£200 × 20%).

Examiner's report – Personal Taxation

May 2007 – Part II LFQ 1

The main problem....was in grossing up the trust income and dividends using the appropriate rates.

Example 1

During 2013/14 Annabelle received the following income:

(a)   Bank interest of £800
(b)   A payment from a discretionary trust of £1,000
(c)   Dividends from HighPay Plc of £450
(d)   A payment from an interest in possession trust of £500 which was paid out of the trust's interest income.

What amounts should Annabelle include in her income tax computation?

5 Step 2: Deductible payments and losses

5.1 Overview of deductible payments

A deduction is available for certain payments from total income to arrive at 'net income'.

The amount of relief available is the gross amount paid in the tax year.

These deductible payments include: [s.24]

(a)   **Gifts of shares and land to charity**
(b)   **Certain interest payments.**

Relief for **non-trade related patent royalty payments** was **abolished** from 5 December 2012.

Relief for losses, such as **property losses** (see later in this Text), is also deducted at Step 2.

5.2 Gifts of shares and land to charity

Relief is available for gifts of certain assets to charity if the asset gifted is: [ss.432 & 433]

(a)   **Quoted shares or securities** (including shares dealt with on the Alternative Investment Market (AIM))
(b)   **UK freehold or leasehold land**.

Relief is given by deducting the market value of the assets (less any consideration given by the charity, plus any incidental costs of making the disposal) **from total income**.

There is no capital gains tax (CGT) on such gifts (see later in this Text).

Exam focus point

Examiner's report – Personal Taxation

November 2009 – Part I SFQ 9

Most candidates realised that there was income tax relief but were vague as to exactly how much; only a small minority knew that it was available for quoted but not unlisted companies.

5.3 Interest payments

Interest payments **paid** in a tax year are deductible from total income when a loan is used for the following purposes:

(a)   **To buy plant or machinery for use in a partnership.** Interest qualifies for three years from the end of the tax year in which the loan was taken out. If the plant is used partly for private purposes, only a proportion of the interest is eligible for relief. [s.388]

(b)   **To buy plant or machinery for employment purposes.** Interest qualifies for three years from the end of the tax year in which the loan was taken out. If the plant is used partly for private purposes, only a proportion of the interest is eligible for relief. Interest relief is not available for a loan to acquire a **car** which an employee uses for business purposes, as a mileage allowance is available for business mileage instead (see later in this Text). [s.390]

(c) **To buy an interest in a close company (ordinary shares)** (other than a close investment holding company) or to lend money to such a company for the purpose of its business. A close company is a company controlled by its shareholder-directors or by five or fewer shareholders.

When the interest is paid the borrower must *either* hold some shares and work full time as a manager or director of the company *or* have a material interest in the close company (ie hold more than 5% of the shares). [s.392]

Relief is not available if Enterprise Investment Scheme (EIS) (see later in this Text) relief is claimed on the shares.

(d) **To buy shares in an employee-controlled company**. The company must be an unquoted trading company resident in the UK with at least 50% of the voting shares held by employees. [s.396]

(e) **To invest in**, or contribute capital or make a loan to, **a partnership**. The borrower must be a partner (other than a limited partner), and relief ceases when he ceases to be one. [s.398]

(f) **To buy shares in or lend money to a co-operative** (a common ownership enterprise). The borrower must work for the greater part of his time in the co-operative or a subsidiary. [s.401]

(g) **To pay inheritance tax**. Interest paid by the personal representatives of a deceased person's estate qualifies for 12 months after the date that the loan was taken out. [s.403]

(h) To replace other loans qualifying under (c) to (f) above.

Exam focus point

If the examiner asks you to give examples of deductible interest payments try looking at **s.383(2) ITA 2007** which sets out the eligible loans on which interest is deductible.

If the interest is paid wholly and exclusively for business purposes the taxpayer can instead deduct the interest when computing his trade profits, rather than from total income. The interest need not fall into any of the categories outlined above.

Interest on a loan taken out by an individual to buy a **letting property** will qualify as an expense when computing property income (see later in this Text).

Where interest is allowable in the computation of **trade profits or property income**, the amount *payable* (on an accruals basis) is deducted rather than interest *paid* in the tax year.

5.4 Limit on income tax reliefs

This section is new

From the 2013/14 tax year there is a **limit on the amount of certain income tax reliefs** that an individual can claim. [s.24A]

Relief is capped at the **higher of**:

(a) **£50,000**, and
(b) **25% of the taxpayer's 'adjusted total income'**.

An individual's adjusted total income is broadly their **total income** (as calculated at Step 1 of the income tax computation above) **for the tax year, plus any amounts donated under the payroll deduction scheme, but reduced by the gross amount of personal pension contributions** (see later in this Text) they may have made. [s.24A(8)]

The affected reliefs include:

• **Property loss relief**, where the loss arose from capital allowances (see later in this Text)

- **Share loss relief** on certain unquoted trading company shares (see later in this Text)
- **Qualifying interest payments**, eg on loans to buy an interest in a close company (see above)

The cap applies to the total of all the affected reliefs claimed in a tax year. **If makes a claim for more than one affected relief, he can choose which one(s) to restrict.** It is most beneficial to restrict those reliefs that can be used in future years (eg property losses) and to take relief for those which would otherwise be lost (eg qualifying interest payments).

Where the taxpayer claims to use one of the above reliefs in an earlier tax year, **relief is capped in that earlier year.**

Example 2

For 2013/14 Adam has earnings of £250,000, but received no other income.

During the year his tax relievable outgoings included a gross contribution of £10,000 to his personal pension scheme and qualifying interest paid on a loan he had taken out three years ago to buy shares in a close company.

What is the maximum relief that Adam can obtain in respect of the loan interest assuming he paid interest of:

(a) £25,000
(b) £55,000, or
(c) £75,000.

---

6 Step 3: Personal allowance and blind person's allowance

6.1 The allowances

The personal allowance and the blind person's allowance are deducted from net income (at Step 3) to arrive at 'taxable income'. The amounts given in the following paragraphs are for 2013/14.

Exam focus point

The amount of personal allowance and blind person's allowance is given in the ATT's tax tables. Find them!

6.2 Personal allowance (PA)

6.2.1 Basic personal allowance

Until 6 April 2013, an individual's personal allowance depended on their age. From that date, the **personal allowance is instead available by reference to the individual's date of birth.**

All individuals (including children) born after 5 April 1948 are entitled to an amount of tax free income, the personal allowance (PA), of £9,440.

If an individual's 'adjusted net income' exceeds £100,000 the personal allowance is reduced by £1 for every £2 of excess income. It can be reduced to nil (once income reaches £118,880), but if any allowance remains it is rounded up to the nearest pound.

Adjusted net income is broadly net income, less a deduction for the **gross** value of: [s.58]

(a) Gift Aid donations (see below)
(b) Personal pension contributions (see later in this Text), and
(c) Trade losses.

Example 3

Bart earns £127,510 in 2013/14 from his employment with Waltrade Ltd. This is his only income in the year. He makes a contribution of £15,000 (gross) to his personal pension.

Calculate Bart's taxable income.

6.2.2 Allowances for older individuals

Individuals born between 6 April 1938 and 5 April 1948 (ie aged 66 to 75 years in 2013/14) are entitled to a higher personal allowance of £10,500 instead of the basic PA.

Where adjusted net income (see above) exceeds £26,100 the allowance is reduced by one half of the excess over £26,100. However, the allowance cannot usually fall below the level of the basic personal allowance (ie £9,440) unless adjusted net income exceeds £100,000, in which case it can be reduced to £nil (see above).

Individuals born before 6 April 1938 (ie aged 76 or over in 2013/14) are entitled to a slightly higher personal allowance of £10,660. This higher allowance works in the same way as above with regard to the adjusted net income limit of £26,100.

Example 4

Geoff is 68 on 13 February 2014. He has income of £28,520. What is his personal allowance for 2013/14?

Exam focus point

Examiner's report – Personal Taxation

November 2010 – Part II LFQ 1

Most candidates dealt with the income restriction to the personal allowance correctly with the exception of the deduction of the grossed up gift aid donation from net income.

6.3 Blind person's allowance (BPA)

A taxpayer who is registered with a local authority as a blind person is entitled to an allowance of £2,160. This is given in addition to the personal allowance.

6.4 Persons resident abroad

In general, non-UK residents are liable to tax on income arising in the UK, but are not entitled to allowances. However, certain people are entitled to allowances despite being non-resident. These are: [s.56(3)]

(a)   Individuals resident in the Isle of Man or the Channel Islands
(b)   Former residents who have left the country for their own or a family member's health reasons
(c)   Current or former Crown servants and their widows or widowers
(d)   Employees in the service of any territory under Her Majesty's protection
(e)   Missionaries
(f)   EEA nationals (ie all 28 EU member states, plus Iceland, Liechtenstein and Norway).

The above rules for non-residents apply both to allowances deducted from net income (the PA and the BPA) and to allowances that reduce tax (eg married couples' allowance, see below).

UK resident, non-domiciled individuals who claim to use the remittance basis of taxation (ie it does not apply automatically) on their foreign income are not entitled to personal allowances (see later in this Text).

6.5 Setting off allowances

As a general principle, personal allowances and other reliefs which are set against an individual's total income may be set off in the way that **minimises the individual's tax liability. Deductible payments, losses and personal allowances should be set against non savings income first then savings income and finally against dividend income.**

Exam focus point

Calculation of allowances is often tested in the short form questions. Make sure you are familiar with the rules.

---

7 Steps 4 & 5: Calculating the tax liability

7.1 The personal tax computation

We have now considered the fundamental elements of the *personal tax computation*. Here is an example of what that computation might look like so far.

Illustration 1

MRS A: INCOME TAX COMPUTATION 2013/14

	£
Employment income – salary (PAYE of £45,960 deducted)	140,200
Property income – rent from cottage	24,100
Taxed income from discretionary trust £1,485 × 100/55	2,700
Total income	167,000
Less: deductible payment (eg qualifying interest paid)	(1,017)
Net income	165,983
Less: personal allowance (adjusted net income > £118,880)	(Nil)
Taxable income	165,983

Income tax is charged on the figure of 'taxable income' according to the type (or 'component') **of income being taxed. Different tax rates apply to non savings, savings income and dividends.**

7.2 Non savings income

In 2013/14 the first £32,010 of non savings income (ie in the **basic rate band**) is taxed at the basic rate of **20%**. Between £32,010 and £150,000 it is taxed at the **higher rate of 40%** and **above £150,000 it is taxed at the additional rate of 45%** (50% in 2012/13).

In the above illustration all of the taxable income is taxed as non savings income:

(a)   On the first £32,010 at the basic rate (20%) = £6,402
(b)   On the next £117,990 (ie up to £150,000) at the higher rate (40%) ie £117,990 @ 40% = £47,196
(c)   On the excess above £150,000 at the additional rate (50%) ie £15,983 @ 45% = £7,192

The total tax liability would be £60,790.

The tax bands and rates are provided in the ATT's tax tables in the examination.

Example 5

Simone's taxable income (ie after the personal allowance) for 2013/14 is £49,035. All of her income is non savings income. Calculate Simone's tax liability for the year.

The tax calculation may be affected by cash payments to charity made under the Gift Aid scheme (see below) **or to personal pension schemes** (see later in this Text).

7.3 Savings income

'Savings income' is taxed after 'non savings income'. There is a **'starting rate band'** that applies only to savings income and, within this band, **up to £2,790 is taxed at 10%.**

If savings income falls in the **basic rate band,** ie £2,791 to £32,010 , it is taxed at **20%.**

If it falls in the **higher rate band,** ie £32,011 to £150,000, it is taxed at **40%.**

If it falls above the **higher rate band,** 45% (50% in 2012/13) tax on the gross amount of the savings income is payable.

However, the 10% starting rate band for savings income is only available if the taxpayer has taxable non-savings income of less than £2,790. Non savings income uses the starting rate band in priority to savings income. So, if a taxpayer has taxable non savings income of, say, £5,000 and savings income of £500, the 10% band is not available and the total income of £5,500 is taxed at 20%.

Interest is paid after the **bank or building society deducts 20% 'at source',** so, as we saw above, if £80 of net interest is received, it must be grossed up at $^{100}/_{80}$ to £100 for inclusion in the income tax computation.

The 20% tax credit is then deducted from the tax liability in the income tax computation. So, to continue our example, a tax credit of £20 can be deducted from the investor's tax liability and **can be refunded if the liability is less than the tax credit** (ie it can create a repayment).

Example 6

Assume that all of Simone's taxable income (Example 5) is savings income. Calculate her tax liability for the year.

7.4 Dividend income

'Dividend income' is taxed as the **'top slice'** of a taxpayer's income, ie after all other income.

Dividends falling in the basic rate tax band are taxed at 10%. Dividends falling into the **higher rate band** are taxed at **32.5%** and if **taxable income exceeds £150,000, they are** taxed at 37.5% (42.5% in 2012/13).

Dividends come with a *notional* 10% tax credit so, as we saw above, if the investor receives a dividend of £90, it must be grossed up at $^{100}/_{90}$ to £100 for inclusion in the income tax computation and has a tax credit of £10. However, since it is not a real tax credit, although it can be deducted from the shareholder's tax liability it **cannot be repaid to him. So, for the full 10% credit to be available, all of the dividend income has to be chargeable to tax**

Deductible payments and the personal allowance must be set against **non savings income in priority to savings income and dividend income.**

Example 7

Brittany received dividends of £49,500 in 2013/14. This was her only income in the year. What is her income tax liability and state the amount of tax credits she will be able to set against this liability?

Exam focus point

If a taxpayer's income includes savings and dividends it is important to adopt a layout which assists in applying these rules. Accordingly three columns, one for non savings income, one for savings income and one for dividends are recommended.

Example 8

Albert has a salary of £12,535, £2,000 (gross) of building society interest and £3,000 (gross) of UK dividends. What is his tax liability?

Example 9

Barry receives net bank interest of £8,000, and UK dividends of £10,800. What is his tax liability assuming he has rental income of:

(a)   £26,185?
(b)   £135,000?

Example 10

Bertha has rental income of £1,500, bank interest (net amount received) of £8,800, and receives UK dividends of £10,800. What is her tax liability?

Example 11

Carol has a salary of £5,540 and received building society interest of £105,000 and a UK dividend of £22,140. How much is Carol's tax liability?

7.5 Gift Aid

7.5.1 Cash donations

A taxpayer receives tax relief for cash payments to UK and broadly EU/EEA charities made under the Gift Aid scheme. [s.414]

7.5.2 Tax relief

All taxpayers are entitled to basic rate (20%) tax relief at source, ie for a donation of £1,000 the taxpayer will pay £800 to the charity. The charity claims the tax deducted by the taxpayer from HMRC.

Higher and additional rate taxpayers are entitled to additional relief through the income tax computation. The actual payment is grossed up by 100/80 and the donor's basic rate and higher rate bands are extended by the gross amount so more income is taxed at the basic/ higher rates rather than the higher/ additional rates. [s.414]

In the following illustration, assume the taxpayer pays a total of £1,920 to charity under Gift Aid:

Illustration 2

MR B: INCOME TAX COMPUTATION 2013/14

		£
Net income (non savings)		48,090
Less: personal allowance		(9,440)
Taxable income		38,650
Tax liability	£	£
Basic rate band:	32,010 @ 20%	6,402
Extended basic rate band: £1,920 × 100/80	2,400 @ 20%	480
Higher rate:	4,240 @ 40%	1,696
	38,650	8,578

So, the taxpayer obtains relief on the Gift Aid donation at the higher rate of £480 (£2,400 × (40 − 20 = 20%)) as income that would otherwise be taxed at 40% is only taxed at 20%.

In total the taxpayer has received tax relief of £960 (£480 at source and £480 in his income tax computation) on a gross gift of £2,400, ie at the rate of 40%. The charity has received £2,400 in total (£1,920 from the taxpayer and £480 from HMRC).

Taxpayers may elect to carry back the Gift Aid payments to the previous tax year. This may enable them to obtain higher rate tax relief in the previous year if their income in the current year is not sufficient to obtain higher rate relief.

A carry back claim must be made no later than the date on which the taxpayer files his return for the earlier year, and in any event no later than the filing date for electronic tax returns for that year (see later in this Text). So, a claim to carry back relief from 2013/14 to 2012/13 must be made by 31 January 2014. [s.426]

Example 12

Zoë earned £50,000 in 2013/14 and expects to earn £30,000 in 2014/15. She has no other income. In May 2014, she paid £8,000 under the Gift Aid scheme. Zoë elects for the gift to be treated as made in 2013/14. Show Zoë's tax liability in both years assuming that 2013/14 rates and allowances continue to apply in future years.

7.5.3 Conditions

The charitable payment must not be repayable to the donor.

Benefits provided by the charity to the donor or any person connected with him must not be worth more than: [s.418]

(a)	For gifts ≤ £100:	25% × the donation
(b)	For gifts between £100 and £1,000:	£25
(c)	For gifts > £1,000:	lower of:
		(i) 5% × the donation and
		(ii) £2,500

The taxpayer must complete a declaration form agreeing to pay the appropriate amount of tax to cover the amount that the charity will reclaim.

If a donor pays insufficient tax during the year his personal allowance must be restricted to ensure the basic rate tax being recovered by the charity is paid.

All cash payments to charity (other than those made under the Payroll Deduction Scheme – see later in this Text) are potentially relievable under the Gift Aid scheme. There are no maximum or minimum thresholds for Gift Aid payments.

8 Step 6: Tax reductions

8.1 Introduction

Tax reductions reduce the tax on the income once it has been calculated. The tax reductions are as follows.

	Tax reduction
Investment under the **Venture Capital Trust Scheme (VCT)** (see later in this Text)	30% of investment (maximum investment = £200,000 per annum)
Investment under the **Enterprise Investment Scheme (EIS)** (see later in this Text)	30% of investment (maximum investment = £1,000,000 per annum
Investment under the **Seed Enterprise Investment Scheme (SEIS)** (see later in this Text)	50% of investment (maximum investment = £100,000 per annum)
Maintenance payments following the breakdown of marriage	10% of payment
Married couple's allowance	10% of allowance

Married couple's allowance and relief for maintenance payments are only available where the individuals concerned were born before 6 April 1935 (ie were aged 79 by the end of the 2013/14 tax year).

8.2 Married couple's allowance (MCA)

8.2.1 The relief

The MCA is available for married couples and same sex couples within a civil partnership. [s.42]

The MCA is only available if either spouse or partner (or both) was born before 6 April 1935 (ie 79 in 2013/14). If this condition is satisfied a minimum allowance is available of £3,040.

The tax reduction is given at 10% so the minimum tax reduction is 10% × £3,040 = £304.

For couples who are married **before 5 December 2005** (the date civil partnerships were introduced), the **tax reduction is automatically allocated to the husband**, while for marriages and civil partnerships entered into **on or after 5 December 2005**, the **tax reduction is allocated to whichever partner has the higher income**.

The maximum value of the MCA is £7,915 if *either* partner is 79 by the end of the tax year **but is subject to an income restriction**.

When adjusted net income exceeds £26,100 , the personal allowance given to someone born before 6 April 1938 is reduced by half of the excess, as explained above. **Once that has been reduced to £9,440 (or lower if the individual has adjusted net income between £100,000 and £118,880), the married couple's allowance is then reduced by the excess restriction, but not to below £3,040.**

For marriages before 5 December 2005, the reduction in the married couple's allowance always depends on the *husband's* adjusted net income. For marriages and civil partnerships entered into on or after 5 December 2005, the restriction to the MCA depends on the adjusted net income of the partner with the higher income.

8.2.2 Elections to transfer the MCA

The wife (or for partnerships/marriages entered into on or after 5 December 2005, the lower earning partner) can unilaterally (ie alone) elect to have half of the MCA tax reduction set against her tax instead of her partner's. The election must be made by the start of the tax year.

Alternatively, the couple can jointly elect, by the start of the tax year, to transfer all of the MCA tax reduction to the wife (or for partnerships/marriages entered into on or after 5 December 2005, the lower earning partner). An election remains in force until revoked, and any revocation applies from the following 6 April. For the year of marriage/partnership, an election may be made during the year.

The elections can only apply in respect of the minimum £3,040 MCA even if a higher allowance is available.

Only if the MCA turns out to be wasted (because either spouse or partner has insufficient tax to reduce) can the excess then be transferred to the other spouse or partner.

8.2.3 The year of marriage

In the year of marriage/civil partnership, the MCA is reduced by $^1/_{12}$ for each full tax month (from the 6th of one month to the 5th of the next) **before the wedding/civil partnership**.

8.2.4 The year of death/separation

If a wife (or for partnerships/marriages entered into on or after 5 December 2005, the lower earning partner) dies during a tax year, her partner receives the personal allowance (PA) and a full MCA for that year. The wife or lower earning partner will have a full PA for the year of death.

When a husband (or for partnerships/marriages entered into on or after 5 December 2005, the higher earning partner) dies the full PA and MCA are available. Any election relating to the MCA becomes void in the year of death. The widowed spouse or partner obtains the PA for the year, as normal, and is entitled to any MCA that becomes surplus.

In the tax year in which separation takes place, the husband or higher earning partner receives the PA plus a full MCA. However, any MCA election remains valid.

8.3 Maintenance payments

Provided the payer or the recipient (or both) was born before 6 April 1935 a tax reduction is available for payments under court orders or written agreements, or for maintenance assessments by the Child Support Agency. [s.453]

All maintenance payments are made gross (without deduction of tax at source) and are not taxable on the recipient.

Provided that the payment is made to the former spouse/partner for the benefit of the former spouse/partner or of a child of the family (and not directly to a child of the relationship), the payer is entitled to claim a tax reduction of 10% of the lower of:

(a)   The payments *due* in the tax year, and
(b)   The minimum value amount of the MCA (£3,040 for 2013/14).

8.4 Giving tax reductions

The tax reduction is calculated and deducted only if the individual has enough tax to reduce.

Illustration 3

Greg's tax liability is £130. During the year he made a small investment of £500 in an EIS company, so he has a tax reduction available to him of £150 (£500 × 30%).

However, this amount can only reduce his tax liability to nil. Greg *cannot* claim a repayment of £20 (£150 – £130).

The tax that can be reduced is the tax as calculated at steps 4 and 5 in the income tax computation (see above).

An individual may be entitled to several different tax reductions. They **must be applied in a set order** as follows:

(a)   Investments under the venture capital trust and then enterprise investment schemes
(b)   Maintenance payments
(c)   The married couple's allowance.

Using the MCA last enables any unused amount to be transferred to the other spouse/partner. The other tax reductions cannot be transferred in this way.

Example 13

Peter, a married man aged 79, pays maintenance of £3,000 a year to a former spouse. His current wife has no income and is younger than him. Show his tax position for 2013/14 if his income consists of:

(a)   Trading profits of £28,980 and rental income of £2,000,
(b)   Trading profits of £9,120 and rental income of £2,000.

9 Step 7: Tax payable

The final step in calculating the tax liability is to add certain tax charges including (see later in this Text): [s.30]

(a)   The pension lifetime allowance charge, and
(b)   The pension annual allowance charge.

The **high income child benefit tax charge** (see later in this Text) **is also added to the tax liability** where applicable.

Any tax already suffered by deduction at source (or already paid on account under self assessment) can then be deducted from the tax liability to arrive at the tax payable by the taxpayer.

We have now completed the steps for calculating income tax.

Example 14

Jack has the following income and outgoings during the year:

	£
Salary (tax deducted under PAYE £47,598)	135,000
UK dividend received (net)	3,600
Building society interest received (net)	14,800
Discretionary trust payment received (net)	5,500
Gift Aid donation (net amount paid)	8,000
Investment in Seed Enterprise Investment Scheme company	15,000

What is Jack's tax payable or repayable for 2013/14?

10 Exempt income

Here is a list of some of the **main types of income that are exempt from income tax**, many of which are covered later in this Text:

(a)   Income arising from Individual Savings Accounts (ISAs) or Junior ISAs

(b)   Interest or terminal bonus on National Savings & Investments certificates and prizes on premium bonds

(c)   Up to £4,250 gross letting income from letting furnished accommodation in the landlord's own main residence

(d)   Dividends on ordinary shares in Venture Capital Trusts (VCTs) (up to the permitted maximum £200,000 investment per year)

(e)   A terminal bonus paid under a 'save as you earn' (SAYE) scheme

(f)   Interest ('repayment' interest) received from HMRC on overpaid tax

(g)   Many social security benefits, eg universal credit, child tax credit and working tax credit

(h)   Qualifying care relief of £10,000 plus £200 a week per child under age 11 and £250 a week per child age 11 and over

(i)   First £30,000 of certain compensation payments received on termination of employment

(j)   Interest on government stocks (eg Treasury stock) held by non-residents

(k)   Employment pensions paid to individuals retiring through work-related illness or injury but only the amount in excess of an ordinary ill-health pension

(l)   Damages (and interest on damages) for personal injuries

(m)   Scholarship income (in the hands of the scholar; taxable on parent if paid by parent's employer)

(n)   Winnings from betting and gaming (including the lottery)

(o)   Gifts.

The last two exemptions in the list do not derive from statute, but from the general principle that income is taxable only if, broadly, it arises from a *source*. Neither gambling winnings nor gifts have a source and hence they are not taxable.

- Income tax is charged on the chargeable income of a chargeable person for a tax year.

- Adults and children are all liable to income tax on their income.

- All components of an individual's income are brought together in a personal tax computation.

- All figures in the computation must be included gross.

- Certain payments can be deducted from total income. The main deductions are donations to charity in the form of shares or land and interest on certain loans.

- *Net income* is a figure representing the taxpayer's assessable income from all sources, after deductible payments.

- The personal allowance is deducted to arrive at *taxable income*. The personal allowance is available to each individual. It is increased for individuals born before 6 April 1948 (subject to their level of income).

- We categorise income into different types: non savings, savings and dividends. Each type of income suffers different rates of tax depending on whether the income falls into the starting, basic, higher or additional rate band. Non savings income is taxed first (at 20%, 40% then 45%) then savings income (at 10%, 20%, 40% then 45%) and finally dividend income (at 10%, 32.5% and 37.5%).

- The 10% band for savings income is only available if taxable non savings income does not exceed £2,790.

- Some interest income is received gross and some net. Interest received net (typically bank and building society interest) must be grossed up by 100/80 for inclusion in the income tax computation.

- Dividends from UK companies are deemed to be received net of a 10% tax credit. They must be grossed up by 100/90 for inclusion in the tax computation.

- Cash donations to charity under Gift Aid are made net (saving basic rate tax at source) and also reduce the higher/additional rate tax bill (by extending the basic rate and higher rate tax bands).

- Tax reductions are deducted in arriving at the *tax liability*. These include the married couples' allowance (only available to individuals aged 79 and over), VCT, EIS and SEIS investments, and certain maintenance payments.

- The *tax payable* is the tax liability less tax suffered at source (and payments on account).

- Certain types of income are exempt from income tax.

Quiz

1. A 'tax year' is a 12-month period running from 1 April to the following 31 March. True/False?

2. The income of a minor child (aged under 18) is always treated as income of his parent. True/False?

3. To what extent are the following individuals liable to UK income tax?

    (a) John Smith, resident and domiciled in UK, who has both UK and foreign source income.

    (b) Johann Schmidt, who has never been to the UK, but who receives rental income from a property in London in addition to his salary from his German employer. Johann has always lived in Germany.

4. Define 'net income'.

5. Daniel is 35, has trade profits of £46,040 and makes a Gift Aid donation of £500 (net). Calculate Daniel's tax liability.

6. On 31 December 2013 an individual receives income from a discretionary trust of £1,815. Show how much must be included in their income tax computation.

7. On 31 December 2013, an individual receives a UK dividend of £832. Calculate the amount that will be shown in the income tax computation.

8. Alison, aged 45, has the following sources of income in 2013/14:

Income from employment (PAYE suffered £14,322)	£61,250
Income from rented properties	£30,000
Interest received on high rate savings bank account	£3,000
UK dividends received	£9,000

    Calculate her tax payable for the year.

9. Sarah is 68 and has net income of £28,320. She makes a donation via Gift Aid to Oxfam of £560. To what personal allowance is Sarah entitled?

10. Jack (aged 64) married Elsie (aged 79) forty years ago. To what allowances and tax reductions is Jack entitled in 2013/14, assuming his net income is £27,200?

11. Oberon (born 4 April 1935) and Titania (born 14 May 1954) married on 24 December 2013. What allowances and tax reductions are they entitled to in 2013/14 assuming Oberon's income is £11,000 and Titania's income is £16,000?

12. Peter (aged 79) and Rita (age 58) separated on 1 July 2013. Thereafter, Peter pays Rita £250 per month in maintenance. Payments are made on the last day of each month.

    (a) Will Peter make the payments net of income tax or gross?
    (b) What tax reduction is Peter entitled to in 2013/14?

1.   False – it runs from 6 April to the following 5 April.

2.   False – the income is only treated as the parent's income (broadly) if it is derived from the parent and exceeds £100 (gross) in the tax year.

3.   (a)   John Smith is liable to UK income tax on all his income, regardless of where it arises.

     (b)   Johann Schmidt, being not resident in the UK, is liable to UK income tax only in respect of income arising in the UK, ie on his UK rental income.

4.   Net income: total income (from all sources) less deductible payments (eg qualifying interest).

5.

	£
Net income	46,040
Less: PA	(9,440)
Taxable income	36,600
Tax:	
£32,010 × 20%	6,402
£625 × 20% (W)	125
£3,965 × 40%	1,586
Tax liability	8,113

(W) Basic rate band extended by gross donation of £625 (£500 × 100/80)

6.   £3,300, ie £1,815 × 100/55

7.   £924 (ie £832 × 100/90)

8.

	Non savings income	Savings income	Dividends
	£	£	£
Employment income	61,250		
Property income	30,000		
Bank interest £3,000 × 100/80		3,750	
Dividends £9,000 × 100/90			10,000
Net income	91,250	3,750	10,000
Less: PA (W)	(6,940)		
Taxable income	84,310	3,750	10,000

	£
Tax:	
£32,010 @ 20%	6,402
£52,300 @ 40%	20,920
£3,750 @ 40%	1,500
£10,000 @ 32.5%	3,250
Tax liability	32,072
Less: tax suffered at source	
tax credit on dividends	(1,000)
tax credit on interest	(750)
PAYE	(14,322)
Tax payable	16,000

	£	£
Working		
Basic PA		9,440
Total income £(91,250 + 3,750 + 10,000)	105,000	
Less: limit	(100,000)	
	5,000	
Restriction (£5,000 ÷ 2)		(2,500)
Available PA		6,940

9.

	£
Personal allowance (born between 6 April 1938 and 5 April 1948)	10,500
Less: ½(£28,320 – £700 (W) – £26,100)	(760)
Available PA	9,740

(W) Gross donation to charity is £560 × 100/80 = £700. This is taken as a notional deduction from net income when calculating the restriction to the PA.

10.

	£
Personal allowance (born after 5 April 1948)	9,440
Married couple's allowance (given by reference to age of elder spouse)	7,915
Less: ½ × (£27,200 – £26,100)	(550)
	7,365

Tax relief restricted to 10%, ie £737

11. *Oberon*:

Personal allowance: £10,660 (born before 6 April 1938)

Titania:

Personal allowance: £9,440 (born after 6 April 1948)

MCA: given as one spouse is 79, apportioned as they married part way through the tax year: £7,915 × 4/12 = £2,638

Tax reduction @ 10% = £264

Note. The marriage took place after 5 December 2005, so the MCA is allocated to the spouse with the higher income, Titania.

12. (a) Gross

 (b) Lower of

  (i) Payments due: £250 × 9 = £2,250, and
  (ii) £3,040

   ie £2,250

   Tax reduction £2,250 × 10% = £225

Solutions to chapter examples

Solution to Example 1

Annabelle must include the following amounts:

(a)   Bank interest: £1,000 (£800 × 100/80)
(b)   Discretionary trust income: £1,818 (£1,000 × 100/55)
(c)   Dividends: £500 (£450 × 100/90)
(d)   IIP trust income: £625 (£500 × 100/80 as paid out of interest income).

Solution to Example 2

Maximum relief:

			£
Higher of:	(i)		50,000
	(ii) 25% × £240,000 (W)		60,000

ie £60,000 ∴

		£
(a)	Maximum relief for £25,000 interest	25,000
(b)	Maximum relief for £55,000 interest	55,000
(c)	Maximum relief for £75,000 interest	60,000

Working – Adjusted total income

	£
Total income	250,000
Less: gross pension contribution	(10,000)
Adjusted total income	240,000

Solution to Example 3

Income tax liability 2013/14

	£
Earnings/ Net income	127,510
Less: personal allowance (W)	(3,185)
Taxable income	124,325

Working

	£	£
Personal allowance		9,440
Total net income	127,510	
Less: gross pension contribution	(15,000)	
Adjusted income	112,510	
Less: limit	(100,000)	
	12,510	
Less: ½ × £12,510		(6,255)
Available PA		3,185

Solution to Example 4

Geoff was born on 13 February 1946 (ie between 6 April 1938 and 5 April 1948) so he is entitled to the higher personal allowance of £10,500. However, his adjusted net income exceeds £26,100 so his available PA is as follows:

	£
Net income	28,520
PA	10,500
Less: ½ × £(28,520 – 26,100)	(1,210)
PA given	9,290

Solution to Example 5

	Income		Tax
	£		£
Basic rate:	32,010	@ 20%	6,402
Higher rate:	17,025	@ 40%	6,810
	49,035		13,212

Solution to Example 6

	Income		Tax
	£		£
Starting rate:	2,790	@ 10%	279
Basic rate:	29,220	@ 20%	5,844
Higher rate:	17,025	@ 40%	6,810
	49,035		12,933

Solution to Example 7

	£
Net income £49,500 × 100/90	55,000
Less: PA	(9,440)
Taxable income	45,560
Income tax:	
£	
32,010 × 10%	3,201
13,550 × 32.5%	4,404
45,560	
Tax liability	7,605

The tax liability can be reduced by tax credits of only £4,556 based on the *taxable* dividend, rather than £5,500 based on the whole dividend received.

Solution to Example 8

	Non savings income	Savings income	Dividends
	£	£	£
Net income	12,535	2,000	3,000
Less: PA	(9,440)	–	–
Taxable income	3,095	2,000	3,000
Income tax:		£	
£			
3,095 × 20% (non savings income taxed first)		619	
2,000 × 20% (savings income taxed second)		400	
3,000 × 10% (UK dividends taxed last (top slice))		300	
8,095			
Tax liability		1,319	

Non-savings income exceeds the starting rate band for savings income of £2,790. All of the savings income is therefore taxed at the basic rate (20%). The £3,000 dividend income also falls within the basic rate band and is taxed at 10%.

Albert has tax credits of £700 (£2,000 × 20% + £3,000 × 10%) which can be offset against his tax liability leaving tax payable of £619 (£1,319 – £700) most of which, if not all, will have been collected under PAYE.

Solution to Example 9

(a) Property income £26,185

	Non savings income	Savings income	Dividends
	£	£	£
Property income	26,185		
Interest (× 100/80)		10,000	
Dividends (× 100/90)			12,000
Less: PA	(9,440)	–	–
Taxable income	16,745	10,000	12,000

Income tax:

	£
16,745 × 20%	3,349
10,000 × 20% (savings income)	2,000
5,265× 10% (dividend income in BR band)	526
32,010	
6,735 × 32.5% (dividend income in HR band)	2,189
38,745	
Tax liability	8,064

UK dividend income in the basic rate band is taxed at 10%. The 32.5% rate applies where it exceeds the higher rate threshold. Barry's tax credits of £3,200 (£10,000 × 20% + £12,000 × 10%) would reduce the liability to tax payable of £4,864 (£8,064 – £3,200).

(b) Property income £135,000	Non savings income	Savings income	Dividends
	£	£	£
Property income	135,000		
Interest (× 100/80)		10,000	
Dividends (× 100/90)			12,000
Less: PA (total income > £118,880)	(NIL)	–	–
Taxable income	135,000	10,000	12,000

Income tax:

	£
32,010 × 20%	6,402
102,990 × 40% (non savings income in HR band)	41,196
10,000 × 40% (savings income in HR band)	4,000
5,000 × 32.5% (dividend income in HR band)	1,625
150,000	
7,000 × 37.5% (UK dividend income at AR)	2,625
Tax liability	55,848

Non savings and savings income in the higher rate band are taxed at 40%. Dividend income in the higher rate band is taxed at 32.5% and at the additional rate of 37.5% where it is in excess of the higher rate band. Barry's tax credits of £3,200 (£10,000 × 20% + £12,000 × 10%) would reduce the tax liability to £52,648 (£55,848 – £3,200).

Solution to Example 10

	Non savings income	Savings income	Dividends
	£	£	£
Property income	1,500		
Interest (× 100/80)		11,000	
Dividends (× 100/90)			12,000
Less: PA	(1,500)	(7,940)	–
Taxable income	Nil	3,060	12,000

Income tax:

	£
2,790 × 10%	279
270 × 20% (savings income)	54
12,000 × 10% (UK dividend income in BR band)	1,200
15,060	
Tax liability	1,533

Bertha's non savings income is below £2,790 so the starting rate band for savings income is available. Her tax credits of £3,400 (£11,000 × 20% + £12,000 × 10%) would reduce the liability to tax *repayable* (ie a refund) of £1,867 (£1,533 – £3,400). Tax credits on dividends are offset in priority to other tax deducted at source to maximise the relief available.

Solution to Example 11

	Non savings income £	Savings income £	Dividends £
Employment income	5,540		
Interest (× 100/80)		131,250	
Dividends (× 100/90)			24,600
Less: PA (£nil as total income > £118,880)	(Nil)	–	–
Taxable income	5,540	131,250	24,600

Income tax:

£		£
5,540 × 20%		1,108
26,470 × 20%		5,294
32,010		
104,780 × 40%		41,912
13,210 × 32.5%		4,293
150,000		
11,390 × 37.5%		4,271
161,390		
Tax liability		56,878

Carol's income exceeds £118,880 so she does not receive a PA. Her tax credits of £28,710 (£131,250 × 20% + £24,600 × 10%) would reduce the liability to tax payable of £28,168 (£56,878 – £28,710).

Solution to Example 12

	2013/14 £	2014/15 £
Employment income	50,000	30,000
Less: personal allowance	(9,440)	(9,440)
Taxable income	40,560	20,560
Tax		
£32,010 / £20,560 × 20%	6,402	4,112
£8,550 × 20%	1,710	
	8,112	4,112

Income is below the higher rate threshold of £32,010 in 2014/15, so if no claim were made no higher rate relief would be available for the Gift Aid donation in 2014/15.

Instead, with a carry back claim, the basic rate band is extended by £10,000 (£8,000 × $^{100}/_{80}$) in 2013/14. The claim allows a further £8,550 of income in 2013/14 to be taxed at 20% rather than 40%, saving tax of £1,710.

Solution to Example 13

	(a) £	(b) £
Trade profits	28,980	9,120
Property income	2,000	2,000
Net income	30,980	11,120
Less: personal allowance (W)	(9,440)	(10,660)
	21,540	460
Income tax		
£21,540 / £460 × 20%	4,308	92
Tax reductions		
Maintenance payment £3,040 (max) × 10%	(304)	(304)
	4,004	nil
Married couple's allowance £6,695 × 10% (W)	(670)	–
Income tax liability	3,334	nil

Tax reductions cannot lead to repayments of tax, so in (b) part of the relief for the maintenance payments and the MCA is wasted. If Peter's wife had income of her own, the surplus MCA (£792) could be transferred to her.

Working

Income restriction:

	(a) £
Net income	30,980
Less: income limit	(26,100)
Excess	4,880
Half	2,440
PA	10,660
Reduction (£2,440 – restricted)	(1,220)
Basic PA	9,440
Maximum MCA	7,915
Excess reduction £(2,440 – 1,220)	(1,220)
Available MCA	6,695

Solution to Example 14

	Non savings income £	Savings income £	Dividends £
Employment income	135,000		
Building society interest (BSI) £14,800 × 100/80		18,500	
UK dividends £3,600 × 100/90			4,000
Discretionary trust payment £5,500 × 100/55	10,000		
Net income	145,000	18,500	4,000
Less: PA (£nil as total income > £118,880)			
Taxable income	145,000	18,500	4,000

Income tax		£	£
Non savings income =	£32,010 × 20%		6,402
	£10,000 × 20% (note)		2,000
	£(145,000 – 32,010 – 10,000) = £102,990 × 40%		41,196
Savings income =	£(150,000 – 145,000) = £5,000 × 40%		2,000
	£10,000 × 40% (note)		4,000
	£(18,500 – 5,000 – 10,000) = £3,500 × 45%		1,575
Dividend income =	£4,000 × 37.5%		1,500
			58,673
Less: tax reduction – SEIS: £15,000 × 50%			(7,500)
Tax liability			51,173
Less: Tax suffered on dividends £(4,000 × 10%)		400	
Tax suffered on salary – PAYE		47,598	
Tax suffered on discretionary trust payment £(10,000 × 45%)		4,500	
Tax suffered on BSI £(18,500 × 20%)		3,700	(56,198)
Repayment due			(5,025)

Note. The basic rate band and higher rate bands are extended by the gross amount of the Gift Aid payment, ie by £10,000 (£8,000 × $^{100}/_{80}$).

Short Form Questions:

1.1 – 1.18 inclusive

Long Form Questions:

1.1	Mr Daphnis
1.2	Mr Rich
1.3	Mr Poor
1.4	Lauren

chapter

2

Investment income

The purpose of this chapter is to help you to:

- identify whether interest is received net or gross
- deal with the taxation of dividend income
- identify specific tax free investments
- set out and apply the rules for the Enterprise Investment Schemes and Venture Capital Trusts
- understand how income from trusts and estates is taxed
- identify miscellaneous income
- understand and apply the anti avoidance rules for pre-owned assets, receipts from close companies, the Accrued Income Scheme and non-qualifying life assurance policies
- understand the tax consequences of owning investments jointly

References: ITA 2007 unless otherwise stated

1 Interest

1.1 General

We have already seen how to tax bank investment income (interest). **The income assessed in a tax year is the full amount received in that year** (with no deductions for expenses).

However, we also need to be able to identify which interest is received net of tax and which is received gross to determine the amount to include in the income tax computation.

1.2 Interest received gross

This includes interest on:

(a)   **National Savings and Investments (NS&I) accounts**
(b)   UK government (Treasury) stocks (issued after 6 April 1998)
(c)   Fixed term (up to 5 years) deposits of £50,000 and over (for accounts opened before 6 April 2012)
(d)   Loans between individuals
(e)   Quoted Eurobonds, ie a quoted corporate bond

The full amount received must be included in the income tax computation.

1.3 Interest received net

Most building society and bank deposit interest is paid net of 20% tax, and must be grossed up by 100/80 for inclusion in the income tax computation.

Interest received from unquoted debentures (unquoted corporate loan notes) is also received net of a 20% tax credit.

Individuals who are not liable to income tax (eg because their allowances cover their income) **can certify their status** (on Form R85) to any bank or building society at which they have an account **and interest will be credited gross**. Should the income later prove to be taxable the individual must declare it on their tax return and tax will be paid under self assessment.

Example 1

Warren receives the following amounts during 2013/14:

(a)	Barclays Bank interest	£1,800
(b)	5% Treasury Stock 2014 interest	£2,500
(c)	NS&I Savings Account interest	£500
(d)	Unquoted corporate loan note interest	£12,000

You are required to state whether the interest from each source would be received net or gross and to calculate the amounts to include in Warren's income tax computation.

Exam focus point

Examiner's report – Personal Taxation

November 2007 – Part I SFQ 9

Too many candidates went down the route of calculating the taxable interest on an accruals basis, thereby not realising that interest is taxed on a receipts basis.

May 2008 – Part I SFQ 3

Very few candidates realised that the interest received in May 2008 would fall to be taxed in part on Mark in the 2008/09 tax year. Many candidates misread the question and tried to calculate the interest for 2007/08.

---

2 Dividends

2.1 General

We have also seen how to tax dividends, which are received net of a deemed (or 'notional') 10% tax credit and are grossed up by $^{100}/_{90}$ for inclusion in the computation. **Remember this tax credit can only reduce the tax liability calculated on taxable income and cannot be refunded to the shareholder.**

The individual is taxed on the amount received during the tax year. The date on the dividend voucher is taken as the date of receipt regardless of when the cheque is cashed or when the bank transfer is made.

2.2 Top slice of income

Dividend income is treated as the top slice of a taxpayer's income.

There are **two main exceptions** to this rule. The following are taxed after dividend income:

(a)   Taxable gains on **life assurance policies** (see below) and

(b)   The **taxable part of payments made on termination of employment** (see later in this Text),

in that order.

Example 2

Jackie receives a salary of £30,000, £15,000 of dividends and a £100,000 taxable termination payment during the tax year. Calculate her tax liability for 2013/14.

---

3 Tax-free investments

3.1 Overview

The following investments are **tax free**:

(a)   NS&I Savings Certificates (including indexed-linked issues) (see below)

(b)   Interest received from Save As You Earn (SAYE) (building society, bank, or NS&I) schemes (see later in this Text)

(c)   Premium Bond winnings

(d)   Income from Individual Savings Accounts (ISAs) (see below)

(e)   Dividends from Venture Capital Trusts (VCTs) (see below)

3.2 NS&I Savings Certificates

These have historically been attractive, particularly to higher and additional rate taxpayers, as **the accumulated interest paid at the end of the period of investment is totally free from income tax and capital gains tax (CGT)**.

There are two types of savings certificates:

(a)   **Fixed interest**, which provide a guaranteed rate of interest, and
(b)   **Index-linked**, which provide protection from inflation.

The maximum holding of each is **£15,000** per individual per issue. There are currently no issues available to new investors.

3.3 Individual Savings Accounts (ISAs)

3.3.1 Overview

ISAs are generally available to individuals **aged over 18** who are **resident in the UK.**

Junior ISAs are available **for children under the age of 18**.

Investment is permitted in cash and shares.

3.3.2 Main features

The main features of ISAs for individuals **age 18 and over** are as follows.

(a)   There is an **annual subscription limit of £11,520, of which no more than £5,760 can be in cash**

(b)   There is **no statutory lock in period** or minimum subscription

(c)   There is **no lifetime limit**

(d)   The account is **completely free of tax** on both income and capital growth

(e)   ISAs are offered and operated by HMRC approved account managers who must agree to operate accounts in accordance with the ISA regulations.

Individuals **under 18 but over 16** are allowed to subscribe up to £5,760 pa in a **cash only ISA** account. This **does not impact the Junior ISA limit** if they already hold one of those accounts (see below).

Once the maximum amount has been subscribed for in any type of ISA for a year, it is not possible to make further investments **even after a withdrawal** is subsequently made.

3.3.3 ISA accounts

There are two types of ISA account:

(a)   **Cash**, including all the kinds of bank and building society accounts as well as NS&I products, supermarket savings accounts and similar, and

(b)   **Stocks and shares**, including shares obtained from approved savings-related share option schemes and share incentive plans (transferred into the shares component at market value) but not shares acquired on a public offer or a demutualisation.

Individuals over 18 can invest in two ISA accounts each year, one cash and one stocks and shares, so long as they keep within the investment limits.

Example 3

James, age 35, is considering putting the following amounts into a cash ISA account:

(a)   £5,760, or
(b)   £2,000, or
(c)   £Nil.

Advise James how much he can invest in a stocks and shares ISA in 2013/14 if he were to go ahead with each of these cash investments.

3.3.4 Tax exemption

Income and capital gains are tax free within an ISA account, even if the investor makes a withdrawal from the account. This tax **exemption ends on the investor's death.**

An investor **cannot put any more money into an existing ISA account if he becomes non-resident** (see later in this Text). The investor can, however, **still keep the account open** and is still entitled to the benefits. If the investor later resumes his UK residence, he can continue to put money in again.

3.3.5 Junior ISAs

Junior ISAs are available for UK resident children **under the age of 18**, born on or after 3 January 2011 or before September 2002. These **replace the Child Trust Fund (CTF),** which was available to children born between 1 September 2002 and 3 January 2011. Junior ISAs are not currently available to children who already have an existing CTF.

As with normal adult ISAs, there are **two types of Junior ISA accounts**, the **cash and the stocks and shares** accounts. Children can hold up to one cash and one stocks and shares Junior ISA at a time. The **maximum amount** that can be paid in total into the accounts each year is **£3,720**.

From **age 16** the child can **also open a normal Cash ISA** without affecting the Junior ISA limit.

Once the child reaches **age 18** the Junior ISA **becomes a normal ISA** (either a cash or stocks and shares ISA as appropriate), and they can **withdraw money** from the accounts without losing the tax exemption.

4 Tax efficient investments

4.1 The Enterprise Investment Scheme (EIS)

4.1.1 Introduction

The Enterprise Investment Scheme (EIS) is intended to encourage investment in the **shares** of **unquoted trading companies by offering income tax and CGT reliefs and exemptions where certain conditions are satisfied.**

The EIS income tax rules are discussed below. The CGT rules are covered later in this Text.

4.1.2 The relief

When an individual subscribes for eligible shares in a qualifying company, the **amount subscribed is treated as a tax reduction (see earlier in this Text), saving income tax at 30%.** [s.158]

There is **no minimum qualifying investment** and the **maximum total investment that can qualify for this income tax relief in a tax year is £1,000,000.**

Relief is usually given on an actual basis so a 2013/14 investment will attract relief against the tax liability for 2013/14. However, a **taxpayer can claim to carry back his investment**, up to the usual limit, to the previous year. [s.158(4)]

Dividends from EIS shares are taxable under the normal rules.

Example 4

Karen has net income (all non savings income) of £60,000 for 2013/14. She invested £100,000 in a qualifying EIS company on 1 September 2013. Calculate Karen's income tax liability for 2013/14.

Exam focus point

Examiner's report – Personal Taxation

November 2010 – Part I SFQ 5

A high proportion of candidates recognised the maximum current year tax relief available, with fewer identifying the possibility of carrying back relief on the excess investment.

4.1.3 The claim for relief

The **claim for relief must be made within five years from 31 January following the tax year** (so by 31 January 2020 for a 2013/14 investment). This is different from the general time limit for taxpayer claims of four years from the end of the tax year (see later in this Text). [s.202]

4.1.4 Withdrawal of relief

If an individual disposes of shares (by sale or gift other than a gift to a spouse or civil partner) **within three years of their issue, the tax reduction obtained may be wholly or partly withdrawn.** [ss.209 & 210]

If the shares are given away (other than to the investor's spouse or civil partner) **within the three years, all of the tax reduction is withdrawn**.

On a **sale** within the three years, the tax reduction to be withdrawn is:

$$\text{Consideration obtained} \times \frac{\text{Tax reduction obtained on issue}}{\text{Issue price of shares}}$$

However, the **withdrawal cannot exceed the tax reduction originally obtained**.

If EIS shares are **disposed of after three years from issue:**

(a)   The **tax reduction is not withdrawn**

(b)   If there is a **gain for CGT purposes** (see later in this Text), **it is exempt**

(c)   Any **loss for CGT purposes is restricted by reducing the issue price, ie the cost, by the tax reduction not withdrawn** (but not so as to create a gain).

When shares issued under the EIS are sold at arm's length at a loss at any time (within or outside the first three years), and the EIS relief is not wholly withdrawn, the **loss may be set against general income (ie in the same way as a trading loss)**, of the current and/or previous year. [s.131]

Example 5

In May 2013, David subscribes £34,000 for shares in an EIS company. David's tax liability for 2013/14 (before tax reductions) is £5,000, reduced to nil by the EIS relief. David did not elect to carry back any of his investment to 2012/13.

In May 2015, David sells half of the shares for £12,000. The other half are sold for £25,000 in June 2016, giving rise to a gain of £8,000.

(a)   How much of the tax reduction is withdrawn on the first sale?
(b)   How is the gain on the second sale treated?

A **transfer of shares between spouses/civil partners does not give rise to a withdrawal of the tax reduction**. The reduction obtained remains associated with the shares, and if the recipient partner disposes of the shares outside the marriage/civil partnership within three years of their issue, it is withdrawn by an assessment on the recipient spouse/partner.

The **death of a shareholder is not treated as a disposal for the purposes of the withdrawal of the tax reduction**..

4.1.5 Investor conditions

Exam focus point

You may find it helpful to read the following EIS sections with your tax legislation ss.156 to 257 ITA 2007 open in front of you. Look at how much information is contained in these sections. Do not learn things that you can easily look up in the legislation, such as the various conditions for the investor and the company, and learn where to find the information instead.

A **qualifying individual is one who is not connected with the company** at any time in the period from two years before the issue (or from incorporation if later) to three years after the issue. An individual is connected with the company in any of the following circumstances: [s.166–170]

(a)   He (either alone or with his associates) broadly holds **more than 30%** of the ordinary shares or can exercise more than 30% of the voting rights in the company or any subsidiary

(b)   He is an **employee or a non-qualifying director** of the company or of a subsidiary, or of a partner of the company or of a subsidiary. **A qualifying director who is also an employee is not treated as connected under this rule**.

(c)   On a winding up of the company or any subsidiary, he (either alone or with his associates) would be entitled to more than 30% of the assets

(d)   He is a **partner** of the company or of any subsidiary

Associates include business partners, spouses, partners in a civil partnership, parents or remoter forebears and children or remoter issue. **An investor's brothers, sisters, uncles, aunts and in-laws are not treated as associates.** [s.253(2)]

A **qualifying director is, broadly, one who only receives reasonable remuneration (including any benefits) from the company**. [s.169]

The investor does not need to be UK resident (see later in this Text) although he must have income which is taxable in the UK in order to benefit from the relief.

Exam focus point

Examiner's report – Personal Taxation

May 2011 – Part II LFQ 3

The least well answered question on the paper. Only a minority picked up that Tasha owned more than 30% of the shares and was therefore unable to benefit from EIS income tax relief. The restriction of Isobel's capital loss for the income tax relief initially obtained, but partially withdrawn, was poorly dealt with.

4.1.6 Company conditions

4.1.6.1 Qualifying company

A **qualifying company** is a company which satisfies all of the following conditions: [s.180]

(a)   It exists wholly to carry on one or more qualifying trades (see below) throughout the three year period commencing with the issue of the shares

(b)   Throughout the 3 year period commencing with the issue of the shares the company must have a **permanent establishment (PE) in the UK**, ie a fixed place of business such as a branch or factory

(c)   The company must be **unquoted** at the time the EIS shares are issued and no arrangements must exist at that time for the company to cease to be unquoted

(d)   **It does not control any other company** (except for qualifying 51% subsidiaries) **and it is not under the control of another company**

(e)   The **assets of the company must not exceed £15 million immediately before and £16 million immediately after the issue**

(f)   The company must have **fewer than 250 full time equivalent employees**

(g)   The company must have **raised not more than £5 million** in venture capital funds in the previous 12 months

(h)   At the date the shares are issued the company must not be in financial difficulty.

4.1.6.2 Qualifying trade

A **qualifying trade is one carried on commercially with a view to profit.** The following activities are excluded. [s.192]

(a)   Dealing in commodities, futures, shares, securities, other financial instruments or land

(b)   Dealing in goods other than in an ordinary trade of wholesale or retail distribution

(c)   Financial activities such as banking, hire purchase and insurance

(d)   Leasing, apart from chartering of ships (other than offshore installations and pleasure craft) for up to 12 months at a time

(e)   The receipt of royalties or licence fees, except in respect of a company's research and development

(f)   The provision of legal and accountancy services

(g)   Property development

(h)   Farming or market gardening

(i)   Holding or managing woodlands or any forestry activity

(j)   Operating or managing hotels

(k)   Operating or managing residential care homes or nursing homes

(l)   Providing certain services for another business [s.199]

(m)   Shipbuilding

(n)   Coal and steel production

(o)   Energy generation or export where the company receives Feed in Tariffs (FiTs), unless commercial electricity generation began by 6 April 2012.

4.1.6.3 Qualifying shares

The **shares must generally be newly issued, fully paid up ordinary shares** which carry **no preferential rights to dividends**, assets or redemption in the three years from the date of issue **unless**:

(a)   The **amount and timing of the payment** of the dividends **does not depend on a decision of the company, the investor or anyone else,** *and*

(b)   The rights to dividends are **not cumulative** (ie the right to receive a dividend cannot roll forward to future periods if the company has insufficient profits to pay the dividend). [s.173]

The shares must be issued to raise money for the purpose of a **qualifying business activity**, which can be to carry on a qualifying trade (see above) *or* carry out research and development intended to lead to such a trade *or* to hold shares and securities in companies carrying out qualifying trades or research and development. [s.174]

The maximum annual amount that a company may raise under the EIS and VCT schemes (see below) is £5 million.

The shares must not be issued **as a result of or in connection with 'disqualifying' arrangements**, ie where the main purpose is to ensure relief is available and either the benefit of the investment is passed to another person, or the business, in the absence of the arrangements, would be carried on by another business. [s.178A]

4.1.2.4 Use of funds

The company must use the money raised from the share subscription for the purpose of the qualifying business activity generally within two years of the date of the share issue, or within two years of commencement of a qualifying activity if later. [s.175]

Exam focus point

Examiner's report – Personal Taxation

May 2008 – Part II LFQ 3

This question caused the most difficulties for candidates for two key reasons. Either candidates did not attempt to answer the question showing a lack of time and/or preparation, or the information provided was not that asked for by the question.

The question specifically stated that the client had already taken advice on whether the company was a qualifying company for EIS purposes; this information was often ignored with candidates outlining the conditions that the company would need to meet.

The question also clearly stated that candidates were not required to consider the withdrawal of any relief given.

With those two statements in mind, the question should have been relatively straightforward for a well prepared candidate to answer. Instead there was evidence of large sections of legislation simply being reproduced as an answer.

4.2 Seed Enterprise Investment Scheme

4.2.1 Introduction

The Seed Enterprise Investment Scheme (SEIS), which is similar in many respects to the regular Enterprise investment Scheme (EIS) (see above), applies to **investments in smaller, early stage companies made between 6 April 2012 and 5 April 2017.** [s.257A]

4.2.2 General requirements

Many of the same **general requirements** as for EIS shares, for example regarding eligible shares, the purpose of the issue etc, also apply to SEIS shares. [s.257C – CF]

4.2.3 The investor

Qualifying investments by individual investors attract **50% income tax relief.** [s.257AB]

The main requirements for a qualifying SEIS investor are that:

- He must **not have a substantial interest** in the issuing company, ie must **own less than 30% of the shares, voting power** or rights on a winding up. [s.257BF]

- Neither the investor nor his associates are employees of the issuing company in the three years beginning with the date the shares are issued. [s.257BA]

Investments by directors of the company are permitted and such directors may also concurrently qualify under the EIS.

The **maximum annual investment limit for the investor is £100,000,** although **unused amounts can be carried back** to the previous year. [s.257AB]

The investor must **claim the relief no more than five years after the self assessment filing deadline** for the year in which the shares are issued, so **by 31 January 2020 for a 2013/14 SEIS investment.** [s.257EA]

Relief may be withdrawn in a similar way as for EIS shares if the shares are disposed of within three years of their issue. [s.257FA]

4.2.4 The company

The main requirements for a SEIS company are that it must: [s.257DA et seq]

- **Trade through a UK permanent establishment**
- Be **unquoted**
- Have **gross assets up to £200,000**, and
- Have **fewer than 25 employees**

The company's main purpose must be to carry on a **new qualifying trade** (as defined for EIS purposes) and there must be a genuine new venture.

A qualifying SEIS company may only **raise up to £150,000 in total** (this is not an annual limit) and must not previously have had EIS or venture capital trust (VCT) (see below) investments. [s.257DL & s.257DK]

The **main differences** between a SEIS and an EIS company are:

- The **funds raised** by a SEIS company **must be used within three years** compared with only two years for an EIS company

- The **company must either use 70% of the funds or have been carrying on the new qualifying trade for at least 4 months before a claim for approval can be made**, while an EIS company must simply have traded or carried on qualifying R&D for four months before a claim for approval can be made. [s.257ED (3)]

4.2.5 Capital gains tax aspects

The **CGT exemption** for disposals of SEIS shares after three years from issue apply as for EIS, ie: [s.150E TCGA 1992]

(a)   If there is a **gain for CGT purposes** (see later in this Text), **it is exempt**

(b)   Any **loss for CGT purposes is restricted by reducing the issue price, ie the cost, by the tax reduction not withdrawn** (but not so as to create a gain).

Where **gains realised from disposals of any assets** during 2013/14 are **reinvested** through the SEIS in the same tax year, **reinvestment relief of up to 50%** (100% in 2012/13) **of the SEIS investment is available to exempt the gain.** [Sch 5BB TCGA 1992]

Illustration 1

In August 2013, Gillian makes the maximum investment in SEIS shares, ie £100,000. She realised a chargeable gain of £125,000 in October 2013 on the disposal of a very valuable painting.

As Gillian has made a gain in 2013/14 and invested in SEIS shares in the same tax year, she can claim SEIS reinvestment relief to exempt part of the gain on the painting. The maximum gain which is exempt is 50% of the qualifying SEIS investment, ie £50,000 (£100,000 × 50%). Consequently, only £75,000 (£125,000 – £50,000) of the gain remains chargeable.

If she had made the same investment and gains in the previous tax year, she would have been able to claim £100,000 reinvestment relief, leaving only £25,000 of the gain chargeable.

CGT is covered in detail later in this Text.

4.3 Venture Capital Trusts (VCTs)

4.3.1 Introduction

Certain income tax and CGT advantages are available to individuals who invest in a Venture Capital Trust (VCT). These tax advantages are intended to encourage investment in unquoted trading companies (broadly EIS type companies) through a listed VCT company, so spreading the investment risk.

4.3.2 Tax reduction on investment

An **individual** who is at **least 18 years of age** who subscribes for **new eligible shares in a Venture Capital Trust** (VCT) can claim income tax relief in respect of his investment. The amount of income tax relief available to such an individual is the lower of: [s.263]

(a) **30% of the amount subscribed for eligible shares in VCTs in the year up to a maximum investment of £200,000** per tax year, and

(b) The individual's income tax liability for the year.

The tax relief is given as a tax reduction in the income tax computation (see earlier in this Text).

4.3.3 Relief on distributions

Distributions (ie dividends) received by an individual in respect of ordinary shares in a VCT are exempt from income tax, provided:

(a) The company was a VCT when the individual acquired his shares, and

(b) The dividend is paid out of profits which accrued to the company in an accounting period ending after its approval as a VCT, and

(c) **The shares in respect of which the dividend is paid were not acquired by the investor in excess of the permitted maximum £200,000** investment for any tax year. [s.709 ITTOIA 2005]

The relief on dividends is available to individuals at least 18 years old on the first £200,000 of ordinary shares **acquired** in each tax year at a time when the company was a VCT. This includes shares acquired by purchase on the Stock Exchange (or by gift, or in any other manner). **It is not necessary for the individual to have subscribed for new VCT shares.**

The 30% tax relief given on the investment, however, is only given on the first £200,000 of new VCT ordinary shares **subscribed** for in each tax year. [s.261]

Illustration 2

Miss Davis bought existing ordinary shares in VCT1 with a value of £30,000 on 1 May 2013. On 1 December 2013 she subscribed £400,000 for new ordinary shares in VCT2.

1. The VCT1 shares will qualify for relief on distributions only as she did not subscribe for these shares and therefore they do not qualify for relief on investment.

2. The first £200,000 of the £400,000 invested in VCT2 shares will qualify for the 30% relief on investment as these shares were subscribed for. Only £170,000 of the investment will qualify for relief on distributions.

4.3.4 Withdrawal of relief

VCT income tax relief is withdrawn if the investor disposes of his shares in the VCT within five years of their issue. A disposal by gift or sale at a profit results in a withdrawal of the full relief.

A disposal by sale for less than the cost of the shares (ie at a loss) results in a clawback of relief equal to the proceeds received, multiplied by 30%. [s.266]

The death of the investor or a disposal to a spouse/civil partner does not result in any withdrawal of relief.

VCT income tax relief is also withdrawn if the VCT loses its approved status within five years after issuing eligible shares to the investor. In such circumstances the investor's full income tax relief is withdrawn. [s.268]

Withdrawals of VCT income tax relief are made by way of an assessment for the year in which the relief was originally given. [s.270]

Investors are required to give notice to an officer of HMRC within 60 days if an event occurs which gives rise to withdrawal of relief. [s.271]

4.3.5 Conditions for relief

VCTs are companies, that are not close companies, that are approved by HMRC. The legislation should primarily be relied on in this area but an outline of the conditions is given below: [s.274]

(a) **The VCT's ordinary shares must be quoted on a stock exchange in the UK, EU or EEA** [s.274]

(b) Its **income has been derived wholly or mainly from shares** or securities

(c) It **has not retained more than 15% of this income**, ie it must distribute 85% of such income and 100% of any other income. However, this distribution requirement is waived if the amount required to satisfy the 15% rule is less than £10,000 per 12 month accounting period

(d) **Not more than 15% of the company's investments is in a company other than another VCT** or a company that would qualify as a VCT if it were quoted

(e) In each accounting period **at least 70% of its investments are in shares in qualifying holdings** (broadly holdings in **unquoted companies which have a PE in the UK and which are not in financial difficulty**) [s.286A & s.286B]

(f) **At least 70% of the company's qualifying holdings has been or will be represented by holdings of eligible shares** [s.274]

(g) **At least 10% of the total amount invested in any company must be in the form of ordinary, non-preferential shares**

(h) The **amount invested** by the VCT in a single company **must not exceed £1 million** in any six month period or year of assessment **if the VCT is a member of partnership or a party to a joint venture.** [s.287]

There are also **conditions which a company whose shares are held by the VCT must comply with** as follows:

(a) The company must have **fewer than 250 full time equivalent employees**

(b) The company must have **raised less than £5 million** in venture capital funds in the previous 12 months

(c) The company (and any qualifying subsidiaries) **must be carrying on a qualifying activity**, which includes a qualifying trade (see below) or preparing to carry on such a trade, and commence it within two years after the date of issue of shares [ss.290 & 291]

(d) **The money raised from the issue of shares must be used for the purposes of its qualifying trade within two years** [s.293]

(e) **The value of the company's assets must not exceed £15m immediately before and £16m immediately after the relevant holding is issued to the VCT** (the 'gross assets' test) [s.297]

(f) There must be **no 'disqualifying arrangements'**, as for the EIS schemes. [s.299A]

HMRC will specify the date from which a VCT is approved. This cannot be earlier than the date on which application for approval was made by the company.

Approval may be withdrawn where a VCT ceases to satisfy the above conditions or fails to satisfy such conditions within the above time periods. A notice of withdrawal of approval normally has effect from the time it is given.

4.3.6 Qualifying trades

All trades (including research and development from which it is intended that a trade will be derived) are qualifying trades except for the prohibited activities mentioned above for EIS. [s.303]

4.3.7 Capital gains tax aspects

Any gains on the first £200,000 of shares purchased (whether subscribed for directly from the VCT company or purchased from a third party) are exempt from CGT and any losses are not allowable. [s.151A(1) TCGA 1992]

CGT is covered in detail later in this Text.

Exam focus point

Examiner's report – Personal Taxation

November 2010 – Part I SFQ 2

The first part of this question was well answered, but many candidates went on to explain about the withdrawal of income tax relief for the second part, when they were asked to comment on the capital gains tax position on sale. Candidates would be advised to read questions carefully as valuable time will have been wasted on this question.

4.4 Pensions

Individuals often save for retirement by investing in a pension. Pensions are extremely tax efficient because:

(a) Tax relief is available for investments (known as 'contributions'), and

(b) Income and gains arising from investments within the pension are not liable to tax. A pension can be thought of as a tax free wrapper around any investments within it.

Pensions are covered in detail later in this Text.

5 Other income

5.1 Trust income

5.1.1 Discretionary trusts

A beneficiary of a discretionary trust is only assessed to income tax on actual distributions received by him from the trust. Each distribution is accompanied by a 45% tax credit.

The trustees advise the beneficiary of the net distribution and associated tax credit by issuing him with a form R185 (Statement of income from trust) after the end of each tax year (see below).

Income from discretionary trusts is always taxed as non savings income, regardless of the type of income received by the trust.

Illustration 3

Dan received a distribution of £16,500 from the Davies Discretionary Trust. This is received net of a 45% tax credit.

He will enter gross income of £30,000 (£16,500 × 100/55) as 'Trust income' in his tax computation, which is taxed as non savings income at his marginal rate of tax (20%, 40% or 45%), and he can deduct the £13,500 tax credit from his liability.

5.1.1 Interest in possession trusts

The **beneficiary** of a non-discretionary trust, ie an interest in possession trust, is known as the **life tenant** and is **subject to income tax on all the income arising in the trust** (rather than on the distributions made by the trust) except where it is needed to meet the income expenses of the trust. The **beneficiary is taxable on the income even if he doesn't actually receive it** from the trustees during the tax year.

Credit is given for any tax suffered or paid by the trustees on the income.

The trustees advise the beneficiary of the net distribution and associated tax credit by issuing him with a **form R185** (Statement of income from trust) after the end of each tax year (see below).

The **income retains its original nature** and is **taxed in the beneficiary's hands at the rates relevant to the type of income received by the trust**. So, rental income received by the trust is assessed on the beneficiary as rental income, bank interest as savings income, and so on.

5.1.2 Statement of income (R185)

The trustees of each type of trust give the beneficiary a 'Statement of income from trust' (Form R185 (Trust Income)) that the beneficiary can use to complete his tax return, which shows the **net income** (ie after tax has been taken off or paid by the trustees) and the **tax credit**.

Example 6

During 2013/14 Lily receives the following income:

Salary (£1,512 tax paid via PAYE)	£17,000
Building society interest	£150
Discretionary trust receipt	£6,600

Lily is also the beneficiary of an interest in possession trust. The trustees sent her a Form R185 (Trust income) for 2013/14 showing £18,000 of net dividend income. However, Lily did not receive the income until 1 May 2014.

Calculate Lily's tax payable or repayable for 2013/14.

Exam focus point

Examiner's report – Personal Taxation

November 2011 – Part II LFQ 2

Generally very mediocre answers; very few made the crucial distinction between Nigel being assessed on the income of the life interest trust as it arose, irrespective of the distributions made, and him only being assessed in relation to the discretionary trust when distributions were received.

5.2 Estate income

5.2.1 Introduction

When someone dies, the assets they own (less liabilities) at the date of death make up their 'estate' for tax purposes.

The deceased is liable for income tax on any income *receivable* up to the date of death, regardless of whether it is actually received before or after death.

The 'personal representatives' (PRs) are taxed on any income receivable during the 'administration period.' This starts on the date of the deceased's death and ends when the administration of the estate is completed.

A PR is a person who acts as executor (named in the deceased's will) or administrator (where the deceased died without having made a will (ie intestate)) of a deceased person's estate.

5.2.2 Specific gifts

A will may specify that a certain beneficiary (or 'legatee') should receive a particular asset or a set sum of money. Where the asset bequeathed is an **income producing asset, eg shares, the beneficiary is taxable on the income receivable on and after the date of death on an arising basis**.

Where the beneficiary is taxable on the income, the income will have first been taxed on the PRs who will provide the beneficiary with a statement of income (R185 (Estate Income)).

This shows:

(a)   The net income (ie after any tax has been taken off) for the beneficiary to report

(b)   Tax credits (eg 20% tax deducted from savings income at source) and tax paid by the PRs, which the beneficiary can deduct from his own liability.

5.2.3 Beneficiaries with an absolute interest in the residue

A beneficiary has an absolute interest in the residue if he is entitled to both the income and capital of the whole (or part) of the residue of the estate (ie whatever is left after specific gifts have been allocated). **The residuary beneficiary is taxable on the income of the residue after setting off the PR's expenses.**

In some cases this will include income that arose before death but is received after death.

Expenses are set against dividend income first, then savings income, then non savings income.

Where the estate administration is carried on over a number of years, it is usual for the PRs to make interim payments to beneficiaries before the administration of the estate is completed. **When the PRs make an interim payment, the residuary beneficiary is taxable on the lower of:**

(a)   **The actual amount received from the estate, and**
(b)   **The estate's distributable income of a particular tax year.**

These interim payments are assessed on *a receipts* basis. They are treated as being made from non savings income, then savings income, and then dividend income. The amount of the receipt is grossed up at the appropriate rate for the type of income in question in the year of receipt by the beneficiary, regardless of the tax actually paid by the PRs.

If there is an excess of income left at the end of the administration period, it is treated as income of the year in which the administration ended, regardless of when it is actually paid over to the beneficiary.

Illustration 4

Paul died on 1 November 2013, leaving his entire estate to his wife, Christa. The PRs received a dividend of £6,750, bank interest of £1,600 and rental income of £3,000 in 2013/14.

The PRs had expenses of £540. They made an interim payment of £4,090 to Christa on 1 April 2014. The administration of the estate ended on 31 December 2014.

The assessable amounts and the statement of income given to Christa for 2013/14 will be as follows:

2013/14

The interim payment of £4,090 is treated as coming from non savings income (ie property income) first, then savings income, then dividend income.

Gross income available for distribution

	Non savings £	Savings £	Dividends £
Rental income	3,000		
Bank interest £1,600 × $^{100}/_{80}$		2,000	
Dividends £6,750 × $^{100}/_{90}$			7,500
Taxable income	3,000	2,000	7,500
Less: expenses (from dividends first) £540 × $^{100}/_{90}$			(600)
Income available for distribution	3,000	2,000	6,900
Less: distributed to Christa 2013/14			
(non savings first, then savings, then dividends)			
£2,400 × $^{100}/_{80}$	(3,000)		
£1,600 × $^{100}/_{80}$		(2,000)	
£ 90 × $^{100}/_{90}$			(100)
£4,090			
c/f to 2014/15	Nil	Nil	6,800

Note. The above shows how the income will be distributed to Christa and is NOT an income tax computation.

2013/14 statement of income

	Net £	Tax £
Non savings income	2,400	600
Savings income	1,600	400
Dividend income	90	10

Christa will use the statement of income to report the income received and tax suffered on her income tax return. The balance of the income will be taxed when it is received or in the year the administration ends, ie in 2014/15.

5.2.4 Beneficiaries with a limited interest in the residue

A beneficiary has a limited interest in the residue if he is only entitled to the income (and not the capital) of the whole (or part) of the residue. He will be taxed on the net income of the estate during the administration period, after the PRs expenses have been deducted. Again, if he is only entitled to part of the income of the estate, he will only be taxed on that part.

The same tax rules used for beneficiaries with absolute interests also apply for those with limited interests.

5.3 Property income

If an individual rents out a property any income received is taxable as **non savings income**. Property income is covered in detail later in this Text.

5.4 Miscellaneous income

Income that is not categorised as from a specific source, eg savings, property or earnings, is taxed as 'miscellaneous income'. Examples of miscellaneous income include:

- Income received by a child but taxed on the parent (see earlier in this Text)
- Loans and benefits received from closely controlled companies (see below), and
- Certain interest taxed under the Accrued Income Scheme (see below).

6 Income tax anti-avoidance rules

6.1 Pre-owned asset tax

6.1.1 Introduction

An **income tax charge**, the **'pre owned asset tax' (POAT),** may apply where, for example, a person makes a **gift of property (including cash) and subsequently benefits from that property (or other property acquired from the proceeds of the original property),** in circumstances where the inheritance tax (IHT) gift with reservation rules do not apply (see below).

The POAT charge broadly applies to **land (including buildings) and chattels (ie personal property). There is no charge if the total taxable amount does not exceed £5,000** (see below).

6.1.2 Land

The rules apply where an **individual occupies land and he had either:**

(a) **Previously owned** the land but had **disposed** of it, or
(b) **Provided consideration used by another person in acquiring the land.**

The taxable amount is the **annual value of the land less any amount paid by the individual for the use of the land.** Payment of **full rent will reduce the taxable amount to nil.**

The land must be formally valued in the first tax year that the POAT charge applies and every five years after that.

6.1.3 Personal property

The rules apply where an individual possesses a **'chattel'** (ie personal property) and he had **either**:

(a) **Previously owned** the chattel but had **disposed** of it, or
(b) **Provided consideration used by another person in acquiring the chattel.**

The taxable amount is the **value of the chattel multiplied by the official rate of interest** (given in the ATT's tax tables that are provided in the exam), **less any amount paid by the individual for the use of the asset.**

As for land, **chattels must be formally valued in the first tax year that the POAT charge applies and every five years** after that.

6.1.4 Exclusions

There are a number of **'excluded transactions'**, which **do not fall within the POAT charge at all**. Such **excluded transactions** include: [para 10 Sch 15 FA 2004]

*   Transactions at **arm's length**
*   Transfers to a **spouse or civil partner**
*   **Small gifts**, of up to £3,000 pa.

As we saw above, there are also a number of **exemptions** that may apply to **exempt the income tax charge where the transaction initially satisfies the POAT conditions**, including: [paras 11 & 13 Sch 15 FA 2004]:

*   Transactions that are **within the IHT gift with reservation provisions**
*   Where the **combined value of all benefits does not exceed the £5,000** *de minimis* limit in the tax year.

Example 7

Joe gifted £400,000 cash to his son, Tony, in June 2008. Tony bought a house with the money in September 2011. Joe moved into the property, which has an annual rental value of £6,000, shortly after and continues to live there. What is the pre-owned asset tax charge for Joe, who has taxable income in 2013/14 of £40,000?

Example 8

Joe also gifted £400,000 cash to his daughter, Caroline, in June 2008. Caroline bought a picture worth £250,000 with the money. The picture currently hangs in Joe's reception room. What is the pre owned asset tax charge for Joe?

6.1.5 Inheritance tax election

An individual caught by the rules can **elect to disapply this income tax charge** by 31 January following the tax year in which the charge arises. The property will instead be within the **gift with reservation rules** for IHT purposes.

Exam focus point

Examiner's report – Personal Taxation

May 2008 – Part I SFQ 10

Very few candidates indicated that they had any awareness that this question was about the pre-owned asset rules. Some went down the route of calculating a tax charge on the basis of William receiving a benefit in kind from his rent free occupation; others saw this as being a question about John's emigration triggering a CGT charge on a gain that had been held over on the gift of the cash to him. Only a very few scored good marks.

BPP
LEARNING MEDIA

6.2 Loans and benefits from closely controlled companies

This section is new

6.2.1 What is a close company?

A closely controlled, or **'close'**, **company** is one which is **under the control of**: [s.439 CTA 2010]

(a)   **Five or fewer participators**, or
(b)   **Participators who are directors, with no limitation on the number**.

A participator is broadly defined as a **shareholder** in the company. [s.454 CTA 2010]

There may be an income tax charge if a participator who is not an employee of the close company receives:

- Some kind of **benefit**, such as a company car, or
- A **loan** from the company.

6.2.2 Benefits provided to participators

Any **benefits** (eg a company car, cheap loan) that a close company provides to a **participator who is not an employee** of the company, cannot be taxable as employment income. Instead, the **cash value of the benefit** (as calculated for employment income purposes – see later in this text) is **treated as a net dividend**. [s.1064 CTA 2010].

This must be **grossed up by 100/90** and **included in the participator's income tax computation, in the same way as if he had received an actual dividend**.

Example 9

Sound Garden Ltd is a close company which prepares accounts to 31 March each year. Shayne and Gail are both shareholders but only Shayne works for the company.

On 1 May 2013 the company purchased two cars. Shayne and Gail were provided with one of the cars each which they can use for private purposes.

Explain the tax position for Shayne and Gail.

6.2.3 Loans to participators

If a participator, who is **not an employee,** is given a **loan at or below the official rate of interest** he is treated as **receiving a net dividend equal to the amount of the taxable benefit** which would arise if he were an employee (see above).

If the company writes off *any* **loan** (including those at a rate at or above the official interest rate) the participator is **treated as receiving a net dividend, equal to the amount written off**. Where the participator is also an employee, it should be noted that the usual employment income benefit on the write off of a loan to an employee does not apply. [s.189 ITEPA 2003]

In both cases the net dividend must be **grossed up by 100/90** and **included in his income tax computation**. The **10% notional tax credit is available** to reduce the individual's tax liability as normal (see above). [s.415 ITTOIA 2005]

The loan can, however, be **ignored** if broadly it is **less than £15,000** and the participator works full time for the company.

Example 10

Newell Ltd, a close company, makes a loan of £50,000 at a 5% interest rate to Graeme, a shareholder, on 10 December 2010. Graeme does not work for the company.

Newell Ltd writes off the loan on 1 March 2014.

Explain the tax position for Graeme assuming he is a higher rate taxpayer in both 2010/11 and 2013/14.

6.3 Accrued income scheme

The Accrued Income Scheme (AIS) applies on the disposal of interest-bearing securities (Treasury stock (gilts) and company loan stock) to ensure that the buyer and the seller are only taxed on the interest relating to the period of time that they have actually owned the securities.

The AIS does not apply to shares.

Interest on securities (sometimes called the 'coupon') is generally paid twice a year.

Illustration 5

James owns £5,000 of 5% loan stock, paying interest on 15 March and 15 September each year. The interest taxable in 2013/14 is:

- £125 (£5,000 × 5% × 6/12) received on 15 September 2013, and
- £125 received on 15 March 2014.

As we saw earlier, interest is usually taxed on the receipts basis. However on a disposal of securities, the AIS allocates the interest on a straight line time basis between the buyer and the seller. The seller is taxed on the interest for the period that has 'accrued' up to the date of disposal, while the buyer is taxed on the income that accrues from the date they purchase the stock.

If an individual sells securities 'cum interest', this means that the buyer receives the next interest payment on the six monthly date, even if he has not owned the securities for that whole six months. The buyer will be taxed on the interest received but will receive relief for the interest relating to the period of time that he did not own the securities.

Illustration 6

An investor purchases £10,000 of 6% loan stock 'cum interest' on 1 July 2013, which pays interest on 1 June and 1 December each year. He will receive the next interest payment of £300 (6% × £10,000 ÷ 2) due on 1 December 2013, which relates to the period since the last payment (1.6.13) until the payment date (1.12.13).

The interest received of £300 is chargeable to tax but, as he has only owned the stock for five months (1.7.13 – 1.12.13), he will receive relief of £50 ($^1/_6$ × £300) for the one month (June) that he didn't own it so will only actually be taxed on interest of £250 (£300 – £50).

The seller will be taxed on that one month's worth of interest (£50) even though he did not own the securities on 1 December 2013. It is taxable as **miscellaneous income** (see above).

Example 11

Ralph purchases £10,000 of 5% Treasury Stock cum interest on 1 February 2013 and sells it cum interest on 1 April 2014. Interest is paid on the stock on 1 May and 1 November each year.

How much interest is taxable on Ralph in 2013/14 and 2014/15?

If an individual sells securities 'ex interest' (ie without the interest), he receives and is taxed on the next interest payment on the six monthly date, even though he no longer owns the stock. He will receive relief for the interest relating to the period of time that he did not own the securities, while the buyer will be taxed on 'miscellaneous' income (see below) equal to the interest relating to the period he owns the stock.

The rules do not apply in a number of situations, for example where an individual has not held securities exceeding £5,000 (nominal value) in the current or previous year.

6.4 Life assurance policies

6.4.1 Qualifying policies

There is no income tax charge on the maturity or encashment of a qualifying life assurance policy.

A policy is qualifying if: [para 1 Sch 15 ICTA 1998]

(a)   The policy secures a capital sum on death, earlier disability, or a date not before the tenth anniversary of taking out the policy

(b)   The premiums are reasonably even and are payable annually or at shorter intervals

(c)   At least a certain capital sum is assured, broadly 75% of the premiums payable.

The **maximum that can be paid into a qualifying policy issued on or after 6 April 2013 is £3,600 in a 12 month period.**

Gifts worth up to £30 that are commonly offered to induce people to take out policies do not make a policy 'non-qualifying'.

Any profit (the excess of proceeds over total premiums paid) **on maturity or encashment of the policy is free of tax so long as premiums have been paid for a minimum of one of the following**.

(a)   **Life of the assured**
(b)   **10 years and**
(c)   **3/4 of the term.**

6.4.2 Non-qualifying policies

Non-qualifying policies include **single premium bonds, investment bonds** or **property bonds**. A lump sum is invested in a life fund, a small part of which buys life cover and the balance is invested. During the term of the policy any investment gains and income are taxed only in the hands of the insurance company.

Withdrawals of up to 5% of the premium per year (on a cumulative basis) **are allowed with no immediate tax liability**. So, in 2013/14 an investor who purchased a £30,000 single premium bond in 2007 can effect a partial surrender for £9,000 (6 years × 5% × £30,000) tax free.

The overall gain on the policy on a **chargeable event** (eg encashment, sale or death of the investor) **is taxed as savings income and comes with a basic rate tax credit (20%).** Top slicing relief (see below) may apply.

When the policy is finally encashed, any tax free withdrawals are added to the amount received on encashment to determine the overall tax liability. There is no starting rate or basic rate liability. In addition, any tax at the higher or additional rate can be reduced by using the following *top slicing* rules:

Step 1 Calculate the **overall profit** from the policy.

(proceeds on encashment *plus* early withdrawals *less* initial premium).

Step 2 **Divide** the overall profit by the **number of complete years since the policy was taken out.**

Step 3 Calculate the increase in the taxpayer's total tax liability that arises from **adding the slice** found in Step 2 to his **other sources of income**. This slice is **taxed as the top slice of income** above all other income, *including dividend income*. Remember that the slice is **only liable to tax at the higher or additional rate.**

Step 4 **Multiply** the increase found in Step 3 **by the number of years** used in Step 2 to find the tax payable.

If, before final encashment, withdrawals exceed the permitted limit, the excess is taxable immediately at the higher or additional rate. Again, top slicing applies. The slice is found by dividing the excess by the number of years since the policy was taken out (or, if appropriate, since the last excess occurred). In calculating the tax on final encashment, the excess(es) are excluded from the calculation of the overall profit since they have already been taxed.

Example 12

An investor took out a single premium policy on 31 October 2007 for £15,000. He withdrew 4% of the premium in each of the next five years and he encashed the policy on 30 June 2013 receiving £20,000. In 2013/14 his other income (all non savings) was £31,740 after deducting his personal allowance.

Calculate the amount of tax payable in respect of the single premium policy.

Exam focus point

Examiner's report – Personal Taxation

November 2011 – Part I SFQ 5

This question caused a lot of problems. Many candidates were unaware of the tax free amount that could be withdrawn every year. As a consequence, many candidates could not calculate the profit made on the bond. This would have given a candidate one half of the marks available.

7 Joint investments

7.1 General principles

Income from investments held in spouses' or civil partners' joint names will usually be split equally between them for tax purposes if they are living together, even if they hold unequal shares in the assets.

They are treated as **owing the property equally except** if the income is: [s.836]

(a)   **Earned** income, eg employment income
(b)   Profits from a business **partnership**
(c)   **Dividends** from jointly owned shares in a **close company**
(d)   Property income from a **furnished holiday letting** (FHL) (see later in this Text).

Where the couple separates, the equal shares rule no longer applies.

7.2 Joint declaration

The couple can make a joint declaration of their actual interests in an asset held in joint names if their actual entitlements to the asset and its income are unequal. **This will result in the income being assessed on each partner according to their actual share**.

Income will be split on the basis of the declaration from the date of the declaration. A declaration in respect of an asset cannot be withdrawn and remains in force until either the marriage/partnership comes to an end or the interests change.

If the interests do change the 'equal shares' rule applies until a further declaration is made. If an asset ceases to be held in joint names, the partner entitled to all the income from the asset will be assessed on it from the date of the change.

7.3 Planning

If one partner's marginal rate of tax (the rate on the highest part of his or her income) is higher than the other partner's marginal rate, **it is sensible to transfer income-yielding assets to the partner with the lower rate**. Income can then, for example, be taxed at 20% instead of at 40% or 45%. However, **an outright gift of the property (with no strings attached) is required.**

Where HMRC feels the split is really tax avoidance, HMRC has the power to reassess the tax liability of both parties for the past four years.

Chapter roundup

- Some interest income is received gross and some net. Interest received net must be grossed up by 100/80 for inclusion in the income tax computation.

- Dividends are received net of a 10% notional tax credit and must be grossed up by 100/90 for inclusion in the tax computation. They are usually taxed as the top slice of income.

- Certain investments (eg NS&I certificates) are completely tax free.

- UK resident individuals over 18 can invest in a cash and/ or stocks and shares ISA. Individuals between 16 and 18 can invest in a cash ISA only.

- Under 18s can invest in a Junior ISA with a maximum annual investment of £3,720.

- There is no income tax on interest or dividends in, nor capital gains tax on disposal of shares from, the ISA.

- Certain income tax and capital gains tax advantages are available to individuals who invest in EIS and VCTs.

- EIS relief applies where an individual subscribes for new ordinary shares in a qualifying company. Qualifying companies are in general unquoted trading companies where the trade is not a 'secure' one ('secure' being dealing in land, finance etc).

- EIS relief allows 30% of the investment as a tax reduction. The maximum investment qualifying for relief is £1,000,000.

- Under certain specific circumstances EIS relief can be clawed back (ie withdrawn) by HMRC.

- The SEIS provides a 50% income tax reduction to investors in smaller, early stage companies. The annual maximum investment qualifying for relief is £100,000.

- A VCT company must meet a number of conditions for approval for VCT relief to be available including that the VCT must be a listed company whose income must derive wholly or mainly from shares and securities.

- The VCT investor will receive a tax reduction for 30% of the amount subscribed up to £200,000 of new VCT ordinary shares subscribed for in each tax year. This relief is withdrawn if the investor disposes of his shares in the VCT within five years of their issue.

- VCT dividends on the first £200,000 of VCT ordinary shares acquired (by subscription or purchase) are exempt from income tax.

- Income from discretionary trusts is always taxed as non savings income. Income from interest in possession trusts is taxed at the beneficiary's tax rates, depending on the type of income.

- When someone dies, the person they leave their assets to (ie the beneficiaries or 'legatees' of their estate) is usually taxable on income arising from the assets they have been left.

- Some income does not fall into a specific category and is taxed as miscellaneous income.

- The pre-owned asset tax is an anti-avoidance income tax charge on benefits received by former owners of property.

- A participator who is not an employee of a close company receiving any benefits (including a cheap loan) from the company, is treated as receiving a distribution (ie dividend). Where any loan to a participator (regardless of whether he is an employee) is written off he is treated as receiving a distribution equal to the amount of the loan written off.

- The accrued income scheme applies on the disposal of interest-bearing securities to ensure that the buyer and seller are only taxed on the interest relating to their period of ownership.

- The gain arising on a non-qualifying life assurance policy is taxed as savings income and comes with a basic rate tax credit. Tax at the higher or additional rate can be reduced by using top slicing relief.

- Married couples and civil partners are taxed equally (ie 50:50) on income from most assets held jointly (except broadly shares in a close company) unless they have notified HMRC of an actual ownership percentage which is different.

1. How will the following sources of interest be taxed?
   (a) NS&I savings account interest
   (b) Current account interest from Lloyds Bank
   (c) Interest on $3\frac{1}{2}$% War Loan
   (d) Interest on NS&I Certificates

2. Glenda is age 70 and has a state pension (received gross) and a small amount of building society interest each year. What advice would you give her on tax recovery?

3. Doreen, aged 30, has the following sources of income in 2013/14:

Income from employment (PAYE suffered £1,512)	£17,000
Income from rented properties	£4,130
Interest received on NS&I savings account	£3,800
UK dividends received	£6,500

   Calculate her tax payable for the year.

4. Mr and Mrs Daniels have three sons, Matthew aged 12, Jason aged 17 and Paul aged 19. Who may invest in an ISA?

5. Which of the following individuals cannot obtain EIS income tax relief?
   (a) An individual who, together with his associates, controls 26% of the voting power in the company
   (b) An unpaid (non-executive) director of the company
   (c) The managing director's secretary.

6. Hadfield Ltd, a close company, provides a car to one of its shareholders, John, who does not work for the company. If John had been an employee the taxable amount included as part of his employment income would have been £3,450. What is the tax position for John, assuming that he is an additional rate taxpayer?

7. Gemma has owned £20,000 of 3% Treasury Stock for many years. She sells the stock cum interest on 31 October 2013 to Mandy. Interest is payable on 1 June and 1 December each year. How much is taxable on Gemma and Mandy in 2013/14?

8. James has an investment property. He pays income tax at 40% on the rental income. His wife Jill has insufficient income to utilise her personal allowance so he wishes to transfer the income to her for tax purposes. Which of the following statements are correct?
   (a) He can transfer the property into her name, on condition she hands over the income to him, so the income will be taxed on her.
   (b) He can transfer the property into her name, let her use the income as she chooses but require her to leave the property to him in her will and the income will be taxed on her.
   (c) He can transfer the property into joint names with his wife, retain a 95% beneficial interest, and thereby transfer half the income to her.
   (d) Under (c) he could declare that 95% of the income was hers.

1. (a) Received gross and taxable in full as savings income.
   (b) Bank interest is received net of 20% tax and the gross amount is taxable savings income.
   (c) Interest on 3½% War Loan, as with most UK government stocks, is received gross.
   (d) Exempt.

2. Glenda is clearly a non-taxpayer so should lodge a form R85 with the building society to be paid her interest gross. This is more efficient from a cash flow perspective than making a claim for repayment of tax which would be required if the interest continued to be paid net.

3.

	Non savings income £	Savings income £	Dividend income £
Employment income	17,000		
Property income	4,130		
NS&I interest (received gross)		3,800	
Dividends £6,500 × 100/90			7,222
Net income	21,130	3,800	7,222
Less: PA	(9,440)		
Taxable income	11,690	3,800	7,222

Tax:	£
11,690 @ 20%	2,338
3,800 @ 20%	760
7,222 @ 10%	722
Tax liability	3,820
Less: tax suffered at source	
tax credit on dividends	(722)
PAYE	(1,512)
Tax payable	1,586

4. All of them. Matthew and Jason, who are both under 18, can open a Junior ISA, although Jason can also subscribe to a regular cash ISA account as he is between 16 and 18.

5. (a) Is fine because he owns ≤ 30%.
   (b) Is fine as a 'qualifying director'.
   (c) Employees are not entitled to relief.

6. John is treated as receiving a gross dividend of £3,833 (£3,450 × 100/90). As he is an additional rate taxpayer he will pay tax at 37.5% and will receive a 10% tax credit as follows:

	£
£3,833 @ 37.5%	1,437
Less: dividend tax credit £3,833 @ 10%	(383)
	1,054

7. Gemma receives the first interest payment on 1 June 2013, ie £300 (£20,000 × 3% × 6/12). This is taxable as interest income.

   She then sells the stock on 31 October 2013 'cum interest', so Mandy receives the next interest payment due on 1 December 2013.

   As Gemma owned the stock from 1 June 2013 to 31 October 2013 she will be taxable on 5 months of interest: £300 × 5/6 = £250. This is taxable as 'miscellaneous' income.

   Mandy will be taxable on the remaining £50 interest (£300 – £250) as interest income.

8. (a) and (b) are False as the property must be transferred without 'strings attached'.
   (c) is True as income on jointly held property is deemed to be shared equally.
   (d) is False. A joint declaration can be made to overturn the 50:50 split assumption but it can only change the split to the actual proportions of beneficial ownership.

Solutions to chapter examples

Solution to Example 1

Source	Net/ gross	Taxable amount
Bank interest	Net	£2,250 (£1,800 × 100/80)
Treasury Stock interest	Gross	£2,500
NS&I savings account interest	Gross	£500
Unquoted corporate loan note interest	Net	£15,000 (£12,000 × 100/80)

Solution to Example 2

	Non savings income £	Dividends £		
Employment income	30,000			
UK dividends £15,000 × 100/90		16,667		
Termination payment	100,000			
Net income	130,000	16,667		
Less: PA (total income >£118,880)	(nil)			
Taxable income	130,000	16,667		
Income tax		£		£
Basic rate band Non savings income = £30,000 × 20%				6,000
Dividends				
£2,010 × 10%				201
Higher rate band £(16,667 – 2,010) = £14,657 × 32.5%				4,764
Termination payment £100,000 × 40%				40,000
Tax liability				50,965

Solution to Example 3

(a) If he puts £5,760 into a cash account he can invest a maximum of £5,760 in a stocks and shares account.

(b) If he puts £2,000 into a cash account he can invest a maximum of £9,520 in a stocks and shares account.

(c) If he does not invest in a cash account he can put the full £11,520 in a stocks and shares account.

Solution to Example 4

Karen's 2013/14 tax liability is:

	£
Net income	60,000
Less: PA	(9,440)
Taxable income	50,560
Income tax:	
£32,010 × 20%	6,402
£18,550 × 40%	7,420
	13,822
Less: Tax reduction: EIS relief (£100,000 × 30% = £30,000, limited to tax)	(13,822)
Tax liability	Nil

The balance of £16,178 (£30,000 – £13,822) can be carried back and set against the previous year's liability.

The rate of relief given is $\dfrac{13,822}{100,000} \times 100 = 13.82\%$. This rate is important if relief is withdrawn in the future.

Solution to Example 5

(a)   The sale is within three years of the subscription for the shares, so the income tax relief is proportionately withdrawn.

The rate of relief originally given was $\frac{5,000}{34,000} \times 100 = 14.7\%$.

The amount of relief withdrawn is: £12,000 × 14.7% = £1,764

(b)   The full gain of £8,000 is exempt as the shares have been held for more than three years.

Solution to Example 6

	Non savings income £	Savings income £	Dividends £
Employment income	17,000		
Interest £150 × 100/80		187	
Discretionary trust income £6,600 × 100/55	12,000		
Dividends (from IIP) £18,000 × 100/90			20,000
Net income	29,000	187	20,000
Less: PA	(9,440)		
Taxable income	19,560	187	20,000

Income tax		£
£19,560 × 20%		3,912
£187 × 20%		37
£12,263 × 10%		1,226
£7,737 × 32.5%		2,515
Tax liability		7,690
Less tax suffered on:		
Dividends £20,000 × 10%		(2,000)
PAYE		(1,512)
Interest £187 × 20%		(37)
Discretionary trust £12,000 × 45%		(5,400)
Tax repayable		(1,259)

Solution to Example 7

Income tax charge: £6,000 @ 40% (higher rate taxpayer)   £2,400

Solution to Example 8

Notional interest: £250,000 @ 4%   £10,000
Income tax charge: £10,000 @ 40%   £4,000

Solution to Example 9

Car provided to Shayne

As Shayne is an employee of the company he will be taxed on the benefit of the car as employment income.

Car provided to Gail

As Gail is not an employee of the company she will be treated as having received a dividend equal to the benefit of the car (as calculated for employment income purposes) grossed up by 100/90.

Solution to Example 10

2010/11

The making of the loan has no tax implications for Graeme as it is made at an interest rate which exceeds the official rate (ie 4%).

2013/14

When the company writes off the loan, Graeme is treated as receiving a gross dividend of £55,556 (£50,000 × 100/90). As he is a higher rate taxpayer he will pay tax at 32.5% (assuming this amount does not take him above the higher rate threshold).

His tax liability is:

	£
£55,556 @ 32.5%	18,056
Less: dividend tax credit £55,556 @ 10%	(5,556)
	12,500

Solution to Example 11

2013/14

Ralph purchases the stock on 1 February 2013 'cum interest', which means that he receives the next interest payment due on 1 May 2013. He will obtain relief for the three months that he did not own the stock.

		£
1.5.13	Interest: 5% × £10,000 × ½	250
	Less: accrued income relief (1 Nov 2012 – 1 Feb 2013)	
	£250 × $^3/_6$	(125)
		125
1.11.13	Interest (owned for the whole 6 months)	250
	Interest	375

2014/15

Ralph sells the stock on 1 April 2014 'cum interest', which means that the purchaser receives the next interest payment due on 1 May 2014. However, as Ralph owned the stock from 1 November 2013 to 1 April 2014 he will be taxable on that five months' worth of interest in 2014/15. As he does not own the stock on 1 May 2014 he cannot be taxed on it as interest. Instead it is taxable as 'miscellaneous' income.

		£
1.5.14	Accrued income (1 Nov 2013 – 1 Apr 2014)	
	£250 × $^5/_6$	£208

Solution to Example 12

	£
Proceeds on encashment	20,000
Add: withdrawals within 5% limit: 5 × 4% × £15,000	3,000
	23,000
Less: initial premium	(15,000)
Overall profit	8,000

The profit is taxed as savings income and comes with a basic rate tax credit. Tax is only payable at the higher and additional rate. If the profit is taxed in full in 2013/14, it is taxed as the top slice of income and therefore £7,730 (£31,740 + £8,000 – £32,010) is taxed at the higher rate. Using the top slicing rules the tax payable is reduced and is calculated as follows:

Number of complete years = 5. One slice = £8,000/5 = £1,600
Tax liability in respect of the policy:

	£
Total income: £31,740 + £1,600	33,340
Less: basic rate band	(32,010)
Slice taxed at higher rates	1,330
Tax @ 20% (40% – 20% credit)	266
£266 × 5 years	1,330

Note. No additional tax is payable on the part of the slice that falls within the basic rate band (ie £270 (£1,600 – £1,330)) as it is covered by the 20% tax credit. In the tax return, relief is given as a deduction of £216 (ie [£7,730 @ 20%] – £1,330).

Short Form Questions:

2.1 – 2.18 inclusive

Long Form Questions:

2.1	Fred
2.2	George and Mildred Roper
2.3	Enterprise Investment Scheme

The purpose of this chapter is to help you to:

- outline the purpose and tax effect of child and working tax credits
- identify taxable and non-taxable social security benefits
- calculate the high income child benefit income tax charge
- calculate qualifying care relief

References: ITEPA 2003 unless otherwise stated

Tax credits and social security benefits

Exam focus point

Tax credits and social security benefits are examinable at the computational level. The ATT has confirmed that candidates must be able to identify whether a benefit is taxable and, if so, correctly include it in the taxpayer's income tax computation.

As indicated below, certain social security benefits are included in ATT's Tax Tables provided in the exam. In other cases the amounts of tax credits and other social security benefits will be provided, where necessary, in the question.

1 Tax credits

1.1 Introduction

Child Tax Credit (CTC) and Working Tax Credit (WTC) are designed to support people with children and working people who are on low incomes. Universal Credit (UC) will begin to replace these credits from October 2013. The Pension Credit is for those who have reached the state pension age (see later in this Text) to provide them with a minimum income.

The term 'tax credits' is a misnomer as they are **not tax credits that appear in the individual's tax computation but are non-taxable (ie exempt) amounts**, payable directly to the individuals who are entitled to receive them.

1.2 Child tax credit

An individual who is **responsible for at least one child** may qualify for Child Tax Credit (CTC). Higher credits are payable to those with lower incomes. The CTC is **not taxable.** [s.677]

The credit, which is paid to the main carer, is **made up of a number of elements** including:

Element	Given
Family element	One per family
Child element	Per child
Disabled child element	In addition, per disabled child
Severely disabled child element	In addition to the disabled element, per severely disabled child

CTC should not be confused with Child Benefit which is paid to all parents with income below £60,000 (see below).

1.3 Working tax credit

Individuals who **work**, but are on a **low income**, may qualify for the Working Tax Credit (WTC). It is often payable **in addition to the CTC** and the amount received **depends upon the income of the family**. The WTC is **not taxable.** [s.677]

The WTC is also made up of a number of elements:

Element	Given
Basic element	One per single claimant or couple
Couple's and lone parent element	In addition to basic, one per couple
Disabled worker element	In addition
30 hour element	In addition to other elements
Severe disability element	In addition to disabled element
Childcare element	% of childcare costs

1.4 Universal credit [SI 2013/376]

Universal credit (UC) begins to replace the CTC, WTC and certain other means-tested benefits, such as income-related employment and support allowance, from October 2013. Any UC received is **exempt** from income tax.

1.5 Pension credit [SI 2002/1792]

Pension Credit is available to people of State pension age (see below). It **guarantees pensioners a minimum income.**

2 Social security benefits

2.1 Introduction

In certain situations individuals may be able to claim State benefits, which **may be either taxable or exempt** from income tax, as set out below. [s.656, 660 & 677]

Where taxable, the amount **accruing in the tax year** is **taxed as 'Social Security income'** in the income tax computation. It is treated as **non savings income**.

> ### Exam focus point
>
> Candidates must know whether a social security benefit is taxable. Find the tables in **ss.660 and 677 ITEPA 2003**, which set out the **taxable and exempt social security benefits** respectively, so that you know where to find them in the exam. Follow through with the legislation as you read through the rest of this chapter.
>
> If needed, you will be given the amount to include in the income tax computation in the question. You are not expected to know the amounts of such benefits, other than those included in ATT's Tax Tables.

2.2 Benefits available following a death

Benefit	Detail	Tax treatment
Bereavement payment [s.677]	One off lump sum	Not taxable
Bereavement allowance [s.660]	Weekly benefit when spouse/civil partner dies	Taxable
Widowed parent's allowance [s.577]	Weekly benefit when spouse/civil partner dies if have child(ren) < 19 years old	Taxable

2.3 Benefits available for illness

Benefit	Detail	Tax treatment
Statutory sick pay (SSP) [s.660]	£86.70 per week if average weekly gross earnings of ≥ £109	Taxable
Employment and support allowance	Paid if SSP is not available: – Contribution based [s.660] – Income-related [s.677]	 Taxable Not taxable

2.4 Benefits available to those needing long term care

Benefit	Detail	Tax treatment
Personal independence payment (PIP) [s.677]	• For individuals < 65 with physical/ mental disability • Replaces disability living allowance	Not taxable
Attendance allowance [s.677]	For individuals ≥ 65 with physical/ mental disability	Not taxable

2.5 Benefits available to carers

2.5.1 Overview

Benefit	Detail	Tax treatment
Carer's allowance [s.660]	For individuals who look after someone needing long term care (see above)	Taxable
Child benefit	See below	Depends on level of income
Qualifying care relief	See below	Tax free up to 'qualifying amount'

2.5.2 Child benefit

The following weekly amounts of **child benefit** are **payable in respect of each qualifying child**:

- £20.30 a week (£1,056 per year) for the eldest child
- £13.40 a week (£697 per year) for each additional child.

Child benefit is generally **not taxable**. [s.677]

However, an **income tax charge applies for higher income taxpayers as follows**: [s.681B]

Adjusted net income	Tax charge
≤ £50,000	None
> £50,000	1% of benefit per £100 of income between £50,000 and £60,000
> £60,000	Full amount of child benefit received in that tax year

Adjusted net income is defined in the same way as for the adjustment to the personal allowance (see earlier in this Text).

The high income child benefit charge must be **disclosed in a specific section of the self assessment tax return** and is **added to the income tax liability. If both** parents **have income over £50,000**, the one with the **higher income must disclose the charge.**

Claimants can **opt not to receive child benefit** at all to avoid the charge.

Example 1

Sara and Terry Evans have two children. Sara receives child benefit of £1,752. Sara is a stay at home mum with minimal income, while Terry runs his own business. His income during 2013/14 is £57,655.

What is the high income child benefit income tax charge on Terry?

2.5.3 Qualifying care relief

Qualifying care relief is available to individuals who provide **foster care for children up to age 18** and receive income for doing so. [s.803 ITTOIA 2005]

Carers can receive a certain **'qualifying amount'** of income for their caring activities **tax free**. The qualifying amount is calculated as follows:

(a)   **£10,000 per household per year**, plus

(b)   (i)   **£200 per week per child under age 11**, and

        (ii)   **£250 per week per child age 11 or over.**

If the carer's **income exceeds the qualifying amount** they have a choice for calculating the tax payable. They can use either:

(a) The **profit method**, which requires the carer to pay tax on their actual fostering receipts less a deduction for actual expenses and capital allowances, or

(b) The **simplified method**, which requires the carer to pay tax on the excess of their actual fostering receipts over the qualifying amount. No account is taken of expenses or capital allowances.

Exam focus point

The ATT has confirmed that only the simplified method of calculating the taxable amount is examinable in the Personal Taxation paper.

The relief is given **in addition to the personal allowance**. Any taxable amount is chargeable at the **non-savings** rates.

Example 2

Melissa is a self employed foster carer. Throughout 2013/14 she looks after two foster children, Elliott, who is 8 and Elise, who is 14. Her total foster care receipts for the year are £35,000. This is her only income during the year.

Calculate Melissa's income tax liability for the year?

2.6 Other benefits

Benefit	Detail	Tax treatment
State pension and State second pension (S2P) [s.577]	Payable at State pension age	Taxable
Statutory maternity pay (SMP) [s.660]	• 90% of average weekly pay for the first six weeks • Standard rate payment for the following 33 weeks of the lower of: – 90% × weekly earnings, and – £136.78	Taxable

Example 3

Diana has worked for Grenfell Ltd for two years. She currently earns £10,400 a year and receives gross interest of £3,250 during 2013/14. She goes on maternity leave on 6 June 2013.

Calculate Diana's income tax liability for 2013/14, clearly showing how much statutory maternity pay Diana is entitled to.

Exam focus point

Examiner's report – Personal Taxation

May 2011 – Part I SFQ 7

Well answered; to save time candidates should be aware that it is acceptable to just write 'taxable' or 'not taxable' against the [social security] payments listed in the question.

- Certain tax credits may be claimed by workers with low incomes and by families with children.

- Various state benefits may be available on death, illness, disability, unemployment and retirement. Some are taxable while others are tax free.

- State benefits and reliefs may also be available to those with children and those who look after the disabled.

- The high income child benefit income tax charge applies where a taxpayer's income exceeds £50,000 and he or his partner receives child benefit.

- Carers receive tax free income for their caring activities under the qualifying care relief provisions.

Quiz

1. Maria is a single parent. During 2013/14 Maria earns £15,000 (£1,112 tax deducted via PAYE) from her job as a secretary and receives rental income of £10,000. She also receives total child and working tax credits of £3,465, and child benefit of £1,056. Calculate Maria's tax payable for 2013/14 .

2. Oliver has total income of £52,000 (all non-savings income) in 2013/14. His wife, Stacey, is a stay at home mum who looks after their two year old son, Scott. Stacey receives child benefit of £20.30 per week. Calculate Oliver's income tax liability.

3. State whether the following social security benefits are taxable or exempt:

    (a) Jobseeker's allowance
    (b) Statutory maternity pay
    (c) Employment and support allowance (income related element)
    (d) Carer's allowance
    (e) Bereavement payment.

1.

	Non savings £	Tax suffered £
Employment income	15,000	1,112
Property income	10,000	
Net income	25,000	1,112
Less: PA	(9,440)	
Taxable income	15,560	
Income tax	£	
£15,560 @ 20%	3,112	
Less: tax suffered at source	(1,112)	
Tax payable by Maria	2,000	

Tax credits and child benefit are not taxable. As Maria's income is below £50,000 there is no high income child benefit charge.

2. Oliver's income in 2013/14 is between £50,000 and £60,000, so there will be a child benefit income tax charge:

	£
Income	52,000
Less: PA	(9,440)
Taxable income	42,560
Tax:	
£32,010 @ 20%	6,402
£10,550 @ 40%	4,220
	10,622
Add: child benefit income tax charge (W)	211
Tax liability	10,833

Working

	£
Income	52,000
Less: threshold	(50,000)
Excess	2,000
÷ £100	20
Charge: 1% × £(20.30 × 52) × £20	211

3. (a) Jobseeker's allowance – Taxable
    (b) Statutory maternity pay – Taxable
    (c) Employment and support allowance (income related element) – Exempt
    (d) Carer's allowance – Taxable
    (e) Bereavement payment – Exempt

Solution to Example 1

	£
2013/14	
Income	57,655
Less: threshold	(50,000)
Excess	7,655
÷ £100 (Note 1)	76
Charge: 1% × £1,752 × £76	1,331

Notes.

(1)   Round down to the nearest whole number at all stages of the calculation.

(2)   The child benefit of £1,752 is exempt income for Sara. The high income child benefit charge must be disclosed by Terry in his 2013/14 income tax return.

Solution to Example 2

Melissa 2013/14

	Non savings £
Foster care receipts (W)	1,600
Less: PA	(9,440)
Taxable amount	Nil

Melissa has no tax liability for the year.

Working

	£	£
Foster care receipts		35,000
Less: 'qualifying amount'		
Fixed amount	10,000	
Amount per child:		
Elliott (< 11): 52 weeks × £200	10,400	
Elise (≥ 11): 52 weeks × £250	13,000	
Total 'qualifying amount'		(33,400)
Taxable amount		1,600

Solution to Example 3

	Non savings £	Savings £
Employment income (W1)	1,733	
Investment income		3,250
SMP (W2)	5,594	
Net income	7,327	3,250
Less: PA	(7,327)	(2,113)
Taxable income	Nil	1,137
Tax liability: £1,137 @ 10% (within starting rate band)		114

Workings

(1)   *Employment income for two months*

   £10,400 × 2/12 = £1,733

(2)   *Statutory maternity pay*

   Diana's weekly wages are £200 (£10,400 ÷ 52). Her maternity pay, all paid during 2013/14, is as follows:

	£
£200 × 90% = £180 × 6 weeks	1,080
£136.78 (ie lower of £180 and £136.78) × 33 weeks	4,514
Total	5,594

Short Form Questions:

3.1 – 3.3 inclusive

Long Form Questions:

3.1	Jonty
3.2	Fiona
3.3	Jane Bradbury

- understand the rules for the taxation of income from land and buildings

- set off property losses correctly

- calculate the amount of a short lease premium that is taxable as income

- identify furnished holiday accommodation

- understand when 'the rent a room' scheme applies

- understand the tax position of landlords living outside the UK

- be aware of the rules for Real Estate Investment Trusts (REITs)

References: ITTOIA 2005 unless otherwise stated

Property income

1 Introduction

All lettings in the UK by an individual landlord are treated as a single business with the profit or loss computed for a tax year on normal business accounting principles – ie **rents and expenses included on an accruals basis**. Profits and losses on individual properties are pooled, so **current year losses are automatically set off**.

Property income is always taxed as non savings income.

Exam focus point

Property income is a core area of the syllabus. It appears within the personal income tax computation and can be set either as a long written or computational question.

A UK resident landlord is taxed on property income from property **within and outside the UK**.

In this chapter we consider the rules for taxing **UK property income**.

2 UK property income

2.1 Calculating property income

The property income taxable on individuals is based on the annual profits arising from the 'business' including:

(a) **Rent** charges
(b) Part of the **premium on the grant of a short lease** (see below).

A person receiving rental income is taxed on the full amount of the profits **accrued in (ie relating to) the tax year**.

2.2 Allowable property expenses

2.2.1 Allowable expenditure

Expenses are allowed (ie are deductible) if they are wholly and exclusively incurred for the 'business' of letting. Expenses such as advertising, accountancy and insurance are allowed but depreciation is not (capital allowances or 'wear & tear' allowances (see below) are given instead).

Bad debts are allowed on business principles, so if a rent payment appears unlikely, the landlord can provide for it in his letting accounts at the end of the tax year.

Both loan (ie mortgage) interest and overdraft interest are deductible in computing property income, provided the related borrowing was applied wholly and exclusively for the purposes of the letting business.

If the landlord has a number of properties he can set off the running expenses incurred on **empty properties** (eg properties under repair between lets), against other property income.

Expenditure on **repairs**, such as painting and decorating, mending broken windows, etc, is generally deductible for income tax purposes so long as there is **no significant improvement** of the property beyond its original condition, as that would be treated as capital expenditure (see below).

2.2.2 Capital expenditure

Capital expenditure on let properties, eg the cost of building an extension, **is generally not deductible** when computing the assessable property income. Instead it will usually be deductible when calculating the capital gain or loss on the eventual **disposal** of the property (see later in this Text).

Illustration

Jerome replaces some roof tiles that were blown off by a storm. This is a repair and is deductible when calculating the property income to include in his income tax computation.

If instead Jerome had taken off the roof and built on another storey, that would be a capital improvement and the expenditure would only be deductible when calculating any gain on a future disposal of the property.

Replacing an item with the nearest modern equivalent, for example replacing single glazed windows with double glazed windows, is **allowable as a repair** for income tax purposes and is not disallowable as improvement expenditure.

Capital allowances (the tax equivalent of accounting depreciation) **are not allowed for expenditure on furniture used in a residential dwelling** (although they may be available for equipment used in the property – see below).

Instead, the landlord can **elect for the 'wear and tear allowance'**. [s.308A]

This allowance is equal to:

10% × [rents – (relevant expenses if paid by the landlord)]

Relevant expenses are utilities, council tax and other expenses, which in the case of furnished lettings, are normally borne by the tenant, eg water rates. [s.308C (5)]

Relief for capital expenditure used to be available on a renewals basis, which meant that the original cost and the cost of any improvements were not deductible for income tax purposes, but the cost of replacing furniture to the same standard was allowed. This was a cumbersome system to administer, and has been abolished from 6 April 2013.

Example 1

Natalie rents out a furnished investment property for the whole of 2013/14 for £1,200 a month, payable on the first day of the month, in advance. The tenants do not pay the rent for April 2014 until 15 April 2014.

During the year she had the following expenses in connection with letting the property:

	£
Mortgage interest	7,200
Repairs and maintenance	565
Water rates	275
Painting and decorating	1,350
Insurance	(see below)
Gardening and cleaning	175

For the year ended 31 December 2013 Natalie paid landlord's insurance premiums totalling £685. For the year ended 31 December 2014 this increased to £755. The tenants pay council tax of £1,650.

Natalie claims the wear and tear allowance.

Calculate Natalie's property income for 2013/14.

2.2.3 Properties used by the landlord

If property is occupied at some time by the owner, the allowable deduction for repairs, insurance, council tax and so on is restricted to a proportion based on the period that the property is available for letting. For example, if HMRC accept that letting took place throughout the year and was occupied by the owner for 4 weeks and by tenants for 30 weeks, 48/52 of the expenses would be allowed. Expenses specific to the letting such as advertising would, however, be allowed in full.

2.3 Capital allowances on equipment

Capital allowances may be claimed on plant and machinery (P&M) used for the maintenance or repair of the properties or plant let as part of the building (eg lawn mowers). They are generally available at 100% for the first £250,000 of expenditure in the year (the 'Annual investment Allowance' (AIA)) and at 18% on the balance and on existing expenditure.

As explained above, capital allowances are not available in respect of furniture and instead the wear and tear allowance is available.

The Landlord's Energy Savings Allowance of up to £1,500 per property is also available (until 31 March 2015) as a deduction from property income to landlords who incur capital expenditure on energy savings items, eg insulation and draught proofing in a dwelling house.

Exam focus point

Examiner's report – Personal Taxation

November 2010 – Part II LFQ 1

The property income was well dealt with although a number of candidates did not take account of the wear and tear allowance.

3 Property losses

Where there is an overall loss:

(a) The **loss is carried forward and set against UK property income** in subsequent years

(b) **Losses** resulting from **capital allowances** can be **set against the taxpayer's general income** for the year of the loss and the following tax year, subject to the **limit on income tax reliefs** (see earlier in this Text). [s.120 ITA 2007)]

The loss relief at (a) above is automatic and no claim is required. Losses under (b) above must be claimed within 12 months from the self assessment filing date for the year of the loss (ie by 31 January 2016 for a 2013/14 loss).

Where a property is let at **less than the full commercial rent** (eg to a relative at a nominal or 'peppercorn' rent), **expenses can only be deducted up to the amount of the rent received** from the property (ie they cannot create a loss that can be set against other property income).

4 Premiums on leases

4.1 Basic principle

A 'lease' is a right to use an asset (in this case a property) for a specified period of time. Any **amount paid up front** by the lessee (the tenant) to the lessor (landlord) for the use of a property is referred to as a **'premium'** and is treated as a capital receipt. There are usually therefore no income tax implications for a premium as it is a capital sum.

However, when a premium is received on the *grant* (that is, by a landlord to a tenant) of a **short lease (50 years or less), part of the premium is treated as rent and is taxed as property income** in the year of grant.

4.2 Amount taxed as income

The premium taxed as property income is the whole premium less 2% of the premium for each complete year of the lease, except the first year. This is expressed as the formula: [s.277(4)]

$P \times \dfrac{50-Y}{50}$, where P = the premium and Y = the number of years on the lease minus 1 year

The balance (ie the capital element) is subject to capital gains tax (see later in this Text).

This rule does not apply on the *assignment* (ie sale) of a lease (one tenant selling his interest in the property to another), nor to the grant of a lease of more than 50 years, which is usually only subject to capital gains tax.

Example 2

Samantha granted a lease to Carrie on 1 March 2014 for a duration of 12 years. Carrie paid Samantha a premium of £42,000. Show Samantha's property income for 2013/14.

This part of the premium is assessed on the receipts basis, ie in full in the year the lease is granted. The accruals concept does not apply.

The balance of the premium (ie the capital element) **is subject to capital gains tax as a part disposal of the freehold or leasehold interest** (see later in this Text). The amount of the premium chargeable to income tax as property income is excluded from the calculation.

4.3 Premiums for granting subleases

A tenant may sublet the property and charge a **premium on the grant of the lease to the subtenant**. This premium is taxed as property income in the normal way, except that where the tenant originally paid a premium for his own original or head lease, relief is given, computed as:

Premium taxable as property income for head lease $\times \dfrac{\text{duration of sub - lease}}{\text{duration of head lease}}$

Example 3

Clive granted a lease to Derek on 1 March 2006 for a period of 40 years. Derek paid a premium of £16,000. On 1 March 2014 Derek granted a sublease to Eric for a period of ten years. Eric paid a premium of £30,000.

Calculate the property income assessable on Derek in 2013/14.

5 Furnished holiday lettings (FHLs)

5.1 Introduction

Income from commercial lettings of furnished holiday accommodation in the UK and other parts of the European Economic Area (EEA) is taxed as property income but, provided certain conditions are satisfied, is mainly treated for most tax purposes as if it were trading income. [s.328]

A 'commercial letting of furnished accommodation' requires the letting to be on a **commercial basis with a view to the realisation of profits, with the tenant being entitled to the use of the furniture.**

Where the taxpayer also has other letting income, he is treated as running a 'business of letting' and a 'business of furnished holiday letting' and the two are computed separately.

Where the taxpayer owns properties in both the UK and the EEA, these are treated as two **separate furnished holiday letting (FHL) businesses.**

Accommodation is only furnished holiday accommodation if it **satisfies three conditions:** [s.325]

(a)   **The availability test** *and*
(b)   **The occupancy test** *and*
(c)   **The pattern of occupation condition.**

5.2 Conditions

5.2.1 The availability condition

The property must be **available for commercial letting to the public for at least 210 days** in a year.

5.2.2 The letting condition (the 'occupancy' test)

The property must be **let for at least 105 days** in the year.

If a landlord has two or more properties and each passes the 210 day test separately, then he can **elect to average the days** so they need only pass the 105 day test on average.

This averaging election must be made by the **anniversary of the self assessment filing date** for the tax year in question, ie by 31 January 2016 for FHL income reported on a 2013/14 tax return.

A landlord may choose to leave particular properties out of the averaging computation if they would pull the average down to below 105 days.

If a property reaches the occupancy threshold in some years but not in others, the taxpayer may make a **'period of grace' election.** This election treats **the property as a qualifying FHL** so long as he **genuinely intended to meet the occupancy threshold** but was unable to do so, for example due to unforeseen circumstances such as adverse weather conditions.

The property **must have reached the occupancy threshold in the year before the election** (year one), either on its own or because of an averaging election.

In addition, if the property **still does not meet the occupancy threshold in the year after making the election** (year three), that year can **also be treated as a qualifying FHL** year. [s.326A]

Example 4

Stef owns a villa in Spain that would otherwise qualify as a FHL. The villa is let as follows:

	Number of days let
2012/13	110
2013/14	78
2014/15	92
2015/16	107

Explain whether and in which years the villa qualifies as a FHL, assuming Stef makes any beneficial elections.

The taxpayer may use a **combination of the averaging and period of grace elections** to ensure a property continues to qualify.

5.2.3 The pattern of occupation condition

If the property is let out to the same person for periods **longer than 31 days**, ie a period of **'longer term occupation'**, in one stretch, **none of the days counts towards the occupation threshold** (unless there are exceptional and unforeseen circumstances, such as where a holidaymaker falls ills and cannot leave the accommodation in time).

If the **total of all or any longer term occupation lettings exceeds 155 days in the year, the property cannot qualify as a FHL** for that period.

The property **can be let to the same person more than once as long as each let is less than 31 days**. All of these lettings together to the same person can total more than 31 days and still count towards the occupation threshold.

Example 5

Darcy lets out his property, which otherwise qualifies as a FHL, to four different families in 2013/14 as follows:

Family	Number of days
Appleby	28
Brandon	30
Cranston	25
Brandon (2nd letting in the year)	29
Delow	32

Explain whether the property will qualify as a FHL in 2013/14.

5.3 Tax treatment

Where the above conditions are fully satisfied the commercial letting of furnished holiday accommodation **is treated as a trade** (but assessed as property income rather than trade profits):

(a) The profits are treated as earned income so the **income qualifies as relevant earnings** for pension purposes (see later in this Text). [s.328]

(b) **Capital allowances are available as for traders, ie an AIA of 100% on the first £250,000 of expenditure and 18% on the balance**. This applies to furnishings etc used in a dwelling. This replaces the wear and tear allowance.

(c) Capital gains tax entrepreneurs' relief, rollover relief, and relief for gifts of business assets, are available when the landlord eventually disposes of the property (see later in this Text).

However, **losses** arising from the letting of a FHL can only be **set against income from that same FHL business**, rather than against general income as for regular trading losses.

6 The rent a room scheme

If an individual lets a room or rooms in his main residence (ie to a lodger), then a special exemption may apply.

If gross rents (ie before deducting expenses) **are less than the limit of £4,250 per property a year, the rents are wholly exempt from income tax** and expenses and capital allowances are ignored. However, the taxpayer may claim to ignore the exemption, for example to generate a loss by taking into account both rent and expenses.

This limit is halved if any other person (including the owner's spouse) also received income from renting accommodation in the property while the property was the owner's main residence.

If gross rents exceed the limit, the taxpayer will be taxed in the ordinary way, ignoring the rent a room scheme, unless he elects for the 'alternative basis'. **If he so elects, he will be taxable on gross receipts less £4,250** (or £2,125 if the limit is halved), with no deductions for expenses or capital allowances.

An election to ignore the exemption or an election for the alternative basis must be made on or before the anniversary of 31 January following the end of the tax year concerned, so by 31 January 2016 for an election relating to 2013/14. An election to ignore the exemption applies only for the year for which it is made, but an election for the alternative basis remains in force until it is withdrawn or until a year in which gross rents do not exceed the limit.

7 Rent paid to a non-resident landlord

Under the **Non Resident Landlord Scheme** (NRLS) the agent for the property (or where there is no agent, the tenant) must **deduct basic rate tax at source before rent is paid** over to a non-UK resident landlord of a UK property. [s.971 ITA 2007]

Any higher or additional rate tax that is payable is dealt with by the non-resident landlord under self assessment.

Rent can be paid gross to the non-resident landlord by agreement with HMRC under the NRLS, as long as the landlord's UK tax affairs are up to date and he undertakes to include tax from property income in the payments on account which he makes under self assessment.

8 Real Estate Investment Trusts (REITs)

A **REIT is a listed company** (AIM does *not* count for this purpose) **owning, managing and earning rental income from commercial or residential property**.

REITs can **elect for their property income (and gains), including that received from other REITs, to be exempt from corporation tax.** The company must **withhold basic rate (20%) tax** from distributions paid to shareholders (who cannot own more than 10% of a REIT's shares) **out of these profits**.

These distributions are **taxed as property income on the investor, not as dividends.**

Distributions by REITs **out of other income** (ie not property income or gains) are **taxed as dividends** in the normal way.

Example 6

Sue has a holding (less than 1%) of shares in The Property Business which is a REIT. During 2013/14 she received a dividend from her investment of £6,400. The REIT paid the dividend out of exempt property income. She also has a salary of £32,000 (tax deducted via PAYE of £4,512) and bank interest income (gross amount) of £1,000 in the year.

Calculate Sue's tax payable.

Exam focus point

Examiner's report – Personal Taxation

November 2008 – Part I SFQ 3

Many candidates were not aware of the features of a REIT, some confusing them with EIS.

- UK property income is calculated as accrued rental income less accrued revenue expenses for each property for a tax year.
- Profits and losses of individual properties are pooled to arrive at the UK property income assessment for the individual.
- A 10% wear and tear allowance is available in respect of furniture for furnished properties.
- Losses on UK properties must be carried forward and set against future UK property profits.
- An element of the premium received by a landlord on the grant of a short lease is taxable as UK property income.
- If a property meets various conditions it may be classified as a Furnished Holiday Let (FHL) so income from it is treated as earned income for pension contribution purposes, capital allowances are available and certain CGT business reliefs are available on disposal of the property.
- Losses from a FHL, however, can only be set against income from that same FHL business and not against general income like normal trading losses.
- FHL properties in the UK and those located elsewhere in the EEA are treated as two separate businesses.
- If an individual rents out a room in their main residence and charges their tenant less than £4,250 pa, this amount is not taxable.
- Dividends from REITs are taxed as property income not company dividends. Basic rate tax (20%) is deducted at source from such distributions.

Quiz

1. David buys a property for letting on 1 August 2013 and grants a tenancy to Ethel from 1 December 2013 at £3,600 pa payable quarterly in advance. How much is taxable in 2013/14?

2. Catherine rents out a furnished property for £16,000 pa and pays the water rates of £320 and council tax of £780 on the property. Calculate the amount of wear and tear allowance she can claim.

3. John pays buildings insurance premiums for 12 months in advance on 1 October each year to cover all his letting properties. He pays £4,800 in 2012 and £5,200 in 2013. How much is deductible from his property income in 2013/14?

4. Debbie lets a flat to her widowed mother for £600 pa when a market rent would be £3,600 pa. Debbie pays all the letting expenses which amount to £1,800 for 2013/14. Explain what relief is available for the loss incurred.

5. Paul grants a lease for 10 years to Graham for a premium of £20,000. How much is assessable as property income and when will it be assessed?

6. Michael owns four holiday cottages in the UK and one in France that would otherwise qualify as FHLs. Each cottage is let for the following number of days:

	Number of days let
Cottage 1	135
Cottage 2	149
Cottage 3	110
Cottage 4	54
Cottage 5 (France)	216

Which of Michael's cottages will qualify as FHLs assuming he makes any beneficial elections?

7. What is the main income tax advantage of a profitable 'furnished holiday letting' business?

8. What is the income threshold for 'rent a room' relief?

1. Rent accrued 1.12.13 – 5.4.14, ie $^4/_{12} \times £3,600 = £1,200$.

2. Wear and tear allowance deductible from rental income:

   $10\% \times £(16,000 - 320 - 780) = £1,490$

3. Insurance premiums accrued in 2013/14

	£
$^6/_{12} \times £4,800$	2,400
$^6/_{12} \times £5,200$	2,600
	5,000

4. There is no loss as the property is let at a non-commercial rent. In this case, only expenses up to the amount of the rent (ie £600) can be set off against the income. This brings the property income assessment down to £Nil.

5. Property income £20,000 × ((50 – 9)/50)   £16,400

   Assessable in the year the lease is granted.

6. Initially it appears that Cottage 4 will not qualify as a FHL as it is not let for at least 105 days. However, Michael can elect to average the number of days his other properties have been let to determine whether Cottage 4 can qualify:

   The UK and EEA properties must be treated as separate businesses, so we take the total number of days that the UK properties have been let, ie 448 days.

   The average is 112 days (448 ÷ 4) so all the properties qualify as FHLs.

7. FHL income qualifies as relevant earnings which gives scope to make higher pension contributions (see later in this Text).

8. £4,250 a year.

Solution to chapter examples

Solution to Example 1

	£	£
Rental income (amount accrued – late payment irrelevant)		14,400
Less: Expenses:		
Loan interest	7,200	
Repairs and maintenance	565	
Water rates	275	
Painting and decorating	1,350	
Insurance ([9/12 × £685] + [3/12 × £755])	703	
Gardening and cleaning	175	
Wear & tear allowance (10% × £[14,400 – 275])	1,413	
Total expenses		(11,681)
Property income		2,719

Note. The council tax is paid by the tenants so does not affect the calculation.

Solution to Example 2

	£
Assessable as property income: £42,000 × ((50 – 11)/50)	32,760

Solution to Example 3

	£
Property income: £30,000 × ((50 − 9)/50)	24,600
Less: allowance for premium paid to Clive by Derek	
(£16,000 × ((50 − 39)/50)) × 10/40	(880)
Amount assessable	23,720

Solution to Example 4

2012/13	The property satisfies the 105 day occupancy threshold
2013/14	The property does not satisfy the 105 day occupancy threshold but Stef can elect for a period of grace as the property had actually reached the threshold in 2012/13
2014/15	If Stef makes the election for 2013/14, the period of grace can continue to apply in 2014/15, even though the property does not actually reach the threshold
2015/16	The villa satisfies the 105 day occupancy threshold

Therefore the property qualifies in all four years.

Solution to Example 5

The lettings to the Appleby and Cranston families qualify as they are less than 31 days each.

The lettings to the Brandon family also qualify as each let is less than 31 days.

The letting to the Delow family cannot be counted as it exceeds 31 days.

The total number of days that are looked at for the purpose of the occupancy test is therefore 112, which is more than 105, so the property as a whole qualifies as a FHL in 2013/14.

Solution to Example 6

	Non savings income £	Savings income £	Total £
Employment income	32,000		
Dividend from REIT – Property income £6,400 × 100/80	8,000		
Interest		1,000	
Net income	40,000	1,000	41,000
PA	(9,440)		(9,440)
	30,560	1,000	31,560

Non savings income £30,560 @ 20%	6,112
Savings income £1,000 @ 20%	200
Tax liability	6,312
Less: tax suffered	
Savings income £1,000 @ 20%	(200)
REIT dividend income £8,000 @ 20%	(1,600)
PAYE	(4,512)
Tax payable	Nil

Note. Dividends from REITs are taxed as property income not as company dividends. Basic rate tax (20%) is deducted at source from such distributions.

Now try the following questions

Short Form Questions:

4.1 – 4.7 inclusive

Long Form Questions:

4.1	Randall
4.2	Corelli
4.3	Mary Taylor

chapter

5

Employment income

The purpose of this chapter is to help you to:

- explain the scope of the charge to income tax on employment income

- identify and calculate the benefits taxable on all employees

- calculate the benefits taxable only on employees paid £8,500 or more pa and directors

- identify tax free benefits available to all employees

- identify the payments and expenses that can be deducted from employment income

- apply the special provisions taxing payments on termination of employment

References: ITEPA 2003 unless otherwise stated

1 Basis of employment income

1.1 Assessable income

Remuneration from an office or employment is taxed as employment income. Employment income is divided into:

(a)   General earnings, and
(b)   Specific employment income

General earnings include:

(a)   Any salary, wages or fee
(b)   Any benefits.

Specific employment income includes:

(a)   Payments made on termination of employment (see below)
(b)   Income from acquisition of shares derived from employment (see later in this Text)
(c)   Pension income received from an unregistered pension scheme.

1.2 The receipts basis

General earnings are assessed as income for the year in which they are received. The date of receipt is the earliest of: [s.18]

(a)   The date of **payment** (or payment on account), or

(b)   The date when a person becomes **entitled** to the payment, or

(c)   In the case of directors only, the earliest of:

    (i)   The date the earnings are credited in the company's records or accounts, or

    (ii)   The end of a period of account if earnings for that period are determined before the period ends, or

    (iii)   The date earnings are determined if the amount is not determined until after the period of account ends.

Taxable benefits (eg company cars) are generally treated as received when they are provided to the employee. If an employer provides a benefit to an employee's family member, the benefit will be taxable on that employee.

Example 1

A director of a company is entitled under his employment contract to a salary of £24,000 pa payable monthly on the last day of each month in equal amounts. Additionally he is entitled to a performance related bonus calculated on each half year's profits. The company prepares accounts to 31 December each year.

His bonus for the six months to 30 June 2012 of £8,000 is determined on 1 November 2012, credited to his account in the company's records on 1 January 2013 and paid to him with his January salary. His bonus of £11,500 for the six months to 31 December 2012 is not determined until agreed by the shareholders at the AGM on 30 April 2013. It is then entered into the company's records and paid with his May salary.

You are required to calculate his taxable employment income for 2012/13 and 2013/14.

If remuneration is received after the employee has ceased to work for that employer it is still taxable, regardless of whether the office or employment is still held at the date of receipt.

2 Taxable benefits assessable on all employees

2.1 The general rules

The general rule for benefits received by excluded employees (ie paid less than £8,500 pa) is that they are **only taxable** if they can be turned into money. The value of such benefits can be thought of as the **'second-hand value'**.

The general rule for non-excluded employees is that the taxable value of the benefit is the cost to the employer of providing the benefit.

For both excluded and non-excluded employees there are now many specific rules, which override the general rules.

The following specific rules for the provision of vouchers, living accommodation and mileage allowances apply to *all* employees regardless of the level of their earnings.

Certain benefits are only taxed on employees earning £8,500 or more and directors (ie non-excluded employees). The specific rules for how to calculate these taxable benefits are set out below.

Any amounts received by an employee in respect of benefits (or expenses – see below) from their employer usually form part of a director's or employee's earnings and must be **reported on Form P11D** (*Expenses and benefits*) or Form 9D for excluded employees. Form P11D is reproduced towards the end of this Chapter.

Any **benefits** that a close company provides to a **participator** (ie broadly a shareholder) **who is not an employee** of the company, cannot be taxable as employment income. Instead, the **cash value of the benefit**, as calculated for employment income purposes, is **treated as a net dividend** (see earlier in this Text). [s.1064 CTA 2010].

Exam focus point

'Benefits' are a core area of the syllabus. Spend time, making sure you understand how to calculate the cash value of benefits.

2.2 Vouchers

If an employee receives a **cash voucher**, he is assessable on the **sum of money for which the voucher is capable of being exchanged**. He is assessed in the year he receives the voucher.

If an employee receives

(a)   Non-cash vouchers (eg book tokens), or

(b)   Credit tokens (eg a credit card)

he is **assessable on the *cost to the employer of providing* the benefit**, unless the benefit itself is exempt (see below).

The following are **examples of tax free vouchers** which are commonly provided, although any other voucher which is used to provide a tax free benefit is also exempt:

(i)   **Child care vouchers** (tax free up to specified limits (see below)).

(ii)   Vouchers in respect of the cost of an **eye test or prescription glasses**.

(iii)   Voucher for a **car parking space** at or near an employee's place of work (eg an NCP season ticket), whether for an employee's own car or a company car.

2.3 Accommodation [ss.104 – 107]

2.3.1 Basic charge

The value of the accommodation benefit provided to *any* employee is the annual value of that property (given in the exam). If the premises are rented rather than owned by the company, then the benefit to the employee is the higher of:

(a)   The rent actually paid by the employer, including a proportion of any premium paid in respect of a lease of ten years or less, and

(b)   The annual value.

The amount of lease premium to include in (a) above is broadly the lease premium divided by the number of years of the lease. [s.105A]

The amount taxable on the employee will be reduced by any contribution he makes for the use of the property and any element of business use.

Example 2

Tony is provided with a company flat.

Annual value	£300
Rent paid by the company	£3,380
Amount paid by Tony to the company for the use of the flat	£520

You are required to show Tony's assessable benefit.

2.3.2 Job related accommodation

There is no taxable benefit if the accommodation provided is job related, ie it is provided in one of the following circumstances: [ss.99 &100]

(a)   Residence in the accommodation is **necessary** for the proper performance of the employee's duties (eg a caretaker), or

(b)   Accommodation is provided for the better performance of the employee's duties and the employment is of a kind in which it is **customary** for accommodation to be provided (eg a vicar or policeman), or

(c)   The accommodation is provided as part of special **security** arrangements in force because of a special threat to the employee's security (eg the Prime Minister).

2.3.3 Expensive accommodation

Where the cost of the living accommodation exceeds £75,000 an additional benefit is charged on the employee or director. The additional benefit is found by applying the following formula: [s.104]

$$ORI \times (C - £75,000)$$

ORI is the official rate of interest at the start of the tax year. The rate is given in the Tax Tables provided in the exam.

C is the 'cost of providing' the living accommodation and is the aggregate of the cost of purchase and the cost of any improvements made before the relevant tax year. It is therefore *not* possible to avoid the charge if the employer purchases a property requiring substantial repairs and 'does it up'. The cost is the net cost, after taking account of any amounts paid by the employee.

If the accommodation was acquired by the employer more than six years before it was first provided to the employee and its original cost, plus improvements, exceeded £75,000, the 'cost of providing' is increased (or reduced if appropriate) **to its market value when first provided to that employee**. Note that regardless of current market value, an additional charge cannot apply if the *original* cost plus improvements is under £75,000.

Where any contribution paid by the employee for the use of the property exceeds its annual value, the excess may be deducted from the additional expensive accommodation benefit.

Example 3

Simon is provided with a house by his employer (not job related accommodation). It was originally made available to him on 1 July 2010, although the company had acquired the house at a cost of £125,000 on 1 April 2007.

On 1 September 2012, £8,000 was spent on extending the property.

For 2013/14, the annual value of the house is £1,400. Simon pays £3,000 for the use of the house to his employer.

You are required to calculate his total benefit for 2013/14 in respect of the house.

2.4 Mileage allowances

Where employers pay mileage allowances to their employees to use their own cars for business travel the employees are taxed on any amounts in excess of the HMRC authorised mileage rates.

The **tax-free limits are 45p a mile for the first 10,000 business miles and 25p a mile thereafter** and are shown in the Tax Tables provided in the exam.

Any amount paid in excess of the limit is taxable on the employee. If the employer pays less than the authorised rates the employee can claim a deduction from their employment income for the shortfall.

The rates take into account depreciation, running expenses etc and the employee cannot claim a deduction for any loan taken out to purchase the car or any capital allowances on the cost of the car.

Any amount paid to the employee for mileage other than on the employer's business (eg for home to office mileage) is always taxable in full.

Example 4

Owen drives 14,000 business miles in his own car. Calculate the taxable benefit or allowable deduction assuming:

(a)   He is reimbursed 45p a mile
(b)   He is reimbursed 25p a mile
(c)   No reimbursement is made.

The employer is only required to report the taxable profit (if any) and the employee will only claim for the shortfall (if any).

Employers can pay employees using their own cars up to 5p a mile tax free for taking fellow employees as passengers on business journeys. An employee cannot claim a deduction against his taxable employment income where he receives either no payment from the employer or less than 5p a mile.

Employers can also pay a tax free mileage allowance to employees using motorcycles and bicycles in the course of their employment as follows:

Motorcycles	24p
Bicycles	20p

These generous rates are intended to encourage the use of more environmentally friendly transport. There is no reduction in the rates for over 10,000 miles (although, in the case of bicycles, this is not likely to be a practical point!).

Exam focus point

Examiner's report – Personal Taxation (old syllabus)

Nov 2001 – Question 1

Some candidates confused the mileage allowance calculation and deducted the excess of the allowance paid over the ... Authorised Mileage allowance from the salary as an expense.

Many candidates were confused over the correct way to calculate the accommodation benefits. The most common error was to restrict the amount of the benefit by one half (on the basis that he spent only half his time in each property?) ...

---

3 Benefits assessable on employees paid £8,500 or more and directors

3.1 Employees paid £8,500 or more and directors

Certain benefits are only assessed on employees who are paid £8,500 or more (ie who are not excluded employees) or directors.

Earnings, for the £8,500 pa test include salary, commissions, fees, reimbursed expenses and also benefits assessable on employees paid £8,500+ pa/directors. In other words, one must *initially assume* that a particular employee is paid £8,500 pa or more in order to determine whether or not he really is in that category. [s.218]

You may find it useful to learn the following proforma:

	£
Employment income (net of occupational pension contributions and payroll giving donations)	X
Reimbursed expenses	X
Benefits as if were paid £8,500 pa or more	X
TEST HERE	X
Less: allowable deductions	(X)
Taxable employment income if the taxpayer is paid £8,500 pa or more	X

The test must be made before making allowance for any deductions (eg expenses).

The £8,500 is pro-rated where the employment is held for less than the full tax year.

The term 'director' refers to any person who acts as a director or any person in accordance with whose instructions the directors are accustomed to act (other than a professional adviser).

A full-time working director, or a director of a non-profit making company or charity, and who, with associates, controls not more than 5% of the voting rights of the company is excluded unless he earns £8,500 pa or more.

3.2 The general rule

The value of a benefit is the cost to the employer *of providing* **that benefit.** So, for example, the taxable benefit where private medical insurance is provided to an employee is the amount paid to the private medical insurer by the employer. There are, however, special rules for a number of specific benefits.

A benefit arises if it is provided 'by reason of the employment' so there is no need for the employer to provide it directly. In addition the rules apply if benefits are provided to members of an individual's family or household.

Where **in-house benefits** are provided, the case of *Pepper v Hart (1992)* established that the cost of **providing the benefit is the marginal (ie additional) cost** and not the average cost. This case involved employees of a public school paying reduced fees for their own children, calculated to cover the extra cost to the school eg food and laundry for the employee's child. They successfully argued that there was no cost to the employer as they had reimbursed the marginal costs. HMRC had wanted to value the benefit by averaging the total school costs over the total number of pupils.

This marginal cost basis is relevant to a wide range of employments and can apply, for example, where employees of transport undertakings (eg British Airways) are allowed to take up unsold seats free or at below the full price.

Exam focus point

Preparation of an income tax computation is a common long form question that can often test the position of a higher paid employee with several benefits. You will be required to calculate the cash value of these benefits using the rules detailed in this chapter. Use a separate working for each benefit.

3.3 Expenses connected with living accommodation

Expenses connected with living accommodation are only assessable on non-excluded employees, or directors. Examples of these expenses are:

(a)   Heating, lighting or cleaning the premises
(b)   Repairing, maintaining or decorating them
(c)   Providing furniture etc normal for domestic occupation (annual value taken as 20% of cost – see below).

Unless the accommodation qualifies as 'job related' (see above) the full cost of additional services (excluding structural repairs) is taxable. If the accommodation is 'job related', however, the taxable value of additional services is restricted to a maximum of 10% of 'net earnings'. For this purpose, net earnings are all amounts taxable as employment income (*excluding* the additional services (a) – (c) above) less any allowable expenses. [s.315]

If the employer pays the council tax due in respect of the property this will also be taxable *unless* **the employee is in job related accommodation.**

Example 5

Mr Quinton is employed as a security guard earning £12,000 in 2013/14. In order to carry out his duties properly he is required to live in a house adjacent to his employer's premises and this is accepted by HMRC as job related accommodation. The house cost £70,000 two years ago. The annual value of the house is £650.

In 2013/14 the company pays an electricity bill of £250, a gas bill of £200, a gardener's bill of £150 and redecoration costs of £1,000. Mr Quinton makes a monthly contribution of £50 for his accommodation. He drives a company car on which the assessable benefit is £2,990.

You are required to calculate the amount assessable as employment income for 2013/14.

3.4 The car benefit rules

Special rules apply for calculating the taxable car benefit where a non-excluded employee is provided with a car by his employer (often referred to as company cars), which can be used for private purposes. [s.121]

(a)   The tax charge arises where the car is provided by reason of the employee's employment, whether it is by the employer or by some other person.

(b)   **The taxable benefit is a percentage, determined by the level of the car's carbon dioxide (CO_2) emissions** (see below) × **the car's list price**. There is **no benefit for electric cars** (until at least 5 April 2015).

(c)   The **list price** of the car is the sum of the following items:

(i)   The list price of the car for a single retail sale in the UK at the time of first registration, including delivery charges and the cost of standard accessories. **Discounts received by the employer are ignored.**

(ii)   The price (including fitting) of all **optional accessories added when the car was first provided** to the employee, excluding mobile telephones, equipment needed by a disabled employee, equipment for the car to run on road fuel gas and, where there is a threat to an employee's physical security, features such as armour-plating and bullet-proof glass.

(iii) The price (including fitting) of **all optional accessories fitted later and costing at least £100 each**, with exclusions as in (ii). Such accessories affect the taxable benefit from and including the tax year in which they are fitted. Accessories that merely replace existing accessories and are not superior to the ones replaced are ignored.

(d)   There is a special rule for classic cars. If the car is at least 15 years old (from the time of first registration) at the *end* of the tax year, and its market value at the end of the year is over £15,000 and greater than the price found under (c), that market value (including accessories) is used instead of the price.

(e)   **If the employee makes a capital contribution** towards the cost of the car or accessories this is **deducted from the list price** for calculating the benefit, subject to a **maximum deduction of £5,000.**

(f)   **The percentage used in the benefit calculation depends on the CO_2 emissions of the car as follows:**

Emissions	Car benefit percentage 2013/14
0g/km	0%
1 – 75g/km	5%
76 – 94g/km	10%
95g/km or more	11% + 1% for every 5g/km in excess of 95g/km
Over 215g/km	35% (maximum)

There is a **3% supplement for diesel cars** (maximum is still 35%).

Example 6

Nigel Issan is provided with a diesel car which had a list price of £22,000 when it was first registered. The car has CO_2 emissions of 178g/km.

You are required to calculate Nigel's car benefit for 2013/14.

(g) **The benefit is reduced on a time basis where a car is first made available or ceases to be made available during the year** or is incapable of being used for a continuous period of not less than 30 days (for example because it is being repaired). If a car is unavailable for less than 30 days and a replacement car of similar quality is provided, the replacement car is ignored and treated as being the usual car.

Exam focus point

Note that where *any* benefit is only available for part of the tax year, the taxable benefit must be time apportioned. Look carefully at the dates given in the question.

(h) **The benefit is reduced by any payment the user is required to make for the private use of the car** (as distinct from a capital contribution to the cost of the car). However, the benefit cannot become negative to create a deduction from the employee's income. **Payments for insuring the car do not count.**

Example 7

Vicky Olvo starts her employment on 6 January 2014 and is immediately provided with a new petrol car with a list price of £25,000. The car was more expensive than her employer would have provided and she therefore made a capital contribution of £6,200. The employer was able to buy the car at a discount and paid only £23,000. Vicky contributed £100 a month for being able to use the car privately. CO_2 emissions are 242g/km per the car's registration document.

You are required to calculate her car benefit for 2013/14.

Exam focus point

Examiner's report – Personal Taxation (old syllabus)

Nov 2006 – Question 1

Some candidates lost a mark in the car benefit calculation as they deducted the employee's contribution *[for use]* from the cost price of the car *[rather than from the benefit]*.

(i) **Pool cars are exempt.** A car only qualifies as a pool car if *all* the following conditions are satisfied: [s.167]

 (i) It is used by more than one director or employee and is not ordinarily used by any one of them to the exclusion of the others.

 (ii) Any private use is merely incidental to business use.

 (iii) It is not normally kept overnight at or near the residence of an employee.

(j) Where an employee has sacrificed salary to obtain private use of a car, the taxable benefit is the higher of salary foregone and the benefit calculated as above.

(k) Employers must make **quarterly returns containing details of cars provided to employees** on form P46 (car). These returns are made for income tax quarters (ending on 5 July, 5 October, 5 January and 5 April), and must be made within 28 days of the end of each quarter.

(l) **The benefit calculated above covers all expenditure by the employer on repairs, servicing, insurance, road fund licence and cleaning.** It does not, however, cover the cost of a driver or chauffeur. Where a driver or chauffeur is provided for both business and private mileage, an agreed proportion of the employer's associated costs would be assessable on the employee.

(m) A **car telephone is exempt** (see below).

(n) **No benefit** arises on the provision of a **car parking space at or near work** (see below).

3.5 The fuel benefit rules

Where **fuel for private motoring** is provided to an employee paid £8,500 pa or more or a director with a company car, he will be assessed on a fuel benefit in addition to the car benefit above.

The fuel benefit charge is based on the same percentage as is used to calculate the car benefit × the base figure. The base figure for 2013/14 is £21,100 and is shown in the Tax Tables provided in the exam. [s.150]

There is no taxable benefit if either **all the fuel was provided for business** travel **or the employee reimburses *all* of the cost of private fuel.**

Any reduction for non-availability of a company car also applies to the fuel benefit. If the car is available for x months but fuel is only supplied for private use for y months ($y < x$) the fuel charge is still $x/12$ of the full charge.

The taxable fuel benefit only applies to company cars. If fuel is provided for an employee's own car, the normal rule of 'cost of providing' applies.

Example 8

An employee was provided with a new petrol car costing £15,000 (the list price) on 1 June 2013. During 2013/14 the employer spent £900 on insurance, repairs and vehicle licence. The employer paid for all petrol (£2,300) without reimbursement. The employee was required to pay the employer £25 per month for the private use of the car.

The car has CO_2 emissions of 115g/km.

You are required to calculate the total assessable benefit for 2013/14 in respect of the car and fuel.

3.6 Company vans

An annual scale charge of £3,000 applies for unrestricted private use of company vans. A further £564 charge applies for the provision of private fuel. [s.155]

This charge only applies to employees who use a company van for **significant** private journeys other than journeys between home and work.

The charge is **pro-rated** if the van is only provided for part of the year or if it is incapable of being used for 30 or more consecutive days. The charge is also reduced by any employee contributions for private use.

There is **no charge for electric vans** (until at least 6 April 2015).

3.7 Private use of employer's assets

3.7.1 Using an employer's asset

The taxable value of the private use of **an employer's assets** (other than cars, vans and accommodation) **is:**

> 20% × the market value of the asset when first used by the employee. [s.205]

If there is any **business use of the asset the benefit is reduced proportionately** (see below for the use of computers).

If the asset is **leased** by the employer and the lease charge is greater than the 20% benefit, that lease charge will be the taxable benefit.

3.7.2 Acquiring an employer's asset

If an asset which has been used by an employee is subsequently acquired by that employee, the assessable benefit on the acquisition is the greater of:

(a)   **The current market value of the asset**, and

(b)   **Market value when first provided less any amounts already assessed as a benefit (at 20%) in respect of use of the asset**.

This rule prevents tax free benefits arising on fast depreciating items by the employee purchasing them at a much reduced second hand value.

Illustration 1

An employer buys a suit costing £200 for use by an employee (who earns £30,000 per annum) on 6 April 2012. On 6 April 2013 the employee purchases the suit for £15, its market value then being £25.

The benefit assessable in 2012/13 is 20% × £200   £40

The benefit assessable in 2013/14 is the greater of:

		£	£
(a)	Market value at acquisition by employee	25	
(b)	Original market value	200	
	Less: assessed in respect of use	(40)	
		160	
	ie		160
	Less: price paid by employee		(15)
	Benefit		145

If the employee does not buy the asset he will continue to be assessed on 20% × the original value **each year** (even if use continues for more than five years). However, it remains tax efficient for assets like suits, which need replacing every two or three years, to be purchased by the employer rather than by the employee out of net income.

3.7.3 Special assets

3.7.3.1 Computers

Where an employer provides an employee with a **computer** to carry out his employment duties but the employee also uses that computer for personal use, there will **only be a taxable benefit if his private usage is 'substantial'**

HMRC considers that where a computer has been provided so that an employee can carry out his employment duties either at home, or whilst travelling or at work, it is **highly unlikely that any private use will be significant when compared with the business need for providing the computer** in the first place. In these circumstances **no tax charge** will arise.

Ilustration 2

Nasreen's employer provided her with a laptop costing £1,200 on 1 May 2013.

If Nasreen's only personal use of the laptop is to, say, check personal emails occasionally she is unlikely to have any taxable benefit.

However, if she uses the laptop for personal purposes for, say, 40% of the time then her taxable benefit will be:

	£
£1,200 × 20% × 11/12	220
Less: business use – 60% × £220	(132)
Taxable benefit	88

3.7.3.2 Bicycles

As the provision of a **bicycle** for home to work travel is a tax free benefit (see below), if an employee buys a bicycle that he has previously used, the **taxable benefit is always the market value when he buys it.**

3.8 Taxable cheap loans

3.8.1 Basic rule

Loans to employees, directors and their families give rise to taxable benefits equal to:

(a) **Any amounts written off, and**

(b) **The amount of interest calculated using the official rate of interest less the amount of interest actually payable by the employee/director.** [s.175]

There is no taxable benefit if the total balance on all loans to the employee did not exceed £5,000 at any time in the year. If the £5,000 threshold is exceeded, a benefit arises on interest on the whole loan, not just on the excess of the loan over £5,000. [s.180]

When a loan is written off there is no £5,000 threshold so writing off a loan of £1 would give rise to a £1 benefit.

Exam focus point

Examiner's report – Personal Taxation

November 2008 – Part II LFQ 1

The most common errors were ... not recognising that the loan, being less than £5,000, was not a taxable benefit.

3.8.2 Calculating the interest benefit

There are two methods of calculating the amount of the benefit.

(a)   **The normal 'averaging method'** takes the average of the amount of loan outstanding at the beginning and end of the tax year (or the dates on which the loan was made and repaid in the tax year) and applies the official rate of interest to it. [s.182]

(b)   **The alternative method calculates interest on a daily basis on the actual amount outstanding.** [s.183]

The normal 'averaging' method applies automatically unless an election is made by the taxpayer or HMRC who normally only make the election where it appears that the 'averaging' method is being deliberately exploited.

Different loans to the same employee are usually treated separately.

Example 9

At 6 April 2013 a cheap loan of £30,000 was outstanding to a director, who repaid £20,000 on 6 December 2013. The remaining balance of £10,000 was outstanding at 5 April 2014. Interest paid during the year was £250.

What is the benefit under both methods for 2013/14?

3.8.3 Exceptions

The following categories of cheap loan can be ignored:

(a)   Loans made on **ordinary commercial terms** [s.176]

(b)   Loans **qualifying for tax relief** (eg loan to buy shares in a close company or to buy a property for letting). Any interest the employee actually pays is relieved as normal (eg as a deduction from total income or as an expense deductible from property income).

   If the loan only partly qualifies for tax relief (eg a loan to buy computer equipment used partly for business purposes and partly privately) it is not exempt.

   Instead the full cash equivalent of the loan should be included as part of the employee's employment income (and reported on form P11D). The employee is deemed to have paid interest equivalent to the cash equivalent of the loan and must then claim any tax relief due in respect of the qualifying element on his self assessment tax return. [s.184]

   In effect, only the private element of the loan interest paid is a taxable benefit. [s.178]

Example 10

Anna, who is single, has an annual salary of £36,000 and a loan from her employer of £24,000 at 1.25% interest to buy a holiday cottage which Anna uses herself and lets to tenants. The net rents (before interest relief) are £4,500 and 15% of general expenses have been disallowed to reflect Anna's occupation.

What is Anna's tax liability for 2013/14?

Exam focus point

Examiner's report – Personal Taxation (old syllabus)

Nov 2003 – Question 1

This question was attempted by almost every candidate and the majority gained over half marks. The computation of George's income and tax liability caused few problems although the calculation and inclusion (or exclusion) of [cheap taxable] loan interest and mileage were the most common areas for error.

---

4 Tax-free benefits – summary

There is a fairly long list of benefits which are **not taxable** on **any** employees, including:

(a) **Accommodation and subsistence:**

   (i) **Job related accommodation** (see above)

   (ii) **Meals in a staff canteen** so long as available to all employees on broadly similar terms (but not where provided as part of a salary sacrifice scheme) [s.317 (4A)]

   (iii) **Incidental overnight expenses** of up to £5 per night for employees working away from home in the UK, or £10 per night if working abroad which would otherwise be taxable (eg laundry, newspapers, telephone calls home). [ss.240 & 241]

   However, where more than one night is spent away, the exemption works on an **aggregate basis**, eg for four nights spent elsewhere in the UK, the overall limit is £20

   (iv) **Subsistence costs** for 'site based employees' (see below)

(b) **Travel:**

   (i) **Provision of a car parking space at or near the place of work**

   (ii) **Mileage allowances for cars etc within the HMRC Authorised mileage rates** (see above)

   (iii) Payment for additional transport costs or the cost of overnight accommodation in a case where public transport is disrupted by industrial action

   (iv) Payment for a **taxi or hired car for an employee who is occasionally required to work late** (after 9pm), in circumstances where either public transport has ceased or it would be unreasonable to expect the employee to use it. If such arrangements occur frequently (more than 60 times a year) or regularly (eg every Friday), then *no* exemption is available

   (v) Reimbursement to a director or employee of costs necessarily incurred in travelling to another company in the same group of which he is a director

   (vi) **Home to site travel costs for 'site based employees'**

   (vii) Provision of **works buses** with a seating capacity of 9 or more which are used mainly to bring employees to and from work

   (viii) The payment of general subsidies to public bus services used by employees to travel to work, regardless of whether the employees pay the same fare as other members of the public or any fare at all

   (ix) Provision of **bicycles and cycling safety equipment** made available for employees mainly to travel **between home and work**

   (x) Provision of **workplace parking for bicycles and motorcycles**

   (xi) Provision of **alternative transport to get car sharers home** when exceptional circumstances, such as a domestic emergency, mean that the normal car sharing arrangements unavoidably break down

(c) **Education and training:**

   (i) Payments made by an employer to an employee attending a **full-time training course** (including a sandwich course) at a university, college, school or similar establishment to cover accommodation, living and travel cost (but excluding tuition fees payable by the employee) provided they **do not exceed £15,480 per academic year** [SP 4/86]

   (ii) Payments made in respect of a past or present employee for the costs of a **qualifying training or retraining course** – full time, day release or block release

(d) **Removal expenses:**

   Up to £8,000 of removal expenses borne by the employer where the employee has to move house on first taking up the employment or on a transfer within the organisation. 'Removal expenses' include for this purpose the reimbursement of interest on a bridging loan, usual professional fees, costs of finding a new home, and replacement of domestic goods such as furniture, curtains and carpets

(e) **Entertainment**:

   (i) **The provision of a Christmas party or alternative annual function, provided that the cost is no more than £150 per head per annum.** If the cost exceeds £150 the whole cost is taxable, not just the excess above £150. Where there is more than one annual event in a tax year there is no taxable benefit if the events cost no more than £150 in total. However if, for example, there are two events which cost £100 and £60 only one of the events would be exempt. The events must also be available to all employees

   (ii) The provision of entertainment by a person who is neither the employer, nor connected with them

(f) **Childcare**:

   (i) **Childcare facilities available to all employees either on the employer's premises or on other premises where the employer is responsible for the financing and management of the facilities**

   (ii) **Other qualifying employer arranged childcare costs or childcare vouchers**

   The childcare must be provided by **officially registered or approved childcare carers** or organisations, including those in the employee's home (eg nannies).

   For anyone **already in a scheme at 6 April 2011, up to £55 per week (£243 per month) is always exempt**.

   For those joining an approved childcare scheme on or after 6 April 2011 the amount that is exempt per week depends on the employee's 'basic earnings assessment', which is the individual's expected earnings for the current tax year.

   This is calculated by adding together the employee's basic earnings and taxable benefits and then deducting excluded income, which includes occupational pension scheme contributions and allowable expense payments (see below). The personal allowance is also deducted where earnings do not exceed £150,000. This earnings figure is then compared with the usual income tax basic rate, higher rate and additional rate bands (see earlier in this Text) to determine the amount of tax relief (see below).

   The **exemption is** as follows: [s.270A & s.318–318D]

	Weekly amount £	Monthly amount £
Basic rate employee:	55	243
Higher rate employee:	28	124
Additional rate employee:	25	110

   These amounts provide all taxpayers with the same tax relief as basic rate taxpayers, ie £11 per week (ie £55 ×20%).

(g) **Health**:

   (i) **Overseas medical expenses** incurred while working abroad as part of the duties of the employment, and the cost of insuring against such expenses

   (ii) Provision of **eyesight tests**, and spectacles, contact lenses etc, where required by health and safety at work legislation. The exemption is available if tests/appliances are made available to all relevant employees

   (iii) One **health screening or medical check up** per tax year

(h) **Home-working**:

   A **tax free allowance of up to £4 per week** is payable to employees to cover the additional household costs of working some or all of the time at home. **No record keeping** is required for the flat-rate £4 per week allowance. For payments above that figure, evidence is required that the payment is wholly in respect of additional household expenses incurred by the employee in carrying out his duties at home

(i) **Miscellaneous:**

(i) **Non-cash long service awards – for service in excess of 20 years, £50 per year of service is tax-free**

(ii) Staff **uniforms**

(iii) Awards under a formally constituted **staff suggestion scheme**

(iv) **Gifts** (other than cash) received by reason of the employment **from someone other than the employer**, provided that they amount to **less than £250** in a tax year from a particular source

(v) Assets or services provided to improve an employee's personal physical security from a threat arising out of his employment

(vi) **Workplace sports or recreational facilities provided by employers for use by their staff generally.** This does not apply where the employer pays or reimburses an employee's subscription to a sports club nor where the facilities are only available to limited groups of employees

(vii) Air miles and car fuel coupons obtained in the course of business travel

(viii) **Premiums providing for liabilities and indemnities insurance cover** for directors and employees; expenditure in discharging an employee's liabilities incurred in his capacity as employee; costs of proceedings relating to such matters (any costs paid by an employee qualify for tax relief)

(ix) **Private use of *one* mobile phone, including a smartphone**; the cost of additional mobile phones is a taxable benefit

(x) Use of shower facilities and changing room on employers' premises which are available to all employees

(xi) **Cheap loans under £5,000** (see above)

(xii) Vouchers provided for any exempt benefit

Exam focus point

Examiner's report – Personal Taxation

November 2011 – Part I SFQ 3

Some candidates thought that both mobile telephones were exempt.

Exam focus point

The above list is not exhaustive, but provides a reasonably comprehensive summary of the tax free benefits of which you need to be aware. The main ones are in bold.

The main legislation relating to exempt employment benefits can be found in Part 4 ITEPA 2003.

---

5 Allowable deductions

5.1 Overview

Three types of expenditure made by employees are deductible from employment income:

(a) **Contributions** (within certain limits) **to a registered occupational pension scheme** (see later in this Text)

(b) **Subscriptions to professional bodies**, if relevant to the duties, and

(c) **Donations to charity** (of any amount) **under an approved payroll deduction scheme**. These may also be referred to as a 'Payroll giving scheme' or a 'Give as You Earn scheme'.

In such a scheme, the employee authorises the employer to deduct the donations from their employment income and pay them over to a government-approved payroll giving agency which then pays the money on to a specified charity or charities.

The employee obtains income tax relief for the donations via the PAYE system. The donations are deducted from the employee's taxable pay to which PAYE is applied. The employee therefore obtains income tax relief at both basic and higher rates depending on the level of his employment income. There is no limit on the amount of donations on which the employee can obtain tax relief under the scheme.

> Donations under the scheme are **added back to the individual's total income** for the purpose of calculating the **limit on income tax reliefs** (see earlier in this Text).

Other claims for deductions are hard to obtain. When they are available, they fall into the following categories:

(a)   **Qualifying travel expenses** (see below)

(b)   Other **expenses incurred *wholly, exclusively and necessarily in* the performance of the duties**

(c)   **Capital allowances on plant and machinery *necessarily* provided for use *in* the performance of the duties**. Note that the plant cannot include the employee's own transport as the depreciation is already factored into the HMRC Authorised mileage rates (see above).

Note that the word **'necessarily'** is particularly restrictive. Trading expenses for a company, sole trader or partner have to satisfy only a 'wholly and exclusively' test and are, therefore, much more likely to be allowable. This partly explains why taxpayers prefer to be self employed rather than employed.

5.2 Travel expenses

A deduction is allowed for travel expenses necessarily incurred on travelling in the performance of the duties of employment. [s.337]

Expenditure 'in the performance of' duties does not include expenditure incurred in order to get into a position to perform duties. **Thus travel to work (ie commuting) is not usually allowable.**

However, **a deduction for commuting costs is available to employees with no permanent workplace. This includes 'site based employees' and those intending to spend less than 24 months at a temporary workplace.**

A deduction is also available for **accommodation and subsistence** if an overnight stay is necessary.

5.3 Other expenses

5.3.1 Reimbursed expenses

Where an employee incurs an expense that is reimbursed by his employer, he must **include the full expense as taxable earnings** and then **claim a deduction for any amount incurred wholly, exclusively and necessarily** in the performance of his duties.

An employer can obtain a **'dispensation'** (notice of nil liability) from HMRC **relieving them from reporting employees' expenses payments on form P11D**. HMRC will issue a dispensation if the employees would ordinarily receive a tax deduction for the expenses (eg salesmen's travel expenses) and the payments are properly controlled. Employees do not have to include any expenses covered by the dispensation on their tax returns.

5.3.2 Round sum allowances

Where an employee is provided with a round sum allowance (ie a lump sum) to cover future expenses, he must include the full allowance as taxable earnings and claim a deduction for any amounts spent that would be deductible from trade profits for his employer on a **'wholly and exclusively'** basis.

A dispensation is not available for round sum allowances.

Example 11

Daniel earns £50,000 pa. His employer gives him a £1,000 round sum allowance to cover his expenses for 2013/14.

He spends it as follows:

	£
Business travel	600
Staff entertaining	180
Client entertaining	150
Unaccounted	70
	1,000

Daniel has no other taxable benefits.

What is Daniel's employment income for 2013/14?

5.4 Form P11D

Employers must submit form P11D to HM Revenue & Customs, listing each employee's **benefits and expense payments** for the tax year (employees paid over £8,500 only).

A copy of the most recent form P11D (for 2012/13) is reproduced on the following pages. We have updated the dates to refer to the tax year 2013/14. The actual 2013/14 versions had not yet been issued at the time of publication of this Text and may be slightly different. You should be able to obtain a copy of the actual 2013/14 versions from the HMRC website (www.hmrc.gov.uk) before your examination.

HM Revenue & Customs

P11D Expenses and benefits 2013-14

Please make sure your entries are clear on both sides of the form.

Employer name

Employer PAYE reference

Employee name

Surname

First name(s)

If a director tick here ☐

Date of birth *in figures (if known)*
| D | D | M | M | Y | Y | Y | Y |

Works number/department

National Insurance number

Gender **M – Male F – Female** ☐

Employers pay Class 1A National Insurance contributions on most benefits. These are shown in boxes which are brown and have a **1A** indicator

A *Assets transferred (cars, property, goods or other assets)* — Cost/Market value — Amount made good or from which tax deducted — Cash equivalent
Description of asset — £ — £ — **13** £ **1A**

B *Payments made on behalf of employee*
Description of payment — **15** £
Tax on notional payments not borne by employee within 90 days of receipt of each notional payment — **15** £

C *Vouchers and credit cards* — Gross amount — Amount made good or from which tax deducted — Cash equivalent
Value of vouchers and payments made using credit cards or tokens (for qualifying childcare vouchers see section M of the P11D Guide) — £ — £ — **12** £

D *Living accommodation* — Cash equivalent
Cash equivalent of accommodation provided for employee, or his/her family or household — **14** £ **1A**

E *Mileage allowance and passenger payments* — Taxable amount
Amount of car and mileage allowances paid to employee for business travel in employee's own vehicle, and passenger payments, in excess of maximum exempt amounts *(See P11D Guide for 2013–14 exempt rates)* — **12** £

F *Cars and car fuel If more than two cars were made available, either at the same time or in succession, please give details on a separate sheet*

	Car 1	Car 2
Make and model		
Date first registered	/ /	/ /
Approved CO$_2$ emissions figure for cars registered on or after 1 January 1998 *Tick box if the car does not have an approved CO$_2$ figure*	g/km ☐ *See P11D Guide for details of cars that have no approved CO$_2$ figure*	g/km ☐ *See P11D Guide for details of cars that have no approved CO$_2$ figure*
Engine size	cc	cc
Type of fuel or power used *Please use the key letter shown in the P11D Guide*		
Dates car was available *Do not complete the 'From' box if the car was available on 5 April 2013 or the 'To' box if it continued to be available on 6 April 2014*	From / / to / /	From / / to / /
List price of car *Including car and standard accessories only: if there is no list price, or if it is a classic car, employers see booklet 480*	£	£
Accessories *All non-standard accessories, see P11D Guide*	£	£
Capital contributions (maximum £5,000) the employee made towards the cost of car or accessories	£	£
Amount paid by employee for private use of the car	£	£
Date free fuel was withdrawn *Tick if reinstated in year (see P11D Guide)*	/ / ☐	/ / ☐
Cash equivalent of each car	£	£

Total cash equivalent of all cars made available in 2013-14 — **9** £ **1A**

Cash equivalent of fuel for each car — £ — £

Total cash equivalent of fuel for all cars made available in 2013–14 — **10** £ **1A**

P11D (2013) HMRC 12/12   5013569

BPP LEARNING MEDIA

G Vans and van fuel

Total cash equivalent of all vans made available in 2013–14	**9** £	1A
Total cash equivalent of fuel for all vans made available in 2013–14	**10** £	1A

H Interest-free and low interest loans

If the total amount outstanding on all loans does not exceed £5,000 at any time in the year, there is no need to complete this section.

	Loan 1	Loan 2
Number of joint borrowers *(if applicable)*		
Amount outstanding at 5 April 2013 or at date loan was made if later	£	£
Amount outstanding at 5 April 2014 or at date loan was discharged if earlier	£	£
Maximum amount outstanding at any time in the year	£	£
Total amount of interest paid by the borrower in 2013–14 – enter "NIL" if none was paid	£	£
Date loan was made in 2013–14 if applicable	/ /	/ /
Date loan was discharged in 2013–14 if applicable	/ /	/ /
Cash equivalent of loans after deducting any interest paid by the borrower	**15** £ 1A	**15** £ 1A

I Private medical treatment or insurance

	Cost to you	Amount made good or from which tax deducted	Cash equivalent
Private medical treatment or insurance	£	– £	= **11** £ 1A

J Qualifying relocation expenses payments and benefits

Non-qualifying benefits and expenses go in sections M and N below

Excess over £8,000 of all qualifying relocation expenses payments and benefits for each move	**15** £ 1A

K Services supplied

	Cost to you	Amount made good or from which tax deducted	Cash equivalent
Services supplied to the employee	£	– £	= **15** £ 1A

L Assets placed at the employee's disposal

	Annual value plus expenses incurred	Amount made good or from which tax deducted	Cash equivalent
Description of asset	£	– £	= **13** £ 1A

M Other items (including subscriptions and professional fees)

	Cost to you	Amount made good or from which tax deducted	Cash equivalent
Description of other items	£	– £	= **15** £ 1A
Description of other items	£	– £	= **15** £
Income Tax paid but not deducted from director's remuneration			Tax paid **15** £

N Expenses payments made to, or on behalf of, the employee

	Cost to you	Amount made good or from which tax deducted	Taxable payment
Travelling and subsistence payments *(except mileage allowance payments for employee's own car - see section E)*	£	– £	= **16** £
Entertainment *(trading organisations read P11D Guide and then enter a tick or a cross as appropriate here)*	£	– £	= **16** £
General expenses allowance for business travel	£	– £	= **16** £
Payments for use of home telephone	£	– £	= **16** £
Non-qualifying relocation expenses *(those not shown in sections J or M)*	£	– £	= **16** £
Description of other expenses	£	– £	= **16** £

6 Payments on termination of employment

6.1 Introduction

Payments on termination of employment fall into one of three categories for taxation purposes:

(a)   **Entirely exempt**
(b)   **Partially exempt**
(c)   **Fully taxable.**

6.2 Exempt payments

The **following types of payment** on termination of employment are **exempt.** [ss.406 – 410]

(a)   A payment **on death**

(b)   A payment on account of **injury or disability**

(c)   A lump sum payment **from or to a registered pension scheme**

(d)   **Legal costs** recovered by the employee from the employer following legal action to recover compensation for loss of employment where the costs are ordered by the court or (for out-of-court settlements) are paid directly to the employee's solicitor as part of the settlement.

In addition, the cost of outplacement (eg counselling) services incurred by the employer for the employee's benefit is exempt.

6.3 Fully taxable payments

Any termination payment not falling within (a) to (d) above but which is made *in return for services* will be fully taxable under normal employment income rules.

The question of whether a payment is made in return for services can be a complex one, but generally, if the **contract of employment provides for payment** to be made on termination of employment, the **payment will be in return for services**. If the contract is silent on this point but a payment is made, **it will be taken to be in return for services if there was a reasonable expectation** that such a sum would be paid. Accordingly, those payments made in return for services are taxed in full as part of the individual's employment income 'general earnings'.

Payments made in return for the employee promising, for example, not to work in a particular area **following the termination of his employment (a 'restrictive covenant')** are always **taxable in full**.

6.4 Partially exempt payments

Other 'termination' (or redundancy) payments, such as compensation for loss of office, are not taxable under the normal employment income rules as general earnings because they are not in return for services. They are, however, taxable as 'specific employment income' and the first £30,000 of such payments is free of income tax. [ss.401 – 403]

Redundancy payments (including statutory redundancy) are exempt from tax as earnings but like other termination payments are taxable under s.402 and the first £30,000 is exempt. [s.309]

Any benefits (eg the provision of a company car) which would be assessable had the employment continued, are taxed in the year in which the benefit is received or enjoyed. The £30,000 exemption is set against cash payments in priority to non-cash payments. [s.404]

Any taxable amount in excess of the £30,000 exemption is taxed as the highest part of an individual's income except for gains on non-qualifying life assurance policies (ie above dividend income).

HMRC may treat termination payments made on or around the time of an employee's retirement as arising from an unregistered pension scheme. These payments are fully taxable, with no £30,000 exemption. HMRC have indicated that a middle-aged man moving on to further full-time employment is obviously not retiring but that they are likely to apply this rule to an older man who has no other full-time employment in prospect.

Example 12

Paula, 37, is made redundant on 10 October 2013 and her termination package includes the following:

	£
Compensation payment for loss of office	50,000
Payment to registered pension scheme	5,000
Company car (market value)	12,000
Statutory redundancy pay	6,000
	73,000

Calculate the amount assessable as employment income in 2013/14.

6.5 Payments in lieu of notice (PILONS)

The tax treatment of a payment made in lieu of the employee working their notice period (a PILON) largely depends on whether the PILON is provided for in the employee's contract.

(a)   **Contractual PILONs**

Where an employee's contract contains a provision that enables a PILON to be made, it is usually fully taxable. However, if the contract simply provides for a **notice period with no further qualification**, then any payment made instead of requiring the employee to work that notice is treated as **liquidated damages for breach of contract** and will come within the £30,000 exemption. [Hunter v Dewhurst (1932)].

(b)   **Discretionary PILONs**

(i)   Where the contract term gives the employer discretion **to make a PILON and the employer exercises that discretion, the payment is usually taxable in full.** [EMI Group Electronics Ltd v Coldicott (1999)]

(ii)   However, **if the employer decides not to exercise their discretion but makes a payment to terminate the contract early instead, this will be treated as a breach of contract.** The payment will be treated as compensation arising from the termination of employment (ie damages), rather than from the employment relationship. **The first £30,000 will be tax free.** [Cerberus Software v Rowley (2001)]

(iii)   Where a PILON is an **automatic response** by the employer, ie it is the employer's custom, habit or **practice or there is an expectation** (not merely a hope, but an 'enforceable contractual certainty') of **receiving it on the part of the employee, the payment may be taxable in full as earnings.** However, if the employer follows a procedure for making a **genuine 'critical assessment'** for each payment, for example using an internal written procedure to assess what payment is to be made to each employee and identifying adjustments typical of a damages payment, the payment will be treated as damages (for constructive dismissal in the Clinton case). [Clinton v HMRC (2009); EIM12977]

(c)   **Non-contractual PILONs**

If there is no contractual term covering the PILON the payment may still be taxable in full if:

(i)   The employer offers a PILON to the employee **in advance of terminating the employment and the employee agrees to take it. This will be treated as a variation of the contract** and the payment will be taxable in full. [SCA Packaging v HMRC (2007)]

(ii)   There is no contractual term but the PILON is an **automatic response** by the employer (see above). In this case it may be treated as an **integral part of the employer/employee relationship** and assessable in full. [EIM12977]

6.6 Taxable date

Payments received under termination settlements are **taxable in the year in which they are received** or enjoyed, rather than being taxed in the year of termination.

Similarly any benefits (eg the provision of a company car) which would have been assessable had the employment continued, are **taxed in the year in which the benefit is received** or enjoyed.

6.7 Termination payments after foreign service

Payments received on termination of an employment which included an element of foreign service may be exempt from tax. Complete exemption is given where the foreign service element is 'substantial'.

For the purposes of this exemption, the employee's period of service is treated as including a substantial element of foreign service where the foreign service comprises: [s.413]

(a) Three-quarters of the whole period of service, or

(b) The last 10 years, where the whole period of service is in excess of 10 years, or

(c) Half of the total period of service, including any 10 out of the last 20 years, where the total period of service exceeds 20 years.

If part of the termination payment is still taxable *after* all other exemptions (eg the £30,000 exemption for compensation payments) and there has been foreign service during the period of employment, a **fraction of the otherwise taxable payment can be deducted** equal to: [s.414]

$$\frac{\text{period of foreign service}}{\text{total service}}$$

Exam focus point

Examiner's report – Personal Taxation

November 2011 – Part I SFQ 8

This question caused problems. Candidates appeared confused on what payments are exempt from income tax. Many stated that all termination payments would be exempt from income tax up to £30,000. Few candidates were able to explain how benefits provided after the termination would be taxed. It is inadequate to state that benefits will be taxed in 'the normal way'.

Chapter roundup

- Employment income includes general earnings and certain other receipts.

- Earnings are assessable in the tax year in which they are received. Earnings are not only wages or salary but also certain benefits and reimbursed expenses.

- The provision of living accommodation (unless it is job related accommodation), credit cards, cash or non-cash vouchers and mileage allowances in excess of the authorised mileage rates gives rise to a taxable benefit for *all* employees.

- The living accommodation benefit is based on the annual value of the property. An additional benefit arises where the cost of the property, or in certain circumstances the market value at the date it is first occupied, exceeds £75,000.

- Relief is given to employees for the cost of using their own vehicle or bicycle for work if any mileage allowance paid is less than the authorised rates. Any excess is taxable.

- To determine whether an employee is a non-excluded employee (ie the £8,500 threshold is exceeded) all reimbursed expenses and benefits are included, but no deduction for expenses or payments (other than occupational pension contributions and payroll deduction scheme charitable donations) are taken into account.

- A director is only treated as an excluded employee if, in addition to receiving earnings of less than £8,500, he both works full-time for the company and controls 5% or less of the ordinary share capital.

- The general rule for valuing benefits for excluded employees is the second-hand value, ie the amount of money into which it can be converted, unless special rules apply.

- The general rule for valuing benefits for employees earning £8,500+ and directors is the employer's cost of provision, unless special rules apply.

- The benefits that are only chargeable on employees paid £8,500+ and on directors are:
  - Expenses in connection with living accommodation
  - The provision of a company car and private fuel
  - The provision of a company van with significant private use
  - Use of assets owned by the employer and
  - Taxable cheap loans.

- Some benefits are exempt for all employees (eg workplace parking).

- Only occupational pension contributions, subscriptions to professional bodies, charitable donations under an approved payroll deduction scheme and expenses incurred 'wholly, exclusively and necessarily' in the performance of the employee's duties can be deducted from employment income.

- Employees can only claim a deduction for commuting costs if they are site based employees or have a temporary workplace (<24 months).

- Certain payments made on the termination of employment are completely exempt, eg on death of the employee.

- The first £30,000 of non-contractual termination payments, including statutory redundancy payments, is tax-free.

1. Describe the basis of assessment for employment income.

2. An employee is provided with a flat by his employer (not job related accommodation). The annual value of the flat is £400; rent paid by the employer amounts to £3,900 per annum.

    How much is included in the employee's earnings in respect of this benefit?

3. The additional charge on 'expensive' accommodation (costing more than £75,000) applies only to employees paid £8,500+ pa and directors. True/False?

4. Megan, an employee, received the following in 2013/14:

	£
Salary	5,560
Company car (benefit)	2,310
Reimbursed expenses (of which 75% are deductible)	880

    Is Megan 'an employee paid £8,500 or more'?

5. Buster is the Managing Director of Buster Braces Ltd and is supplied with a Bentley (3 litre, petrol engine) which has a list price of £82,000 in 2010. It has CO_2 emissions of 180g/km. He was disqualified for dangerous driving so is supplied with a chauffeur at the company's expense (full salary costs for 2013/14 are £13,500). The car is fitted with a telephone which Buster uses both for business and privately. All running costs are borne by the company. Buster did 12,000 miles in 2013/14, of which 3,000 miles were for business. What is the total taxable benefit?

6. A video recorder costing £500 was made available to Gordon by his employer on 6 April 2012. On 6 April 2013, Gordon bought the recorder for £150, when its market value was £325. What assessable benefit arises in 2013/14 if Gordon's annual salary is £15,000?

7. The first £5,000 of an interest free loan is exempt from tax. True/False?

8. How much of a termination payment, brought within the charge to employment income by virtue only of s.402 ITEPA 2003, is exempt from tax?

9. Is a taxable fuel benefit reduced by any reimbursement by the employee of the cost of fuel provided for private mileage?

1. Employment income is assessed on the receipts basis, ie on amounts received during the tax year, regardless of when it is earned.

2. £3,900, being the higher of the annual value and rent actually paid.

3. False. Only those in occupation of 'job related' accommodation can avoid the additional charge.

4. Yes

		£
Earnings:	Salary	5,560
	Car benefit	2,310
	Reimbursed expenses	880
	TEST HERE (>£8,500)	8,750
	Less: allowable expenses (£880 × 75%)	(660)
	Employment income	8,090

5.

	£
Car benefit (W)	22,960
Fuel benefit (£21,100 × 28%)	5,908
Telephone benefit (one phone is exempt)	nil
Chauffeur £13,500 × $\frac{9,000}{12,000}$	10,125
Total benefit	38,993

Working

	£
List price £82,000 × 28%	22,960
(11% + ((180 − 95) ÷ 5) = 28%)	

6. Benefit is based on the higher of:

		£	£
(a)	Current MV		325
(b)	Original MV	500	
	Less: already assessed (in 2012/13)		
	£500 × 20%	(100)	
			400

ie £400

The assessable benefit after deduction of the amount paid (£150) is £250.

7. False – only if the loan is less than £5,000 is it exempt.

8. £30,000.

9. No. It is only reduced if the employer is fully reimbursed, in which case the fuel benefit is nil.

Solution to Example 1

	£
2012/13	
Basic salary paid 30 April 2012 to 31 March 2013 inclusive	24,000
Bonus for six months to 30 June 2012	
– determined before the end of the period of account	
∴ 'received' on 31.12.12	8,000
Employment income 2012/13	32,000
2013/14	
Basic salary (30 April 2013 to 31 March 2014 inclusive)	24,000
Bonus for six months to 31 December 2012	
– not determined until the AGM and payable subsequently	
therefore 'received' 30 April 2013	11,500
Employment income 2013/14	35,500

Solution to Example 2

			£
Benefit: greater of			
– annual value	£300		
– rent paid	£3,380		3,380
Less: reimbursed to the company			(520)
Taxable benefit			2,860

Solution to Example 3

Basic charge:

	£
Annual value	1,400
Less: contribution, £3,000 restricted to	(1,400)
	nil

Additional charge:

	£	£
Cost including improvements £(125,000 + 8,000)	133,000	
Less:	(75,000)	
Excess	58,000	
£58,000 × 4%		2,320
Less: balance of contribution £(3,000 – 1,400)		(1,600)
Taxable benefit		720

Solution to Example 4

		£
Authorised mileage rates:	10,000 × 45p	4,500
	4,000 × 25p	1,000
Total allowable mileage deduction		5,500

(a)	Taxable benefit: (45p × 14,000 =) £6,300 – £5,500	£800
(b)	Deduction: £(14,000 × 25p =) £3,500 – £5,500	£(2,000)
(c)	Deduction:	£(5,500)

Solution to Example 5

	£	£
Salary		12,000
Car benefit		2,990
Net earnings		14,990
Accommodation benefit:		
Annual value – exempt (job related)	nil	
Additional services:		
Electricity	250	
Gas	200	
Gardener	150	
Redecorations	1,000	
	1,600	
Restricted to 10% of £14,990	1,499	
Less: employee's contribution (12 × £50)	(600)	899
Employment income		15,889

Solution to Example 6

Car benefit £22,000 × 30% (11% + ((175 – 95) ÷ 5) + 3%)	£6,600

Note that 178g/km is rounded down to 175g/km to be exactly divisible by 5.

Solution to Example 7

	£
List price (N1)	25,000
Less: capital contribution (maximum)	(5,000)
	20,000
£20,000 × 35% (N2)	7,000
3/12 × £7,000 (N3)	1,750
Less: contribution to running costs (£100 × 3)	(300)
Car benefit	1,450

Notes

(1) The discounted price is irrelevant
(2) 11% + ((240 – 95) ÷ 5) = 40% restricted to 35% max
(3) Only available for 3 months in the year (6 January – 5 April)

Solution to Example 8

Car was available for 10 months.

	£
List price £15,000 × 15% (11% + (115 – 95 ÷ 5))	2,250
£2,250 × $^{10}/_{12}$	1,875
Less contribution (10 × £25)	(250)
	1,625
Fuel benefit £21,100 × 15% × $^{10}/_{12}$	2,637
Total taxable benefit	4,262

If the contribution of £25 per month had been towards the petrol, the benefit assessable would have been £4,512 (£1,875 + £2,637). If the cost of private petrol had been fully reimbursed by the employee, there would have been no fuel benefit at all.

Solution to Example 9

Averaging method

$$4\% \times \frac{(30,000 + 10,000)}{2}$$

	£
	800
Less: interest paid	(250)
Taxable benefit	550

Alternative method

	£
£30,000 × $\frac{8}{12}$ (6 April 2013 – 5 December 2013) × 4%	800
£10,000 × $\frac{4}{12}$ (6 December 2013 – 5 April 2014) × 4%	133
	933
Less: interest paid	(250)
Taxable benefit	683

The taxpayer will use the average method but HMRC can elect for the alternative method if it wishes.

Solution to Example 10

	£
Salary	36,000
Cheap taxable loan (include full cash equivalent): £24,000 × (4 – 1.25 =) 2.75%	660
Employment income	36,660
Property income: (£4,500 – [£24,000 × 2.75% × 85%]) (Note)	3,939
Net income	40,599
Less: Personal allowance	(9,440)
Taxable income	31,159

Income tax

	£
£31,159 × 20%	6,232

Note. The employer includes the full cash equivalent of £660 on the employee's P11D and the employee can take a tax deduction in his tax return for the £3,939 qualifying (85%) element.

Solution to Example 11

	£	£
Salary and round sum allowance – employment income		51,000
Less: expense deduction:		
Round sum allowance	1,000	
Less: Disallowed expenditure for the employer		
Client entertaining	(150)	
Unaccounted	(70)	
		(780)
		50,220

Note. Client entertaining is never deductible as a trading expense for the employer.

Solution to Example 12

	£
Compensation payment	50,000
Payment to registered pension scheme – exempt	–
Company car	12,000
Statutory redundancy pay	6,000
	68,000
Less: exemption	(30,000)
Assessable	38,000

Short Form Questions:

5.1 – 5.23 inclusive

Long Form Questions:

5.1	Mr Thomas
5.2	Alf
5.3	Mr Bjork
5.4	HiTech Computers
5.5	Grovelands
5.6	Mr Morris

Employer share schemes

1 Introduction to share schemes

Share schemes are an important element in the remuneration package of not only key executives but the workforce as a whole. They can provide both a reward for contributions made to the company's success and an incentive to maintain and improve its performance. The legislation provides for beneficial tax treatment for various schemes approved by HMRC.

Share schemes fall into **two main categories:**

(a)   Schemes where **shares are allocated or transferred directly to employees** or directors (share incentive schemes), and

(b)   Schemes which provide for the **granting of share options** (share option schemes).

A share option is a right to buy shares in the future at a price fixed at the time the option is granted. Assuming that the market price of the shares either is or will in the future be above the option price, an employee will then be able to acquire shares at a discount to their full value at the time the option is exercised. The employee does not have to exercise the option (ie buy the shares) if the shares have gone down in value.

The legislation provides for **beneficial tax treatment for various schemes approved by HMRC** and a new tax-favoured status of 'employee shareholder', which applies from 1 September 2013.

In this chapter, we consider the **tax implications of both unapproved and approved share schemes.**

2 Unapproved share incentive schemes

2.1 Free or undervalue shares given directly by the employer

2.1.1 General position

If an employer (former, current or prospective) gives shares or securities to an employee or director in the employer company ('Employment Related Securities') at **below their market value there is an income tax charge** (and possibly a National Insurance Contribution charge – see below) **at the date of acquisition**. This is based on the **difference between market value and the amount (if any) the employee pays for the shares.**

2.1.2 Employee shareholder status

This section is new

'Employee shareholder' status is a new category of employment whereby an employee gives up certain employment rights in exchange for shares worth at least £2,000.

From 1 September 2013, when shares are provided to an employee who has agreed to be an **'employee shareholder'**, he is **deemed to have made a payment of £2,000,** for those 'employee shareholder status' shares, so the **value subject to income tax and NIC at the date of acquisition is reduced by that deemed amount.** [s.226A]

In addition there is **no taxable employment benefit** where the employer **provides the employee with the services of an independent adviser in relation to the employee shareholder agreement.**

Example 1

Jared is given 10,000 shares worth £5,000 by his employer.

What amount must be included as employment income in respect of the shares for 2013/14 assuming:

(a)   Jared signs an employee shareholder agreement with his employer on 1 November 2013?

(b)   He does not sign an employee shareholder agreement?

A **capital gains tax (CGT) exemption** is also available on the **disposal of employee shareholder status shares.** CGT is covered in detail later in this Text.

Neither the deemed payment nor the CGT exemption is available if the employee (or persons connected with him) has a **material interest (ie ≥25%)** in the company at **any time in the 12 months before the acquisition** of the employee shareholder shares.

3 Unapproved share option schemes

An unapproved option is simply an option that has not been granted under a scheme approved by HMRC.

There is no income tax (or NIC) at the date the employer *grants* the unapproved option.

When the employee *exercises* the option (ie buys the shares at the price set out in the option), there is an income **tax charge** (and possibly an NIC charge – see below) **on the difference between the market value of the shares at the time of the exercise of the option and the cost of the shares** (plus the cost of the option if the employee had to pay the employer for the option at the date of grant).

Example 2

On 1 December 2013 James exercised options under an unapproved share option scheme run by his employer and acquired 1,000 shares at the option price of £3 per share. The market value at that date was £5 per share.

Calculate the amount assessable to income tax in respect of the exercise of the options.

The base cost of the shares for capital gains tax (CGT) purposes is the market value at the date of the exercise.

4 Approved share schemes

4.1 Introduction

There are four types of HMRC approved share schemes currently available which **attract income tax and NIC advantages. These are:**

(a) **Share incentive plans** (SIP)
(b) Savings related share option schemes (**Save As You Earn** or 'SAYE')
(c) **Company share option plans** (CSOP)
(d) **Enterprise Management Incentive** schemes (EMI).

Each of the schemes have detailed rules which must be met for the scheme to receive HMRC approval. **These rules must also continue to be met when options are granted or exercised, or shares issued if these share transactions are to receive the favourable tax treatment under the approved schemes.**

If the **scheme rules are not met when a transaction occurs**, eg on the grant of an option, then the transaction is **treated as though it relates to an unapproved share scheme** and the tax implications for unapproved schemes, as set out above, apply instead.

Exam focus point

Do not try to remember all of the detailed rules of each of the approved schemes. **Locate the relevant provisions for each scheme in your legislation** so that you know where to find them if you need to.

However you must understand how each of the schemes operate, the main qualifying conditions and the tax implications for each of the schemes.

4.2 Share incentive plans (SIPs)

4.2.1 What is a SIP?

An approved share incentive plan (SIP) is a tax efficient way for employees to own shares in their employer company. **Employees can buy shares out of their pre-tax remuneration and there is usually no income tax (or NIC) when the employee takes the shares out of the plan.** [ss.488 – 515 and Sch 2]

The scheme is operated by creating a trust ('the plan') that acquires shares in the employer company using funds from that company. The trustees then award the shares to the employees in accordance with the employer's instructions and hold the shares within the plan on behalf of the individual employees.

4.2.2 SIP shares

There are four ways in which an employee can obtain plan shares (all shares are held within the plan): [s.64 Part 8, Sch 2]

(a)	**Free** shares:	An employer can give up to £3,000 worth of shares per tax year to an employee.
(b)	**Partnership** shares:	An employee can buy shares out of pre-tax remuneration up to a value of the lower of £1,500 and 10% of salary per tax year.
(c)	**Matching** shares:	An employer can match the partnership shares bought by the employee by giving him up to 2 free shares for every partnership share purchased.
(d)	**Dividend** shares:	An employee can use any amount of dividends (previously limited to £1,500) from the plan shares each tax year to reinvest in further plan shares.

The shares must **be fully paid up ordinary shares, not redeemable and may be subject to restrictions**. [paras 26 & 28 Sch 2]

The shares used in a plan must either be **shares in a company quoted on a recognised stock exchange**, or the subsidiary of such a company, or shares in an unquoted company which is not controlled by another company. [para 27, Sch 2]

4.2.3 Employees receiving shares

The employer company must offer all employees (even part time) the opportunity to participate in the scheme. The company can specify a minimum employment period before an employee is allowed to participate but this must not be longer than 18 months. [paras 8 & 16, Sch 2]

Employers must award 'free' shares to employees on similar terms based on objective criteria (eg based on level of remuneration or length of service). **The employer can make the award conditional on the meeting of performance targets** by the employee or his team, but the different targets set must be broadly comparable, with a similar chance of being met. There must be no deliberate weighting of rewards in favour of directors and more highly paid employees. [paras 9 & 10, Sch 2]

4.2.4 Tax advantages of a SIP

The tax advantages are summarised in the table below as follows:

	Free shares	Partnership shares	Matching shares	Dividend shares
Tax on award	None	None – tax relief for salary used to buy shares	None	None
Tax on removal of shares from plan within 3 years of award	On market value when taken out	On market value when taken out	On market value when taken out	Original dividend taxable but in year when shares taken out of plan if removed within holding period
Tax on removal between 3 and 5 year of award	On lower of: – value at award, and – value on removal	On lower of: – salary used to buy shares, and – value on removal	On lower of: – value at award, and – value on removal	None
Tax on removal after 5 years	None	None	None	None

If no income tax is due when the employee removes the shares from the plan after five years, **there is also no NIC charge** (see later in this Text).

4.2.5 Capital gains tax aspects of SIPs

The base cost of the SIP shares for capital gains tax (CGT) purposes (see later in this Text) **is the market value at the date the employee takes them out of the plan (ie on removal).** So, when the employee sells the shares they are liable to CGT on any increase in value arising between taking them out of the plan and the date of sale.

The employee can **avoid CGT by keeping the shares in the plan until just before they plan to sell them.**

Exam focus point

Examiner's report – Personal Taxation

November 2008 – Part II LFQ 3

Part A1 was rarely answered well with candidates making vague comments about tax being due and most missing the distinction between shares being within the plan for less than 3 years as opposed to between 3 and 5 years. For Part A3 few candidates realised that the base cost was uplifted to market value on withdrawal from the SIP.

November 2010 – Part II LFQ 3

Candidates did not differentiate between shares that had been held in the scheme between 3 and 5 years, and those that had been held for less than 3 years. Few candidates could give the base cost of the shares (part 4).

4.3 Savings related share option schemes (SAYE)

4.3.1 How the SAYE scheme works [Sch 3]

The savings related share option scheme (or 'Save As You Earn' (SAYE) scheme) allows an **employee or director to save a fixed amount** of between £5 (company cannot set the minimum at more than £10) and £250 per month **for a three or five year contract**, in a contractual savings scheme set up by their employer. Seven year contracts are available but no additional contributions may be made after five years. These seven year contracts have been withdrawn with effect from 23 July 2013.

At the beginning of the savings period, the employer grants the employee an option to buy shares in the employer company when the savings period ends, at a price set in the option.

At the end of the contractual period, the employee can withdraw his contributions, together with a tax free bonus dependent on the length of the contract. He can choose to use this money to buy the shares at the option price (ie 'exercise' the option), or simply take the money.

4.3.2 Scheme conditions

4.3.2.1 General conditions

(a)   **The scheme shares are to be paid for out of participants' savings (plus bonuses) under an SAYE scheme, approved by HMRC for that purpose. The amount repayable under the scheme must be as near as possible to the option price.** [para 25, Sch 3]

(b)   **Rights under the scheme must not be exercisable before the 'bonus date'** (ie when the SAYE repayments fall due). This depends on when the SAYE bonus is taken, ie at three or five or seven years. The decision on whether to take the bonus must be made when the option is acquired. [para 26, Sch 3]

Note that with the 'seven year scheme' contributions were made for five years and the repayment and bonus was taken after seven years. There is currently no bonus for any of the schemes.

(c)   **The price at which the shares may be acquired on exercise must be stated when the option is obtained, and cannot be less than 80% of the then market value.** [para 28, Sch 3]

(d)   If the participant **dies before the bonus date, the option** *must* **be exercised within 12 months of death**. Where he dies within 6 months of the bonus date, the option may be exercised within 12 months after the bonus. [para 32, Sch 3]

(e)   **If the participant ceases to be eligible for the scheme within three years of obtaining the option, the option cannot be exercised unless loss of eligibility resulted from cessation of employment due to injury, disability, redundancy, retirement or certain cash takeovers of the company.** Where the option can be exercised this must be done within six months of loss of eligibility. [para 34, Sch 3]

(f)   Schemes may be extended to other group companies. Schemes are then 'group schemes' with 'participating companies'. [para 3, Sch 3]

4.3.2.2 Scheme shares

The shares subject to the scheme must be: [para 18, Sch 3]

(a)   **Ordinary shares of the employer company**, a company which controls it, or a consortium member of the employer company, or the employer's holding company

(b)   **In a company which is not under the control of another company**, unless either they are quoted shares or the controlling company is a quoted company which is non-close

(c)   **Fully paid, irredeemable and may be subject to restrictions, for example the risk of forfeiture** (eg where the employees are required to sell all their shares on ceasing employment).

4.3.2.3 Scheme members

Those eligible to participate in a SAYE scheme: [para 6, Sch 3]

(a)   **Must be employees or full-time directors** of the company concerned (or, in group schemes, of a participating company), and

(b)   **Must be chargeable on their income from that employment as earnings**.

Every employee (whether full or part time) and every full time director *must* **be eligible to participate.**

All eligible persons must be able to obtain and exercise rights on similar terms, and those who participate in the scheme must actually do so, but there may be variations between participants in respect of remuneration, length of service etc.

Note that there is **no longer a restriction on the interest a person may have in a close company** in the previous 12 months (previously a maximum of 25%). [para 10 Sch 3]

4.3.3 Tax advantages of the SAYE scheme

There is usually no income tax (or NIC) on the grant or exercise of a SAYE option provided the options are exercised in accordance with the provisions of the approved scheme (see below) no sooner than three years after the options were granted. [s.519]

4.3.4 Capital gains tax aspects of the SAYE scheme

The base cost of the shares for capital gains tax (CGT) purposes is the **amount the employee pays for the shares (ie the exercise price)**. So, when the employee sells the shares they are liable to CGT on any increase in value between that price and the value on the date of sale.

4.4 Approved company share option plans (CSOP)

4.4.1 How the CSOP works [Sch 4]

Just as with an unapproved scheme, in an approved company share option plan (CSOP) the **employer company simply 'grants' an option to the employee to buy shares in the future at a price set at the date of grant**. However, there are certain tax advantages as the scheme must satisfy a number of conditions to be 'approved' by HMRC.

The CSOP is not linked to, and is more flexible than, the SAYE scheme (see above). **It does not need to be made available to all employees,** ie the employer can reward key employees by granting them CSOP options.

In order to be approved, and benefit from the tax advantages of the plan (see below) **the options must satisfy certain conditions.**

4.4.2 Conditions for approval

The main conditions for approval, in summary, are:

(a)   Only **full time directors** (full time means 25 hours a week excluding meal breaks) and **employees** (full time or part time) may participate. [para 8, Sch 4]

(b)   **An individual is not eligible to participate** if he is able to exercise rights under the scheme at any time when he has, or has within the last 12 months had, a **30% interest** (previously 25%) **in the ordinary share capital of a close company** whose shares may be acquired under the scheme. Any shares that an individual, or an associate of his, may acquire on the exercise of a share option are included in this test. [para 10, Sch 4]

Illustration 1

Jake holds 21% of his employer company's shares. If the company grants him an option to acquire a further 10% he will exceed the material interest threshold.

If he wishes to exercise his option in accordance with the approved scheme rules, he must sell more than a 1% shareholding and then wait 12 months.

(c)   The value of the shares, measured at the time the options are granted, over which an individual holds options **cannot exceed £30,000.** If shares are subject to any restrictions (eg on the freedom to dispose of the shares – see below) they must be valued ignoring those restrictions for the purposes of determining if the £30,000 limit has been met. [para 6, Sch 4]

(d)   The scheme shares must broadly be **ordinary shares** of:

   (i)   The **granting company**, or
   (ii)   A **company controlling the granting company.**

(e)   The scheme shares must be **quoted on a recognised stock exchange** or **in a company which is not under the control of another company.** [para 17, Sch 4]

(f)   Scheme shares must be **fully paid up, irredeemable and may be subject to restrictions.** [paras 18 & 36, Sch 4]

(g)   The **price at which shares may be acquired on the exercise of the option rights**, along with details of any restrictions, must be stated at the time that the option rights are granted, and the price must not be **manifestly less than the market value of the shares** at that time, ignoring any restrictions. [para 22, Sch 4]

4.4.3 Tax implications of the CSOP scheme

4.4.3.1 Tax advantages

There is **no income tax or NIC on either the grant or exercise** of a CSOP option provided:

(a)   The options are **exercised in accordance with the provisions of the approved scheme** (see above) and

(b)   The option rights are **exercised no earlier than three years or later than ten years after the date on which they were granted.** [s.524]

This applies even if the employee pays much less for the shares than they are worth when he buys them (ie when he 'exercises' his option), provided the price at which the shares may be acquired is not manifestly less than their value at the date the option is granted (see above).

The above **tax advantages still apply to an employee who has exercised options within three years** of them being granted where:

(a)   He was **required to exercise options** under the rules of the scheme **because he had ceased to be an employee** of the company, and

(b)   He had **ceased** to be employed **because of, for example, injury, disability, redundancy, retirement** or certain cash takeovers of the company, and

(c)   He **exercised the options within six months of ceasing to be an employee**.

4.4.4 Tax charge on grant

Where the **total of the consideration given for the option (if any) plus the price at which the shares are to be purchased under the option is less than the market value of the shares at the date that the option is granted, the discount is taxed as employment income of the director or employee in the year of grant.** [s.526]

It is unlikely, but possible that this charge can apply if the option is granted within the terms of an approved scheme. Note that the scheme approval condition in (g) above requires that the price at which shares may be acquired on the exercise of the option must not be *manifestly* **less than the market value** of the shares at the date the option is granted. Accordingly, it is **possible that shares could be issued at less than market value and still be within the terms of the approved scheme** (ie not manifestly less than market value), in which case the discount is charged to income tax. [s.526]

If the price paid for the shares on exercise is manifestly less than market value at the date the option is granted then the shares have not been issued in accordance with the terms of an approved CSOP. The shares are then taxed according to the rules for unapproved share option schemes (see above) and not in accordance with the tax rules in this section on CSOPs.

4.4.5 Capital gains tax aspects of the CSOP scheme

The base cost of the shares for capital gains tax (CGT) purposes is the **amount the employee pays for the shares (ie the exercise price).** So, when the employee sells the shares they are liable to CGT on any increase in value between that price and the value on the date of sale.

In practice, the cost of exercising the option (ie buying the shares) is usually funded from the sale proceeds.

Example 3

On 1 December 2013 Patrick exercised options under an approved share option scheme run by his employer and acquired 1,000 shares at the option price of £3 per share. The market value at that date was £5 per share.

Patrick had been granted the options in December 2009 and the market value of the shares at that date was £3.

Calculate the income tax charge assuming Patrick is a higher rate taxpayer.

Example 4

Last year, Cathy's employer granted her an option over 10,000 shares under its approved company share option scheme. At that date the market value of the shares was £2 per share.

Her employer is about to grant a further option to Cathy under the same scheme, up to the maximum permitted value.

Calculate the maximum market value of shares over which Cathy's employer can grant the options, assuming the current market value of the shares is £1.25.

4.5 Enterprise management incentives (EMIs)

4.5.1 How the EMI works [Sch 5]

The EMI scheme enables small trading companies to attract and retain high calibre staff. There are similarities with the approved company share option plan (CSOP) (see above) but the reliefs are more carefully targeted and the conditions harder to satisfy.

Under an EMI scheme a **trading company** with **gross assets not exceeding £30 million** can award **key employees** with **share options worth up to £250,000 each** at the time the option is granted. The maximum value of options which may be granted at any time under an EMI scheme is £3 million.

The scheme is administratively simple to operate. There is **no approval procedure** to follow. Instead, the company enters into a share option agreement with each employee separately and **notifies the details to HMRC within 92 days**.

The company must comply with certain further conditions. Principally it must be carrying on a **trade which would qualify under the EIS rules** (see earlier in this Text).

The scheme is restricted to companies with **fewer than 250 full time equivalent employees**.

Provided the **rules of the scheme are met the employee receives favourable tax treatment** in respect of the shares issued under the scheme.

4.5.2 Tax implications of the EMI

There is **no income tax (or NIC) on the grant** of a qualifying EMI option.

There is **no income tax (or NIC) when qualifying options are exercised if the exercise price was set at a price at least equal to the market value of the shares at the date of grant.** [s.530]

However, **if the options were granted at a discount to the market value at the date of grant there is an income tax charge** (and possibly an NIC charge – see below) **when the options are exercised on the lower of:** [s.531]

(a)   **The discount** (ie the difference between the market value of the shares at the date of grant and the price paid for the shares (the 'exercise' price)), and

(b)   **The difference between the market value of the shares at the date of exercise and the exercise price.**

If the shares are 'readily convertible assets' (see below), **any income tax/NIC charge is collected through the PAYE scheme** operated by the employer.

Any other provisions relating to share schemes may still apply to EMI options, such as the charge on the lifting of restrictions (see below).

Illustration 2

Beckham Ltd, an unquoted company, grants options to Mr Posh, an employee, in December 2008. The options give Mr Posh the right to buy 30,000 shares at £3.50 each. The market value of the shares at the date the option is granted is also £3.50. Mr Posh has until December 2017 to exercise his options.

Under an EMI scheme there is never an income tax charge at the date the options are granted.

Assuming Mr Posh exercises his options and purchases the shares in July 2014 when the market value of the shares is £6.00 per share, there is no income tax on the exercise of the option. There is only an income tax charge on exercise if the options were issued at a discount, ie less than £3.50.

Mr Posh's only tax charge is to capital gains tax when he disposes of the shares. The base cost of the shares is £3.50 per share (the amount he paid for them).

Illustration 3

In Illustration 2 above, assume that Mr Posh is actually granted an option to purchase 30,000 shares at £3.00 each.

The company is granting an option at a discount of 50p per share. There is never an income tax charge on the grant of the option (even though the shares are issued at a discount) under an EMI scheme. The only time an income tax charge arises is on the exercise of the option.

Mr Posh exercises his option in July 2014, and purchases 30,000 shares at £3.00. Assume that the market value at this point is £4.50.

Because the options were granted at a discount there is a tax charge on the exercise of the option.

The tax charge is based on the lower of:

(i)   The market value at the date of grant, *or*
(ii)   The market value at the date of exercise

In this case the market value at the date of the grant is lower at £3.50. The income tax charge is therefore:

30,000 shares × (£3.50 − £3.00) = £15,000

NIC is also due if the shares are readily convertible assets (see below). However, as Beckham Ltd is an unquoted company, the shares are unlikely to be readily convertible and there is no NIC charge.

4.5.3 Conditions for qualifying options

The tax advantages set out above only apply to options which meet the following conditions:

(a)   **An option must be capable of being exercised within 10 years of being granted and must actually be exercised within 10 years.** There is, however, no minimum period before options can be exercised. [Para 36 Sch 5 & s.529]

(b)   The options must be over **fully paid up ordinary shares in the company**. Redeemable or convertible shares cannot be used but the company can set certain conditions on the shares the employee will acquire, such as limited voting rights. [para 35 Sch 5]

Example 5

Thomas, an additional rate taxpayer, was granted 10,000 share options in his employer company, Rona Ltd (a trading company), on 15 March 2010, under its Enterprise Management Incentive scheme. At that time, the shares were valued at £5.00 each and the exercise price was set at £5.50 each.

Thomas exercised his options on 15 November 2013, by which time the shares were worth £15 each.

State the income tax implications of receiving and exercising the EMI options.

4.5.4 Conditions for the company

The stated purpose of EMI relief is to encourage highly talented individuals to join small companies and help them to grow and succeed. The **company could be quoted or unquoted when the options are granted** but the company must meet the following conditions:

(a) **The gross assets of the company must not exceed £30 million.** Where the company is a parent company the limit applies to the group as a whole. In practice, HMRC define gross assets as all assets shown on the balance sheet drawn up in accordance with standard accounting practice. [SP 5/98]; [para 12, Sch 5]

(b) The company **must not be under the control of any other company** with control defined by reference to s.995 ITA 2007 (not ss.450 & 451 CTA 2010). [para 9, Sch 5]

(c) A group may offer EMI share options to employees employed in either the parent or a subsidiary, but the options can only be in the parent company's share capital, and all the subsidiaries must be qualifying companies.

(d) A company must be **mainly carrying on a qualifying trade.** The excluded activities list includes items such as financial activities and property development. Where the company carries on any excluded activities of an incidental nature, this will not disqualify it from issuing EMI options, provided its main activities fall within the permitted trades. [paras 13-23, Sch 5]

(e) In the case of a group the qualifying trades test will be applied to the group as a whole, as if the group was collectively carrying on a single business. [para 14, Sch 5]

(f) The company need not be resident in or incorporated in the UK, but it **must have a permanent establishment** (ie a fixed place of business, for example a branch) **in the UK** for EMI relief to be available. [para 14A, Sch 5]

(g) The company must have **fewer than 250 full time equivalent employees.** [para 12A, Sch 5]

4.5.5 Conditions for the employee

There is no restriction on the number of employees who may participate, and the scheme extends to any employee, not just key employees. The purpose of the grant must be to recruit or retain the employee. The following conditions apply to each employee seeking the relief:

(a) **The employee must be employed by the company or, where appropriate, the group for at least 25 hours a week** or, if less, for at least 75% of their working time. 'Working time' for this purpose includes paid work as an employee or a self employed person. [paras 25-27, Sch 5]

(b) **The employee must not have a material interest in the company.** For EMI purposes this means he must not control 30% or more of the ordinary share capital of the company. [paras 28-33, Sch 5]

(c) **The employee can hold EMI share options with a value of up to £250,000 each at the date of the grant(s).** If the limit is exceeded the first £250,000 is still covered by the scheme. The excess is subject to the unapproved share option rules. **If the employee holds any options under a Company Share Option Plan (CSOP), the £250,000 limit is reduced by the value of those options.** If CSOP options are subsequently granted so that the value of EMI and CSOP options exceed £250,000, this is a disqualifying event (see below). [para 5, Sch 5]

(d) An employee can receive no more than **£250,000 of EMI options in a three year period,** commencing when options taking him up to the £250,000 limit were granted. So, if an employee receives an option over £250,000 of shares and exercises it wholly or partly after one year, he must wait a further two years before further options can be granted even though he has come below the limit. [para 6, Sch 5]

(e) The employee **can hold options under the approved SAYE scheme** (see above) as well as EMI scheme options.

4.5.6 Withdrawal of EMI relief

Income tax (and NIC) relief under the EMI scheme **ceases to be available** (either to employees in general or an individual employee, as appropriate) on the occurrence of the following disqualifying events: [ss.532–539]

(a)   The company breaks the qualifying trade condition

(b)   The company is acquired by another company which does not satisfy the qualifying trade test

(c)   The employee is granted an option under the company share option plan scheme which takes the total value of options over £250,000

(d)   The employee no longer meets the 75% working time test

(e)   The company alters the terms of the option or its share capital such that the scheme no longer meets the requirements for approval.

Following a disqualifying event, the employee must exercise his options within 90 days (previously 40 days), to obtain the favourable tax treatment outlined above.

4.5.7 Capital gains tax aspects of the EMI

The base cost of the shares for capital gains tax (CGT) purposes depends on whether or not income tax was paid at the date of exercise.

If no income tax was paid when the option was exercised, the base cost of the shares is the amount the employee paid for the shares (ie the exercise price).

If, on the other hand, income tax *was* paid when the option was exercised, the base cost is the market value of the shares at the date of exercise (ie the exercise price plus the amount subject to income tax).

Exam focus point

The capital gains tax entrepreneurs' relief conditions are relaxed for shares acquired via an EMI option. However, entrepreneurs' relief is not examinable in the Personal Taxation paper, so this relief is not considered further here.

Exam focus point

Examiner's report – Personal Taxation

May 2011 – Part II LFQ 4

This question was the weakest question for almost all candidates and the standard of response was disappointing. It was not expected that candidates would have memorized the EMI rules, but that a well prepared candidate would be able to obtain the relevant information from legislation in the exam.

---

5 Restricted shares [ss.422-432]

Exam focus point

It is unlikely that there will be a computational question dealing with restricted shares in the exam. It is more likely that you will be expected to recognise when a tax charge would arise and briefly explain how it would be calculated.

The computations in the illustrations below are to aid your understanding of the restricted shares provisions.

5.1 Introduction

Employment-related securities are restricted if **restrictions have been imposed**, directly or indirectly, by any contract, agreement, arrangement or condition and the **market value of the securities is less than it would be if there were no restrictions.**

The restricted securities regime is broadly designed to **charge income tax on any untaxed value of restricted securities (which includes company shares, loan stock and options) owned by an employee when the restrictions on those securities are lifted or they are sold.**

The **definition of 'restricted'** is very wide and covers **any restriction that reduces the value of a security**, for example:

- The **risk of forfeiture**, eg the employee must give the shares back if he does not complete a minimum period of service with the employer, and

- **Restriction on freedom to retain or dispose of securities, or to exercise rights**, eg the employee is not allowed to sell the shares for three years.

5.2 Charge on acquisition

If shares (or securities) are subject to restrictions that depress their value, and they are acquired for less than their actual market value, taking account of the restrictions, **there is an income tax charge on acquisition**, as above, based on that market value less any consideration paid.

However, if the shares are restricted by a risk of forfeiture and the forfeiture period lasts less than 5 years, there is no income tax charge at acquisition (but see below for employee elections).

Illustration 4

A company gives shares worth £5 to an employee, which are subject to restrictions that stop the employee selling their shares to anyone, at any time, except purchasers approved by the company. The restrictions reduce the value of the shares to £3.

In this case the employee will pay income tax on £3, ie the restricted value.

The shares were given to the employee for no consideration so income tax is charged on the full restricted market value.

5.3 Charge on lifting of restrictions

There is also an income tax charge (a post acquisition charge) when the restrictions are lifted or varied, or when, prior to this, the restricted shares are sold. The amount charged to tax as employment income at that time is the **proportion of value that escaped tax on acquisition as a result of the restrictions, plus that same proportion of any growth in value since acquisition.**

Illustration 5

Following on from the illustration above, let's assume the employee sells the shares for £9 when the whole company is sold (so the restrictions no longer apply).

On acquisition the amount of untaxed value due to the restrictions was 40% (ie (£5–£3)/£5).
On disposal the employee will pay income tax on:

	£
The untaxed part of the value at acquisition: 40% × £5	2.00
Plus 40% of the growth in value since acquisition £40% × (£9 – £5)	1.60
Total charged to income tax	3.60

Note that this is the same as 40% of the proceeds on sale (40% × £9 = £3.60).

5.4 Income tax elections

Instead of paying income tax on a chargeable event (ie on acquisition or the lifting of restrictions), the employee and employer can elect up front to pay tax on the unrestricted market value of the shares at acquisition. This avoids the risk of a substantial income tax charge arising in the future because of a large increase in the share value. [s.431]

Instead any growth in value will be subject to capital gains tax (CGT), which is generally chargeable at a lower rate than income tax and various reliefs may be available to reduce the tax liability (see later in this Text). However, this may mean that the employee pays more tax than finally proves necessary if the value of the shares does not increase as expected, as any 'overpaid' tax cannot be refunded.

Illustration 6

A company gives shares worth £5 to an employee, which are subject to restrictions that stop the employee selling their shares to anyone except purchasers approved by the company. The restrictions reduce the value of the shares to £3. The employee and employer jointly elect for the employee to be taxed on the unrestricted market value of the shares.

The employee will pay income tax on £5 in the tax year of acquisition, ie the unrestricted value, and there will be no future income tax charges in respect of the shares.

We saw above that if a risk of forfeiture lasts less than 5 years there is no income tax charge on acquisition. However, it is possible for the employee and employer to make an election to ignore this income tax exemption and instead be charged up front. Any future growth in value of the shares will then be subject to CGT rather than income tax with the same advantages as described above.

Both elections must be made within 14 days of the transaction. This short time period is designed to stop taxpayers monitoring the share value to decide whether to make an election. [s.425]

Example 6

In May 2013 Sophia bought shares from her employer for £5,000 at a time when they were valued at £15,000. The value was restricted due to limitations on the disposal of the shares and the unrestricted market value of the shares at acquisition was £50,000.

State the amount chargeable to income tax on the acquisition of the restricted shares in May 2013, and explain the election that is available at the date of acquisition and why Sophia may wish to make the election.

5.5 Approved share schemes

As we saw above, **shares acquired under the four approved schemes may be subject to restrictions**. However in the case where shares are acquired within the terms of the share scheme, such that no income tax arises on the acquisition, the employer and employee are **deemed to have made an election under s.431** (see above). Consequently, the employee is deemed to have acquired the shares at their market value, ignoring the effect of the restrictions. [s.431A]

5.6 Conversion of convertible shares

Where shares (or securities) are acquired that are convertible into other shares (or securities) the value of the right to convert is disregarded at acquisition.

Instead **income tax is charged on the gain arising from the conversion**. So, if ordinary shares are converted into preference shares the charge is made on the difference in market value between the two types of shares at that date (not any gain arising since acquisition).

6 National insurance contributions (NIC) and share schemes

If there is an income tax charge in respect of acquiring shares through a share scheme, Class 1 National insurance contributions (NIC) (see later in this Text) may also be due, but only if the shares are 'readily convertible assets', ie they can be sold on a stock exchange.

The NIC charge follows the income tax charge so there is never an NIC (or income tax) charge on the acquisition of shares at market value, or on the grant or exercise of options where options are granted at market value at the date of grant and exercised under the terms of an HMRC approved share scheme .

There may, however, be an NIC charge (if the shares are readily convertible assets):

(a)   On the **exercise of an unapproved share option.**

(b)   On the **exercise of an Enterprise Management Incentive (EMI) option** if, at the date of grant, the exercise price was set at lower than market value.

(c)   On the **withdrawal of shares from a Share Incentive Plan (SIP)** within the five year holding period.

(d)   On the exercise of a SAYE option if, at the date of grant, the exercise price was set at less than 80% of the market value.

(e)   On the **receipt of free or cheap shares** provided directly by the employer (unless as part of an employee shareholder agreement where the **value of the shares does not exceed the £2,000 limit**).

(f)   On the **grant of a CSOP option** where the **price which is to be paid for the shares is less than the market value of the shares at the date that the option is granted.**

Exam focus point

Examiner's report – Personal Taxation

November 2010 – Part II LFQ 3

Few candidates stated there would be a NIC charge on the exercise of the options...

May 2011 – Part II LFQ 4

Part 2 then asked for tax illustrations, including NIC (which many candidates chose to ignore).

Chapter roundup

- Where shares are obtained in an employer company at below their market value there is usually an income tax charge and an NIC charge (if the shares can be sold on a stock exchange) at the date of acquisition, on the difference between the market value and price paid.

- An employee shareholder, ie an employee who agrees to give up certain employment rights, is deemed to have paid up to £2,000 for shares received from his employer. There are also CGT benefits to such shares.

- There is no charge to income tax when share options are granted under an unapproved share option scheme. However, gains realised on the *exercise* of an unapproved share option are subject to income tax, based on the market value of the shares acquired less the cost of the shares and the option.

- A SIP allows employees to acquire shares in their employer company whilst avoiding income tax, NIC and capital gains tax. Employees can obtain free shares from the employer, purchase partnership shares from pre-tax salary, the employer can match the partnership shares, and dividends can be reinvested in further shares.

- A SAYE scheme is an option scheme that must be available to all employees and be linked to a contractual savings scheme, which the employee can use to buy shares on exercising the option. There is no income tax or NIC on grant. The price at which shares may be acquired must be stated at the time the option is granted and must be at least 80% of the market value of the shares at that time.

- Under the CSOP scheme there is no charge to income tax or NIC when the options are granted or when the options are exercised if the price at which the shares are acquired is equal to their market value at the date the option is granted.

- Under an EMI scheme options over shares worth up to £250,000 per employee may be granted, up to a maximum of £3 million. There is no income tax or NIC charge on the grant of the option, and a charge only arises on exercise if the exercise price was set at less than the market value of the shares at the time the options were granted.

- Where employment related securities are subject to restrictions which reduce their value there may be an income tax charge on acquisition (based on their restricted value) and also when the restrictions are lifted. Alternatively an election can be made to pay income tax on their unrestricted value at acquisition.

- If income tax is payable in respect of a share scheme Class 1 NIC may also be due but only if the shares are readily convertible assets.

1. Emma, Fiona and Gillian all participate in their employer's approved share incentive plan. On 1 June 2011 they were each awarded free shares worth £3,000.

    Assume they withdraw their shares as follows.

	Date withdrawn	Value when withdrawn £
Emma	1 May 2014	3,500
Fiona	1 July 2014	3,650
Gillian	1 July 2016	4,000

    Which withdrawals suffer an income tax charge and on what value? Give your reasons.

2. On 1 November 2013, Dean exercised options in a share option scheme run by his employer and acquired 2,000 shares at the exercise price of £4 per share. The market value at that date was £6 per share. The options had been granted in November 2009 when the shares were valued at £4.

    Calculate the income tax liability as a result of the above assuming Dean's other income in the year is £50,000 and

    (a) The scheme has HMRC approval, or
    (b) The scheme is unapproved.

3. John was granted unapproved share options over 10,000 shares in his employer's company in May 2006. The market value at the date of grant was £2.00 per share and the exercise price was set at £1.50 per share. John exercised the options in July 2013 when the market value was £3.00 per share.

    Assuming John's other income for the year was £60,000, calculate his income tax liability in respect of the exercise.

1.   Emma: charge on £3,500 (market value when taken out)
     Withdrawal within 3 years

     Fiona: charge on £3,000 (lower of value on award and on withdrawal)
     Withdrawal 3 – 5 years

     Gillian: no charge
     Withdrawal after 5 years

2.   (a)   No IT due on exercise of shares in an approved scheme where options are exercised after 3 years but
           before 10 years of the date they were granted, and the shares were issued at their market value at the date
           the options were granted.

     (b)   Income tax on exercise

	£
MV of shares at exercise (£6 × 2,000)	12,000
Less exercise price (£4 × 2,000)	(8,000)
	4,000

           IT due @ 40% = 1,600

3.   As these are unapproved share options, the income tax liability on exercise is:

	£
MV of shares at exercise (£3 × 10,000)	30,000
Less exercise price (£1.50 × 10,000)	(15,000)
Employment income	15,000
Tax @ 40% (higher rate taxpayer)	6,000

     Note. There is no income tax charge on grant.

Solution to chapter examples

Solution to Example 1

(a)   Employee shareholder agreement

	£
MV of shares	5,000
Less: deemed payment	(2,000)
Employment income	3,000

(b)   No employee shareholder agreement

	£
MV of shares	5,000
Less: amount paid for the shares	(Nil)
Employment income	5,000

Solution to Example 2

	£
Market value at exercise (£5 × 1,000)	5,000
Exercise price (ie price paid by James) (£3 × 1,000)	(3,000)
Amount subject to income tax	2,000

Solution to Example 3

£Nil. This is an approved scheme and the options were exercised more than three years after they were granted, at a price which was equal to the market value of the shares when the options were granted so there are no income tax charges.

Contrast this with James's position in the previous example.

Solution to Example 4

	£
Maximum value for options	30,000
Less: value of existing option: 10,000 × £2	(20,000)
Maximum remaining value	10,000
£10,000 ÷ £1.25	8,000

The option can therefore be granted over 8,000 shares.

Solution to Example 5

There are no income tax implications when options are granted under an EMI scheme.

There are also no income tax implications on exercise in this case as the exercise price was set at above the market value of the shares at the date of grant (there is instead a capital gains tax charge).

Solution to Example 6

Sophia will pay income tax on the £10,000 difference between the restricted value of the shares (£15,000) and their acquisition price (£5,000).

Sophia and her employer can make an election so that Sophia instead pays income tax on the unrestricted market value of the shares at acquisition (£50,000). By making the election Sophia can avoid a large income tax liability if the shares increase substantially in value in the future. Instead, any increase in value will be subject to a lower tax rate as a capital gain.

Now try the following questions

Short Form Questions:

6.1 – 6.4 inclusive

Long Form Question:

6.1	Sue

National insurance contributions

Exam focus point

The topics in this chapter are examinable at the principle level. Candidates are expected to have an awareness of NIC and the main thrust of the NIC provisions without necessarily knowing the details of those provisions.

1 An overview of the NIC system

The Treasury maintains a National Insurance Fund to provide 'contributory benefits' such as the State retirement pension, jobseeker's allowance, various bereavement benefits, employment support allowance (ESA) and certain sickness and maternity benefits.

Collection is administered by the National Insurance Contributions Office (NICO), which is an Executive Office of the HMRC.

However, most of the actual collection is made by HMRC, either as part of the process of self assessment or through the Pay As You Earn (PAYE) system.

There are **four** main Classes of NIC (Classes 1A and 1B are a subset of Class 1 NICs) as follows:

Class 1 Payable in respect of the **'earnings'** of employed earners. The employee makes 'primary' contributions and the employer makes 'secondary' contributions.

Class 1A Payable by employers only on (most) **taxable benefits** provided to employees (other than excluded employees) unless already caught under Class 1 or Class 1B.

Class 1B Payable by employers on the **grossed-up value of earnings included in a PAYE settlement** (an arrangement entered into with HMRC for the employer to settle the employee's tax liability on small and irregular benefits).

Class 2 Flat rate payable weekly by the **self employed based on their accounting profits**, unless these are below a small earnings threshold.

Class 3 Paid **voluntarily** by those not paying Class 1, 2, or 4, to preserve rights to contributory benefits.

Class 4 Payable by the **self employed in addition to Class 2**, and are a **percentage of taxable profits**.

2 Class 1 contributions

2.1 Employed earners

Employees (including directors) and their employers pay Class 1 NI contributions.

Both *primary* (employee's) and *secondary* (employer's) Class 1 contributions are payable where the employed earner:

(a)   **Is aged 16** or over, and
(b)   Is paid an amount equal to or greater than the current earnings threshold (see below).

Only secondary contributions (ie employer's only) are payable if the employed earner has reached pensionable age.

2.2 Earnings for NIC

Earnings include an employee's gross cash pay, eg salary, bonus, commission, tips and expenses.

If a reimbursed expense has a business purpose it is not treated as earnings. For example, if an employee is reimbursed for business travel or for staying in a hotel on the employer's business this is not normally 'earnings'.

The NIC treatment broadly follows the income tax treatment, so if a payment is taxable for income tax purposes it is usually part of earnings for Class 1 NIC purposes.

Earnings does not usually include taxable benefits, eg company cars, but does include non-cash vouchers, any non-business credit card charges and the settlement of an employee's personal liabilities (eg telephone bills). **Instead there is usually a Class 1A NIC charge on taxable benefits** – see below.

In addition, 'earnings' can include employment income from share schemes if there is also an income tax charge (see earlier in this Text).

Example 1

Justin earns an annual salary of £40,000.

During 2013/14 his employment income also included the following:

Bonus (received June 2013)	£5,000
Company car (taxable benefit figure)	£2,100
Company car petrol (taxable benefit figure)	£2,535
Car parking space at work (cost to employer)	£875
Reimbursed expenses (£575 spent for private purposes)	£1,275

How much of Justin's employment income will be treated as earnings for Class 1 NIC purposes?

2.3 Types of Class 1 contributions

2.3.1 Primary contributions

Employed **earners whose earnings exceed the primary threshold** (PT) of £7,755 (£149 per week for 2013/14), must pay a percentage of their earnings above that threshold as primary Class 1 NIC.

Any earnings between the PT and the upper earnings limit (UEL) £41,450 (£797 per week) are chargeable at 12%, and earnings above the UEL are chargeable at 2%. [s.6]; [s.8]

Note that the PT (£7,755) is much lower than the income tax personal allowance (£9,440) in 2013/14.

2.3.2 Secondary contributions

Employers are required to pay secondary Class 1 NIC. This is **13.8% of earnings above the secondary earnings threshold (ST) of £7,696 (£148 per week for 2013/14).** There is no reduction in the rate for earnings above the upper earnings limit. [s.7]; [s.9]

Note that the **earnings threshold for secondary contributions is different from that for primary contributions.**

2.4 Rates of Class 1 contributions

The weekly, monthly and annual earnings thresholds and upper earnings limit (UEL) and the rates of NIC are shown in the Associations' Tax Tables.

In summary, the weekly rates for Class 1 **primary** contributions are:

Earnings	Primary contributions
Below £149 per week	Nil
Between £149 and £797 per week	12% on the amount above £149
Above £797 per week	12% on the amount between £149 and £797 and 2% on the amount above £797

Example 2

Calculate the primary Class 1 NIC due in 2013/14 for the following employees:

Employee 1	£60 per week
Employee 2	£328 per week
Employee 3	£950 per week

In summary, the weekly rates for Class 1 **secondary** contributions are:

Earnings	Secondary contributions
Below £148 per week	Nil
Over £148 per week	13.8% on the amount above £148

Example 3

Continuing Example 2, calculate the secondary Class 1 NIC due in 2013/14 for the same employees.

An employee who earns **below the primary earnings threshold (PT) but above the lower earnings limit (LEL)** (£109 per week or £5,668 annually for 2013/14) **qualifies for contributory state benefits** even though they do not pay NIC.

2.5 Contracting out of S2P

When an individual **retires** and has paid sufficient NIC throughout their working life they become entitled to receive the **basic state pension and the state second pension** (S2P). An individual may, however, decide to **leave the S2P scheme during their working life** (ie **'contract out' of S2P**) if they are a member of their employer's final salary (ie defined benefits) occupational pension scheme (see later in this Text). This is known as 'contracting out'.

When an individual contracts out of S2P, he and his employer pay lower rates of Class 1 NIC each earnings period and receive a rebate between the lower earnings limit and the earnings threshold. The rates are given in the ATT's Tax Tables.

In 2013/14 an employee in a contracted out final salary scheme pays **10.6% rather than the usual 12% on earnings between the PT and UAP and receives a rebate of 1.4% on earnings between the LEL and the PT.** They then pay at the **usual 12% rate on earnings between the UAP and the upper earnings limit (UEL) and at 2% on earnings above the UEL.**

The employer also pays a **reduced rate of 10.4% on earnings between the ST and the UAP**, rather than 13.8%, receives a **rebate of 3.4% on earnings between the LEL and the ST,** and pays at **13.8% over the UAP.**

3 Class 1A NIC

3.1 Background

Employers are liable for Class 1A contributions on most benefits provided to directors and employees with earnings over £8,500 pa. [s.10]

Class 1A NICs are payable by **employers only**, not by employees.

3.2 Scope of Class 1A NIC

An employer must pay Class 1A NICs on all benefits except those which are exempt from income tax (such as a mobile telephone) and those which are liable to Class 1 NICs (such as non-cash vouchers).

The NIC treatment broadly follows the income tax treatment, so if a benefit is taxable for income tax purposes it is usually liable to Class 1A NIC.

Class 1A NICs are **not payable on benefits received by excluded employees (ie earnings < £8,500).**

Example 4

How much of Justin's (Example 1) employment income is liable to Class 1A NICs? Who must pay the liability?

3.3 Computation of Class 1A NIC liability

The Class 1A NIC liability is calculated as 13.8% of the amount of the benefit as measured for income tax purposes. This will be as shown on the annual return form P11D.

However, not all items included on the P11D are liable to Class 1A NICs. In particular remember that if the employer provides vouchers or settles an employee's personal liability (eg telephone bill) these 'benefits' are subject to Class 1 primary and secondary contributions rather than Class 1A (see above).

Illustration 1

Adrian, an employee with an annual salary of £40,000, received the following benefits and expenses during 2013/14 as calculated for employment income purposes.

	£
Car benefit	6,600
Car fuel benefit	4,200
Cheap loan	800
Private medical insurance (employer's scheme)	560
High Street store vouchers	40
Payment of professional subscription*	200
Membership of local golf club (contracted for by employer)	600
Travelling expenses*	1,000

*Adrian was entitled to claim a full income tax deduction for these expenses.

The Class 1A NIC liability for 2013/14 is calculated as follows:

Benefits liable to Class 1A NICs:

	£
Car benefit	6,600
Car fuel benefit	4,200
Cheap loan	800
Private medical insurance	560
Membership of local golf club	600
	12,760

Class 1A NIC liability £12,760 × 13.8% = £1,761

Note. The vouchers are subject to Class 1 NIC, not Class 1A NIC. The medical insurance and golf club membership are subject to Class 1A because the employer contracted for these. If the employee had contracted for the benefits and then claimed reimbursement from his employer, this would have been subject to Class 1 primary and secondary NIC instead as a reimbursement of an employee liability.

4 Class 1B NIC

A PAYE settlement agreement (PSA) enables employers to **settle an employee's income tax and NIC liabilities on certain minor or irregular taxable benefits and expenses on the employee's behalf.** It also saves the employer having to calculate income tax and NIC through the PAYE system, entering the benefits/expenses individually on forms P11D or P9D and paying Class 1A NIC on them at the end of the tax year.

Where an employer has a PSA with HMRC, he is liable to Class 1B contributions on the amount of the earnings in the PSA which would otherwise be chargeable to Class 1 or Class 1A NICs, together with the total amount of income tax payable under the PSA.

5 Class 3 NIC

Class 3 is a voluntary contribution usually paid by individuals who do not already pay any of the other classes of NIC. For 2013/14 the weekly rate is £13.55. Class 3 contributions can only be made to create entitlement to a limited range of benefits (eg the retirement pension and bereavement benefits).

6 Maximum contributions and deferral

National insurance contributions are payable by an individual in respect of **each employment** (and self employment).

Where an individual has **more than one employment** (or is employed and also in self employment) **it is possible that he could pay more national insurance** than someone earning the same total income from only one employment/self employment.

To ensure this does not occur there is a maximum amount of contributions payable, known as the **'annual maxima'**.

Where the employee expects that the annual maxima limit will (or may be) exceeded for a particular tax year, NICO may agree to defer payment of one or more class of contribution until the precise liability can be determined.

Where an individual has more than one employment and believes that, even if deferment is granted, he **will still pay Class 1 contributions equal to at least 52 weekly contributions on earnings at the upper earnings limit, he may apply to NICO not to collect primary Class 1 contributions at the main rate** (ie at 12%) in respect of at least one of his employments.

If NICO grants deferment the employee **must still pay Class 1 contributions at the additional rate** (ie at 2%) on earnings above the primary earnings threshold.

At the end of the tax year if maximum contributions have been paid, the earnings in respect of which deferment was granted are **formally excepted from liability at the main rate**. If they have not been paid (because the earner's expectations were false), the shortfall is collected directly from the individual.

Chapter roundup

- Employees and employers both pay Class 1 contributions on the employee's 'earnings', but at different rates.

- Lower NIC rates are payable if the individual contracts out of S2P.

- Class 1A contributions are payable by employers where a taxable benefit is provided to a director or £8,500 + employee.

- Class 1B contributions are payable by employers when a PSA is in place.

- The 'annual maxima' rules prevent those who hold more than one employment from paying excessive contributions. Deferment of payment may be granted in appropriate circumstances.

Quiz

1. Ursula's employer provided her with living accommodation (not job related) during 2013/14. The taxable benefit is £2,200. She also had the use of a company credit card which she used solely for business purposes. During 2013/14 the credit card bill came to £14,500. What class of NIC is payable for each of the benefits and who is responsible for paying the liability?

2. Only employers pay Class 1A and Class 1B NICs? True/ False.

3. What class or classes of NIC do employed individuals pay?

1. The living accommodation benefit is liable to Class 1A NIC. This is payable by Ursula's employer.

    The credit card bill would usually be liable to Class 1 NIC, payable by both Ursula and her employer. However, all her expenditure was for business purposes so the NIC liability is £Nil.

2. True. Employees do not pay Class 1A or 1B NIC.

3. Employed individuals pay Class 1 NIC only. Their employers may also be required to pay Class 1A on benefits and/or Class 1B on items included in a PSA.

Solutions to chapter examples

Solution to Example 1

Justin's Class 1 NIC earnings are as follows:

	£
Salary	40,000
Bonus	5,000
Non-business expenses	575
Total earnings	45,575

Taxable benefits (the company car and fuel) are not earnings for Class 1 NIC purposes. They are however subject to Class 1A NIC payable by the employer only. The car parking space is not subject to any NIC as it is not taxable for income tax purposes – it is an exempt benefit.

The business element of the reimbursed expenses is not part of earnings as it is an allowable deduction from employment income for income tax purposes.

Solution to Example 2

	Primary contributions
Employee 1	
£60 per week	Nil
Employee 2	
£328 per week	
£(328 – 149) × 12%	£21
Employee 3	
£950 per week	
£(797 – 149) × 12% (maximum)	£78
£(950 – 797) × 2%	3
	£81

Solution to Example 3

		Secondary Contributions
Employee 1		
£60 per week		Nil
Employee 2		
£328 per week	£(328 – 148) × 13.8%	£25
Employee 3		
£950 per week	£(950 – 148) × 13.8%	£111

Solution to Example 4

Liable to Class 1A NIC:	£
Company car benefit	2,100
Fuel benefit	2,535
Car parking space (exempt)	Nil
Total	4,635

The employer pays the Class 1A NIC liability.

Short Form Questions:

Q7.1 – Q7.3 inclusive

Long Form Question:

Q7.1	Mr Howe

chapter

8

Pensions

The purpose of this chapter is to help you to:

- understand the tax treatment of pensions
- calculate and explain the tax relief available for pension contributions
- understand the tax consequences of taking funds out of a pension at retirement age

References: FA 2004 unless otherwise stated

1 Introduction

1.1 Types of pension

An employer may set up an occupational pension scheme for its employees. The scheme may either require contributions from employees or be 'non contributory'. The employer may use the services of an insurance company (an insured scheme) or the National Employment Savings Trust (NEST) or may set up a totally self administered pension fund.

Certain employers **must provide a pension scheme** for its employees. This is known as automatic enrolment. [Pensions Act 2008]

In all other cases **any individual with or without earnings, or even without any taxable income, can pay into a personal pension**. An employee can obtain tax relief on contributions to both their employer's occupational pension scheme and a personal pension scheme, subject to the rules below.

The same set of tax rules apply to all personal and employer provided pensions.

1.2 Taxation of the pension fund

The premiums (ie contributions) go into a fund that is invested and is ultimately used to provide a pension.

Income and gains within the pension are not liable to tax. It might help to think of a pension fund as a tax free wrapper around any investments within the fund.

1.3 State pension

Individuals must also provide for a pension by **contributing to the State pension scheme through their National Insurance Contributions** (NICs). The State scheme has no impact on income tax during an individual's working career.

2 Contributions

2.1 Introduction

An individual can contribute to any number of pension schemes, out of both income or capital, and to both occupational and personal schemes, and will obtain tax relief so long as he stays within the contribution limits (see below).

The payments can even be made on behalf of another (eg a parent for a child, or a husband for a wife).

In addition to the annual contributions limits, tax relief on contributions into a pension scheme may be restricted by the **annual allowance** and the **lifetime allowance**.

2.2 Tax relief

2.2.1 Amount of tax relief

Each year, tax relief is available to an individual for pension contributions up to the higher of:

(a)   **100% of relevant earnings (salary and other earned income), and**
(b)   **£3,600**.

However where total contributions in the year exceed the annual allowance (see below) there is an income tax charge, which effectively withdraws part of the tax relief previously given on contributions paid into a pension scheme.

2.2.2 Relief for contributions to occupational pension schemes

2.2.2.1 Employee contributions

Occupational pension scheme contributions made by the employee are usually paid gross. The gross amount of the contributions is deducted from employment income on the face of the income tax computation.

2.2.2.2 Net pay arrangements

Employers usually operate **net pay arrangements**, ie they **deduct gross pension contributions from the employee's earnings before operating PAYE**. The individual therefore obtains basic, higher and additional rate tax relief, if appropriate, at source.

2.2.2.3 Employer contributions

Contributions paid by the employer on behalf of the employee are deductible for the employer when calculating their taxable profits.

Employers with **250 or more employees** must **automatically enrol certain members of staff into a qualifying pension scheme** and **make a contribution towards it**. The employer can use either an existing pension scheme for this purpose or the National Employment Savings Trust (NEST), a pension scheme that has been established for this purpose for any employer who chooses to use it. [Pensions Act 2008]

Employer contributions to any occupational pension (or personal pension – see below) **scheme are not taxable benefits for the employee. They are, however, added to the employee's own contributions when determining if the 'annual allowance'** (see below) **has been exceeded.**

2.2.2.4 Additional voluntary contributions

An employee who feels that his employer's scheme is inadequate may make **additional voluntary contributions** (AVCs), either to the employer's scheme (in-house AVCs) or to a separate scheme operated by an insurance company (freestanding AVCs). In-house AVCs are deductible from the employee's taxable pay for PAYE purposes, but only to the extent that they, plus any contributions by the employee to the employer's scheme, do not exceed the maximum amount that qualifies for tax relief (see above).

Freestanding AVCs are similar to personal pension scheme contributions (see below) **and are paid net of basic rate tax.**

2.2.3 Relief for contributions to personal pension schemes

All contributions made to personal pension schemes are paid net of basic rate tax. The pension scheme then recovers the basic rate tax from HMRC. So, for every £80 contributed in a tax year, the government contributes a further £20. In this way, all taxpayers obtain basic rate tax relief.

Tax relief at higher rates is obtained by increasing a taxpayer's basic rate and higher rate tax limits by the amount of the gross contribution (like we did with Gift Aid – see earlier in this Text).

As contributions to personal pension schemes (unlike contributions to occupational schemes) are not deducted from total income in the income tax computation the **gross amount** is deducted in the adjusted income computation when calculating:

(a)   The restriction for the personal and married couple's allowances, and
(b)   The limit on income tax reliefs (see earlier in this Text).

This ensures that a taxpayer's allowances and tax reliefs are the same regardless of whether his pension contributions are to an occupational or personal pension scheme.

Even those with no or little income can **contribute up to £3,600 to a personal pension scheme** each year.

An individual's **employer can make contributions to his personal pension** scheme. Such contributions are **not taxable benefits** for the employee although they **are added to the employee's own contributions when determining if the 'annual allowance'** (see below) has been exceeded.

Exam focus point

Do not confuse the way in which tax relief is obtained for the two different types of pensions. Personal pension scheme contributions are paid **net** and relief is given at source and by extending the basic rate and higher rate limits of higher and additional rate taxpayers. Occupational pension scheme contributions are usually made **gross**, out of pre-tax salary, so relief is given immediately at the employee's highest tax rate.

2.3 Annual allowance

2.3.1 What is the annual allowance

The **annual allowance** is the maximum amount of contributions that can be made **tax free** each year during the 'pension input period'. The **annual allowance is £50,000** and is given to you in the ATT's Tax Tables.

The **pension input period (PIP) is the same as the tax year**, unless the individual nominates a different period. The end date of the pension input period determines the tax year that any excess value will be tested against the annual allowance. There **must be one pension input period ending in every tax year**. [s.238]

If the contributions into the scheme during the pension input period exceed the annual allowance there is an income tax charge on the excess (see below).

2.3.2 Unused annual allowance

Any **unused annual allowance is carried forward for three years**, so even where contributions exceed £50,000 in a pension input period, there may not be an annual allowance charge if the individual has not used all of their annual allowance in the previous three tax years. In this case, the **current year's allowance is set off first, then any unused allowance from the earliest of the three tax years in priority to later years**.

The annual allowance charge rules changed in 2011/12 and consequently there are special transitional rules which apply to the carry forward of relief in the three years before that tax year. The **available allowance for the years 2008/09 to 2010/11 is deemed to be £50,000 each year**. The earliest year from which an unused annual allowance can be carried forward is 2008/09.

Where actual contributions in the years **2008/09 to 2010/11 exceed £50,000**, the **excess does not utilise any unused brought forward allowance**. Unused brought forward amounts are only utilised **from 2011/12 onwards**.

An unused annual allowance can only be carried forward **from a year in which the individual was actually a member of a registered pension scheme**, but it is not necessary that a contribution was paid in that year. [s.228A]

2.3.3 Calculating the annual allowance charge

If total contributions **in the pension input period exceed the current year and any brought forward unused annual allowance there is an income tax charge on the excess.**

Total contributions include contributions by the taxpayer and also contributions by third parties, such as an employer or spouse.

The income tax charge is calculated by **treating the excess contributions as the taxpayer's top slice of income (above all other sources, including termination payments).** For example, if the taxpayer has part of the basic rate band remaining, after taking account of his taxable income, the amount of excess contributions equal to the basic rate band remaining is taxed at 20%. Any remaining excess contributions are then taxed at the higher rate and additional rates as appropriate. [s.227]

Remember that the **basic rate and higher rate limits are extended for personal pension contributions and, if relevant, Gift Aid donations** (see earlier in this Text).

The annual allowance charge effectively **claws back the tax relief** given on the excess pension contributions.

The tax is **added to the taxpayer's income tax liability** at Step 7 in the income tax calculation (see earlier in this Text).

Example 1

Carol has total income in 2013/14 of £145,000. During her pension input period for 2013/14 she makes a net contribution to her personal pension of £52,000. She has made the same level of contributions in each of the last five years.

Calculate Carol's annual allowance charge.

Example 2

David has total income in 2013/14 of £292,150. During his pension input period for 2013/14 he makes a net contribution to his personal pension of £125,000. He has made the same level of contributions in each of the last five years.

Calculate David's annual allowance charge.

Example 3

Steven has made the following gross contributions to his personal pension:

2010/11	£27,000
2011/12	£60,000
2012/13	£40,000

In 2013/14 Steven wishes to make a large pension contribution to use up any brought forward annual allowance. What is the maximum contribution he can make before incurring the annual allowance charge?

Example 4

Daphne has earnings of £610,000 for the 2013/14 tax year and makes contributions of £21,500 (gross amount) each month to her registered personal pension scheme during the year. She has made the same level of contributions for the past five years.

Required

(a) State the maximum amount of gross pension contributions for which Daphne will be entitled to tax relief and the actual amount she will have paid into the pension scheme during the year.

(b) Explain how tax relief is given for contributions to personal pension schemes and calculate her income tax liability for 2013/14.

The annual allowance charge **does not apply** in the tax year in which an individual **dies**, so there is no charge even if contributions exceed £50,000 in that year.

2.4 Lifetime allowance

The '**lifetime allowance**' is the maximum amount that can be accumulated in a pension scheme during lifetime, without incurring tax charges. The **lifetime allowance for 2013/14 is £1.5 million** and is given to you in the ATT's Tax Tables.

If this amount is exceeded there is a **tax charge when benefits are taken from the pension scheme fund**. If the benefit is taken as a lump sum the charge on the excess is 55%, otherwise the income tax charge is 25%. The tax charge is added to the taxpayer's tax liability which has been calculated on their income to arrive at their total tax liability for the year (see earlier in this Text).

Example 5

Emma turned 60 on 1 July 2013 and decided to vest her pension benefits on that date. She has a defined contribution pension fund that was valued at £1,650,000 on 1 July 2013. Emma took the maximum tax free lump sum of £375,000 (ie 25% of the lifetime allowance of £1,500,000) and also took the excess of the fund over the lifetime allowance as a lump sum. She used the balance of the fund to buy an annuity.

How much is the total lump sum that Emma will receive from the pension scheme administrators and how much tax must they pay to HMRC on Emma's behalf?

3 Drawing a pension

3.1 Pension age

The minimum age that an individual can receive a pension (including a tax free lump sum, see below) from either an occupational or a personal pension scheme is 55.

Employees can draw part of their pension from a company occupational pension scheme whilst they are still working full or part time for the same employer so long as they have reached the requisite age.

Individuals receive the state pension when they reach the state pension age. For men the **state pension age is currently 65 and between 60 and 65 for women**. It will reach 65 for all women by November 2018 and will increase to 66 between December 2018 and October 2020 for both men and women.

3.2 Tax free lump sum

Individuals can usually take a tax free lump sum of as much as 25% of their pension fund, subject to a maximum of 25% × the lifetime allowance.

There is **no maximum age** for taking the tax free lump sum.

3.3 Balance of the pension fund

There are a number of alternative ways of taking the balance of the pension fund:

(a)   Take a **scheme pension** – secure for life

(b)   Buy an **annuity** – providing a secure, regular (usually monthly) income for life

(c)   Receive a **single cash lump sum at age 60 or over where the pension is small, or 'trivial'** (ie valued at up to £18,000), 25% of which will be tax free (see above)

(d)   Draw a **capped amount of income** (maximum broadly 120% of the equivalent annuity) directly from the pension (a **drawdown pension**)

(e)   Draw an **unlimited amount of income** directly from the pension so long as the equivalent annuity is at least £20,000 a year (a **flexible drawdown pension**).

'Drawing income' means that the individual can receive a **regular income from the pension fund while the fund remains invested.** Although the fund may continue to grow, it could also fall, so a drawdown pension is a riskier choice.

3.4 Taxation of pension income

Apart from the tax free lump sum (above) all other income taken from a pension (including the state pension) is taxed as non savings income.

The amount accruing over the tax year (rather then the amount actually received) is taxable as 'pension income' in the income tax computation (although in the exam this is usually the same figure).

Chapter roundup

- Employees can contribute to their employer's occupational pension scheme and/ or a personal pension. Other individuals can only contribute to a personal pension.

- Income and gains within a pension are tax free. The pension is effectively a tax free wrapper.

- Contributions can be made on behalf of another person and out of income or capital.

- Tax relief for pension contributions made by individuals is given on the higher of 100% of relevant earnings and £3,600.

- Occupational pension scheme contributions are paid gross. Tax relief, at basic, higher and additional rates, is obtained by deducting the contributions from taxable employment income.

- Contributions paid by employers are deductible for the employer and a tax free benefit for the employee. They count towards the annual and lifetime allowances.

- Additional voluntary contributions (AVCs) can be made either to the employer scheme or a separate scheme.

- Basic rate tax relief on personal pension schemes is given at source. The contributions are paid into the scheme net of basic rate tax and HMRC pay the additional 20% to the scheme. Higher and additional rate tax relief is given by extending the basic and higher rate tax limits.

- The 'annual allowance' is the maximum amount that can be paid into a pension tax free each year (currently £50,000).

- Contributions in excess of the annual allowance are taxed on the individual taxpayer as if they were the taxpayer's top slice of income.

- Any unused annual allowance can be carried forward for three years.

- The 'lifetime allowance' is the maximum amount that can be accumulated in a pension during lifetime (currently £1.5m).

- When drawing a pension a tax free lump sum of up to 25% × the fund is available. There is flexibility regarding how to take the balance of the pension.

- The pension on retirement is treated as non savings income of the taxpayer.

Quiz

1. What is the maximum amount that can be contributed by an individual to a pension for which tax relief is available?

2. Harry has been a member of a pension scheme for the past five years but has not made any pension contributions in that time. What is the maximum gross amount he can pay into a pension in 2013/14 without incurring any pension charges?

3. What is the lifetime allowance for 2013/14?

1. The higher of £3,600 and 100% × relevant earnings.

2. Harry can pay in up to the annual allowance, ie £50,000. However, as he has made no contributions in the previous three years the unused relief is carried forward so he can pay in £200,000 in total (£50,000 + £150,000).

3. £1,500,000.

Solution to chapter example

Solution to Example 1

The net contribution of £52,000 is grossed up by 100/80 to £65,000 for the purposes of extending the basic and higher rate limits, and for calculating the personal allowance and annual allowance charge.

The extended basic rate limit is £97,010 (£32,010 + £65,000) and the extended higher rate limit is £215,000 (£150,000 + £65,000).

Excess pension contributions are £15,000 (£65,000 – £50,000). There is no brought forward annual allowance as contributions have been £65,000 (gross) in the last five years.

	£
Total income	145,000
Less: personal allowance (Note)	(9,440)
Taxable income	135,560
Less: higher rate band (extended basic rate band fully used)	(215,000)
Higher rate band remaining	(79,440)

The excess contributions of £15,000 all fall within the remaining higher rate band of £79,440 , so are taxed at 40%.

The annual allowance charge is £6,000 (£15,000 @ 40%)

Note. Full personal allowance is available as adjusted net income is £80,000 (ie £145,000 – £65,000)

Solution to Example 2

The net contribution of £125,000 is grossed up by 100/80 to £156,250 for the purposes of extending the basic and higher rate limits, and for calculating the personal allowance and annual allowance charge.

The extended basic rate limit is £188,260 (£32,010 + £156,250) and the extended higher rate limit is £306,250 (£150,000 + £156,250).

Excess pension contributions are £106,250 (£156,250 – £50,000). There is no brought forward annual allowance as contributions have been £156,250 (gross) in the last five years.

	£
Total income	292,150
Less: personal allowance (Note)	(Nil)
Taxable income	292,150
Less: higher rate limit (extended basic rate band fully used)	(306,250)
Higher rate band remaining	(14,100)

Excess contributions of £14,100 are taxed at 40% and the remaining £92,150 (£106,250 – £14,100) fall into the additional rate band and are taxed at 45%.

The annual allowance charge is:

	£
£14,100 @ 40%	5,640
£92,150 @ 45%	41,467
Annual allowance charge	47,107

Note. No personal allowance is available as adjusted net income exceeds £118,880 (ie £292,150 – £156,250 = £135,900)

Solution to Example 3

Steven's unused annual allowance brought forward from 2010/11 – 2012/13 is £23,000. This is calculated as follows:

	£
2010/11: £50,000 – £27,000	23,000
2011/12: £50,000 – £60,000	(10,000)
	13,000
2012/13: £50,000 – £40,000	10,000
c/f	23,000

This gives a total unused annual allowance of £73,000 in 2013/14 (£23,000 + £50,000).

This is the maximum gross contribution that Steven can pay into his pension without having to pay the annual allowance charge. His contribution is matched first with the 2013/14 annual allowance, then that of 2010/11 and finally with that of 2012/13. If Steven contributes less than £73,000 then part of the unused 2010/11 annual allowance of £13,000 may be wasted as it cannot be carried forward to 2014/15.

Solution to Example 4

(a) As Daphne's earnings are £610,000, all of the contributions of £258,000 (£21,500 × 12) qualify for tax relief.

She will have paid £206,400 (£258,000 less 20% basic rate tax) to the pension scheme.

(b) Basic rate tax relief has been given at source. Higher and additional rate tax relief will be given by extending Daphne's basic and higher rate tax bands for 2013/14 to £290,010 (£32,010 + £258,000) and £408,000 (£150,000 + £258,000) respectively.

However, there will be a tax charge on the excess of the contributions above the annual allowance of £50,000 (there is no unused relief from the previous three years as contributions were £258,000 in those years). The excess contributions are £208,000 (£258,000 – £50,000) and are taxed as Daphne's top slice of income.

Her income tax liability for the tax year 2013/14 is:

	£
Employment income	610,000
Less: personal allowance (adjusted net income > £118,880 (£610,000 – £258,000))	(NIL)
Taxable income	610,000
Income tax:	
£290,010 at 20%	58,002
£117,990 at 40%	47,196
£202,000 at 45%	90,900
	196,098
Add: annual allowance charge (no remaining basic or higher rate bands)	
£208,000 @ 45%	93,600
Tax liability	289,698

Solution to Example 5

	£
Payable to Emma:	
Maximum tax free lump sum	375,000
Excess of fund over the lifetime allowance as a lump sum: £1,650,000 – £1,500,000	150,000
Taxable at 55% (as taken as lump sum): £150,000 × 55%	(82,500)
Pension scheme administrators will pay Emma	442,500

They will pay the tax of £82,500 to HMRC on Emma's behalf.

Now try the following questions

Short Form Questions:

8.1 – 8.6 inclusive

Long Form Questions:

8.1	Mr Matthews (Pilot Paper)
8.2	Ed & Joan
8.3	Dwaine Pipe

9

Overseas aspects
of income tax

The purpose of this chapter is to help you to:

- determine, and explain the significance of, an individual's residence and domicile status
- outline the scope and basis of assessment of overseas and UK income
- understand the remittance basis of taxation for non-UK domiciled individuals
- identify which non-UK residents can receive UK personal allowances
- calculate double taxation relief

References: ITTOIA 2005 unless otherwise stated

1 Residence and domicile

1.1 Introduction

Earlier in this Text we saw that a taxpayer's **residence** and **domicile** had important consequences in establishing the treatment of his UK and overseas income. The rules are now set out in detail.

Exam focus point

From 6 April 2013 the concept of 'ordinary residence', which used to be a key part of determining an individual's liability to UK tax, has been abolished. From that date liability is established by reference only to an individual's domicile status and his residence status. The latter is determined using the new statutory residence test, which replaces guidance in HMRC's booklet HMRC6, which did not have the force of law and subsequently led to many high profile legal cases.

1.2 Residence

1.2.1 Statutory residence test

The **statutory residence test** (SRT) applies from 6 April 2013 to determine whether an individual is UK resident or non-UK resident for income tax, capital gains tax and inheritance tax purposes. It replaces guidance in HMRC's booklet HMRC6, which did not have the force of law and subsequently led to many high profile legal cases. [Sch 45 FA 2013]

The SRT is broken down into **three steps**:

- An **automatic overseas** test
- An **automatic UK residence** test, and
- A **sufficient ties** test.

The operation of the SRT can be summarised as follows, with further details below:

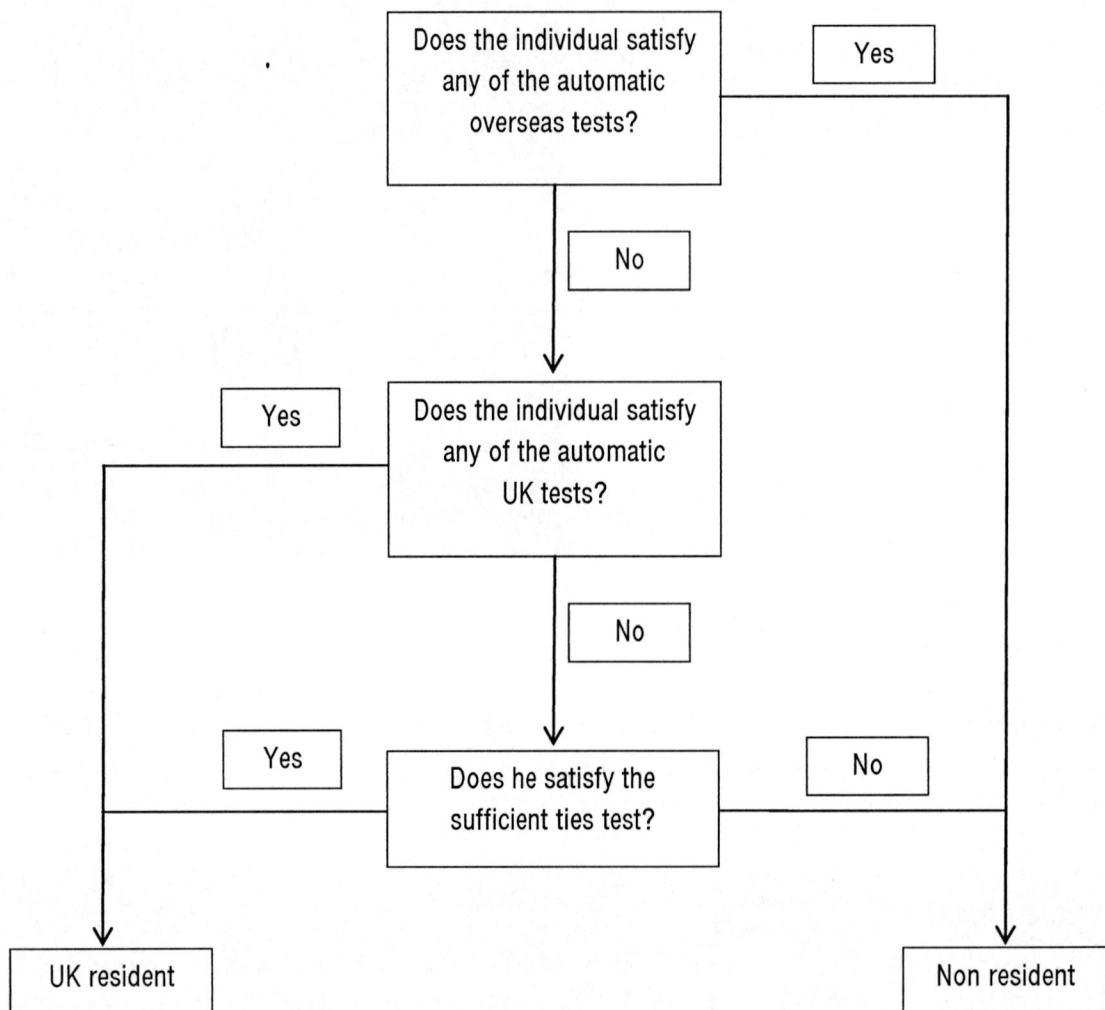

```
                    ┌──────────────────────────┐
                    │  Does the individual      │      ┌──────┐
                    │  satisfy any of the        │─────▶│ Yes  │
                    │  automatic overseas tests? │      └──────┘
                    └──────────────────────────┘            │
                              │                              │
                           ┌──────┐                          │
                           │  No  │                          │
                           └──────┘                          │
                              │                              │
  ┌──────┐    ┌──────────────────────────┐                  │
  │ Yes  │◀───│  Does the individual      │                  │
  └──────┘    │  satisfy any of the        │                  │
              │  automatic UK tests?       │                  │
              └──────────────────────────┘                  │
                           │                                 │
                        ┌──────┐                             │
                        │  No  │                             │
                        └──────┘                             │
                           │                                 │
  ┌──────┐    ┌──────────────────────────┐   ┌──────┐       │
  │ Yes  │◀───│  Does he satisfy the      │──▶│  No  │       │
  └──────┘    │  sufficient ties test?     │   └──────┘       │
              └──────────────────────────┘                  │
       │                                                     │
       ▼                                                     ▼
 ┌──────────────┐                               ┌──────────────┐
 │ UK resident  │                               │ Non resident │
 └──────────────┘                               └──────────────┘
```

There are also special rules that enable an individual to **split a tax year** into a UK resident and non-UK resident part, as well as rules for income and gains that arise during a period of **temporary non residence** (see below).

1.2.2 Automatic overseas tests

The first step is to determine whether the individual satisfies any of the **automatic overseas tests. If he meets any of the following tests he will be treated** as **not resident** in the UK: [paras 12 – 14 Sch 45 FA 2013]

Test 1   Was **resident in the UK for one or more of the three previous tax years** (ie is now leaving the UK) and **spends fewer than 16 days** in the UK in the current tax year

Test 2   Was **not resident in the UK for any of the previous three tax years** (ie is now arriving in the UK) and **spends fewer than 46 days** in the UK in the current tax year

Test 3   **Leaves the UK to carry out full-time work abroad**, ie he satisfies **all** the following conditions:

    (a)   He **works an average of 35 hours a week overseas**, excluding:

        (i)   Sick leave days
        (ii)   Annual or parenting leave days
        (iii)   Gaps of up to 15 days between employment, and
        (iv)   Any days when he works in the UK

    (b)   There must be **no significant breaks**, ie periods of at least 31 non-work days overseas

    (c)   He spends **fewer than 91 days in the UK**

    (d)   He has **no more than 30 UK work days**.

The **terminology** relating to these tests (eg days spent in the UK, work day) is explained in detail below.

Illustration 1

Janette, has previously always been resident in the UK. During the 2013/14 tax year, however, she spent only 10 days in the UK.

As Janette was resident in one or more of the three tax years before the current tax year (ie in 2010/11, 2011/12 and 2012/13) but spent fewer than 16 days in the UK in 2013/14, she is automatically not UK resident for 2013/14.

If the individual **does not meet any of the automatic overseas tests**, the individual is **automatically UK resident if he meets any of the automatic UK tests.**

1.2.3 Automatic UK tests

If the individual **does not meet any of the automatic overseas tests** the next step is to **consider if he meets any of the following automatic UK tests**, in which case he will be treated as **UK resident:** [paras 7 – 9 Sch 45 FA 2013]

Test 1   He **spends 183 days or more** (ie more than six months) in the UK during the tax year

Test 2   There is a **period of at least 91 consecutive days, at least 30 days of which fall in the tax year**, when:

    (a) He **has a home in the UK** in which he spends a sufficient amount of time, ie is **present (ie there in person, no matter the length of time) on at least 30 days**, and

    (b) Either:

        (i)   He **has no overseas home**, or

(ii) He **has an overseas home or homes at which he is present for fewer than 30 days in the tax year** (the 'permitted **amount** of time')

Illustration 2

Jane has been resident in the UK for the last 30 years. She has a home in the UK throughout the 2013/14 and 2014/15 tax years. She is present in that home on more than 30 days during the 2013/14 tax year.

Jane acquires an overseas home on 1 March 2014 and is present there on 30 days in 2013/14 tax year.

Jane does not satisfy any of the automatic overseas tests in 2013/14 as she spends more than 16 days in the UK (having been UK resident in previous tax years) and is not leaving the UK to carry out full time work. So we must consider if she meets any of the automatic UK tests.

Although there is a period of 91 consecutive days, 30 of which fall in 2013/14, when Jane had both a UK home and an overseas home, there is also a period of at least 91 consecutive days (6 April 2013 to 28 February 2014) when she had a UK home (in which she spent sufficient time in 2013/14) but no overseas home.

Jane is therefore resident in the UK for 2013/14 under the second automatic UK test

---

Test 3 He **works full-time in the UK, which for these purposes means:**

(a) He must **work sufficient hours** in the UK (similar to overseas test 3, above), **over a period of 365 days**

(b) With **no significant breaks** from UK work, ie periods of at least 31 non-work days in the UK

(c) **All or part of the 365-day period falls within the tax year** in question

(d) **More than 75% of the individual's working days** in the 365-day period are **UK work days** (see below).

Illustration 3

Marcus travels to the UK on 1 July 2013 to start a secondment with a UK company on the following day. The secondment ends on 1 July 2014 but he does not leave the UK until 6 August 2014. This is 401 days after he arrived in the UK.

Over the 365 day period to 30 June 2014 Marcus met the full-time work criteria and has not taken a significant break from his UK work during this period. Part of this period of 365 days falls within the 2013/14 tax year and part falls within the 2014/15 tax year.

Over the period of 365 days ending 30 June 2014 Marcus works for over three hours on 240 days, 192 (80%) of which are days when Marcus worked for more than three hours in the UK. At least one day when Marcus does more than three hours work in the UK falls within the 2013/14 tax year so he is resident in the UK under the third automatic UK test for 2013/14.

There is also at least one day when Marcus does more than three hours work in the UK within 2014/15, so he also meets the third automatic UK test for that year.

Example 1

Sierra was born in and has lived in Spain all her life. In July 2012 she visits London on holiday and decides to emigrate to the UK.

She lives in her Spanish house (her only home) until she sells it on 15 January 2014 and arrives in the UK on 22 January 2014. She stays in a hotel until 14 February 2014, when she moves into a flat in London, which is now her only home. She signs a lease for one year. During the 2013/14 tax year Sierra is present in her Spanish home on 285 days, and in her London flat on 51 days.

You are required to explain, giving reasons, whether Sierra is UK resident in 2013/14.

If the individual meets **none of the automatic overseas tests and none of the automatic UK tests**, he must look at the **'sufficient ties' test**.

1.2.4 Sufficient ties tests

1.2.4.1 The ties

The **sufficient ties test** compares the number of days spent in the UK against the following **connection factors (known as ties). The fewer number of days that an individual spends in the UK the more ties they need to have to be treated as UK resident.** [paras 17 – 19 & 31 – 38 Sch 45 FA 2013]

(a) **UK resident family,** eg spouse, civil partner, common law partner, child under 18 (although if a child is in full time education in the UK he is not counted so long as he does not spend more than 21 days in the UK outside of term time).

(b) **UK work,** whether employment or self-employment, of **more than 3 hours a day for a combined period of at least 40 days** (which do not need to be continuous days) in the tax year. Travelling time (where paid for by an employer) and job related training count as 'work' for these purposes.

(c) **Accommodation** in the UK, including a **holiday home** or a **property owned by someone other than the individual**. This tie is satisfied if the property is available for a **continuous period of at least 91 days in the year,** and the individual **spends at least:**

　　(i) **One night** in it, or

　　(ii) **16 nights** in it if the accommodation **belongs to a close relative** (ie a parent, grandparent, brother or sister, child or grandchild aged 18 or over)

　　Gaps in the availability of the accommodation of up to 15 days count towards the continuous period of availability.

(d) **More than 90 days spent in the UK in either or both of the previous two tax years.**

(e) **Country tie,** ie has he **spent more days in the UK at midnight** than in any other country in the current year? This tie **only applies to individuals who have been resident in one or more of the previous three tax years** (see below).

1.2.4.2 Ties for individuals coming to the UK

An individual who was **not UK resident in any of the previous three tax years,** ie he is arriving in the UK for the first time, or after a long period of absence, must determine whether he has any of the above ties.

The **number of ties** that must apply in order for the individual **to be treated as UK resident in the current tax year depends on the number of days spent in the UK** as follows:

Number of days spent in the UK	UK ties and residence status
Fewer than 46	Always non-resident
Between 46 and 90	Resident if has 4 ties
Between 91 and 120	Resident if has 3 ties
Between 120 and 182	Resident if has 2 ties
183 or more	Always UK resident

1.2.4.3 Ties for individuals leaving the UK

The sufficient ties test is **more stringent** if the individual has been **resident in the UK in one or more of the previous three tax years** (ie he is leaving the UK) as:

(a)   He needs **fewer ties**, and **fewer days spent in the UK**, to be treated as UK resident in the current tax year, and

(b)   He must consider the **additional 'country' tie**. Even if he spends the same number of days in another country as he does in the UK, he will still satisfy the UK country tie.

The **number of ties** required for a 'leaver' to be treated as UK resident are as follows:

Number of days spent in the UK	Number of ties to be UK resident
Fewer than 16	Always non-resident
Between 16 and 45	Resident if has 4 ties
Between 46 and 90	Resident if has 3 ties
Between 91 and 120	Resident if has 2 ties
Between 120 and 182	Resident if has 1 tie
183 or more	Always UK resident

1.2.5 Terminology

1.2.5.1 What is a 'day spent in the UK'?

Any day where an individual is **present in the UK at midnight** is counted for residency purposes. However he **does not need to count the first 60 days that he spends in the UK due to circumstances beyond his control**, such as serious illness. [para 22 Sch 45 FA 2013]

However, if the individual has:

*   Been **UK resident in at least one of the three previous tax years**

*   Has **at least three UK ties**

*   Been **present in the UK in that year for more than 30 'qualifying days'** (ie days when he is present in the UK at some point, but not at the end of the day)

he must **include any 'qualifying days' over the 30 day threshold** when calculating his total number of days spent in the UK. He can ignore these deemed days, however, when calculating the number of days he has for the 90-day tie.

Example 2

Rick was resident in 2012/13. However in 2013/14 he does not meet any of the automatic UK or overseas tests and only spends 35 days in the UK where he was present at the end of the day. However, he was also present in the UK on 57 other days, leaving the UK before the end of the day. He has three ties under the sufficient ties test.

You are required to explain whether Rick is UK resident in 2013/14.

Transit days, ie days when the individual arrives in the UK as a passenger and leaves the UK the next day, **do not count towards the total day count** for the SRT, provided he does not engage in activities unrelated to simply passing through the UK, such as meeting with friends.

1.2.5.2 What is a 'work day'?

A **work day** is a day during which an individual works for **more than three hours**. This is important for:

(a) The **third automatic overseas test** – to meet the test, the individual **must not work more than three hours a day in the UK on more than 30 days** in the tax year

(b) The **third automatic UK test** – to meet the test, the individual **must spend more than 75% of the days, on which he works for at least three hours, in the UK**

(c) The **work tie** – to have the tie, the individual must **work more than three hours a day in the UK on 40 days or more.**

1.2.6 Split year treatment

Usually an individual is either **resident or non-resident for a complete tax year**. However, a UK resident individual can **split the tax year** into a **UK resident part** and a **non-resident part** when he: [Part 3 Sch 45 FA 2013]

(1) **Leaves the UK** part-way through the tax year and

Cases 1 & 2 He or his partner **starts to work full-time overseas, or**
Case 3 He **ceases to have a home** in the UK

(2) **Comes to the UK** part-way through the tax year and

Case 4 **He starts to have his only home in the UK, or**
Case 5 **He starts full-time work in the UK, or**
Cases 6 & 7 **He ceases (or his partner ceases) working full-time abroad, or**
Case 8 **He starts to have a home in the UK.**

The individual is taxed on income received during the **UK part of the year as a UK resident**, and is charged to UK tax as a **non-UK resident in respect of the overseas part**. The taxation of different sources of income is explained in detail below.

Exam focus point

The ATT has confirmed that candidates need only be able to outline the circumstances in which the tax year can be split and are not required to know the detailed rules for the Personal Taxation paper.

1.2.7 Temporary non-residence

If an individual returns to the UK after a period of temporary non-residence, he may be taxable on certain income (and gains – see later in this Text) **received in that period.**

An individual is treated as 'temporarily non-resident' if:

(a) He **becomes non-resident,**

(b)   He was **UK resident for at least four out of the seven tax years (whether full or split years) before the year of departure from the UK,** and

(c)   He remains **non-resident for five or fewer complete calendar years.**

The individual is treated as **temporarily non-resident between the date he ceases being UK resident and the day before the UK residence resumes** and is **liable to tax in the year** (or part year in the case of a split year) **of his return** to the UK on, for example, the following:

- Certain pension payments, lump sums and other charges, eg withdrawals from a flexible drawdown pension
- **Remitted foreign income** (for remittance basis users – see below)
- **Chargeable event gains** (in respect of non-qualifying life assurance policies), and
- **Capital gains** (see later in this Text).

The income (or gain) is treated as **arising in the tax year that the individual returns to the UK.**

1.3 Domicile

1.3.1 General principles

Broadly speaking, a person is domiciled in the country in which he has his permanent home. Domicile is distinct from nationality or residence. A person may be resident in more than one country, but at any given time he can only be domiciled in one.

A person acquires a *domicile of origin* at birth; this is normally the domicile of his father and therefore not necessarily the country where he himself was born. **A person retains this domicile until he acquires a different domicile of choice.** A domicile of choice can be acquired only by individuals aged 16 or over.

If, before reaching that age, **the person** (eg father) **whose domicile determined the minor's own domicile, acquires a new domicile of choice,** the minor's domicile changes similarly – *domicile of dependency*.

To acquire a domicile of choice a person must sever his ties with the country of his domicile of origin and settle in another country with the clear intention of making his permanent home there. Long residence in another country is not in itself enough to prove that a person has acquired a domicile of choice there unless it can be regarded as indicating intention; there has to be evidence that he firmly intends to live there permanently.

Whether someone is domiciled is only important if they have income (or gains) from an overseas source during the tax year.

2 Taxation of income

2.1 Overview

2.1.1 Effect of residence and domicile status

Generally, **UK residents are liable to UK income tax on their worldwide income (ie all UK and overseas income)** while **non-residents are liable to UK income tax only on income arising in the UK.**

A non-UK resident's income tax liability on their UK income is broadly **limited to any tax deducted at source.** So, where interest is received gross (eg NS&I accounts), the interest is not taxed but if the interest is received net (eg bank interest), the interest is taxable but the tax liability is limited to the basic rate tax deducted at source. [s.811 ITA 2007]

UK residents who are not UK domiciled may be taxable on their foreign income on the remittance basis (see below), ie only to the extent that such income is brought (either actually or effectively) into the UK (see below).

The diagram below provides a broad **summary** of how an individual is taxed, based on his residence and domicile status. The detail for specific types of income is covered further below.

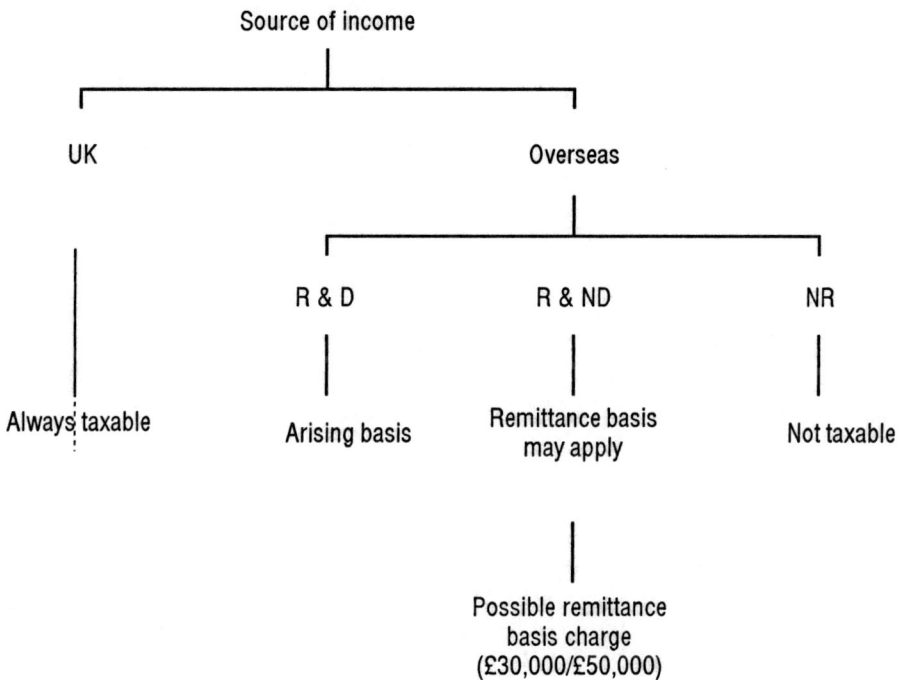

2.1.2 What is overseas income?

Overseas income is income arising outside the UK and includes:

(a) **Interest** from foreign savings accounts
(b) **Dividends** from overseas companies
(c) **Rent** from property abroad,
(d) Foreign **pension** income, and
(e) **Employment income** from working overseas.

Anyone who fails to declare all their overseas income and gains faces a penalty of up to 200% of the tax due (see later in this Text).

2.1.3 Basis of taxation

2.1.3.1 Arising basis

For UK residents, tax is chargeable on 'the full amount of the income arising' in the tax year, that is, regardless of whether the income has been or will be received in the UK.

2.1.3.2 Remittance basis

UK residents who are **not UK domiciled may be taxable on the remittance basis,** ie only when they bring the income into the UK (see further below).

2.2 Taxation of property income

2.2.1 UK property income

Income from UK property is always taxable in the UK, regardless of the residence position of the recipient landlord. It can never be 'disregarded' income (see below).

A **UK property loss cannot be set against overseas rental income**, or *vice versa*.

The rules for the Non Resident Landlord Scheme (NRLS) were covered earlier in this Text.

2.2.2 Overseas property income

As a UK resident is taxable on his worldwide income he is taxable on any income arising from land or property situated overseas. The taxable overseas property income is calculated using the same rules as for UK property income (see earlier in this Text). **The furnished holiday lettings rules apply to qualifying properties situated in the EEA.**

Where the landlord is **not UK domiciled the remittance basis may apply** (see below).

All income arising to one landlord from overseas property, even if in different countries, is treated as derived from a **single business** which is **separate and distinct from any UK property income.** In addition, **furnished holiday lettings income from EEA properties must be kept separate from other overseas property** income.

Therefore, there is no possibility of obtaining relief for a UK property loss against overseas rental income, or *vice versa*.

Losses arising from the letting of overseas property may be used in the same way as for a UK property business, ie carried forward for offset against future overseas property business profits.

If the landlord is **not resident** in the UK there is **no UK tax liability** in respect of **overseas** property income.

2.3 Taxation of interest and dividend income

2.3.1 UK interest and dividends

A non-UK resident's tax liability is limited to the income tax deducted from 'disregarded income' or the tax credit it carries. [s.811 ITA 2007]

'Disregarded income' includes UK savings and dividend income but does not include trading, employment or rental income.

Bank and building society interest can be received gross (and so will have no UK tax liability) if the recipient is not resident in the UK (for the whole tax year).

Interest that arises on UK government 'Free of Tax to Residents Abroad' (FOTRA) securities (ie UK Treasury Stock) is not taxable if received by an individual who is not resident in the UK.

If income tax is limited in this way the **personal and married couples' allowances are not available.** If the level of income that cannot be disregarded is high, it may be more tax efficient for the individual to claim personal allowances and include their entire UK income in their tax computation.

UK businesses and public bodies are required to provide details of payments of interest and other savings income to residents of EU member states. [EU directive 2003/48/EC]

2.3.2 Overseas interest and dividends

Overseas interest (whether bank interest or interest from securities) and dividends are taxed on a UK resident on an **arising basis as either savings or dividend income, unless the remittance basis applies** (ie he is not UK domiciled) in which case they are taxed as **non savings income**, ie at 20%, 40% and 45% and only when they are remitted to the UK.

Dividends from overseas companies which are taxed on the arising basis are taxed in a similar way to UK dividends, ie at 10% in the basic rate band and at the higher and additional rates of 32.5% and 37.5% respectively.

A 10% non-refundable tax credit is available to individuals receiving dividends from non UK resident companies if the overseas country is a 'qualifying territory' (ie has a double taxation agreement with the UK that contains a non-discrimination provision). [ss.397A & 397AA]

The gross amount of foreign dividend received in the UK (ie including any foreign tax) must be included in the UK income tax computation, grossed up at 100/90 (see further below). This applies whether the dividends are taxed on an arising basis or on the remittance basis.

Example 3

During 2013/14 Steve receives dividends of £27,540 from his holding in Boke Inc, a company resident in the United States. The dividend is paid net of 15% withholding tax. The USA is a qualifying territory for UK tax purposes.

What is the taxable dividend that Steve must include in his income tax computation?

2.3.3 Summary

The following is a summary of the tax treatment of UK and overseas investment income (including property income):

Residence and domicile status	Investment income	
	UK income	Overseas income
R, D	Arising basis	Arising basis
R, ND	Arising basis	Possible remittance basis
NR (D or ND)	Arising basis – limited to tax deducted at source if disregarded income (see above)	Not taxable

2.4 Taxation of pension income

2.4.1 UK pension income

Anyone in receipt of a UK pension is taxable on that income. If it is also taxed in another country, **double taxation relief** may be available (see below).

2.4.2 Overseas pension income

Foreign pension income is taxable on UK residents. However, **only 90% of the amount arising is taxed if the individual is taxed on an arising basis** (and not the remittance basis). The full amount of the pension remitted to the UK is taxable if the individual is taxed on the remittance basis. [s.575(2) ITEPA 2003]

2.5 Taxation of employment income

2.5.1 Basis of tax charge

The taxation of employment income is **different from the taxation rules that apply to other types of income** (above).

Tax is charged on employment income depending on:

(a) **Where the duties are performed**

(b) **The residence and domicile status of the employee**, and

(c) In some cases, the **residency of the employer.**

As a general rule, **earnings from duties performed in the UK are taxable in the UK and UK residents are taxed on all their earnings wherever their duties are performed.** However there are also additional rules for specific circumstances which are covered below.

2.5.2 UK resident and domiciled employee

If the employee is **resident and domiciled in the UK for the entire tax year** then **all his earnings are taxable**, wherever the duties are performed. However, if he can **split the tax year** (see above), any **earnings relating to the overseas part of that year,** as determined on a 'just and reasonable' basis, are **not taxable unless they relate to duties performed in the UK.** [s.15 ITEPA 2003]

2.5.3 Non-UK resident employee

If the employee is not resident then only earnings for UK duties are taxable, on an arising basis. [s.27 ITEPA 2003]

2.5.4 UK resident but not UK domiciled

This section is new

If the employee is resident but not domiciled in the UK:

(a) His **UK earnings** are **taxable on an arising basis**, and

(b) His income from **overseas duties** may be **taxable on the remittance basis** if either:

  (i) He has been **non-resident for any three consecutive years out of the previous five tax years** [ss.26 & 26A ITEPA 2003]

  (ii) Or the earnings are 'chargeable overseas earnings', ie: [ss.22 & 23 ITEPA 2003]

   • The **duties** of the employment are performed **wholly outside of the UK,** *and*
   • The **employer is based outside the UK**.

If **split year treatment** applies, the amount of foreign earnings taxable on the remittance basis is the amount **attributable to the UK resident part of the year**, as determined on a 'just and reasonable' basis; the amount attributable to the non-UK resident part of the year is not taxable in the UK.

If the employee **does not satisfy either (i) or (ii) above** then his income from overseas duties are **fully taxable in the UK** on an arising basis.

Illustration 4

In 2013/14 Serge is UK resident but not UK domiciled. He claims to use the remittance basis.

During the year he has earnings in respect of his UK duties of £140,000, which his German employer pays into a UK bank account, and earnings in respect of duties performed wholly outside the UK of £65,000, which are paid into his overseas bank account. He does not remit any of the foreign earnings of £65,000 to the UK.

His earnings of £140,000, for duties performed in the UK, are taxable on an arising basis.

Assuming his UK residency status over the past few years has been as follows he will only be taxable on his foreign earnings of £65,000 when he remits them to the UK:

2008/09 – Not resident
2009/10 – Not resident
2010/11 – Not resident
2011/12 – UK resident
2012/13 – Not resident
2013/14 – UK resident

This is because he has been non-resident for three consecutive years (2008/09 – 2010/11) in the five years before the 2013/14 tax year.

If he had not satisfied this three-year non-residency period, his foreign earnings would still be taxable on the remittance basis as they are chargeable overseas earnings ie duties are performed wholly outside the UK, and he has a non-UK employer.

If split year treatment applies in 2013/14, only the foreign earnings attributable to the UK resident part of the year, if any, would be taxable.

2.5.5 Practical application of the rules

Consider the case of someone leaving the UK to work abroad:

(a)   If the taxpayer becomes non-resident for the period of the contract there is then no question of UK tax arising on the overseas income. If the taxpayer has UK income, he may set his UK personal allowances against it.

(b)   If the individual remains resident in the UK he is taxable on his worldwide earnings, unless he is non-UK domiciled, has 'chargeable overseas earnings' and has claimed the remittance basis.

2.5.6 Income tax exemption for migrant workers

A non-UK domiciled individual with UK employment is **exempt from UK income tax** if his **foreign taxed earnings do not exceed £10,000, his other foreign taxed income does not exceed £100, he has no higher-rate liability, and he does not complete a self assessment tax return.** [s.828A ITA 2007]

2.5.7 Expenses for overseas employment duties

2.5.7.1 Introduction

As we have already seen, the cost of travelling to the site at which the duties of an employment are to be performed is not normally a deductible expense. However, there are a number of special provisions granting relief where foreign travel is involved. We consider first the position of UK employees going to work abroad.

2.5.7.2 UK employees working overseas

An individual who is **resident in the UK** is entitled to a **tax deduction** for the following expenses:

(a)   Where the duties of employment are **performed wholly outside the UK:**

(i)   The **cost of travelling to and returning from an overseas location.** This applies whether the employee bears the costs or they are reimbursed by the employer. [s.341 ITEPA 2003]

(ii)   **Board and lodging outside the UK where the cost is borne by the employer** (either directly or by reimbursement if incurred initially by the employee). No deduction is allowed if the employee bears the cost himself. [s.376 ITEPA 2003]

(b)   Where the duties of employment are **performed partly outside the UK a deduction is available for the cost of travelling to and returning from an overseas location provided the overseas duties can only be performed outside of the UK.** No deduction is allowed if the employee bears the cost himself. [s.370 ITEPA 2003]

A tax deduction is also available for the cost of certain journeys by the employee's spouse/civil partner and any minor (aged under 18) children, but only where the employee's period of absence from the UK is **at least 60 continuous days.** A deduction is available for: [s.371 ITEPA 2003]

(i)   The **cost of the return journey, where the spouse/partner and/or children accompany the employee when he first leaves the UK**

(ii)   The travel costs of visiting the employee during his time abroad.

The relief is a **deduction against the employee's earnings** and therefore **only applies where the costs are paid by the employer, and is restricted to the cost of up to two outward and two return journeys by the same person in a tax year.** This relief does **not** extend to other costs incurred in connection with the visit, eg additional accommodation.

Remember also, from earlier in this Text, that the **reimbursement of incidental overnight expenses** (eg laundry, newspapers, telephone calls home) **of up to £10 per night** whilst working abroad and overseas medical expenses are **exempt benefits** (see earlier in this Text).

2.5.8 Travelling expenses of employees coming to the UK

2.5.8.1 Introduction

Special relief for travelling expenses is available to **individuals who are not domiciled in the UK but who come to the UK to carry out the duties of their office or employment.**

The **relief is only available for a limited time period and provided certain conditions are met** (see below).

2.5.8.2 Allowable expenses

The allowable expenses mirror quite closely those available to UK employees going overseas, described above. The following expenses are **deductible from employment income received for the UK duties:**

(a)   The **cost of travelling from the employee's usual home overseas to the UK and returning home** at the end of his UK duties, and [s.373 ITEPA 2003]

(b)   Where the **employee remains in the UK for at least 60 continuous days, the cost of return journeys by his spouse/civil partner and minor children**, either accompanying him on his arrival or visiting him subsequently. As before, visits are limited to two inward and two return journeys by the same person in any one tax year. [s.374 ITEPA 2003]

The **above expenses must be borne by the employer**, either directly or by reimbursement as the deduction is only available against the amount of taxable income arising as a result of the provision or reimbursement of the travel expenses.

2.5.8.3 Conditions

Relief is only available for the above **expenses incurred during the five year period**, commencing with the date the employee arrives in the UK, and provided the employee was either:

(a)   Not resident in the UK in either of the two tax years preceding that in which the date of arrival falls, or
(b)   Not physically present in the UK at any time during the two years immediately before the date of arrival.

If a non-domiciled employee's removal expenses are reimbursed by his employer, up to £8,000 is exempt (ie not a taxable benefit).

Example 4

Roger is employed as a systems analyst by a UK merchant bank. He is offered a four month secondment, from 1 October 2013 to 31 January 2014, under a separate contract with the company's US subsidiary. All of his duties under this contract will be performed outside the UK.

The agreed salary under the US contract is £8,000, plus reimbursement of Roger's return fare to the US company's Boston office from the UK. The US company will also meet Roger's hotel bill and reimburse certain incidental expenses.

Roger is domiciled and resident in the UK.

During the course of the contract, Roger's hotel bill amounts to £6,500, in respect of his room and meals, and £500 in respect of various incidental expenses, eg telephone calls and newspapers. The bill is entirely met by the employer.

The following travel expenses are reimbursed to Roger:

	£
Return air fare: London – New York	600
Transfer between airport and hotel	50
	650

What are Roger's taxable earnings after any allowable deductions for UK tax purposes from the US contract?

3 Remittance basis

3.1 Availability of the remittance basis

The remittance basis for overseas income, which allows such income to be **taxed only when the taxpayer brings it into the UK,** is only available to individuals who are **not UK domiciled.**

3.2 Automatic application of the remittance basis

A non-UK domiciled individual is automatically taxed on the remittance basis where:

(a)   He has **unremitted income and gains below £2,000** (provided he is not exempt under s.282A – see above), or [s.809D ITA 2007]

(b)   He: [s.809E ITA 2007]

   (i)   **Has either no UK income or gains, or only has taxed UK investment income of £100 or less**

   (ii)   **Makes no remittances** of foreign income or gains during the tax year, and

   (iii)   **Either**

   –   **Has been resident in the UK for not more than six out of the last nine years,** or
   –   **Is under 18 throughout the year.**

The individual does not need to make a claim or submit a self assessment tax return to be able to use the remittance basis. He must, however, notify HMRC if he wishes the arising basis to apply instead. [ss.809D(1B) & 809E(1) ITA 2007]

3.3 Claiming to use the remittance basis

In all other cases, a non-UK domiciled individual must make a claim to use the remittance basis and is known **as a 'remittance basis user' (RBU).**

RBUs do not receive the personal or blind person's allowance, or the married couple's allowance tax reduction.

A claim must be made each year that the individual wishes to be taxed on the remittance basis. If the individual does not make a claim, the arising basis applies to their foreign income.

3.4 Additional remittance basis charge

3.4.1 General principles

Where an individual makes a remittance basis claim (ie is a RBU), he must also pay an additional tax charge for **every** year he chooses to be taxed on the remittance basis if he:

(a)   Is **over the age of 18**, *and*
(b)   Has been **resident in the UK for at least seven out of the last nine tax years**.

The basic 'remittance basis charge' (RBC) is £30,000 and is in addition to the tax due on remitted income (and gains).

Individuals who have been UK **resident for at least 12 years out of the previous 14 tax years** must pay a **higher RBC of £50,000 per year**.

3.4.2 Nominated income

A remittance basis user must 'nominate' unremitted offshore income (or gains), which is effectively subject to UK tax in the year on an arising basis, to create the £30,000 or £50,000 remittance basis charge.

Nominated income and gains are not taxed again when they are remitted to the UK.

Example 5

Sophia, age 32, has been UK resident for the last 15 years, but is not UK domiciled. She receives overseas bank interest of £250,000 (gross) during the tax year but only remits £60,000 to the UK. She has no other unremitted income or gains and makes a remittance basis claim for the year. She is a higher rate taxpayer.

You are required to calculate Sophia's income tax liability. Ignore double tax relief.

3.4.3 Tax planning issues

If, in a particular year, it would be more beneficial for the individual to pay tax on their worldwide income and gains than to pay the RBC, he **may choose not to claim the remittance basis**.

3.5 Temporary non-residents

Where a **temporarily non-resident individual (see above) is taxed on the remittance basis** (see below) and **remits income during a period that he is non-resident**, that income is **taxable in the tax year that they return**. [s.832A].

Illustration 5

Damien left the UK to become resident overseas on 12 May 2011 and HMRC confirmed his residence status as 'not resident'. He had been UK resident for the previous ten years but was non-UK domiciled.

During 2013/14 he made a remittance of £10,000 of foreign income, which had arisen in 2010/11 but was not taxed in that year as Damien had claimed the remittance basis. Damien was not resident when the income was remitted to the UK, so it would also not have been taxed during 2013/14.

Damien returned to the UK on 4 June 2015.

As he had been resident for at least four out of the seven years before his departure and returned to the UK within five years he is treated as only temporarily non-resident. He is therefore taxable on the remitted income in the tax year that he returns to the UK, ie in 2015/16.

3.6 When is income remitted to the UK?

An 'actual' remittance takes place where actual monies are brought into the UK. Remittances of capital are not taxed as income. For this reason it is essential that RBUs keep foreign income and capital in separate bank accounts, and remit only from the capital account.

Foreign income (or gains) are **remitted** to the UK if:

(a)   They are **brought to, or received in or used in** the UK. This includes buying assets outside the UK with untaxed foreign money and bringing them into the UK. There is an exemption for certain items such as personal effects (eg jewellery) and assets that are only in the UK to be repaired. [809X ITA 2007]

(b)   A **service is provided in the UK which is paid for overseas using foreign income** (or gains).

(c)   They are **used overseas in respect of a 'relevant debt' in the UK**, ie a debt that relates to property brought to or used in the UK, or a service provided in the UK, for example, paying loan interest, whether inside or outside the UK, on an overseas mortgage taken out to purchase a residential UK property.

There may also be a remittance where an asset is received or used in the UK and it **derives from foreign income** (or gains). For example if an individual purchases an asset overseas using untaxed foreign money, and gives that asset to his spouse, who then brings that asset to the UK, it is regarded as derived from the individual's foreign income and he is treated as having made a taxable remittance.

3.7 Remittance basis exemptions and reliefs

3.7.1 Money paid directly to HMRC

Funds remitted to the UK, directly to HMRC, to pay the remittance basis charge (RBC – see above) **are treated as if they had not been remitted to the UK.** [s.809V(1) ITA 2007]

The amount remitted often includes an **amount in respect of the liability relating to the following year's RBC** (**'payments on account'** – see later in this Text). **If the individual chooses not to be taxed on the remittance basis in the following year** and receives a refund of the amount paid in advance this is usually **treated as a remittance.** However, the refunded amount is not treated as a remittance if he **takes funds offshore** equal to the 'relevant amount' by **15 March following the end of the tax year for which the payments on account were made** ('tax year two'). [s.809UA ITA 2007]

The **relevant amount** is the **lower** of:

(a)   The **amount of foreign income and gains used to make payments on account**, and
(b)   The **RBC** that the individual paid in the original tax year.

The individual must **complete a tax return for tax year two**, and make a **claim for the amounts not to be treated as a remittance by 5 April** following the end of tax year two. [s.809UA(3) ITA 2007]

Remittances of foreign income or gains to pay **any other UK tax liability**, eg income tax on remitted amounts, are **chargeable to UK tax as remitted income or gains of the tax year in which the tax is paid to HMRC.**

3.7.2 Exempt property

The following **transactions involving 'exempt property' are not treated as remittances:** [s.809X ITA 2007]

(a)   Bringing any property into the UK for **public display** at an **approved establishment,** such as a gallery or museum, or in transit to or from such display, for **no more than two years** [ss.809Z & 809Z1 ITA 2007]

(b)   Bringing clothing, footwear, jewellery, and watches into the UK for **personal use** [s.809Z2 ITA 2007]

(c)   Bringing any property to the UK for **repair** [s.809Z3 ITA 2007]

(d)   Bringing property into the UK **temporarily,** ie for **no longer than 275 days** [s.809Z4 ITA 2007]

(e)   Where the **notional amount remitted** (ie by bringing items of property, other than money, that derive from foreign income or foreign chargeable gains into the UK) is **less than £1,000** per item. [s.809Z5 ITA 2007]

If any of the above items of **exempt property is sold, or the conditions for exemption no longer apply, it is treated as being remitted at that time.** [s.809Y ITA 2007]

3.7.3 Reliefs

3.7.3.1 Business investment relief

Where an individual brings **overseas income or gains** into the UK to make a **'qualifying investment',** ie in an unquoted trading company (including AIM-listed companies and those that undertake commercial property development or letting) he can make a **claim so that the transaction is not treated as a remittance.** [s.809VA ITA 2007]

The foreign income or gains **must be invested within 45 days of being remitted** to the UK and, **once the invested funds are encashed, they must be** removed **from the UK within 45 days or reinvested in another qualifying investment.**

3.7.3.2 Sale of exempt property

If the individual **sells exempt property** (see above) there is **no remittance,** provided the individual receives the **entire proceeds of sale by the first anniversary of 5 January following the tax year in which the property is sold,** and takes the **sale proceeds offshore within 45 days of receipt.** [s.809YA ITA 2007]

3.7.3.3 Loss, theft or destruction of exempt property

This section is new

From 6 April 2013, the **loss, theft or destruction of exempt property no longer triggers a taxable remittance.** [s.809Y(4A) ITA 2007]

In addition, the **receipt of any compensation (ie insurance) payment** in connection with exempt property is **not a remittance provided the payment is taken offshore, or used to make a qualifying investment, within 45 days** of receipt. [s.809YF ITA 2007]

If **temporarily imported property, or property that was brought to the UK for public display,** has been **lost or stolen, and is subsequently recovered,** there is **no taxable remittance** so long as the **item is taken offshore within 45 days.** [s.809Z4(3B) ITA 2007]

4 Personal allowances

4.1 Allowances for non-UK residents

In general, non-UK residents are liable to tax on income arising in the UK, but are not entitled to allowances. However, certain people are entitled to allowances despite being non-resident. These are:

(a)   Individuals resident in the Isle of Man or the Channel Islands
(b)   Former residents who have left the country for their own or a family member's health reasons
(c)   Current or former Crown servants and their widows or widowers
(d)   Employees in the service of any territory under Her Majesty's protection
(e)   Missionaries
(f)   European Economic Area (EEA) nationals. [s.56 ITA 2007]

Commonwealth citizens qualify for a personal allowance if broadly they are already entitled to them under one of the categories listed above. [Sch 1 FA 2009]

The EEA covers Austria, Belgium, Bulgaria, Croatia, Cyprus, Czech Republic, Denmark, Estonia, Finland, France, Germany, Greece, Hungary, Iceland, Ireland (Eire), Italy, Latvia, Liechtenstein, Lithuania, Luxembourg, Malta, Netherlands, Norway, Poland, Portugal, Romania, Slovakia, Slovenia, Spain and Sweden as well as the United Kingdom.

Non-residents who can claim personal allowances may use them against any income chargeable to UK tax.

4.2 Allowances for remittance basis users

If a non-UK domiciled individual **claims the remittance basis** for his income, he is **not entitled to a personal allowance or to the married couples' allowance**. Individuals to whom the remittance basis automatically applies (see above) do not lose these allowances (see above).

5 Double taxation relief (DTR)

5.1 Introduction

As we have seen, **UK tax applies to the worldwide income of UK residents and the UK income of non-residents**.

When other countries adopt the same approach it is clear that some **income may be taxed twice**:

(a)   **Firstly in the country where it arises**
(b)   **Secondly in the country where the taxpayer is resident.**

Double taxation relief (DTR) may avoid the problem, or at least diminish its impact.

5.2 Double taxation agreements

Typical provisions of double taxation agreements based on the OECD Model Agreement are as follows:

(a)   **Total exemption** from tax is given in the country where income arises in the hands of, for example:

    (i)   Visiting diplomats
    (ii)   Teachers on exchange programmes

(b)   **Preferential rates of withholding tax** are applied to, for example, payments of rent, interest and dividends. The usual rate is frequently replaced by 15% or less

(c)   DTR is given to taxpayers in their country of residence by way of a **credit for tax suffered in the country where income arises**

(d)   There are **exchange of information clauses** so that tax evaders can be chased internationally

(e)   There are rules to determine a person's residence and to prevent dual residence (tie-breaker clauses)

(f)   There are clauses which render certain profits taxable in only one rather than both of the contracting states

(g)   There is a non-discrimination clause so that a country does not tax foreigners more heavily than its own nationals.

5.3 Unilateral relief

If no relief is available under a double taxation agreement, UK legislation provides for **unilateral (ie one way) relief**. This is also known as credit relief.

Foreign income must be included **gross (ie inclusive of foreign tax) in the UK tax computation**. A deduction is then available for the **lower of**:

(a) The **UK** tax
(b) The **foreign** tax.

The maximum double taxation relief (DTR) available for **overseas dividends** is **limited to the UK tax paid less the dividend tax credit**, ie for a higher rate taxpayer in 2013/14 the maximum DTR is 22.5% of the gross dividends and for an additional rate taxpayer is 27.5%.

Example 6

Tim, a UK resident higher rate taxpayer, received a dividend of £14,400 from Haki Inc, a USA resident company during 2013/14. The dividend was paid net of 20% withholding tax. The USA is a qualifying territory for UK tax purposes.

You are required to calculate Tim's higher rate tax liability, after DTR, in respect of the dividend.

The UK tax on the foreign income is the difference between:

(a) The UK tax before DTR on all income including the foreign income
(b) The UK tax on all income except the foreign income.

In both (a) and (b), we take account of tax reductions.

Example 7

Jane is resident and domiciled in the UK. She has the following income for 2013/14:

	£
UK salary	37,352
Interest on foreign debenture (net of foreign tax at 5%)	5,700
Foreign rents (net of foreign tax at 60%)	1,500

Assuming that maximum DTR is claimed, show her UK tax liability.

Exam focus point

Examiner's report – Personal Taxation

November 2010 – Part I SFQ 3

This question was well answered with the exception of the unilateral tax relief available on the overseas income. Very few candidates were able to properly apply this relatively straightforward method of double tax relief.

5.4 Expense relief

Where there is no point in claiming credit relief as above, perhaps because trading losses have eliminated any liability to UK tax, **the taxpayer may elect for expense relief instead**. No credit is given against the UK tax liability for foreign tax suffered, instead only the income *after* foreign taxes is brought into the tax computation.

5.5 Other matters

If foreign taxes are **not relieved** in the year in which the income is taxable in the UK, there is **no relief for the unused amount** in any earlier or later year.

Credit relief, whether under a treaty or unilateral, is **ignored** when working out the tax which remains to be reduced by tax reductions.

Taxpayers who have claimed relief against their UK tax bill for taxes paid abroad must notify HMRC in writing of any changes to the foreign liabilities if these changes result in the DTR claimed becoming excessive. This rule applies to all taxes not just income tax.

Exam focus point

Examiner's report – Personal Taxation (old syllabus)

May 2000 – Question 5

This was the least popular question to answer, and although there were a few good answers, the majority were confused over the difference living abroad would make to the UK tax liability of Mr and Mrs Little. Very few explained the basis of determining the UK residence status of an individual or the taxation of rental income for an overseas landlord. Most candidates explained the position regarding personal allowances correctly, and the taxation of foreign income on returning to the UK.

However, several candidates wasted time explaining the potential capital gains tax liability on the rental properties when this was not required by the question.

Chapter roundup

- An individual's residence status is determined using the statutory residence test.

- Usually an individual is resident or not resident for a complete tax year, but HMRC will split a tax year in certain circumstances.

- Domicile indicates one's permanent home:

    - *Domicile of origin:* usually an individual's father's domicile is his first domicile.

    - *Domicile of dependence:* a minor child (< 16) changes his domicile if the person on whom he is dependent (usually his father) changes his domicile.

    - *Domicile of choice:* an adult can change his domicile if he severs ties with his previous country and settles in another country. This can be difficult to establish.

- An individual who is UK resident and UK domiciled is liable to UK income tax on his worldwide income (ie UK and overseas) on an arising basis.

- A UK resident individual who is not UK domiciled is liable to UK income tax on:

    - UK income – arising basis

    - Overseas income – arising basis unless claims remittance basis (or it applies automatically)

- An individual who is not UK resident is only liable to UK income tax on income arising in the UK.

- There is no further tax liability on interest and dividend income for a non resident, as it is restricted to the amount of the tax credit. If UK interest is paid gross to a non resident, it is tax free.

- Income from UK property is always taxable in the UK, even on landlords who are not UK resident.

- UK residents are taxed on income from property situated overseas. Overseas property income is calculated using the same rules as for UK property income. Losses on UK property income cannot be set against profit on overseas property income or vice versa.

- An individual who is UK resident and UK domiciled is liable to UK income tax on all his employment income (UK and overseas) on an arising basis.

- An individual who is UK resident but not UK domiciled is liable to UK income tax on all his employment income unless he satisfies certain conditions and claims the remittance basis for his overseas earnings.

- Special relief is available for certain expenses of both UK individuals working abroad and also overseas individuals working in the UK.

- An individual claiming the remittance basis who is over 18 *and* who has been UK resident in seven out of the previous nine tax years is subject to a £30,000 additional tax charge. The charge increases to £50,000 for individuals who have been UK resident for at least 12 out of the previous 14 tax years.

- Certain non-UK resident individuals may be entitled to receive UK personal allowances.

- Double tax relief (DTR) is available where income is taxed both in the UK and in another country.

Quiz

1. Meredith, age 37, is domiciled in the United States of America, but has been resident in the UK since 2010. To what extent is Meredith charged to UK income tax on rental income from letting a property in New York?

2. Hector, who is resident and domiciled in the UK, receives a pension of £8,000 per annum from his former employer, a Canadian company based in Montreal. Hector used to work in Montreal.

    To what extent is Hector charged to UK income tax on the pension?

3. Outline the circumstances in which the remittance basis applies automatically.

4. Henri has been resident in the UK since 2000/01. He is not UK domiciled. The majority of his income, £80,000 of gross interest income, arises outside the UK, which he does not bring into the UK. He earns £60,000 from his UK employment.

    Should Henri make a claim for the remittance basis for 2013/14 (ignore DTR)?

1.   Meredith can make a claim to use the remittance basis so that she is only taxed on rental income she remits to the UK. She will not need to pay the additional annual remittance basis charge in 2013/14 as Meredith has not been resident in the UK for at least seven out of the nine previous years.

2.   Hector is taxed on an arising basis, but only on 90% (ie £7,200) of the amount.

3.   The remittance basis applies automatically if the individual has unremitted foreign income and gains below £2,000.

      It also applies automatically if the individual's only UK income is £100 or less of taxed investment income, he does not remit any foreign income or gains during the tax year, *and* he has been UK resident for less than seven out of the last nine years (or is under the age of 18 throughout the year).

4.   As Henri has been resident in the UK for at least 12 out of the last 14 tax years, he must pay the higher £50,000 remittance basis charge if he claims to use the remittance basis.

      His tax liability without the claim would be £49,598 (W1), while his tax liability making the claim would be £67,598 (W2).

      Therefore it is not beneficial for him to make the claim.

      Workings

      (1)   *Arising basis*

	Non savings £	Savings £
Salary	60,000	
Overseas interest		80,000
Net income	60,000	80,000
Less personal allowance (no PA as income > £118,880)	(Nil)	
Taxable income	60,000	80,000
Tax:		
£32,010 × 20%		6,402
£27,990 × 40%		11,196
£80,000 × 40%		32,000
Tax liability		49,598

      (2)   *Remittance basis*

	Non savings £
Salary	60,000
Net income	60,000
Less personal allowance (no PA as claiming remittance basis)	(Nil)
Taxable income	60,000
Tax	
£32,010 × 20%	6,402
£27,990 × 40%	11,196
Add remittance basis charge	50,000
Tax liability	67,598

Solution to Example 1

Sierra does not meet any of the automatic overseas tests in 2013/14, as she has not previously been resident in the UK and spends more than 46 days in the UK in 2013/14. So we must look at the automatic UK tests.

As there is a period of 91 consecutive days, falling partly within the 2013/14 tax year (the period starting on 14 February 2014) when she has a home in the UK and no home overseas and she is present in that UK home during 2013/14 on at least 30 days, Sierra is resident under the second automatic UK test for 2013/14.

Solution to Example 2

Rick is a 'leaver' for the SRT, so he requires at least four ties to be treated as UK resident as he has been present for between 16 and 45 days. As he only has three ties under the sufficient ties test he will, at first glance, be non-resident under the SRT.

However, as he was resident in the previous tax year, has at least three ties under the sufficient ties test, and been present in the UK on more than 30 'qualifying days', he must apply the deeming rule.

Rick has a total of 62 days in the UK (ie 35 when he was present at midnight and 27 (ie 57 – 30) qualifying days).

As he has now been present for between 46 and 90 days, he only requires three UK ties so will be resident under the sufficient ties test.

Solution to Example 3

	£
Gross foreign dividend: £27,540 × 100/85	32,400
Add: UK tax credit £32,400 × 10/90	3,600
Taxable foreign dividend (ie £27,540 × 100/85 × 100/90)	36,000

Solution to Example 4

The earnings from the US contract are computed as follows:

	£	£
Salary		8,000
Expenses borne by US company (£500 < £10 per night ∴ exempt)		6,500
Reimbursed travel expenses		650
		15,150
Less: claim under s.341 & s.376 ITEPA 2003		
– travel expenses	650	
– board and lodging	6,500	
		(7,150)
Net earnings		8,000

Solution to Example 5

Sophia is taxable on the remitted income as she has made a remittance basis claim. In addition, as she is over 18 and has been resident in the UK for at least 12 out of the last 14 years she is also subject to the higher £50,000 remittance basis charge.

She does not receive the personal allowance because she is a remittance basis user (although she would not have been eligible for the PA as her income, on an arising basis, would have exceeded £118,880).

Her liability is:

	£
Tax on remitted income: £60,000 × 40%	24,000
Add: remittance basis charge	50,000
Total income tax due	74,000

Sophia must also nominate £125,000 (£125,000 × 40% = £50,000) of the unremitted overseas bank interest to create the £50,000 remittance basis charge. This interest will not be taxed again when it is remitted to the UK.

Solution to Example 6

	£	£
Gross foreign dividend: £14,400 × 100/80	18,000	
Add: UK tax credit £18,000 × 10/90	2,000	
Taxable foreign dividend (ie £14,400 × 100/80 × 100/90)		20,000
Tax @ 32.5%		6,500
Less DTR – lower of:		
(i) Foreign tax: £18,000 × 20%	3,600	
(ii) UK tax: £6,500 − £2,000 (ie £20,000 × 22.5%)	4,500	
ie		(3,600)
Less 10% UK tax credit		(2,000)
Tax due		900

Solution to Example 7

	Non savings £	Savings £	Total £
Salary	37,352		
Overseas interest £5,700 × 100/95		6,000	
Overseas rents £1,500 × 100/40	3,750		
Net income	41,102	6,000	47,102
Less personal allowance	(9,440)		(9,440)
Taxable income	31,662	6,000	37,662

	£	£
Non-savings income		
£31,662 × 20%		6,332
Savings income		
£348 × 20%		70
£5,652 × 40%		2,261
Tax liability		8,663
Less: Double taxation relief:		
Rents (W)	1,500	
Interest (W)	300	
		(1,800)
Tax due		6,863

Working

Since the rents are taxed more highly overseas, these should be regarded as the top slice of UK taxable income. Taxable income excluding the rents is £33,912 and the UK tax on this is:

	£
£32,010 × 20%	6,402
£1,902 × 40%	761
Total	7,163

The UK tax on the rents is £1,500 (£8,663 − 7,163). Since foreign tax of £2,250 (60% of £3,750) is greater, the DTR is the smaller figure of £1,500.

Foreign interest was taxed abroad at the rate of 5% (£300). Since the UK rate is clearly higher (taxed at 20%) the DTR given is limited to £300.

Short Form Questions:

9.1 – 9.5 inclusive

Long Form Questions:

9.1	Ricardo Garcia
9.2	Paul Thomson

Personal Taxation

Part B:
Capital Gains Tax

The purpose of this chapter is to help you to:

- identify the basic charging provision and basis of assessment to CGT

- identify chargeable persons, occasions and assets

- identify exempt assets

- outline the rules for payment of CGT

- identify the overseas aspects of CGT

References: TCGA 1992 unless otherwise stated

1 The charge to tax

1.1 Basic charging provision

Capital gains tax (CGT) is charged on the total amount of chargeable gains made by a chargeable person in a tax year after deducting:

(a)   Any **allowable capital losses of the same tax year**, and

(b)   Any **allowable capital losses brought forward from earlier years**

Gains and losses of the same tax year are netted off. If gains exceed losses, there is a net chargeable gain for the tax year. If losses exceed gains, there is a net allowable loss (see later in this Text).

1.2 Basis of assessment

Individuals who are UK resident are liable to CGT on the disposal of assets situated anywhere in the world.

If an individual is **not UK resident** he is **not generally chargeable to UK CGT**.

An individual who is **not UK domiciled may be taxable on the remittance basis in respect of his foreign gains** (see below).

The concepts of residence and domicile have the same meaning as for income tax purposes (see earlier in this Text).

1.3 Annual exempt amount

Each individual is allowed to make an amount of gains each tax year that is not taxable. This 'annual exempt amount' is £10,900 for 2013/14. It is deducted from net chargeable gains to give the taxable gain for the tax year.

Non-UK domiciled individuals who claim to be taxed on a remittance basis are not entitled to an annual exempt amount.

1.4 Rates of CGT

Gains **are taxed as the 'top slice' of income.** If the gains fall **within the individual's basic rate band, after taking his income into account, they are taxed at 18%.** Gains falling above the **basic rate band are taxed at 28%.**

Example 1

Cheryl has taxable income of £22,010 in 2013/14.

She realises a gain on the sale of an asset in May 2013 of £15,000, and a further gain of £35,000 on a disposal in January 2014. Cheryl has no capital losses in 2013/14 or earlier years.

What is Cheryl's CGT position?

2 Chargeable persons, disposals and assets

2.1 Persons chargeable to CGT

The following are examples of **persons chargeable to CGT**:

(a)   Individuals
(b)   Partners (who are individually responsible for their share of partnership gains)
(c)   Trustees.

The following are examples of **persons exempt from CGT**:

(a)   Charities using gains for charitable purposes
(b)   Registered pension funds
(c)   Persons who are not resident in the UK.

2.2 Disposals chargeable to CGT

A **chargeable disposal** includes:

(a)   A **sale** of an asset or part of an asset

(b)   A **gift** of all or part of an asset

(c)   The **receipt of insurance proceeds** on the loss or destruction of an asset

A **chargeable disposal occurs on the date of contract**, which may in some circumstances differ from the date of actual transfer. Where the contract is conditional, the date of disposal is taken as the date on which the condition is satisfied. However, when a capital sum is received under (c) above, the disposal takes place on the day the sum is *received*.

Where a disposal involves an acquisition by someone else ((a) or (b) above), the date of acquisition for the recipient of the asset is the same as the date of disposal.

The following are not treated as disposals:

(a)   **Passing of assets on death** (the heirs inherit assets as if they bought them at death for their then market value ('probate value'), but there is no disposal for the deceased on the death)

(b)   Transfers of assets as security for a loan or mortgage.

Gifts to charities and housing associations are generally not chargeable to CGT.

Exam focus point

Examiner's report – Personal Taxation (old syllabus)

November 2004 – Question 5

This question was fairly popular but there were few good answers. Many candidates did not appear to know that the gift of an asset to the charity was not chargeable to capital gains tax and could be used as a deduction from income. Several stated that it would qualify for gift relief....

2.3 Assets chargeable to CGT

All forms of property, wherever in the world they are situated, are chargeable assets for CGT purposes unless they are specifically designated as non-chargeable in the legislation.

Gains on disposal of the following assets are **exempt**:

(a)   Motor vehicles (eg **cars**) suitable for private use

(b)   NS&I certificates, premium bonds and SAYE deposits

(c)   Foreign currency bank accounts [s.252]

(d)   **Foreign currency for private use** [s.269]

(e)   Betting and **lottery winnings**

(f)   **Medals** etc awarded for bravery (unless purchased)

(g)   **Damages** for personal or professional injury

(h)   **Life assurance policies** (exempt in the hands of the original beneficial owner)

(i)   Works of art, scientific collections etc provided they are of national importance and are given for national purposes (breach of any conditions imposed will nullify the CGT exemption)

(j)   **Principal (or main) private residence**

(k)   Gilt edged securities (ie **Treasury stock**) and **qualifying corporate bonds** (loan stock)

(l)   **Wasting chattels** (tangible movable property with a life of 50 years or less, eg a racehorse)

(m) **Debts** other than debts on a security

(n) **Pension** and annuity rights

(o) Investments held in an **individual savings account** (ISA)

(p) Certain **employee shareholder status** shares.

3 Administration of CGT

CGT is chargeable for tax years, like income tax. Any gains arising in the year from 6 April 2013 to 5 April 2014 are charged in 2013/14.

There is one payment of CGT due on 31 January after the end of the tax year, ie 31 January 2015 for 2013/14. There are no payments on account for CGT.

It may also be possible to **pay CGT in instalments** (see later in this Text).

Exam focus point

CGT is administered through the self assessment system alongside compliance for income tax. The self assessment system is covered in detail later in this Text.

---

4 The overseas aspects of CGT

4.1 Liability to CGT

Individuals are liable to CGT on the disposal of assets situated anywhere in the world if they are resident in the UK at any point in the year in which the gain is made.

Individuals who arrive in or leave the UK during the year may be able to **split the tax year** for CGT purposes, ie they are charged to CGT only in respect of disposals made after the date of arrival or before the date of departure.

4.2 Non-UK domiciled individuals

If a person is UK resident but is not UK domiciled, he may be able to use the remittance basis of taxation either automatically or by making a claim. Where a non UK domiciled individual makes a remittance basis claim it applies to both their foreign income and foreign gains. The remittance basis was covered in detail earlier in this Text.

If the remittance basis applies, the individual's gains on the disposal of assets located overseas (see below) are only chargeable to CGT when the gains are *remitted* (ie brought in) to the UK.

If a non-UK domiciled individual over the age of 18 makes a claim to use the remittance basis (ie it does not apply automatically) and he has been **UK resident for at least seven out of the previous nine tax years**, he must also pay the **£30,000 remittance basis charge (RBC)**. Once he has been **UK resident for at least 12 out of the last 14 tax years the charge increases to £50,000**. This is the RBC that we covered earlier in this Text and is not an additional charge specifically in relation to capital gains.

There are **special rules for capital losses** made by non-UK domiciled individuals. These are covered in the next chapter.

4.3 Non-UK resident individuals

Normally a disposal of assets situated in the UK is not a chargeable event if the vendor is not resident in the UK at the time of disposal. However, a liability to CGT may arise if the person is **carrying on a trade, profession or vocation in the UK through a permanent establishment** and an asset which has been used for the purpose of the permanent establishment is either disposed of or removed from the UK.

A charge will also arise if the UK trade, profession or vocation ceases. In this case, and in the case of removal of assets from the UK, there is a deemed disposal of assets at their market value.

Exam focus point

Examiner's report – Personal Taxation

May 2008 – Part I SFQ 6

... part (b) caused problems for a small minority of candidates who thought that all disposals of UK assets would be chargeable, irrespective of the residence of the taxpayer.

4.4 Temporary non-residents

Temporary non-residents may be taxable on gains realised whilst they are abroad on the same basis as they are for income (see earlier in this Text), **ie if:**

(a)   They **become non-resident,**

(b)   They were **UK resident for at least four out of the seven tax years (whether full or split years)** before the year of departure from the UK, and

(c)   They remain **non-resident for five or fewer complete calendar years.**

Net gains realised in the year of departure are taxed in that year unless the individual can split the tax year. This applies whether the absence is temporary or permanent.

Subsequent gains (or losses) arising on **disposals of assets owned before departure are chargeable (or allowable) in the tax year of return** as if they were gains/losses of that year. This also applies where the individual can split the tax year in the year of departure, such that gains arising in the overseas (NR) part are also taxed in the tax year of return.

Gains on assets acquired in the non-resident period are not included in the above charge nor are gains which are already chargeable because they arise on a permanent establishment's assets (see above).

Exam focus point

Examiner's report – Personal Taxation

November 2009 – Part I SFQ 6

Most candidates realised that this was a question about temporary non-residence although few picked up all the marks available; the points most often missed were that the rules only apply if resident for 4 or more of the 7 years prior to the year of departure and only to assets that had been acquired before leaving the UK.

4.5 Double taxation relief

If a gain on the disposal of an overseas asset is taxed both overseas and in the UK, double taxation relief (DTR) is available.

DTR applies in the same way as for income tax, ie relief is given for the lower of the UK and overseas tax.

An individual may deduct capital losses (see later in this Text) **and the annual exempt amount in a way that minimises his CGT liability.**

Example 2

Geraldine who is UK resident makes a gain on a UK asset of £30,000 in July 2013 and on a non-UK asset of £20,000 in October 2013. She paid foreign tax of £10,000 on the non-UK asset. She has taxable income of £16,370 in the year. Calculate the CGT payable.

4.6 Location of assets

For CGT purposes assets are **located** as follows:

(a)	**Immovable** property (eg a house)	–	where physically located
(b)	**Tangible movable** property (ie chattels)	–	where physically located at time of disposal
(c)	A **debt**	–	where the creditor is resident
(d)	**Government securities** (eg Treasury stock)	–	within country of that government
(e)	**Shares and securities**	–	in a UK incorporated company are located in the UK other shares/securities are located where registered
(f)	**Goodwill** of a business	–	where business is carried on
(g)	**Patents**	–	where registered

BPP
LEARNING MEDIA

- CGT is charged on 'chargeable gains' that arise when a 'chargeable person' makes a 'chargeable disposal' of a 'chargeable asset'.

- Individuals are entitled to an annual exempt amount for each tax year.

- The rate of CGT depends on the individual's taxable income. Any gains falling within any remaining basic rate band are taxed at 18%. Gains in excess of the basic rate band are taxed at 28%.

- A disposal occurs not only when there is a sale of an asset but also when there is a gift or a capital sum is received (eg insurance money received when an asset is damaged or destroyed).

- Certain assets, such as cars, are exempt from CGT.

- CGT is due on 31 January following the tax year. On certain occasions the CGT may be paid by instalments.

- CGT is charged on persons who are resident in the UK and persons only temporarily abroad. A tax year may be split into resident and non-resident parts.

- A UK resident person is chargeable to CGT on disposals of their worldwide assets.

- UK resident persons who are not UK domiciled may be able to use the remittance basis (either automatically or by making a claim) so that foreign gains are taxed only when they are remitted to the UK.

- Individuals who make a claim to use the remittance basis must also pay the £30,000 or £50,000 remittance basis charge on unremitted foreign income and gains if they are over 18 and have been UK resident for at least seven of the last nine tax years or 12 out of the last 14 tax years respectively.

- Double taxation relief may be available to reduce the tax liability when the same gain is taxed in two countries.

Quiz

1. Martha has chargeable gains (before deduction of the annual exempt amount) of £28,400, all arising from disposals that took place in August 2013. Calculate her CGT liability for 2013/14 assuming she has total income (before the personal allowance) of £41,100.

2. Which of the following constitute chargeable disposals for CGT?

   (a) A gift of shares
   (b) A sale of 2 acres of land out of a plot of 10 acres
   (c) The demolition of a building.

3. Which of the following are chargeable assets for CGT purposes?

   (a) Proceeds from backing the winner of the Grand National
   (b) Damages awarded in an action for libel
   (c) A diamond necklace
   (d) A vintage Rolls Royce.

4. By what date is CGT is due for 2013/14?

5. In which country are the following assets situated?
   (a) A villa in Portugal
   (b) Securities issued by the government of Italy, purchased through a UK agent
   (c) Shares in a company which is UK resident for tax purposes but which is incorporated in and has its share register maintained in Jersey, Channel Islands
   (d) A diamond necklace owned by a UK resident but which is kept in the vaults of a French bank.

1.

Martha – 2013/14	£
Chargeable gains	28,400
Less: annual exempt amount	(10,900)
Taxable gain	17,500
CGT:	
£32,010 – (£41,100 – £9,440) = £350 @ 18%	63
£17,500 – £350 = £17,150 @ 28%	4,802
Total CGT	4,865

2. All of them.

3. (c) only – (a), (b) and (d) are exempt assets.

4. 31 January 2015

5.
- (a) Portugal (where immovable property is physically located)
- (b) Italy (country of government issuing the securities)
- (c) Jersey (where company is registered)
- (d) France (where movable property is physically located)

Solutions to chapter examples

Solution to Example 1

	£
Chargeable gain £(15,000 + 35,000)	50,000
Less: Annual exempt amount	(10,900)
Taxable gain	39,100

CGT payable:
Basic rate band remaining = £32,010 – £22,010 = £10,000

	£
£10,000 @ 18%	1,800
£39,100 – £10,000 = £29,100 @ 28%	8,148
Total CGT	9,948

Solution to Example 2

	UK £	Non-UK £
Chargeable gain	30,000	20,000
Less: Annual exempt amount (Note)	(10,900)	
Taxable gain	19,100	20,000

CGT payable:
Basic rate band remaining = £32,010 – £16,370 = £15,640

	UK £	Non-UK £
£15,640 @ 18%	2,815	
£19,100 – £15,640 = £3,460 @ 28%	969	
£20,000 @ 28%		5,600
CGT	3,784	5,600
Less: DTR lower of:		
(i) UK tax: £5,600		
(ii) Overseas tax: £10,000		
ie		(5,600)
CGT due	3,784	

Note. It is beneficial to set the AEA against the UK gain to keep the UK tax on the overseas gain as high as possible and the UK tax on the UK gain as low as possible.

Now try the following questions

Short Form Questions:

10.1 – 10.5 inclusive

Long Form Questions:

10.1	Peter Jones
10.2	Simon James

11

Computing gains and losses

The purpose of this chapter is to help you to:

- set out the basic CGT computation
- understand how to set off capital losses
- use the valuation rules for specific assets (eg shares)
- identify connected persons and understand the consequences of transfers between them
- understand the value at which transfers take place between husband and wife/civil partners
- apply the part disposal rules
- understand the tax treatment of debts and loans

References: TCGA 1992 unless otherwise stated

1 Calculating a gain or loss

1.1 The CGT computation

A chargeable gain or allowable loss is calculated as follows:

	£
Disposal consideration (or market value)	X
Less: costs of disposal	(X)
Net proceeds	X
Less: allowable costs	(X)
Chargeable gain (allowable loss)	X/(X)

Exam focus point

In computational CGT questions, if an individual disposes of several assets in the tax year, you must calculate the gain/loss on each asset individually using the above proforma.

1.2 Disposal consideration

Normally, it is the actual consideration passing between the parties which is taken into account. However where the disposal is not a bargain at arm's length (ie a gift or sale between connected parties, see below) **the disposal is deemed to take place at market value.**

If the **proceeds are payable in instalments**, there is **one disposal for CGT**. The total amount receivable is the disposal proceeds figure in the gain calculation. It may be possible to **pay the tax due in instalments** (see later in this Text). [s.280]

1.3 Costs of disposal

These may include:

(a) Valuation fees
(b) Estate agency fees
(c) Advertising costs
(d) Legal costs

These costs are deducted from gross proceeds of sale.

Exam focus point

Examiner's report – Personal Taxation

November 2008 – Part I SFQ 10

Few candidates were able to gross up the disposal proceeds for the selling fees.

1.4 Other allowable costs

Allowable costs include:

(a) **Original cost of acquisition** (or market value at the date of acquisition where the disposal was not a bargain at arm's length)
(b) **Incidental costs of acquisition** (similar to costs of disposal)
(c) **Capital expenditure incurred in enhancing the asset** (see below).

1.5 Enhancement expenditure

Enhancement expenditure means capital expenditure which enhances the value of the asset and is *reflected in the state or nature of the asset at the time of disposal*. Certain costs are specifically excluded from this category as follows:

(a) Cost of repairs and maintenance
(b) Cost of insurance
(c) Any expenditure which is treated as a deduction for the purposes of income tax, and
(d) Any expenditure transferred out of public funds eg council grants.

Example 1

Fred bought an asset on 15 February 1986 for £5,000. Enhancement expenditure of £2,000 was incurred on 10 April 1987. Fred sold the asset for £20,500 on 20 December 2013. Incidental costs of sale were £500.

You are required to calculate his chargeable gain.

---

2 Capital losses

2.1 Current year losses

Losses arising in one tax year must be set against gains of that year, even where this takes the gain below the level of the annual exempt amount.

Example 2

George has chargeable gains for 2013/14 of £10,000 from a disposal in July 2013 and allowable losses of £6,000 from a disposal in December 2013. How will he take relief for the losses?

Example 3

Martin has chargeable gains of £15,000 arising from a disposal on 15 May 2013, further gains of £18,000 from a disposal on 28 October 2013 and allowable losses of £10,000 from a disposal on 16 April 2013. Show Martin's CGT liability for 2013/14 assuming he has taxable income of £50,000.

2.2 Losses carried forward

If current year losses exceed current year gains, the excess is automatically carried forward against the first net chargeable gains arising in a future year.

Brought forward losses are used only to the extent that they reduce chargeable gains down to the annual exempt amount. No set off is made if net chargeable gains for the current year do not exceed the annual exempt amount.

Example 4

Bob makes a gain of £11,800 on 25 June 2013. He has losses brought forward of £6,000. How will Bob take relief for these losses?

Example 5

Tom makes chargeable gains of £5,000 in September 2013 and has losses brought forward from 2012/13 of £4,000. How will Tom take relief for these losses?

2.3 Losses in the year of death

The *only* (examinable) time that an individual may carry *back* capital losses is on death. Losses (in excess of gains) arising in the tax year in which an individual dies can be carried back to the previous three tax years on a LIFO basis (ie most recent year first). Losses are utilised so as to reduce chargeable gains for each of the years to an amount equal to the annual exempt amount of that year.

This will result in a repayment of CGT that has already been paid.

Example 6

Joe dies on 1 January 2014. His chargeable gains and allowable losses for recent years, before taking account of annual exempt amounts, have been as follows:

		Gain /(Loss)	Annual Exempt Amount
		£	£
2013/14	Gains	2,100	10,900
	Losses	(12,000)	
2012/13	Gains	10,800	10,600
2011/12	Gains	7,200	10,600
2010/11	Gains	20,500	10,100

You are required to show how the losses arising in 2013/14 are utilised.

2.4 Share loss relief

Relief is available for losses arising on the disposal of shares in certain unquoted trading companies (broadly EIS type companies – see earlier in this Text). [s.131 ITA 2007]

The capital loss is computed as normal but is instead **deducted from the taxpayer's general income in**:

(a)   The tax year in which the disposal takes place, and/or
(b)   The previous tax year.

A **claim** must be made by the anniversary of 31 January following the end of the tax year of the loss, so by 31 January 2016 for a loss arising in 2013/14.

The taxpayer cannot choose the amount of loss to relieve, but can choose whether to set a loss first against the current year's income and then against the previous year's income, or the other way round.

Exam focus point

Examiner's report – Personal Taxation (old syllabus)

November 2004 – Question 5

Many failed to notice that the loss on the shares in Wonder Fabrications could be set against income which therefore meant that for many candidates the answer produced a capital gains tax liability.

2.5 Losses of non-UK domiciled individuals

A non-UK domiciled individual who does not need to make a claim to use the remittance basis (ie it applies automatically) or who chooses to be taxed on an arising basis, can **set capital losses from assets situated overseas ('overseas losses') against his gains, as normal**.

However, **if the individual has had to make a claim to use the remittance basis** (see earlier in this Text) he can only obtain relief for his overseas losses if he chooses to make an **irrevocable overseas losses election**. [s.16ZA]

The individual must make the election in the first year that he claims the remittance basis (even if he has no overseas gains or losses in that year). If he does not make the election none of his foreign losses are allowable losses for as long as he remains non-UK domiciled.

Where the election is made, capital losses (both UK and overseas) must be allocated in the following order:

(a)   Against **foreign chargeable gains** that are **remitted** to the UK, then
(b)   Against **foreign chargeable gains** that are **not remitted** to the UK, then
(c)   Against **UK chargeable gains.**

Only losses allocated under (a) and (c) are actually offset in the CGT computation. **Losses cannot be set against remitted foreign chargeable gains that accrued in an earlier year.** This is in line with the general principle that losses cannot usually be carried back.

Where a loss is set against an unremitted gain under (b), that gain is **permanently reduced** by the loss, so a future remittance of that gain would not be subject to UK tax.

Example 7

Sergio, 34, has been UK resident for four years but is not UK domiciled. In 2013/14 he has the following gains and losses:

	£
Gains on sale of UK shares	30,000
Loss on sale of UK shares	(5,000)
Gain on sale of overseas house	10,000
Loss on sale of overseas shares	(15,000)

Sergio remits £2,000 of the overseas gain on 12 August 2013. He makes a capital losses election as this is the first year that he has had to claim the remittance basis.

Show Sergio's chargeable gains.

---

3 Valuation of assets

3.1 The basic rule

Where it is necessary to use the market value, rather than the actual consideration in the CGT computation (eg on a gift or a sale between connected parties), the value to use is **the price that the asset might reasonably be expected to fetch on a sale in the open market.**

3.2 Shares and securities

Quoted shares and securities are valued at the **lower of two figures** as quoted in The Stock Exchange Daily Official List as follows:

(a)   **'Quarter-up' rule:** add a quarter of the difference between the lower and the higher quoted prices to the lower quoted price, or

(b)   'Average rule': take the **average of highest and lowest marked bargains** (ignore marked special prices).

Example 8

Shares in A plc are quoted at 100–110p. The marked bargains for that day were 99p, 102p and 110p. What value will the shares have for CGT purposes?

Unquoted shares are much harder to value than quoted shares. Values are usually agreed with HMRC's special Shares and Assets Valuation division.

3.3 Negligible value claim

If an asset becomes worthless, the owner may make a claim to treat the asset as though it had been sold and then immediately reacquired at its current market value. This gives rise to an allowable loss. This 'negligible value' claim is often used for shares. [s.24(2)]

The claim can be backdated up to two tax years, provided that the asset had become negligible in value at that time, eg in 2013/14 a claim can be made that an asset's value became negligible in 2011/12, which crystallises an allowable loss in 2011/12.

If the asset is subsequently sold, the base cost of the asset is the value at the time of the negligible value claim.

Example 9

Rhona owns shares in Alf Ltd which she purchased in 1986. Following a sudden change in the company's business in the summer of 2012 the shares plummeted in value and the company went into liquidation. Rhona only learnt of the liquidation in May 2013.

Explain the relief available to Rhona in respect of the Alf Ltd shares.

3.4 Probate value

Where an individual **inherits an asset on the death** of another person they are treated as acquiring that asset at the **market value at the date of death**. This is known as the **'probate value'** and is the individual's **base cost when they eventually sell the asset**.

4 Connected persons

4.1 Introduction

If a transferor and transferee are 'connected' persons any transaction is treated as taking place at market value, regardless of any actual price paid.

If a loss results, it can only be set off against gains arising in the same or future years from transactions with the *same* connected person *while they remain connected*. [s.18]

Exam focus point

Examiner's report – Personal Taxation

May 2011 – Part II LFQ 2

A significant number of candidates also failed to identify that an acquisition from a connected party would be deemed to be at market value for tax purposes.

4.2 Definition of connected persons [s.286]

An individual is connected with:

(a)   His **spouse** or civil partner
(b)   His **relatives** (brothers, sisters, ancestors and lineal descendants)
(c)   The **relatives of his spouse**/civil partner
(d)   The **spouses of his relatives and his spouse's/civil partner's relatives**
(e)   **Business partners**, partners' spouses/civil partners and partners' relatives
(f)   **Trustees** of any settlement of which the individual is the settlor.

A **company** is connected with another person if:

(a)   That person has **control** of the company, or
(b)   He and persons connected with him together have control of it.

A company is connected with another company if:

(a)   The same person has control of both companies, or
(b)   One person has control of one company and persons connected with him have control of the other.

Exam focus point

Examiner's report – Personal Taxation

November 2009 – Part I SFQ 2

There was general uncertainty as to whether the uncle and trustees were connected, and very few candidates even considered whether the company was connected.

4.3 Series of disposals to connected persons ('linked transactions')

A taxpayer might attempt to avoid tax by disposing of his property piecemeal to persons connected with him. For example, a majority holding of shares might be broken up into several minority holdings, each with a much lower value per share, and each of the shareholder's children could be given a minority holding.

To prevent the avoidance of tax in this way, **where a person disposes of assets to one or more persons, with whom he is connected, in a series of linked transactions, the disposal proceeds for each disposal are a proportion of the value of the assets taken together.** [s.19]

So, in the example of the shareholding, the value of the majority holding would be apportioned between the minority holdings.

Transactions are linked if they occur **within six years of each other**.

Illustration 1

Gil owned 10,000 shares in Grissom Ltd, an unquoted company. Three years ago he had made a gift of 3,000 shares in Grissom Ltd, to his son, Greg. At that date the 3,000 shares were worth £15,000.

On 5 May 2013 he gifted a further 6,000 shares in Grissom Ltd to Greg, at which date the value of those shares was £48,000.

On each occasion there is a deemed disposal of the shares at market value. However, as the transactions are linked (transfers to the same connected person within six years) the market value used in the calculation is a proportion of the value of the total number of shares gifted, ie 9,000 shares.

Assuming that the value of 9,000 shares was £63,000 at the date of the first gift and £99,000 at the date of the second gift, the market values to be used in Gil's CGT computations would be as follows:

First gift: $\dfrac{3,000}{9,000} \times £63,000 = £21,000$ (not £15,000 – this figure would have been used in the original computation)

Second gift: $\dfrac{6,000}{9,000} \times £99,000 = £66,000$ (not £48,000)

Note that if the company is a trading company, the transfers may be eligible for gift relief (see later in this Text).

---

5 Married couples and civil partners

5.1 Introduction

A husband and wife (or partners in a civil partnership) are taxed as two separate people. Each has an annual exempt amount, and losses of one cannot be set against gains of the other.

Disposals between a husband and wife (or civil partners) living together do not give rise to chargeable gains or allowable losses. The disposal is said to be on a 'no gain/no loss' basis. The acquiring spouse/partner takes over the base cost of the disposing spouse/partner.

These no gain/ no loss provisions **do not apply to transfers of exempt employee shareholder status shares** (see earlier in this Text). This enables the transferring spouse to benefit from the **CGT exemption** available for exempt employee shareholder shares valued at less than £50,000, and the transferee spouse to take the shares at their market value on the date of the transfer. [s.58(2)]

Example 10

Jacob gave his wife Leah a painting in July 2010. Its market value was £50,000. He had acquired the painting in February 2002 for £10,000. Leah sold the painting in July 2013 for £75,000.

Calculate Leah's chargeable gain.

A couple is treated as living together unless they are separated under a court order or separation deed, or are in fact separated in circumstances which make permanent separation likely. **A transfer in the tax year of separation is therefore treated as a no gain/no loss transfer.**

From the beginning of the next tax year, the spouses/civil partners are **connected** persons **until their divorce is finalised** (ie when they receive the 'decree absolute'), after which time disposals are taxed using the normal rules.

5.2 Jointly owned assets

Where an asset is jointly owned, the spouses/civil partners' actual interests determine the tax treatment, so if there is evidence that a wife's share is 60%, then 60% of any gain or loss is attributed to her. **If there is no evidence of the actual interests, HMRC accept that the asset is held in equal shares.**

Where an income tax declaration has been made (see earlier in this Text) stating how income from the asset is to be shared for income tax purposes, there is a presumption that the same split applies for CGT purposes.

5.3 Tax planning issues

If a spouse who is making other substantial gains wishes to dispose of an asset on which a gain will arise, and the other spouse has his/her CGT annual exempt amount available, **the asset could first be transferred, at no gain/no loss, to the spouse with the annual exempt amount who can then sell the asset.** The transfer must have 'no strings attached' to be effective for tax purposes.

6 Part disposals

6.1 General rules [s.42]

The disposal of part of a chargeable asset is a chargeable event for CGT purposes. The chargeable gain (or allowable loss) is computed by **deducting only a fraction of the original cost of the whole asset.** The fraction is:

$$\frac{A}{A+B} = \frac{\text{value of the part disposed of}}{\text{value of the part disposed of} + \text{market value of the remainder}}$$

The balance of the cost is used when the rest of the asset is sold.

Example 11

Mr Heal possesses a set of four Chippendale chairs (treated as a single asset for CGT purposes) which originally cost him £27,000 in March 1986. He sold one of the chairs at auction in July 2013 for £20,000, before auction expenses of 10%. The market value of the three remaining chairs together is £46,000.

You are required to calculate Mr Heal's chargeable gain.

6.2 Small part disposals of land [s.242]

If the consideration on the part disposal of land is small *and* the total consideration in that tax year from all disposals of land does not exceed £20,000, the taxpayer may claim for there not to be a part disposal and instead to **deduct the 'small' sale proceeds from the base cost** of the land rather than calculate the gain on the part disposal.

'Small' is defined as not more than 20% of the total market value of the land (A + B) immediately before the disposal.

Example 12

Tony sells 2 acres of land out of a plot of 20 acres for £10,000 in 2003/04 (his only disposal that tax year). The market value of the 20 acre plot was £80,000 immediately prior to the sale. The remaining 18 acres are sold in August 2013 for £100,000.

Date of acquisition:	30 April 1986
Original cost:	£45,000
Date of part disposal:	30 April 2003
Date of final disposal:	30 August 2013

Assume Tony made a claim in respect of the part disposal under s.242 TCGA 1992.

You are required to show the adjustment to Tony's base cost on the sale in 2003/04 and his chargeable gain in 2013/14.

Example 13

Brian made the following disposals:

(1) On 23 May 2013 he sold a warehouse, which was used in his trade, at auction for £70,000 (gross). The auction house charged him a commission of 10% on the sale. The warehouse had cost him £10,000 in May 1986.

(2) On 2 November 2013 he sold a tenanted cottage for £258,200 before costs of sale, which amounted to £1,200. He had inherited the cottage, which was one of a pair, on the death of his grandfather in October 1986. They were valued as a pair for probate purposes at £254,000. The value of the cottage retained by him was estimated at £222,500 when he sold the other one.

He has capital losses brought forward of £35,000 at 6 April 2013. His taxable income for the year was £29,010.

You are required to compute his capital gains tax liability.

7 Debts and loans

7.1 Debts

7.1.1 Introduction

Debts are specifically included in the definition of chargeable assets.

7.1.2 Ordinary debts

The original creditor (ie lender) does not make a chargeable gain or an allowable loss on a disposal of the original debt (unless it is a debt on a security – see below).

If someone purchases the debt from the original lender and then disposes of it, he is liable to tax on any gain or entitled to an allowable loss. The satisfaction (ie payment) of a debt is treated as a disposal.

However, if the debt was acquired from the original lender and is disposed of at a loss by someone connected with that lender, the loss is not allowable.

Illustration 2

Fred lends £10,000 to Tom. Fred assigns (ie sells) the debt to Harry for £9,000. Tom repays the full amount lent to Harry.

Whether or not Harry is connected with Fred, Harry has made a disposal and realised a gain of £1,000.

7.2 Debt on a security

A 'debt on a security' is not necessarily a 'secured' debt (ie its payment is not secured on another asset, for example a mortgage is secured on the property over which it is given).

To be a debt on a security it must be:

- **Capable of being held as an investment**
- **Marketable** (ie be capable of being realised at a profit)
- **From an institution** (not from an individual)
- **Evidenced in writing**
- **Loan stock** (ie a loan to a company).

If the original lender disposes of a debt on a security there is a chargeable gain or an allowable loss because they are generally commercial investments. In all other ways a debt on a security is treated in the same way as an ordinary loan.

Exam focus point

Examiner's report – Personal Taxation

November 2011 – Part II LFQ 1

Part 5 was often not answered and those candidates that did attempt it often incorrectly thought that a debt on a security referred to borrowing that was secured on a specific asset..

7.3 Loans to traders

7.3.1 Introduction

Although the original lender is not usually entitled to an allowable loss when a debt becomes irrecoverable, relief is available for certain loans to traders, and for guarantees in respect of such loans. The lender must claim the relief.

7.3.2 Qualifying loans

A qualifying loan must satisfy the following conditions: [s.253(1)]

(a) **The money lent is used by the borrower wholly for the purposes of a trade (not involving lending money) carried on by him**, including furnished holiday lettings, *and*

(b) **The borrower is resident in the UK, *and***

(c) **The debt is *not* a debt on a security.**

The lender can make a claim for loss relief if:

- The loan capital (ie principal) has become irrecoverable, and
- He has not assigned the right to recover the amount, and
- The lender and the borrower were **not spouses** or civil partners either when, or after, the loan was made.

The date of the 'disposal' is the date of the claim, although the lender can specify an earlier time (not more than two years before the beginning of the tax year in which the claim is made) so long as the above conditions were satisfied at that earlier time.

> ### Exam focus point
>
> Examiner's report – Personal Taxation
>
> November 2011 – Part II LFQ 1
>
> In part 4, a significant number of candidates referred to the loss being available by reason of a negligible value claim rather than as a result of the loss being on a loan to a trader; many also thought that the resulting loss would be relievable against income.

Chapter roundup

- CGT is a tax on the increase in value of assets between acquisition and disposal.

- Disposal proceeds are actual money received (including amounts received by instalment or not received until a condition is satisfied) or market value if an asset is gifted or sold to a connected party.

- Allowable expenditure includes the acquisition cost, enhancement expenditure and incidental costs of acquisition or disposal.

- Chargeable gains and losses arising in a tax year are netted off.

- Excess allowable losses must be carried forward and set against chargeable gains arising in a subsequent year to bring the chargeable gain down to the level of the annual exempt amount.

- Losses incurred in the year of death can be carried back against gains arising in the preceding three years on a LIFO basis.

- Losses on certain unquoted shares may be set against general income.

- If a non-UK domiciled individual makes an election in the first year that he is entitled to make a remittance basis claim he can obtain relief for losses on foreign assets. Otherwise he will never be able to use his foreign capital losses.

- A loss arising on a transaction between connected persons may only be set off in restricted circumstances.

- Shares are valued at the lower of the quarter-up and average bargain values.

- No gain/no loss disposals effectively transfer base costs between spouses and civil partners.

- For a part disposal, allowable expenditure is apportioned between the part disposed of and the part retained using the formula: $\frac{A}{A+B} \times cost$.

- In the case of a 'small' part disposal of land the taxpayer may elect that no part disposal takes place. Instead allowable expenditure is reduced by the 'small' disposal proceeds. 'Small' means the disposal proceeds do not exceed 20% of A + B and the proceeds from the part disposal (and from all land disposals in the tax year) do not exceed £20,000.

- Only the disposal of a debt on a security gives rise to a gain or loss to the original lender. Usually there is no chargeable gain or allowable loss unless the lender purchased the debt.

- In certain cases a taxpayer can claim an allowable capital loss for irrecoverable loans made to traders.

Quiz

1. Yvette buys a 2% shareholding in Blanche Ltd, a trading company on 9 August 2005 for £125,000. She sells the shares on 12 December 2013 for £160,000. Show her taxable gain after the annual exempt amount.

2. Philip has chargeable gains of £13,500 and allowable losses of £2,300 in 2013/14. Losses brought forward at 6 April 2013 are £7,000. What amount is chargeable to CGT in 2013/14? What are the losses carried forward?

3. Losses arising in the year in which an individual dies are set first against gains arising in the year of death. Any excess losses may then be carried back and set against gains of the four preceding years, using gains of a more recent year before those of an earlier year. True/False?

4. Compute the CGT value of the following shares in quoted companies:

   (a)   Z plc – quoted prices : 250p to 260p
          marked bargains : 248p, 254p and 262p

   (b)   Y plc – quoted prices : 402p to 420p
          marked bargains : 380p (special), 390p and 410p

5. With which of the following persons is Joe connected for CGT purposes?

   (a)   His son Eddie
   (b)   His cousin Frank
   (c)   A company, Joe Ltd, of which he owns 95% of the ordinary share capital and voting power
   (d)   His brother Ray's wife

6. Richard, a higher rate taxpayer, sells 4 acres of land in May 2013 out of a plot of 10 acres for £38,000. Costs of disposal amount to £3,000. The 10 acre plot cost £41,500 in 1990. The market value of the 6 acres remaining is £48,000.

   Compute his capital gains tax liability.

1.

	£
Proceeds	160,000
Less: cost	(125,000)
Chargeable gain	35,000
Less: annual exempt amount	(10,900)
Taxable gain	24,100

2.

	£
Gains in year	13,500
Losses in year	(2,300)
	11,200
Losses brought forward (£11,200 – 10,900)	(300)
	10,900
Annual exempt amount	(10,900)
Chargeable amount	nil

Losses carried forward at 5 April 2014
£(7,000 – 300) = £6,700.

3.   False – the carry back period is three years only.

4.   (a)   Z plc : lower of

   (i)   250p + ((260–250p)/4) = 252.5p

   (ii) $\dfrac{248+262}{2}$ = 255p

   ie 252.5p per share

   (b)   Y plc : lower of

   (i)   402p + ((420 – 402p)/4) = 406.5p

   (ii) $\dfrac{390+410}{2}$ = 400p

   ie 400p per share

5.   Joe is connected with all except (b), his cousin.

6.

	£
Proceeds	38,000
Less: costs of disposal	(3,000)
	35,000
Less: allowable cost : £41,500 $\times \dfrac{38,000}{38,000+48,000}$	(18,337)
Chargeable gain	16,663
Less: Annual exempt amount	(10,900)
Taxable gain	5,763
CGT @ 28% (higher rate taxpayer)	1,614

Solutions to chapter examples

Solution to Example 1

The computation of the chargeable gain will be as follows:

	£
Disposal proceeds	20,500
Less: incidental costs of sale	(500)
Net proceeds	20,000
Less: allowable costs £(5,000 + 2,000)	(7,000)
Chargeable gain	13,000

Solution to Example 2

As the losses are *current year* losses they must be fully relieved against the £10,000 of gains to produce net gains of £4,000, despite the fact that net gains are now below the annual exempt amount, part of which will be wasted.

Solution to Example 3

	£
Chargeable gains	33,000
Less: current year loss	(10,000)
Net gains	23,000
Less: annual exempt amount	(10,900)
Taxable gain	12,100
CGT @ 28% (no basic rate band left)	3,388

Solution to Example 4

Bob's loss relief can be restricted to £900 so as to leave net gains of:

£(11,800 – 900) = £10,900

which will be exactly covered by his annual exempt amount.

The remaining £5,100 of loss relief (ie £6,000 – £900) is carried forward to 2014/15.

Solution to Example 5

His gains of £5,000 are covered by his annual exempt amount for 2013/14. He will therefore carry forward all of his £4,000 loss brought forward to 2014/15.

Solution to Example 6

Loss relief is:

	£	Gains £	Losses £
2013/14			
Gains	2,100		
Less: losses	(12,000)		
Loss available for c/b			9,900
2012/13			
Gains	10,800		
Less: loss c/b	(200)	10,600	(200)
Less: AEA		(10,600)	
Taxable gain		nil	
Loss available for c/b			9,700

2011/12		
Gains		7,200
Less: AEA (part)		(7,200)
Taxable gain		nil
2010/11		
Gains	20,500	
Less: loss c/b	(9,700)	(9,700)
	10,800	
Less: AEA	(10,100)	
Taxable gain	700	
Unrelieved loss		nil

This will generate a repayment of any CGT that may have been paid in the earlier years.

Solution to Example 7

As Sergio makes an overseas loss election he can set his overseas and UK losses against his gains. The losses must be offset in a particular order:

		£
(i)	Remitted overseas gain	2,000
	Less: losses (W)	(2,000)
	Chargeable gain	Nil
(ii)	Unremitted overseas gain (£10,000 – £2,000)	8,000
	Less: losses (W)	(8,000)
	Reduced permanently to:	Nil
(iii)	UK gain	30,000
	Less: losses (W)	(10,000)
	Chargeable gain	20,000
Total chargeable gains ((i) £nil + (iii) £20,000)		20,000

Working

	£
2013/14 capital losses £(15,000 + 5,000)	20,000
Less: set against (i)	(2,000)
Less: set against (ii)	(8,000)
Less: set against (iii)	(10,000)
Loss c/f	Nil

The annual exempt amount is not available to reduce either the UK or overseas gains as Sergio has claimed to use the remittance basis. However, Sergio does not have to pay the remittance basis charge as he has not been UK resident for at least seven out of the last nine years.

Solution to Example 8

The valuation of the shares in A plc for CGT purposes will be the lower of:

(a) $100 + 1/4 (110 – 100) = 102.5$, and

(b) $\frac{110+99}{2} = 104.5$

The market value for CGT will therefore be 102.5p (ie £1.025).

Solution to Example 9

As the shares have become worthless Rhona can make a negligible value claim for 2012/13 or a later year until the liquidation is complete. She can use the loss against her gains (or her income if they are qualifying shares for share loss relief purposes).

Although Rhona discovers the information in 2013/14, and usually a negligible value claim can be backdated two years, the shares were not of negligible value in 2011/12. So 2012/13 is the earliest year for the claim.

Solution to Example 10

The transfer from Jacob to Leah is automatically at no gain/no loss.

	£
The base cost for Leah is:	
Original cost to Jacob	10,000

Note. The market value of the painting at transfer is irrelevant.

When Leah sells the painting, a gain will arise:

	£
Proceeds	75,000
Cost (as above)	(10,000)
Chargeable gain	65,000

Solution to Example 11

	£
Disposal proceeds	20,000
Less: incidental costs of sale	(2,000)
Net proceeds	18,000
Less: cost (W)	(8,182)
Chargeable gain	9,818

Working

The cost of the single chair being sold is: $\dfrac{A}{A+B} \times cost$

$$\frac{20,000}{20,000+46,000} \times £27,000 = £8,182$$

Solution to Example 12

		£
(a)	*No part disposal*: adjustment to cost instead	
	Original cost	45,000
	Proceeds from part disposal (small as < 20% × £80,000 and < £20,000)	(10,000)
	Allowable base cost c/f	35,000
(b)	*Subsequent disposal*	£
	Proceeds	100,000
	Less: allowable cost (above)	(35,000)
	Chargeable gain	65,000

Solution to Example 13

Summary

		£
Chargeable gains:	Warehouse (W1)	53,000
	Cottage (W2)	120,568
		173,568
Less: loss b/f		(35,000)
Net gains		138,568
Less: annual exempt amount		(10,900)
Taxable gain		127,668
CGT payable:		
£3,000 (£32,010 − £29,010) @ 18%		540
£124,668 (£127,668 − £3,000) @ 28%		34,907
Total CGT		35,447

Workings

		£
(1)	*Warehouse*	
	Proceeds (net) £(70,000 – 7,000)	63,000
	Cost	(10,000)
	Chargeable gain	53,000

		£
(2)	*Cottage (part disposal)*	
	Proceeds	258,200
	Less selling costs	(1,200)
	Net proceeds	257,000
	Cost: $\dfrac{258,200}{258,200+222,500} \times £254,000$	(136,432)
	Chargeable gain	120,568

Now try the following questions

Short Form Questions:

11.1 – 11.12 inclusive

Long Form Questions:

11.1	Dorrit
11.2	Harbottle

12

Shares and securities

The purpose of this chapter is to help you to:

- understand the need for and apply the matching rules
- calculate the share pool holding
- calculate the gain where a reorganisation of share capital takes place
- identify gilts and qualifying corporate bonds (QCBs)
- calculate the gain where a reorganisation involves QCBs

References: TCGA 1992 unless otherwise stated

1 The need for special rules

Shares present special problems when computing gains or losses on their disposal. Suppose that a taxpayer buys some quoted shares in X plc on the following dates:

		Cost £
5 May 1985	100 shares	150
17 January 1987	100 shares	375
2 May 2000	100 shares	1,000

On 15 June 2013, he sells 220 of his shares for £3,300. To determine his chargeable gain, we need to be able to work out which shares out of his three original holdings were actually sold. Since one share is identical to any other, it is not possible to work this out by reference to factual evidence.

As a result, it has been necessary to devise **'matching rules'**. These allow us to **identify which shares have been sold and so work out what the allowable cost (and the gain) on disposal should be**. These rules are considered in detail below.

2 Share matching rules

For individuals, the matching of shares sold is in the following order:

(a)   Shares acquired on the **same day** (average cost)
(b)   Shares acquired in the **following thirty days** on a FIFO (first in, first out) basis
(c)   Shares from the share pool (average cost) which contains all shares acquired prior to the disposal date.

The matching rules **do not apply to employee shareholder status shares** (see later in this Text). [s.236E]

Example 1

George bought the following shares in Red plc:

Date	No.	Cost £
1.5.08	9,000	18,000
20.2.14	2,000	5,000
12.3.14	5,000	12,000

He sold 10,000 shares on 20 February 2014 for £30,000.

Show George's gain on sale.

3 The share pool

3.1 The composition of the share pool

The share pool contains all shares of the *same* class in the *same* company that were acquired before the disposal date.

The share pool is also referred to as the 's.104 pool' or 's.104 holding', indicating where in TCGA1992 the relevant legislation can be found.

3.2 The calculation of the share pool value

In order to compute the value of the share pool, **two columns are required showing**:

(a)   The **number of shares**

(b)   The aggregated **cost** of the shares.

The pool is constructed by adding the number and cost of shares acquired prior to the date of disposal to the relevant columns, and deducting the number and cost of the shares (calculated using average cost) disposed of.

Example 2

Oliver bought 1,000 shares in Juland plc for £2,750 in August 1985, another 1,000 for £3,250 in December 1987 and 2,000 more shares in July 1989 at a cost of £4,000.

On 9 July 2013 Oliver disposed of 3,000 shares for £18,000.

Compute the chargeable gain on disposal.

---

4 Reorganisations

4.1 Introduction

There are several circumstances where a company will reorganise its share capital including:

(a)   **Bonus issues** (or scrip issues)
(b)   **Rights issues**
(c)   **Capital distributions**
(d)   **Reorganisations**
(e)   **Takeovers.**

The effects of such transactions on an individual is that his existing, original holding is in some way altered. The problem so far as CGT is concerned is usually how to apportion the original base cost between the original shareholding and whatever the shareholding is after the reorganisation.

4.2 Bonus issues

Bonus shares are free shares, issued at no cost, to existing shareholders. When a company (quoted or unquoted) issues bonus shares, the **size of the shareholder's original holding is increased but there is no need to adjust the original cost.**

The bonus issue shares are treated as having been acquired at the date of each original acquisition of the underlying shares. The normal matching rules then apply.

Example 3

Show how the disposal of the ordinary shares of X plc would be matched assuming the following transactions had taken place:

6.4.85   Purchase of 800 shares
6.4.90   Purchase of 600 shares
6.5.01   Purchase of 1,000 shares
1.7.13   Bonus issue of 1 for 4
6.7.13   Sale of 2,200 shares.
15.7.13   Purchase of 200 shares

4.3 Rights issues

4.3.1 Effect of a rights issue

The difference between a bonus issue and a rights issue is that in a **rights issue the new shares are paid for so we must adjust the original cost.**

Example 4

Julia had the following transactions in the shares of T Ltd:

July 1985	purchased 1,500 for	£3,750
July 1990	purchased 1,000 for	£3,000
May 2001	purchased 2,000 for	£8,000
June 2002	takes up 1 for 4 rights issue at £4.20 per share	
October 2013	sells 5,625 for	£50,400

Compute the chargeable gain or allowable loss arising.

4.3.2 Sale of rights nil paid

Where the shareholder does not take up his rights to buy new shares but instead sells that right to a third party, the proceeds received from the third party are treated as a capital distribution (see below) and the **proceeds are dealt with under the part disposal rules** (see earlier in this Text) where A = the proceeds received and B = the MV of the existing shareholding.

However, if the proceeds are **'small'** (ie less than the higher of £3,000 or 5% of the value of the shares (A+B) at the time of the rights issue), there is **no part disposal and instead the 'small' proceeds can be deducted from the cost.**

Alternatively, if the **proceeds** from the sale of the rights are **greater than the full original cost** of the shares, an election can be made to **use the full cost of the shares in calculating the gain.** The base cost carried forward will then be nil.

4.4 Capital distributions

For CGT purposes, a capital distribution (such as a payment received on a liquidation) is a **repayment of share capital.** The way in which the distribution is dealt with depends on the size of the distribution.

The normal rule is that the **distribution will be treated as a part disposal of the asset** where A = the capital distribution received and B = the MV of the shareholding after the distribution.

If, however, the **distribution is 'small', defined as less than the higher of £3,000 or 5% of the value of the shares (A+B)**, there is no part disposal and instead **the 'small' distribution proceeds can be deducted from the cost.**

Example 5

Barr holds 1,000 shares in Woodleigh plc for which he paid £10,000 in October 1988. The company is now in liquidation and in July 2013 the liquidator made a distribution of £4 per share.

Show how this will be treated if the market value of the shares after the distribution is either:

(a)   £61,000, or
(b)   £80,000 and in December 2013 Barr received a final distribution of £90,000.

Where the proceeds from a distribution are greater than the full original cost of the shares, the taxpayer may elect to have the **full cost** set against the part disposal proceeds. Therefore on a later disposal of the shares, allowable cost will be nil.

4.5 Reorganisation of shares

A reorganisation takes place where new shares, or a mixture of new shares and securities (debentures), are issued in exchange for the original shareholding. **A reorganisation does not in itself amount to a disposal of the original shareholding. Instead the new holding is regarded simply as having been acquired on the same date and for the same consideration as the old**. The problem is how to apportion the original cost between the different types of capital issued on reorganisation.

If the new shares and/or securities are *quoted*, then the original cost is apportioned by reference to the market values of the new types of capital on the first day of quotation after the reorganisation.

Example 6

Dan owns ordinary shares in Sullivan plc, purchased as follows:

1985	2,000	shares costing	£1,750
1987	3,000	shares costing	£13,250

In August 2013 there was a reorganisation whereby each ordinary Sullivan plc share was exchanged for 2 'A' ordinary shares (quoted at £2 each) and 1 preference share (quoted at £1 each).

Show how the original costs will be apportioned.

Where the new holding comprises **unquoted** shares or securities, the original cost is again apportioned on the basis of the market value of those new shares or securities. However in this case it is the market value **at the date of the subsequent disposal** which is used. Therefore if the shares are sold a few at a time, a separate calculation is needed for every subsequent disposal.

Example 7

An unquoted company reorganises its share capital in August 1990, so that for every 10 ordinary shares, a shareholder receives:

6	'A' ordinary shares
14	5% preference shares

Samuel originally owned 10,000 ordinary shares in the company which he acquired in 1986 for £16,000. In September 2013 he sells 7,000 of his preference shares, at which time the market value of the preference shares is £1.25 each and of the 'A' ordinary shares, £3.50 each.

Compute the allowable cost to set against proceeds from the September 2013 disposal.

4.6 Takeovers

When a company is taken over and the shareholders of the old company receive shares in the new company in exchange for their old shares this is known as a **'paper for paper' takeover,** and there is **usually no CGT liability.** For both quoted and unquoted shares **the new holding is deemed to have been acquired on the same date and at the same cost as the *original* holding.**

This treatment does not apply to exempt employee shareholder status shares (see later in this Text).

If part of the takeover consideration is in cash, then a liability will arise on the proportion of the gain that the cash element bears to the overall consideration and the normal part disposal rules will apply, where A = the cash received and B = the MV of the shares received.

If the cash received is **'small'**, ie not more than the higher of £3,000 and 5% of the total value on the takeover (A+B), then the **small distribution rules apply** and the cash received will be deducted from cost for the purpose of further disposals.

These takeover rules apply where the company issuing the new shares (the acquiring company) **takes over more than 25% of the ordinary share capital** of the old company (the target company) or where the acquiring company makes a general offer to shareholders in the target company which would, if accepted, give the acquiring company control of the target company.

Example 8

Le Bon holds 10,000 £1 shares bought originally for £2 each in Duran plc, a quoted company. In May 2013 the board of Duran plc agrees to a takeover bid by Spandau plc under which shareholders in Duran plc are to receive 3 Spandau plc shares plus £1.50 cash for every 4 shares held in Duran plc. Immediately following the takeover, the shares in Spandau plc are quoted at £5 each.

Show Le Bon's chargeable gain.

Note that 'paper for paper' transactions are only treated as not giving rise to any immediate CGT liability if the transactions are entered into for *bona fide* commercial reasons and not for tax avoidance motives.

5 Reorganisations involving gilts and qualifying corporate bonds

5.1 Definition and treatment

The disposal of gilts or qualifying corporate bonds (QCBs) does not usually give rise to a chargeable gain or an allowable loss.

Gilts include Treasury Loans, Treasury Stock, Exchequer Loans, Exchequer Stock and War Loans.

A QCB is a security (ie debenture, or loan note/stock) that: [s.117]

(a) Represents a '**normal commercial loan**'. This excludes any bonds which are convertible into shares, or which carry the right to excessive interest or interest which depends on the results of the issuer's business;

(b) Is **expressed in sterling** and for which no provision is made for conversion into or redemption in another currency.

5.2 Tax treatment on reorganisations involving QCBs

Special rules apply when a reorganisation or takeover involves QCBs issued in exchange for shares.

When QCBs are issued, the chargeable gain which would have arisen if the shares had been sold for cash at their market value at the time of the reorganisation must be calculated. This gain is then 'frozen' (ie not charged) until the QCB is redeemed, sold or given away.

If the disposal is a no gain/no loss disposal to a spouse/civil partner, the gain does not become chargeable until a disposal outside the marriage/partnership.

If the reorganisation is followed by the owner's death while he still owns the QCBs, the gain never becomes chargeable.

Example 9

Mr Holland bought 10,000 shares (a 25% shareholding) in Tilbrook plc in June 1990 for £18,000. On 19 May 2013, Tilbrook plc was taken-over by Difford Group plc and Mr Holland received:

- 20,000 ordinary shares in Difford Group plc
- £10,000 8.5% QCB loan stock in Difford Group plc
- £10,000 cash.

On 19 May 2013, the ordinary shares in Difford Group plc were quoted at £2.50 and the QCB Loan Stock at £1.50.

Show the gains arising as a result of the above.

Exam focus point

You should assume (and state your assumption) that loan notes (ie loan stock/ debentures) qualify as QCBs in your exam unless told otherwise.

- Special matching rules apply to identify which shares an individual is selling out of a holding acquired at different times.

- Disposals by an individual are matched with his acquisitions in the following order:
    - Same day acquisitions (average cost)
    - Acquisitions in the next thirty days (FIFO)
    - The share pool (also known as the s.104 pool) (average cost)

- Bonus and rights issues are broadly treated as acquired at the same date as the original holding to which they relate.

- Where shares are converted into other shares, no disposal takes place, and the new shares take over the original shares' acquisition date and cost.

- On a takeover, 'paper for paper' transactions (ie shares received in exchange for other shares) are not usually chargeable disposals.

- If both cash and shares (or securities) are received on a takeover, there is a part disposal in respect of the cash element.

- Disposals of gilts and QCBs are exempt from capital gains tax. Losses are not allowable.

- If a QCB is received in exchange for shares on a reorganisation, the gain is calculated at the date of the reorganisation but is frozen and not charged until a later disposal of the QCB.

Quiz

1. Set out the order of matching for 5,000 shares sold by an individual on 7 November 2013, if acquisitions have been made as follows:

	No of shares
30 October 1985	3,000
4 April 1986	2,000
30 September 1989	2,000
10 July 1991	1,000
7 November 2013	1,000
30 November 2013	2,000

2. A capital distribution is treated as small if it amounts to less than the higher of £X and Y% of the value of the shares. What are X and Y?

3. Reggie owns 5,000 ordinary shares in Perrin plc (a quoted company) which cost him £7,000 in 1986. Perrin plc is the subject of a takeover bid by Marwell plc (also a quoted company) which offers, in exchange for each Perrin plc ordinary share:

    2 Marwell plc £1 ordinary shares – valued at 75p each
    £1 Marwell plc loan stock – valued at 80p

    Compute the base costs for any later disposal of the new shares and loan stock owned by Reggie and calculate the gain, if any, arising at the time of the takeover.

1. (a) 1,000 shares acquired on disposal date (7.11.13)
    (b) 2,000 shares acquired in next 30 days (30.11.13)
    (c) 2,000 (out of 8,000) shares from the share pool

2. $X = 3,000$, $Y = 5$.

3. Market value of new holdings:

		£
Ordinary shares:	$5,000 \times 2 \times 75p$	7,500
Loan stock:	$5,000 \times 80p$	4,000
		11,500

Base cost of Perrin plc shares (£7,000) is allocated in the ratio 7,500 : 4,000, ie

Base cost of Marwell plc shares:

$$£7,000 \times \frac{7,500}{11,500} = \underline{£4,565}$$

The loan stock is (presumably) a qualifying corporate bond (QCB) so, at the date of the takeover, the gain arising in respect of the QCBs received will be frozen:

		£
Proceeds (MV)		4,000
Less: cost	$£7,000 \times \dfrac{4,000}{11,500}$	(2,435)
Frozen gain		1,565

This will crystallise when the loan stock is redeemed or sold in the future. Any actual gain arising on that redemption/ disposal will be exempt (or any loss not allowable).

Solution to Example 1

Matching:

20.2.14	2,000 shares (same day)
12.3.14	5,000 shares (next 30 days)
1.5.08	3,000 shares (share pool)
	10,000

Note. We do not need to construct a share pool as there is only one acquisition before the date of disposal.

Gains

	£	Gains £
20.2.14 holding		
Proceeds $\dfrac{2,000}{10,000} \times £30,000$	6,000	
Less: cost	(5,000)	1,000
12.3.14 holding		
Proceeds $\dfrac{5,000}{10,000} \times £30,000$	15,000	
Less: cost	(12,000)	3,000
Share pool		
Proceeds $\dfrac{3,000}{10,000} \times £30,000$	9,000	
Less: cost $\dfrac{3,000}{9,000} \times £18,000$	(6,000)	3,000
Total gains		7,000

Solution to Example 2

Share pool:

	No of shares	Cost £
August 1985	1,000	2,750
December 1987	1,000	3,250
July 1989	2,000	4,000
	4,000	10,000
Disposal: July 2013		
Cost: $\dfrac{3,000}{4,000} \times 10,000$	(3,000)	(7,500)
Pool c/f	1,000	2,500

	£
Proceeds	18,000
Cost (above)	(7,500)
Chargeable gain	10,500

Solution to Example 3

Order of matching:

(i)   *Next 30 days*

		No. of shares
Purchase	15.7.13	200
Disposal	6.7.13	(200)

(ii)   *Share pool*

		No. of shares
Purchase	6.4.85	800
Purchase	6.4.90	600
Purchase	6.5.01	1,000
		2,400
Bonus issue (1 for 4)		600
		3,000
Disposal 6.7.13		(2,000)
Pool c/f		1,000

   Note. The bonus issue is not treated as a separate acquisition, but is matched with previous acquisitions.

Solution to Example 4

Share pool:

	No. of shares		Cost
			£
Purchase July 1985	1,500		3,750
Purchase July 1990	1,000		3,000
Purchase May 2001	2,000		8,000
	4,500		14,750
Rights issue (1 for 4)	1,125	× £4.20	4,725
	5,625		19,475
Disposal October 2013	(5,625)		(19,475)
	–		–

Calculate gain:

	£
Proceeds	50,400
Cost	(19,475)
Chargeable gain	30,925

Solution to Example 5

(a)   The distribution of £4,000 is not small (ie it is > 5% × £65,000 (£61,000 + £4,000) = £3,250) so there is a part disposal. A = distribution received. B = market value of the shares after the distribution

	£
Disposal proceeds (distribution received)	4,000
Less: cost £10,000 × $\frac{4,000}{61,000+4,000}$	(615)
Chargeable gain	3,385

(b)   The first distribution is less than 5% of the value of the shares (£84,000 (£80,000 + £4,000) × 5% = £4,200).
      The small distribution reduces the cost used when he receives the final distribution:

	£	£
Disposal proceeds (final distribution received)		90,000
Less: cost	10,000	
Less: small distribution	(4,000)	(6,000)
Chargeable gain		84,000

Solution to Example 6

The value of the new holding is:

	£
10,000 'A' ordinary shares at £2	20,000
5,000 preference shares at £1	5,000
	25,000

The original costs will be apportioned 20,000 : 5,000 as follows:

Share pool:

	No of shares	Cost
		£
Purchase 1985	2,000	1,750
Purchase 1987	3,000	13,250
	5,000	15,000

Apportioned cost:

10,000 new 'A' ordinary shares: $\dfrac{20,000}{25,000} \times £15,000 = \underline{£12,000}$

5,000 new preference shares: $\dfrac{5,000}{25,000} \times £15,000 = \underline{£3,000}$

Solution to Example 7

Original cost: 10,000 ordinary shares = $\underline{£16,000}$

Market values of new holdings in September 2013:

	£
6,000 'A' ordinary shares @ £3.50 each	21,000
14,000 5% preference shares @ £1.25 each	17,500
	38,500

Allowable cost of shares sold:

$\dfrac{7,000}{14,000} \times \dfrac{17,500}{38,500} \times £16,000 = £3,636$

Solution to Example 8

Total value of the takeover package due to Le Bon on the takeover:

		£
Shares	3/4 × 10,000 (= 7,500) × £5	37,500
Cash	1/4 × 10,000 × £1.50	3,750
		41,250

The share for share element of the takeover does not give rise to a CGT disposal. The new shares in Spandau plc simply take on the acquisition date and original cost of the old shares in Duran plc.

Since the cash (£3,750) exceeds the higher of £3,000 and £2,063 (5% × £41,250), ie £3,000, it cannot be deducted from the acquisition cost. There is therefore a part disposal.

	£
Disposal proceeds (cash received)	3,750
Less: apportioned cost:	

$$\dfrac{\text{Cash received}}{\text{Cash received} + \text{value of shares received}} \times \text{original cost}$$

	£
$\dfrac{3,750}{3,750+37,500} \times 10,000 \times £2$	(1,818)
Chargeable gain	1,932

Note. The base cost of the shares is £18,182 (£20,000 – £1,818)

Solution to Example 9

Value received on takeover:

	£
Ordinary shares (20,000 × £2.50)	50,000
QCB loan stock (£10,000 × £1.50)	15,000
Cash	10,000
Total	75,000

Original cost of Tilbrook plc shares allocated as follows:

	£
Ordinary shares in Difford Group:	
$\dfrac{50,000}{75,000} \times £18,000$	12,000
QCB loan stock in Difford Group	
$\dfrac{15,000}{75,000} \times £18,000$	3,600
Cash	
$\dfrac{10,000}{75,000} \times £18,000$	2,400
Total	18,000

Gain on receipt of cash:

	£
Proceeds	10,000
Less: cost (above)	(2,400)
Chargeable gain	7,600

Gain on receipt of QCB:

	£
Proceeds (MV of QCB)	15,000
Less: cost (above)	(3,600)
Frozen gain	11,400

This gain is frozen until the loan stock is disposed of.

New ordinary shares:

This is a 'share for share' disposal so no gain arises. The new shares in Difford Group plc are treated as having been acquired in June 1990 for £12,000.

Short Form Questions:

12.1– 12.3 inclusive

Long Form Questions:

12.1	Julie Green (Pilot Paper)
12.2	Mr Jones
12.3	Richard Price
12.4	Eric James

BPP
LEARNING MEDIA

13

Chattels and wasting assets

- define the terms 'chattel' and 'wasting asset'
- calculate the gain or loss on the disposal of chattels
- understand the taxation of wasting assets that are not chattels
- understand and apply the rules for the taxation of leases

References: TCGA 1992 unless otherwise stated

1 Chattels

1.1 Definition

A *chattel* is an item of tangible movable property (it can be moved, seen and touched). Chattels include antiques, stamp collections and works of art.

'Wasting' chattels are generally exempt from CGT. A *wasting* asset is one with an estimated life of 50 years or less, for example a racehorse.

All items of plant and machinery are regarded as having an estimated life of 50 years or less, so are wasting chattels and are exempt from CGT (although see below for assets used in a business).

Wasting chattels include:

(a)   Clocks and watches [CCH IR Int 86, Tolleys RI 88]
(b)   Taxi cabs
(c)   Guns
(d)   Racehorses.

1.2 Gains

If a chattel is not a wasting asset, any gain arising on its disposal will still be exempt from CGT if the gross proceeds and cost are both £6,000 or less.

If sale proceeds exceed £6,000, but the cost is less than £6,000, the gain is limited to:

5/3 × (gross proceeds − £6,000).

Example 1

Adam purchased a Chippendale chair on 1 June 1985 for £800. On 10 October 2013 he sold the chair at auction for £6,480 net of the auctioneer's 10% commission. Show the chargeable gain arising.

Exam focus point

Examiner's report – Personal Taxation (old syllabus)

May 2002 – Question 2

... The gain on the sale of the vase was calculated correctly in many cases but there were a few who muddled the chattel relief calculation. The vintage car was treated correctly in most cases, but there were a few who appeared to consider that because the car was 'vintage' it became chargeable. ...

1.3 Capital losses

Where a chattel is sold for less than £6,000, but cost more than £6,000, any allowable loss is restricted to the amount that would arise if it were sold for gross proceeds of £6,000.

Example 2

Eve purchased a manuscript on 1 July 1984 for £8,000 which she sold in October 2013 at auction for £2,800. Costs of disposal were £280. Compute the gain or loss arising.

A loss cannot be turned into a gain under this provision. If a real loss arises, but substituting £6,000 for the sale proceeds produces a theoretical gain, then there is no allowable loss or chargeable gain.

Exam focus point

The CGT treatment of non-wasting chattels may be examined in the short form or part of long form questions. The tricky bit is spotting that the asset in question is a non-wasting chattel. Look out for assets with relatively low values.

1.4 Plant and machinery

There are special rules for plant and machinery qualifying for capital allowances (CAs). They are strictly wasting chattels but they are *not* exempt from CGT. Instead the CGT treatment is as follows:

Proceeds < Cost	**No allowable loss** for CGT (relief already given by CAs).
Proceeds ≤ £6,000, Cost ≤ £6,000	**Exempt**.
Proceeds > £6,000, Cost < £6,000	**Chargeable** (regardless of expected useful life). Any CAs given will have been clawed back as a 'balancing charge'. Apply the non wasting chattels' restriction to the gain if appropriate.

Example 3

Suppose the asset sold by Adam in Example 1 was plant and machinery. How much is the chargeable gain?

2 Wasting assets (other than leases)

Special rules apply to wasting assets that are not chattels. An example of an 'intangible' wasting asset is a copyright.

The allowable expenditure in respect of a wasting asset is deemed to waste away to nothing over its predictable life on a straight line basis.

Example 4

Sarah acquired a copyright for £20,000 for use in her trade on 10 May 2004 when it had 15 years to run. On 9 August 2013 she sells the copyright for £17,500. What is her chargeable gain?

3 Leases

3.1 Introduction

A lease is the right to occupy land for a fixed period of time. **For CGT purposes a distinction is made between a long lease which has more than 50 years to run and a short lease which has 50 years or less to run.**

There are five different situations to consider:

(a)   **Assignment** (ie sale) of a **long lease**
(b)   **Assignment** of a **short lease**
(c)   **Granting** (ie sub-letting) of a **long lease out of a freehold** or out of a long head lease
(d)   **Granting** a **short lease out of a freehold** or out of a long head lease
(e)   **Granting** a **short lease out of a short head lease.**

The duration of the lease is usually determined by the period specified in the lease.

3.2 Assignment of a long lease

This is the simplest case, since the assignment (sale) of a long lease is the same as a **disposal of the whole asset.** Any gain on disposal will be chargeable to CGT (subject to any private residence exemption – see later in this Text). **The gain is calculated in the same way as for any other asset.**

3.3 Assignment of a short lease

A lease which has 50 years or less to run at the date of disposal is a wasting asset. As we saw above, when calculating the gain on the disposal of a wasting asset only a **certain proportion of the original cost is deductible** as the rest of it will have wasted away. In the case of short leases the proportion is determined by a table of percentages contained in Schedule 8 TCGA 1992. [para 1 Sch 8]

The allowable proportion is given by X/Y × original cost where X is the percentage relating to the number of years left for the lease to run at the date of the assignment, and Y is the percentage relating to the number of years the lease had to run when first acquired by the disposer.

The table only provides percentages for exact numbers of years. Where the duration is not an exact number of years the relevant percentage is found by **adding** one twelfth of the difference between the two years on either side of the actual duration for each extra month. **Odd days of 14 or more count as a month.**

Exam focus point

The lease percentages are reproduced in the Association's Tax Tables available to you in the examination.

Example 5

Mr A acquired a 20 year lease on 1 August 2004 for £15,000. He assigned it on 1 August 2013 for £19,000.

You are required to compute the chargeable gain.

3.4 Grant of a long lease

If the taxpayer grants a lease out of his freehold or long lease, this is treated as a part disposal. Where the lease is granted for 50 years or more, the gain on the part disposal is calculated using the usual part disposal rules. **The gain will be calculated by deducting the following proportion of the original cost from the proceeds:**

$$\text{Original cost} \times \frac{A}{A+B}$$

where **A** is the premium paid for the lease, and **B** is the value of the remainder, in this case the value of the right to get the property back on the expiry of the lease, known as the *reversionary interest*. This will be given to you in the examination.

Example 6

Mr B acquired a freehold property for £18,000 on 1 January 1986. On 1 July 2013 he granted a 60 year lease for a premium of £20,000. At the time of the grant the value of the reversion was £25,000.

You are required to compute any chargeable gain arising.

3.5 Grant of a short lease out of a freehold or long lease

If **a short lease is granted out of a freehold or long head-lease, part of the premium is assessable as property income** (see earlier in this Text) **and must be excluded from the CGT computation**. The proceeds figure used in the CGT computation is the 'capital element' of the premium (ie the total premium less the amount assessable as property income). We must also adjust the allowable cost by using the following formula:

Original cost $\times \dfrac{a}{A+B}$

where **a** is the capital element of the premium, **A** is the total premium, and **B** is the value of the reversionary interest.

Example 7

Assume the facts as in the previous example, except that the lease is for 30 years rather than 60.

3.6 Grant of a short lease out of a short lease

If **a short lease is granted out of a short head lease, part of the premium will be assessable as property income** (see earlier in this Text) which must be excluded from the CGT computation.

We do this by initially **using the full amount of the premium as the consideration for CGT purposes. The cost is then adjusted using the lease percentage table in Schedule 8. The allowable proportion is given by** $\dfrac{X-Y}{Z} \times$ **original cost** where:

- **X** is the percentage relating to the number of years **left for the lease to run at the date of grant of the sublease**
- **Y** is the percentage relating to the number of years left to run at the date **when the sublease expires**, and
- **Z** is the percentage relating to the number of years the lease had to run **when first acquired**.

After calculating the gain, **deduct the amount chargeable as property income to arrive at the chargeable gain**. This deduction cannot turn a chargeable gain into an allowable loss, nor can it increase the amount of an allowable loss.

Example 8

On 1 June 2008, Amy paid a premium of £30,000 to acquire a 30 year lease on a property. On 1 June 2013, she granted a 10 year sub-lease over the whole property in return for a premium of £40,000. The rent payable under the sub-lease was the same as the rent payable under the original lease.

Calculate Amy's chargeable gain.

Exam focus point

Examiner's report – Personal Taxation

November 2008 – Part II LFQ 2

Question 2 was tricky, as lease questions are likely to be. However there were relatively easy marks to be gained, especially in parts 1 and 3. Part 3 was generally the area where candidates gained most of their marks, reflecting the fact that this part required next to no knowledge of lease CGT calculations. Candidates who did not panic at the thought of a long question on leases but just did the basics well could get reasonable marks on this question.

- Chattels are 'tangible moveable property', ie assets which can be moved, seen and touched.

- 'Wasting chattels', ie those with a predictable life of 50 years or less, are exempt from CGT unless they qualify for capital allowances (when a gain is chargeable, but a loss is not allowable).

- The following summarises the rules relating to disposals of non wasting chattels.

Proceeds	Cost	CGT implications
$\leq$ £6,000	$\leq$ £6,000	Exempt
> £6,000	> £6,000	Gain calculated in normal way
> £6,000	< £6,000	Gain calculated in normal way but restricted to $^5/_3 \times$ (gross proceeds – £6,000)
< £6,000	> £6,000	Loss is restricted by deeming gross proceeds to be £6,000

- The cost of a wasting intangible asset (eg a copyright) wastes away over time, so only the cost remaining at the date of disposal can be deducted in the CGT computation.

- When considering the tax consequences of transactions involving leases, it is essential to ascertain whether the transaction involves the assignment (sale) of an existing lease, or the grant (sub-letting) of a lease out of a freehold or a long lease.

- An assignment involves transferring the lease from one person to another, with the transferor entirely disposing of his interest.

- The grant of a sub-lease is treated as a part disposal of the lease. Where a lease is granted for 50 years or less part of the premium received will be subject to a charge as property income, with the balance chargeable to CGT.

- The following table summarises the different ways in which leases are treated for CGT purposes.

	Type of lease	Treatment
Assignment	Lease > 50 years	Disposal of whole asset – normal CGT computation
	Lease $\leq$ 50 years	Allowable cost calculated according to lease percentage table
Granting of leases	Sub-lease > 50 years	Normal part disposal rules
	Sub-lease $\leq$ 50 years, out of freehold or headlease > 50 years	Part disposal rules with proceeds reduced by amount charged as property income. Capital element of premium used in top line of part disposal formula
	Sub-lease $\leq$ 50 years, out of head lease $\leq$ 50 years	Full premium used as proceeds. Adjust cost using lease percentage table. Deduct property income assessment

Quiz

1. What is a wasting asset?

2. Robert sells a gun for £15,000 that he bought at auction for £1,000 four years ago. What is the chargeable gain/allowable loss?

3. Micky sells an antique vase in August 2013 for £8,000, having acquired it in November 1999 for £5,800.

   Compute the chargeable gain.

4. Petra sells a diamond ring, which she inherited from her aunt, for £5,000. Probate value of the ring was £7,600. What is the allowable loss on sale?

5. State how your answer to Question 4 above would differ if the probate value of the ring had been £4,600.

6. Assignment of a lease with 40 years to run is the disposal of a wasting asset. True/False?

7. Danny assigns a lease on 30 November 2013 which he acquired on 31 May 2007, at which time it had exactly 30 years to run. If Danny paid £55,000 for the lease in May 2007, compute the allowable cost for the disposal on 30 November 2013.

8. Edward grants a 60 year sub-lease out of his 999 year head lease for a premium of £80,000. Edward's head lease was acquired by him two years ago at a cost of £105,000. If the value of the reversionary interest is agreed to be £40,000, how much of Edward's original cost is allowable against the premium received on the grant of the sub-lease?

9. Show how your answer to Question 8 above would differ, if the sub-lease had been for a duration of only 40 years instead of 60.

1. A wasting asset is one with an estimated life of 50 years or less.

2. Nil – a gun is a wasting chattel so is exempt from CGT.

3.

	£
Proceeds	8,000
Less: cost	(5,800)
	2,200

The chargeable gain cannot exceed:

5/3 (£8,000 – 6,000) = £3,333

Chargeable gain (lower gain) = £2,200

4.

	£
Deemed proceeds	6,000
Less: cost (probate value)	(7,600)
Loss	(1,600)

5. As proceeds and original cost (ie, probate value in this instance) are less than £6,000, the gain is exempt. There is therefore neither a gain nor a loss.

6. True

7. This is the sale of a short lease so we need to adjust the cost using the percentages from the table. The allowable cost is: $£55,000 \times \dfrac{X}{Y}$

    X: % for 23 years 6 months = 78.055 + ($^{6}/_{12}$ (79.622 – 78.055)) = 78.839

    Y: % for 30 years = 87.330

    Therefore, allowable cost = $£55,000 \times \dfrac{78.839}{87.330} = £49,652$

8. This is the grant of a long lease from a longer head lease so there is a part disposal:

    Allowable cost = original cost $\times \dfrac{A}{A+B}$

    ie $£105,000 \times \dfrac{80,000}{80,000+40,000} = £70,000$

9. This would be the grant of a short lease from a long head lease so there we need to use a modified part disposal calculation:

    Allowable cost = original cost $\times \dfrac{a}{A+B}$

    Where a = capital element of the premium (ie not charged as property income)

	£
Full premium	80,000
Less: amount taxed as property income ($£80,000 \times \dfrac{50-39}{50}$)	(17,600)
Capital element	62,400

    Allowable cost: $£105,000 \times \dfrac{62,400}{80,000+40,000} = £54,600$

Solutions to chapter examples

Solution to Example 1

	£
Gross proceeds (£6,480 × $\frac{100}{90}$)	7,200
Less: incidental costs of sale (10%)	(720)
Net proceeds	6,480
Less: cost	(800)
	5,680

Restricted to a maximum of 5/3 × £(7,200 – 6,000) = £2,000

Solution to Example 2

Eve has a loss that must be calculated using deemed gross proceeds of £6,000.

	£
Deemed disposal proceeds	6,000
Less: incidental costs of disposal	(280)
	5,720
Less: cost	(8,000)
Allowable loss	(2,280)

Solution to Example 3

Chargeable gain	£2,000

Exactly the same calculation as Example 1

Solution to Example 4

	£
Disposal proceeds	17,500
Less: cost	
$£20,000 \times \dfrac{5\frac{3}{4}}{15}$	(7,667)
Chargeable gain	9,833

Note. The sale proceeds are for the time remaining in respect of the copyright (ie 5.75 years) so we match this to the cost of what is left (ie 5.75 years worth of 15 years' cost). The remainder of the cost has wasted away.

Solution to Example 5

	£
Disposal proceeds	19,000
Less: cost	
$£15,000 \times \dfrac{11 \text{ years}}{20 \text{ years}}$, ie $\dfrac{50.038}{72.770}$	(10,314)
Chargeable gain	8,686

50.038 = percentage for 11 years (time left on lease at disposal on 1.8.13)

72.770 = percentage for 20 years (time on lease when purchased on 1.8.04)

Solution to Example 6

	£
Disposal proceeds (full premium)	20,000
Cost:	
$£18,000 \times \dfrac{20,000}{20,000 + 25,000}$	(8,000)
Chargeable gain	12,000

Solution to Example 7

	£
Premium (A)	20,000
Less: amount taxed as property income ($£20,000 \times \dfrac{50-29}{50}$)	(8,400)
Capital element of premium (a)	11,600
Less: cost:	
$£18,000 \times \dfrac{11,600\,^*}{20,000\,^* + 25,000}$	(4,640)
Chargeable gain	6,960

Note. The numerator (top number) of the part disposal fraction is the *capital element* of the premium (a), whilst the denominator (bottom number) is the total premium (A).

Solution to Example 8

Amy's allowable expenditure on the grant of the sub-lease is:

$£30,000 \times \dfrac{81.100 - 61.617}{87.330}$ (see working) = £6,693

The amount of the premium chargeable as property income is:

	£
Premium (full)	40,000
Less: amount taxed as property income ($£40,000 \times \dfrac{50-9}{50}$)	(32,800)
Capital element of premium	7,200

Amy's gain is therefore:

	£
Premium	40,000
Less: allowable expenditure	(6,693)
Gain	33,307
Less: chargeable as property income	(32,800)
Chargeable gain	507

Working for percentages:

61.617 = 15 years	Time left on lease when 10 year sublease ends on 1 June 2023
81.100 = 25 years	Time left on lease when sublease granted on 1 June 2013
87.330 = 30 years	Time on lease when purchased on 1 June 2008

> Now try the following questions

Short Form Questions:

13.1 – 13.7 inclusive

Long Form Questions:

13.1	Doug
13.2	Mr Cole
13.3	CGT leases

14

The purpose of this chapter is to help you to:

- calculate the relief available on the disposal of an individual's home
- identify an individual's principal private residence (PPR) where he owns more than one home
- calculate the further relief available where a residence is let as residential accommodation
- understand how business use of a property impacts on the availability of PPR relief

References: TCGA 1992 unless otherwise stated

Principal private residence relief

1 General principles

1.1 Overview

A gain arising on the sale of an individual's only or main private residence (principal private residence) is exempt from CGT. Any loss is not allowable. The exemption applies to both leasehold and freehold property.

1.2 Relief for actual occupation

The basic rule is that the gain is wholly exempt where the owner has occupied the whole of the residence throughout his period of ownership. Where occupation has been for only part of the period, the exempt proportion of the gain is: [s.223]

$$\text{Total gain} \times \frac{\text{period of occupation}}{\text{total period of ownership}}$$

A further proportionate restriction is made where only part of the property has been occupied as his residence, eg where part is used exclusively for business purposes.

The last 36 months of ownership is exempt in all cases if at some time the residence has been the taxpayer's main residence. [s.223(1)]

There is no exemption for a property that is acquired wholly or partly for the purpose of making a gain on a subsequent disposal. However, it is difficult for HMRC to prove such an intention.

1.3 Deemed occupation

The period of occupation is also deemed to include certain periods of absence, provided the individual had no other exempt residence at that time and the **period of absence was at some time both preceded by and followed by a period of actual occupation**.

The periods of *deemed occupation* are: [s.223(3)]

(a) **Any period** (or periods taken together) of absence, for any reason, **up to three years**. Where the period exceeds three years, three years out of the longer period are deemed to be a period of occupation;

(b) **Any periods** during which the owner was **required by his employment to live abroad**;

(c) **Any period** (or periods taken together) **not exceeding four years** where the owner was:

    (i) **Self-employed and forced to work away from home** (UK and abroad)

    (ii) **Employed and required to work elsewhere in the UK** (overseas employment is covered by (b) above)

The above periods apply even if the residence is let while the owner is away.

Although deemed periods of occupation must usually be preceded and followed by a period of actual occupation, the **re-occupation requirement is waived by extra-statutory concession where the individual has been required to work abroad or elsewhere in the UK (paras (b) and (c) above) and is unable to return home** because the terms of his employment require him to work elsewhere.

Also by HMRC concession, a house is treated as occupied as the owner's main residence for a period of up to 12 months (or longer if there is a good reason) if he was prevented from living in the house because it was being built or altered or because necessary steps were being taken to dispose of their previous residence. [ESC D49]

Exam focus point

Examiner's report – Personal Taxation

November 2009 – Part I SFQ 7

... the most frequently omitted point was reference to the fact that the first period of deemed occupation only qualifies because there is actual occupation both before and after. A significant minority overlooked the requirement for there to be actual occupation after the period working overseas to enable that period to qualify for deemed occupation.

Example 1

Arnold purchased a house in July 1985 for £50,000. He lived in the house until June 1987 and then moved to a rented apartment until June 1991. He then worked abroad for ten years before returning to the UK to live in the house again in July 2001. He stayed in the house for six months before moving out to live with friends until the house was sold on 23 December 2013 for £150,000.

Calculate any chargeable gain arising on disposal.

1.4 Disposal of a garden

The exemption covers a **garden and grounds up to half a hectare** (slightly over one acre), but it can exceed half a hectare if the house is **sufficiently large** to warrant it.

Where the main residence is sold along with only part of the garden, leaving the rest of the garden to be sold separately (for development purposes) at a later date, the **PPR exemption will not be available on the later sale** as the garden is no longer part of the individual's main residence.

2 More than one residence

2.1 Election for residence to be treated as main residence

Where a person has more than one residence, he may, by notice to HMRC, nominate which is his main residence. The notice must be given within two years of the second property being used as a residence. The nomination may be varied at a later date.

The individual **must actually reside in both residences**, at least from time to time. Any period of ownership of a residence not nominated as the main residence will be a chargeable period. An election can have effect for any period beginning not more than two years prior to the date of the election. If there is a **change in the combination of residences, a new two year period begins.**

If **no election** is made then **HMRC can determine, based on all the facts, whether the property is the taxpayer's PPR.** The taxpayer may appeal against the decision to the Tax Tribunal.

2.2 Job related accommodation

A person lives in **job related accommodation** (see earlier in this Text) where:

(a)   It is **necessary** for the proper performance of his duties; or

(b)   It is provided for the **better performance of his duties** and it is one of the kinds of employment in which it is customary for employers to provide accommodation; or

(c)   There is a **special threat** to the employee's security and use of the accommodation is part of security arrangements.

An individual living in job related accommodation will be treated as occupying any second house that he owns and where he intends, in due course, to occupy the house as his only or main residence. It is not necessary to establish any form of actual residency in such cases. The benefit of this rule also applies to self employed persons living in 'job related' accommodation (eg tenants of public houses).

2.3 Husband and wife and civil partners

Where spouses (or civil partners) live together, only one residence can qualify as the main residence for PPR relief.

When an **inter-spouse transfer takes place following separation**, not only is the usual 36 month relief available, but the **former marital home can also continue to be treated as the only or main residence of the transferor** until the earlier of:

(a)   The date of transfer, or

(b)   The date upon which the **recipient ceases to use the property as their main or only residence,**

even where this is longer than the usual 36 months. [s.225B]

3 Letting relief

Gains may also be exempt where they relate to a period while the property is let, up to a certain limit. The two main circumstances in which letting relief will apply are: [s.223(4)]

(a)   When the owner is absent and **lets the property during his absence,** and

(b)   When the owner **lets part of the property while still occupying the rest of it.** In this case the owner will get full PPR relief on the part he has occupied and letting relief on the rest of the property.

In both cases **the letting must be for *residential* use** and the last 36 months of ownership of the property will qualify for full relief even if the whole or part of the property is let during that period.

Letting relief is restricted to the lowest of:

(a)   **The gain relating to the letting period** (and not already covered by the deemed occupation provisions),

(b)   **The gain that is already exempt under the PPR provisions,** and

(c)   **£40,000.**

Letting relief cannot turn a gain into an allowable loss, nor increase an existing loss.

Where a **lodger** lives as a member of the owner's family, sharing their living accommodation and eating with them, no part of the accommodation is treated as having ceased to be occupied as the owner's main residence. The question of letting relief does not therefore arise and **full PPR relief would be available** on disposal.

Similarly where lodgers are taken in under the 'rent a room' scheme – which gives income tax exemption on £4,250 of gross rental income (see earlier in this Text) **– it will not lead to a restriction of PPR. Again letting relief will not be relevant.**

Exam focus point

PPR relief and letting relief are regularly examined in the long form questions of Personal Taxation either computationally or in a written question. Make sure you are familiar with the deemed occupation periods and letting relief. This is all in s.223 TCGA 1992.

Example 2

Miss Coe purchased a house on 1 May 1985 for £90,000 and used it as her main residence. She sold it on 30 September 2013 for £384,000, having let half of it from 1 January 1987 to 30 September 1991. She then lived in the whole of the property until sale.

Calculate the chargeable gain arising.

4 Business use

Where part of a residence is used *exclusively* for business purposes the gain attributable to that part will always be taxable. There is no relief on the business element for the last three years of ownership.

Example 3

Mr Woof purchased a property for £35,000 on 1 December 1985 and began operating a veterinary practice from that date in one third of the house. He sold the house on 1 December 2013 for £130,000. He continued to operate the veterinary practice from new premises which he rented.

Compute the chargeable gain, if any, arising on disposal.

Chapter roundup

- Gains arising on the disposal of a dwelling house are exempt from CGT if the house was the individual's only or main residence throughout the period of ownership.

- Where the house is not owner-occupied throughout the period of ownership only the proportion of the gain attributable to the period of owner-occupation is exempt.

- Certain 'periods of absence' are deemed to be periods of occupation. The last 36 months of ownership are always treated as a period of occupation.

- Although gardens of up to one half hectare (possibly more) are also covered by the private residence exemption, the disposal of part of a garden, following the disposal of the house, attracts no relief.

- Where an individual owns more than one residence he may, within two years of the second being used as a residence, nominate one as his main residence.

- A married couple (or civil partners) may have only one qualifying residence.

- Where the house or part of it is let as residential accommodation, letting relief may be available up to a maximum of £40,000.

- Where part of a house is *used exclusively* for business purposes, the gain attributable to the business use portion is not eligible for PPR relief.

Quiz

1. Provided the property has at some time been the owner's principal private residence, the last ... months of ownership is always an exempt period. How many months?

2. In what circumstances is the following requirement ignored: that in order for a period of absence to be treated as deemed occupation, the taxpayer must actually occupy the property at some time *after* the period of absence?

3. Where an individual sells one of two properties which he owns, both of which he has occupied from time to time as a residence, what is the CGT position, assuming he has failed to make any election?

4. Ruth sells a house which has been partly occupied by her as her principal private residence and partly let to students as residential accommodation.

   The facts are:

   - Gain before PPR relief: £155,000.
   - Occupied solely by Ruth as her PPR from 1 July 1991 (date of purchase) to 30 June 1992
   - Occupied from 1 July 1992 to 31 December 2013 (date of sale) 20% by Ruth, 80% by students.

   Calculate:

   (a) The PPR exemption, and
   (b) The chargeable gain after all exemptions and reliefs.

5. Hannah has always used one room of her house exclusively as an office – HMRC has agreed that this amounts to 10% of the whole property. If the gain on the sale of the property is £124,000, calculate the chargeable gain on the assumption that Hannah owned the property from 1 July 1990 to 30 November 2013.

BPP
LEARNING MEDIA

Solutions to Quiz

1. 36.

2. By concession, where the taxpayer has been absent either because he was working abroad or because he was working elsewhere in the UK, and he is prevented from re-occupying the property because the terms of his employment require him to work elsewhere.

3. HMRC will determine, based on the facts, whether the property sold is or is not the taxpayer's principal private residence. The taxpayer has a right of appeal to the Tax Tribunal.

4. Gain before relief: £155,000

			PPR	Let period
(a)	PPR exemption:			
	(i)	1.7.91 – 30.6.92: 100% exemption	12m	
	(ii)	1.7.92 – 31.12.10: 20% exemption (222m)	44m	178m
	(iii)	1.1.11 – 31.12.13: 100% exemption (last 36 months)	36m	
			92m	178m

    Total ownership = 270m

    PPR exemption:

	£
$\frac{92}{270} \times £155,000$	52,815

    (b) Chargeable gain:

	£
Gain before relief	155,000
Less: PPR exemption	(52,815)
Gain attributable to letting period	102,185
Less: s.223 TCGA 1992 relief – *lowest* of:	
– £40,000	
– £52,815 (PPR relief)	
– £102,185 ($\frac{178}{270}$ × £155,000) (relates to let period)	(40,000)
Chargeable gain	62,185

5.

	£
Gain before relief	124,000
Less: PPR exemption	
£124,000 × 90%	(111,600)
Gain after PPR	12,400

Solution to Example 1

(a) Exempt and chargeable periods

		Exempt months	Chargeable months
(i)	July 1985 – June 1987	24	–
(ii)	July 1987 – June 1991	36	12
(iii)	July 1991 – June 2001	120	–
(iv)	July 2001 – December 2001	6	–
(v)	January 2002 – December 2010	–	108
(vi)	January 2011 – December 2013	36	–
		222	120

(b) *Explanations*

(i) July 1985 – June 1987

A period of actual owner occupation.

(ii) July 1987 – June 1991

Deemed occupation for up to '3 years of absence for any reason'. The period is both preceded and followed by actual owner occupation.

(iii) July 1991 – June 2001

Deemed occupation as the owner is required by his employment to live abroad. The period is both preceded and followed by a period of actual owner occupation.

(iv) July 2001 – December 2001

A period of actual owner occupation.

(v) January 2002 – December 2010

Not occupied. Deemed occupation for up to '3 years of absence for any reason' has already been used.

(vi) January 2011 – December 2013

Covered by the final 36 months exemption.

(c) *Calculation of the chargeable gain*

	£
Disposal proceeds	150,000
Less: cost	(50,000)
Gain before PPR relief	100,000
Less: exempt under PPR provisions	
222/(222 + 120) × £100,000	(64,912)
Chargeable gain	35,088

In this example, had Arnold gone straight to live with friends in July 2001 instead of having six months occupation he would have lost not only the extra six months, but also the periods from July 1987 to June 2001, as the property was not occupied again by the owner prior to sale so these two periods of absence would lose their 'deemed occupation' status.

Solution to Example 2

	£	£
Disposal proceeds		384,000
Less: cost		(90,000)
Gain before PPR relief		294,000
Less: PPR exemption		
$£294,000 \times \dfrac{284}{341} \dfrac{(W1)}{(W2)}$	(244,856)	
$£294,000 \times \dfrac{57}{341} \dfrac{(W3)}{(W2)} \div 2$	(24,572)	
		(269,428)
Left in charge		24,572
Less: letting relief		
lowest of:		
(a) gain relating to letting period: £24,572	(24,572)	
(b) PPR relief given: £269,428		
(c) £40,000		
Chargeable gain		NIL

Workings

		Months
(W1)	Period not let and fully occupied as PPR: 1.5.85 – 31.12.86	20
	1.10.91 – 30.9.13	264
		284

(W2) Period of ownership: 1.5.85 – 30.9.13   = 341 months

(W3) Period let: 1.1.87 – 30.9.91   = 57 months

Note. Miss Coe cannot claim exemption for part of the period of letting under the 3 year absence rule since during this time she has a main residence which qualifies for relief (ie the rest of the house).

Solution to Example 3

	£
Disposal proceeds	130,000
Less: cost	(35,000)
Gain before PPR relief	95,000
Less: PPR exemption £95,000 × ²/₃	(63,333)
Chargeable gain	31,667

PPR exemption is lost on one third owing to use of that part exclusively for business purposes. Note that the exemption is restricted for business use for the *whole* period of ownership, including the last 36 months.

Now try the following questions

Short Form Questions:

14.1 – 14.3 inclusive

Long Form Questions:

14.1	Owning two homes (Pilot paper)
14.2	Peter Stamp
14.3	Mr Richman

chapter

15

The purpose of this chapter is to help you to:

- understand and apply the gift relief rules in appropriate situations

- understand the CGT reliefs available under the Enterprise Investment and Venture Capital Schemes

- understand the exemption available for employee shareholder status shares

- understand the tax treatment when insurance money (ie compensation) is received when an asset is damaged or destroyed

References: TCGA 1992 unless otherwise stated

Other CGT reliefs

1 Introduction to CGT reliefs

In this section we consider CGT reliefs that are available to 'defer' or exempt gains arising on the disposal of certain assets.

We have already considered Principal Private Residence relief, which exempts or reduces the gain arising on the sale of a taxpayer's main residence. In this chapter we consider the CGT reliefs under the three venture capital schemes and the new employee shareholder status scheme, which provide for the exemption of gains on the disposal of shares in certain circumstances, and the deferral of gains on any asset where funds are reinvested in EIS and SEIS scheme shares.

Also in this chapter we consider the circumstances in which a chargeable gain may be deferred on the gift of an asset and when compensation is received when an asset is damaged or destroyed. When a gain is deferred it is transferred, usually to another asset, until some later date.

In all cases the gain on disposal of the asset is calculated in the normal way and then the appropriate relief is applied.

2 Gift relief

2.1 General principle

If an individual makes a gift of a qualifying business asset gift relief may be available. The transferor's gain, calculated using proceeds equal to market value, is reduced by the relief and the transferee acquires the asset at that market value less the transferor's deferred gain. [s.165]

A partial claim is not allowed, for example, to ensure sufficient gains remain to be covered by losses or the annual exempt amount.

The transferor and transferee, who must be resident in the UK, must make a joint claim for the relief within four years of the end of the tax year. So, for a gift in 2013/14 the claim must be made by 5 April 2018.

2.2 Assets attracting gift relief

The relief only applies if the gifted property is: [s.165 (2)]

(a)   An **asset used in a trade**, profession of vocation carried on by:

    (i)   The transferor, or

    (ii)   The transferor's personal company (a company in which 5% or more of the voting rights are controlled by the individual), or

    (iii)   A trading company owned by a holding company which is the transferor's personal company,

or

(b)   **Shares or securities of a trading company** (or the holding company of a trading group) where:

    (i)   The shares are **not quoted** on a recognised stock exchange, or

    (ii)   The **company** (or holding company) **is the transferor's personal company** (ie transferor can exercise at least 5% of the voting rights).

    The fraction CBA/CA must be used to calculate the eligible gain – see below.

Gift relief is also available where *any* asset is gifted to a trust (other than to a disabled person's trust) as there is also an inheritance tax (IHT) charge. [s.260(2)]

Exam focus point

Examiner's report – Personal Taxation

May 2011 – Part I SFQ 10

A significant minority failed to grasp what the 'four potential gift scenarios' were which made it difficult for them to present a cohesive answer. Generally poorly answered, especially in relation to the possibility of claiming holdover relief on a gift into trust.

2.3 Gifts of shares

When an individual makes a gift of shares, we use the matching rules as normal (see earlier in this Text) to calculate the gain.

If they are shares in the individual's personal company (ie he can exercise at least 5% of the voting rights) only the gain relating to the proportion of the chargeable business assets of the company can qualify for gift relief.

It is necessary to apportion the gain in the ratio of total chargeable business assets (CBAs) to total chargeable assets (CAs) (ie the fraction $^{CBA}/_{CA}$) using the market value of the assets at the date of disposal of the shares (often given in the form of a balance sheet extract).

A CA is any asset chargeable to capital gains tax. Assets that are exempt from CGT (eg cash, stock, debtors, motor cars and items of plant and machinery with cost and value of less than £6,000) are ignored.

A CBA is a chargeable asset used in the trade or the business. Shares and other assets held as investments, such as rental property, cannot be CBAs.

The gain attributable to the value of chargeable non-business assets will not attract gift relief so this element always remains chargeable.

If the shares are in a holding company, the apportionment is made by reference to the chargeable assets of the whole trading group.

Gift relief is **not available on gifts of shares to companies**.

Example 1

On 6 August 2013 Henry gave his 8% shareholding in a trading company to his brother resulting in a gain of £60,000. The market value of the shares was £150,000. The market value of the company's total chargeable assets at the time of the sale amounted to £40,000 of which the market value of total chargeable business assets was £30,000.

You are required to calculate the chargeable gain arising to Henry and the base cost of the shares for his brother, assuming all available reliefs are claimed.

Example 2

Mr McGregor owns 10% of the shares of an unquoted trading company. On 1 January 2014, the company's net assets were:

	£
Plant*	50,000
Factory	1,470,000
Investments (shares)	80,000
Net current assets	300,000
	1,900,000

* made up of items with a market value of more than £6,000 each.

Mr McGregor bought the shares in 1985 for £200,000 and gave them to his son on 1 January 2014 when their market value was £950,000.

You are required to calculate the chargeable gain.

Exam focus point

The CBA/CA rule only applies to gains on the disposal of personal company shares. The individual can claim to defer the whole gain if it is not his personal company.

Examiner's report – Personal Taxation

November 2009 – Part I SFQ 3

Most candidates were aware of the need to do a CBA/CA calculation, albeit many included motor cars and debtors as both CAs and CBAs. Most knew to apply the resulting restriction to the gain, although some applied it just to the cost in the gain calculation. Every single candidate who got the calculation correct also knew that a joint election was required.

2.4 Gifts of business assets with non-business use

If an individual makes a gift of a business asset, the amount of the gain that can be deferred is reduced if the asset has not been used in the transferor's trade (or that of his personal company) **throughout his period of ownership.** The reduction is pro rata on a time basis.

If the asset is a building, part of which was used for a non-business purpose during the period of ownership, a 'just and reasonable' restriction will apply.

Example 3

Keith gives a factory to his son realising a chargeable gain of £50,000. He has owned the factory for 8 years and has used it in his trade for 5 years. For the other 3 years it was let as a warehouse.

You are required to calculate what part of the gain is eligible for gift relief and what part is immediately chargeable.

Remember, in the case of a gift of shares (see above), the deferred gain is restricted if the company owns non-business chargeable assets at the date of the gift.

2.5 Sales at an undervalue

If the disposal involves actual consideration which is less than the market value (ie a sale at an undervalue rather than an outright gift), then **the gain that can be held over (ie deferred) is the gain *less* the excess of the actual consideration over allowable costs.** This excess is immediately taxable.

Example 4

On 1 August 2013 Angelo sold shares in his personal trading company valued at £200,000 to his son Michael for £50,000. Angelo had originally purchased the shares in July 1986 for £30,000. Michael sold the shares for £195,000 in October 2014. Angelo and Michael jointly elect for relief under s.165 TCGA 1992.

You are required to compute any chargeable gains arising.

Exam focus point

Gift relief is an extremely examinable topic both computationally and in written questions. Make sure you know which assets qualify for the relief (see s.165) and how much gain can be deferred in both the case of an outright gift and a sale at undervalue.

2.6 Anti-avoidance: the emigrating donee

Consider the situation where a gift relief claim is made but then the recipient emigrates. When they eventually sell the asset there will be no UK CGT, as they will not be resident, so the deferred gain will never become chargeable.

Anti-avoidance rules apply to ensure that this deferred gain will eventually crystallise so **where the recipient becomes not resident in the UK, the deferred gain will be assessed on them immediately before they become not resident.** This rule only applies **if the recipient leaves the UK within six tax years of the end of the year of the gift.** [s.168]

Where the recipient disposes of the asset before ceasing to be resident, the deferred gain crystallises so there is no charge on emigration. A disposal to the recipient's spouse/civil partner before emigration, however, does not count, unless the spouse/civil partner then disposes of the asset to a third party.

If the tax payable by the recipient has not been paid within a year of the due date, HMRC may collect it from the transferor instead. The transferor has the right to recover the tax from the recipient.

If the recipient ceases to be resident because he takes up full time employment abroad, then, provided residence in the UK is resumed within three years and the asset is not disposed of in the meantime, the deferred gain will not be taxed in the way described above.

2.7 CGT instalments

There is an option to pay the CGT due by instalments where a gift of certain assets (eg land or unquoted shares) **either does not qualify for gift relief, or gift relief has been claimed but some part of the gain remains taxable** (eg where there has been a sale at below market value, or the CBA/CA restriction applies for shares). [s.281 TCGA 1992]

The details of the CGT instalment option are covered later in this Text.

3 Enterprise Investment Scheme (EIS) CGT reliefs

3.1 Disposals of EIS shares

3.1.1 Introduction

Where shares qualify under the Enterprise Investment Scheme (EIS) for income tax relief (see earlier in this Text), **special rules apply when the investor disposes of those shares.** [s.161 ITA 2007]

3.1.2 Disposal of EIS shares at a gain

Where the shares are disposed of after the 'relevant period' (broadly, three years after the issue of shares), any gain is exempt from CGT. [s.150A]

If the shares are disposed of within the relevant period at a gain, a normal CGT computation is used, ie ignore the fact that the EIS shares ever qualified for income tax relief.

3.1.3 Disposal of EIS shares at a loss

Where EIS shares are sold at a loss (whether within or outside the relevant period) the loss is allowable but the cost of the shares is reduced by the amount of the EIS income tax relief attributable to the shares.

If the disposal occurs within the relevant period, so all (or some) of the income tax relief is withdrawn, the cost of the shares is not (or only partially) affected.

Illustration

During 2013/14 Martin invested £35,000 in EIS shares and received income tax relief of £35,000 × 30% = £10,500.

He sells the shares in February 2015 for £15,000. This leads to a withdrawal of EIS relief of £15,000 × 30% = £4,500.

Gain:	£	£
Disposal proceeds		15,000
Less: Cost	35,000	
EIS relief given (and not withdrawn) £(10,500 – 4,500)	(6,000)	(29,000)
Allowable loss		(14,000)

If the shares had instead been sold outside the relevant period (ie so that there was no withdrawal of income tax relief), the allowable loss would instead be:

	£	£
Disposal proceeds		15,000
Less: Cost	35,000	
EIS relief (none withdrawn)	(10,500)	(24,500)
Allowable loss		(9,500)

Share loss relief is available for a loss arising on the disposal of EIS shares. This means it can be set against general income of the same and/or preceding year. (see earlier in this Text). [s.131 ITA 2007]

3.2 EIS CGT deferral relief

3.2.1 General provisions

If an individual makes a gain on the disposal of *any* asset, the gain may be deferred (ie delayed) if the individual subscribes for Enterprise Investment Scheme (EIS) shares. [Sch 5B]

The EIS shares do not need to qualify for the EIS income tax reduction (see earlier in this Text) **for this deferral relief to be available.** So the investor can be 'connected' with the company (ie he can own more than 30% of the shares and can be an employee) and he can invest more than the maximum allowed under the income tax rules (£1,000,000 for 2013/14).

3.2.2 Amount of relief

For every £1 invested in EIS shares, the investor can defer £1 of gain.

He can defer up to the full amount he subscribes for his shares, although he can specify a lower amount in his claim to take into account the availability of losses and the annual exempt amount.

The gain is deferred and is 'frozen' until, usually, the EIS shares are sold (see below).

Example 5

Robert made a gain of £196,000 on the disposal of a holiday cottage in 2013/14. He subscribed for some shares in a company which qualified under the EIS rules. How much should Robert claim to defer if:

(a)   The shares cost £200,000 and Robert wants to take the maximum deferral relief possible?
(b)   The shares cost £170,000 and Robert wants to take the maximum deferral relief possible?
(c)   The shares cost £200,000 and Robert has no other chargeable gains?

3.2.3 Conditions

3.2.3.1 The gain to be deferred

The gain must either arise on:

(a)   **The disposal of an asset or**
(b)   **On a gain, previously 'frozen' under these rules, crystallising (ie coming back into charge).**

3.2.3.2 The investor

The investor must be **UK resident when he makes the gain and also when he subscribes for the EIS shares.**

3.2.3.3 The company

The company must be a qualifying company under the EIS income tax rules (broadly an unlisted company carrying on a qualifying trade) (see earlier in this Text).

3.2.3.4 The shares

The investor must subscribe for the shares directly from the company (and not just purchase them on the open market) wholly in cash.

The shares must: [para 1(2)(a) Sch 5B & s.173 ITA 2007]

(a)   Be **new ordinary shares**, fully paid up
(b)   Not be redeemable before the termination date (generally three years after their issue)
(c)   Not have preferential rights to dividends or assets on a winding up within that period.
(d)   Be subscribed and issued for genuine commercial purposes (not for the avoidance of tax)
(e)   Be issued to raise money for a qualifying business activity.

Deferral relief will be withdrawn if the money raised is not used for the qualifying business activity within two years of the issue of the shares.

3.2.3.5 Time for investment

The investor must subscribe for the shares within the period of one year before and three years after the gain to be deferred accrues. [para 1(3) Sch 5B]

3.2.3.6 The claim

The claim must be made by the **fifth anniversary of 31 January following the end of the tax year in which the EIS shares are issued** (ie by 31 January 2020 for gains deferred in respect of EIS shares issued in 2013/14). [Sch 5B Para 6]

3.2.4 Taxing the deferred gain

The deferred gain will crystallise (ie come back into charge) if: [para 3(1) Sch 5B]

(a)   **The investor disposes of the shares to anyone, except to his spouse or civil partner**

(b)   **The investor's spouse or civil partner disposes of the shares, and they had acquired the shares from the investor**

(c)   **The investor becomes non resident within the three years following issue of the shares (the 'relevant period'),** unless he is employed full time abroad for up to three years and keeps the shares until he returns to the UK

(d)   **The investor's spouse or civil partner becomes non resident** within the relevant period (except as in (c) above), if they acquired the shares from the investor

(e)   **The shares cease being 'eligible shares'**, eg the company ceases to be a qualifying company or the money subscribed is not used for a qualifying business activity. However, if a company becomes listed this does not result in the gain coming back in charge unless there were arrangements in place at the outset for it to become listed.

The deferred gain becomes chargeable in the year of the event, not the year when it originally arose (if different). The gain is charged on the person holding the shares at that date, whether the investor or his spouse or civil partner if the shares have been passed to them.

4 Seed Enterprise Investment Scheme (SEIS) CGT reliefs

4.1 Disposals of SEIS shares at a gain

Where **shares qualify under the Seed Enterprise Investment Scheme (SEIS) for income tax relief** (see earlier in this Text), any **gain** arising on a disposal of those shares after three years is **exempt** (in the same way as for EIS shares – see above) so long as the SEIS conditions have been satisfied throughout the period. [s.150E]

4.2 Disposals of SEIS shares at a loss

Where SEIS shares are sold at a loss, the **allowable loss for CGT purposes is reduced**, in the same way as for EIS shares (see above), **to take account of any income tax relief received.**

4.3 SEIS reinvestment relief

Where an individual makes a gain on the **disposal of an asset during the 2013/14 tax year, up to £50,000 of the gain is exempt** from CGT if he makes a **qualifying SEIS investment during that same tax year.** It is also possible to make a claim to **carry back relief for a reinvestment to exempt a gain of the previous year** so long as a carry back claim has been made for income tax purposes. [Sch 5BB]

The **maximum SEIS reinvestment relief claim is limited to 50%** of the amount reinvested (maximum £100,000), in SEIS shares in the year.

In 2012/13, the first year of the scheme, 100% of the amount reinvested in SEIS shares, up to the maximum £100,000 investment, was available to defer gains of the same tax year.

Example 6

Ricky subscribed for shares worth £70,000 in an SEIS company on 14 May 2013. On 28 October 2013 he made a gain of £200,000 on the disposal of an investment property.

What is the maximum SEIS reinvestment relief Ricky can claim in 2013/14?

EIS deferral and SEIS reinvestment relief cannot be claimed in respect of the same expenditure.

5 Venture Capital Trust (VCT) CGT disposal relief

Any gain is exempt (and any loss is not allowable) on the disposal of VCT shares so long as the company was a VCT company both when the shares were acquired and at the date of the disposal. [s.151A]

This disposal relief is **available whether the taxpayer subscribed for the shares directly from the company or acquired them from a third party.**

However, the relief is only available **to the extent that the shares did not exceed the 'permitted maximum'** in the tax year of purchase (currently £200,000). [s 151A(6)]

6 Employee shareholder status exemption

This section is new

Any gain on the first disposal of **employee shareholder status shares** by the employee shareholder is **exempt** from capital gains tax if, **when the shares were acquired,** their **total value does not exceed £50,000.** [s.236C]

This amount is based on the unrestricted value of the shares, and takes into account all employee shareholder status agreements with the same, or associated, employer.

The **base cost** of the shares in the gain calculation is the **amount chargeable to income tax, less the £2,000** income tax-free amount (see earlier in this Text).

If the shares' **value exceeds £50,000 when they were acquired,** only the **proportion** of the gain relating to the first £50,000 is exempt.

7 Compensation and insurance monies

7.1 Destroyed assets

If an asset is destroyed or lost (and not merely damaged) **any insurance monies (ie compensation) received will be chargeable to CGT. However, if the proceeds are used to replace the asset within twelve months any gain can be deducted from the cost of the replacement asset.** If only part of the proceeds are used, the gain immediately chargeable is limited to the amount not spent. The rest of the gain is then deducted from the cost of the replacement. [s.23(4)]

The date of disposal is the date that the compensation is received and not the date that the asset was lost or destroyed.

Example 7

Alison bought a painting in January 1990 for £10,000. It was destroyed in a fire in May 2013 and she received £80,000 from the insurance company two months later. In March 2014 she bought another painting for £75,000 and made a claim under s.23(4) TCGA 1992.

Show Alison's CGT position in respect of the above.

7.2 Damaged assets

If an asset is damaged and insurance money (compensation) is received as a result, there is a part disposal, where A is the insurance money received and B is the value of the damaged asset. The taxpayer can avoid a part disposal computation by electing for the insurance money to be deducted from the cost of the asset ('rolled over') **so long as the asset is non wasting and:**

(a)   Not more than the higher of £3,000 or 5% of the insurance money is *not* used in restoring the asset; or
(b)   The insurance money is less than the higher of £3,000 or 5% of the value of the asset (ie is 'small'). [s.23(1)]

If (a) and (b) do not apply there will be a part disposal calculation, although the taxpayer can elect for this to apply only to the part of the proceeds not used in the restoration. In this case B (in the part disposal formula) is the value of the restored asset. The allowable cost will include the costs of restoration (enhancement expenditure).

Again, the date of disposal is the date that the compensation is received and not the date that the asset was damaged.

Example 8

Mr Jones bought a building which cost £40,000 on 15 August 1993. On 10 September 2013 it was damaged in a fire and, as a result, £33,000 insurance proceeds were received. Of this £20,000 was used to restore the building; the market value of the building immediately after restoration was £62,000.

You are required to calculate the chargeable gain arising on disposal and the base cost of the building for future computations assuming Mr Jones elects for there to be a part disposal only in respect of the money not spent on restoring the building.

Exam focus point

Examiner's report – Personal Taxation

May 2011 – Part I SFQ 8

Poorly answered; most candidates were aware that somehow the £15,000 that was not used in restoration had to be taxed but there was little clarity beyond that.

Chapter roundup

Gift relief

- Gift relief applies mainly to gifts and sales at an undervalue of business assets, including certain shares.

- Gift relief is also available where *any* asset is gifted to a trust (other than to a disabled person's trust) as there is also an inheritance tax (IHT) charge.

- The transferor's gain is effectively transferred to the donee because the base cost of the asset for the donee is reduced by the deferred gain (ie the gift relief claimed).

- On a sale at an undervalue any real profit (ie actual consideration less original cost) remains chargeable. The balance of the gain can be deferred.

- Gift relief is restricted where there has been non-business use of an asset or where shares in the transferor's personal company are gifted and there are non-business chargeable assets (ie investments) held by the company.

- The emigration of the recipient of the gift within six years will result in the crystallisation of the chargeable gain. An exception is made for individuals employed abroad on a temporary basis.

Enterprise Investment Scheme

- A gain on the disposal of shares that qualified for EIS income tax relief, and were held for at least three years, is exempt from CGT.

- A gain on disposal of any asset may be deferred if the individual reinvests the amount of the gain in shares in a qualifying EIS company.

- Relief is given on a £1 for £1 basis (although it is possible to specify a smaller amount in the claim to preserve losses or the annual exempt amount).

- There are detailed conditions to be satisfied regarding the shares, the investor and the EIS company.

Seed Enterprise Investment Scheme

- A gain on the disposal of shares that qualified for SEIS income tax relief, and were held for at least three years, is exempt from CGT.

- SEIS reinvestment relief provides an exemption where gains up to £50,000 (ie 50% of £100,000 maximum SEIS investment) arising in 2013/14 are reinvested in SEIS shares during 2013/14 or 2012/13.

Venture Capital Trust Scheme

- A gain on the disposal of qualifying VCT shares is exempt.

Employee shareholder status shares

- A gain arising on the disposal of employee shareholder status shares is usually exempt.

Compensation

- If an asset is destroyed or lost a gain is calculated when insurance money is received, unless the money is spent replacing the asset within 12 months.

- If an asset is damaged there is a part disposal when insurance money is received, unless the money is spent restoring the asset. If only part of the money is spent the gain can be deferred.

1. The gift relief election for gifts between individuals must be made jointly by the transferor and the transferee. True/False?

2. In what circumstances may the gain on a gift of a business asset between individuals be *fully* (as opposed to only partially) deferred?

3. On 15 May 2013 Philippa makes a gain on the sale of a painting of £60,000. Philippa makes no other disposals during 2013/14 and has capital losses brought forward of £12,000. What is the minimum investment she can make in qualifying EIS shares to reduce her gain to nil, assuming she wishes to fully utilise her capital losses?

4. Where an asset is completely destroyed there is a part disposal of the asset. True/False?

5. Kate sells a painting on 12 June 2013 for £120,000 making a gain of £40,000. If she makes an investment of £50,000 in qualifying SEIS shares in September 2013 the gain of £40,000 will be frozen until the SEIS shares are sold. True/False?

6. Kelly makes a gain of £35,000 on the disposal of all of her employee shareholder status shares, which were all acquired on the same day. The shares were valued at £100,000 when Kelly acquired them. The entire gain of £35,000 is exempt. True/False?

1.   True.

2.   (a)   There is no actual consideration, or there is a sale at an undervalue and the actual consideration is less than the transferor's base cost.

      (b)   The whole of the asset has been used throughout the transferor's period of ownership in the transferor's (or his personal company's) trade.

3.   Philippa can claim EIS deferral relief if she invests in qualifying EIS shares. To reduce her taxable gains to nil she can make a minimum investment of:

      £(60,000 – 12,000 – 10,900) = £37,100.

      Her gains computation would be as follows:

	£
Gain before relief	60,000
Less: EIS deferral relief (ie amount spent on subscribing for EIS shares)	(37,100)
	22,900
Less: capital losses b/f	(12,000)
	10,900
Less: annual exempt amount	(10,900)
Taxable gain	–

4.   False. There is a part disposal if the asset is only damaged.

5.   False. SEIS reinvestment relief is only available at 50% in respect of the gain of £40,000 (ie £20,000 relief) in 2013/14. In addition, that £20,000 is exempt, it is not simply frozen until the SEIS shares are sold, as it would be if the reinvestment had been in EIS shares.

6.   False. The exemption is only available for the first £50,000 of shares acquired so only £17,500 of the gain (ie £35,000 × 50/100) is exempt.

Solutions to chapter examples

Solution to Example 1

	£
Total gain (on shares)	60,000

Proportion relating to chargeable business assets eligible for relief:

$$£60,000 \times \frac{30,000}{40,000} = £45,000$$

	£
Less: gift relief	(45,000)
Chargeable gain relating to other chargeable non-business assets	15,000

Base cost of shares for Henry's brother:

	£
Market value at date of gift	150,000
Less: gain deferred by gift relief	(45,000)
Cost c/f	105,000

Solution to Example 2

	£
Total chargeable business assets are:	
Plant	50,000
Factory	1,470,000
	1,520,000

	£
Total chargeable assets are:	
Plant	50,000
Factory	1,470,000
Investments	80,000
	1,600,000

Gain on sale of shares

	£
Disposal proceeds (use market value)	950,000
Less: cost	(200,000)
Gain before gift relief	750,000

Eligible for relief:

$$£750,000 \times \frac{1,520,000}{1,600,000} = £712,500$$

	£
Less: gift relief	(712,500)
Chargeable gain	37,500

Solution to Example 3

	£
Total gain	50,000
Less: 3/8 of £50,000 for letting	(18,750)
Gain eligible for gift relief	31,250
Chargeable gain £(50,000 – 31,250)	18,750

Solution to Example 4

(a) *Angelo's CGT position*:

	£
Disposal proceeds (market value)	200,000
Less: cost	(30,000)
Gain before relief	170,000
Less: gain deferred:	
Gain less: actual proceeds *less* cost (chargeable now)	
£170,000 – £(50,000 – 30,000)	(150,000)
Chargeable gain £(50,000 – 30,000)	20,000

(b) *Michael's CGT position*:

	£
Disposal proceeds	195,000
Less: base cost = MV at gift *less* gain deferred	
£(200,000 – 150,000)	(50,000)
Chargeable gain	145,000

Solution to Example 5

(a) £196,000. The cost of the shares exceeds the gain, so the whole gain can be deferred.

(b) £170,000. The cost of the shares is less than the gain, so the claim is restricted to the amount subscribed for the shares. The rest of the gain (£26,000) is chargeable (unless he subscribes for more EIS shares).

(c) Robert should claim to defer £185,100. This is calculated as follows:

	£
Gain before relief	196,000
Less: EIS deferral relief	(185,100)
Chargeable gain	10,900
Less: annual exempt amount	(10,900)
Taxable gain	nil

Solution to Example 6

Ricky can make a claim for £35,000 SEIS reinvestment relief (ie £70,000 × 50%).

Solution to Example 7

	£
Gain on destruction of original painting ('disposal' date is **July** 2013 (Note))	
Proceeds	80,000
Less: cost	(10,000)
	70,000
Less: gain deferred balancing figure ie £(70,000 – 5,000)	(65,000)
Chargeable gain*	5,000

* Proceeds not reinvested (ie £80,000 – £75,000)

	£
Base cost of new painting:	
Price paid	75,000
Less: gain deferred	(65,000)
Revised base cost c/f	10,000

Note. The date of disposal is important as this determines the tax year in which the gain is taxed.

Solution to Example 8

	£
Chargeable gain	
Compensation received	33,000
Less: used in restoration	(20,000)
Consideration for part disposal	13,000
Allowable cost:	
$(40,000 + 20,000) \times \dfrac{13,000}{13,000 + 62,000}$	(10,400)
Chargeable gain	2,600

	£	£
Base cost of restored building		
Original cost	40,000	
Cost of restoration	20,000	
		60,000
Less: Insurance money not used in part disposal computation	20,000	
Cost used in part disposal computation	10,400	
		(30,400)
Base cost c/f		29,600

Now try the following questions

Short Form Questions:

15.1 – 15.9 inclusive

Long Form Questions:

15.1	Fran & Anna
15.2	Joe Bloggs
15.3	P J Laval
15.4	Simon
15.5	Emily
15.6	Peter
15.7	Sarah Stone

Personal Taxation

Part C:
Administration

- understand when an individual must notify HMRC of their liability to income tax and capital gains tax

- recognise the different tax return filing deadlines

- explain how an individual pays his income tax and capital gains tax liability

- understand the penalties for not notifying, filing or paying on time

- outline the way amendments are made to the return

- understand the requirements for keeping information records

- explain how taxpayers can claim reliefs

- understand HMRC's powers to obtain information and to inspect documents and premises

- describe the procedure at an appeal hearing before the Tribunals

References: TMA 1970 unless otherwise stated

Administration of income tax and CGT

1 Introduction

Personal tax compliance for income tax and capital gains tax (CGT) is administered through the self assessment system. The major burden is placed on the taxpayer and his advisers.

In practice many taxpayers arrange for their tax adviser to prepare and submit their tax returns. It is important to realise that the taxpayer is still the person *responsible* for submitting that return and for paying whatever tax becomes due – **the tax adviser is only acting as the taxpayer's *agent*,** and as such cannot take over the taxpayer's duties and responsibilities. Contractual obligations and professional requirements however ensure that the tax adviser performs competently.

References in this section to income tax include (where appropriate) Class 4 National Insurance Contributions (NIC).

2 Notification of liability to income tax and CGT

2.1 Who must notify?

Individuals who are chargeable to income tax or CGT for any tax year and who have not received a notice to file a tax return must notify their chargeability to HMRC **within six months from the end of the tax year,** ie by 5 October 2014 for 2013/14. [s.7(1) & (2)]

If a person has **no chargeable gains** and is **not liable to higher or additional rate tax,** he does not need to notify HMRC if all his income: [s.7(3)-(7)]

(a)   Is subject to Pay As You Earn (PAYE) (ie is **employment income**)

(b)   Has had (or is treated as having had) **income tax deducted at source,** or

(c)   Is **UK dividend income.**

2.2 Penalties for failure to notify chargeability

2.2.1 Overview

One set of penalty rules applies across the taxes, including income tax and capital gains tax, for failures to notify chargeability to tax that result in a loss of tax. [Sch 41 FA 2008]

The rules apply to **failures by either the taxpayer or his tax adviser,** unless the taxpayer can show that he took all reasonable steps to avoid the failure.

Higher penalties apply if the failure to notify involves income or gains arising in certain foreign countries. [para 6 – 6D Sch 41 FA 2008]

> ### Exam focus point
> Do not try and memorise all the different penalties – use your legislation (Paras 6 & 13 Sch 41 FA 2008) to help you.

2.2.2 Amount of penalty

Penalties are **behaviour related,** increasing for more serious failures, and are **based on the 'potential lost revenue'.**

The 'potential lost revenue' is broadly **the amount of tax outstanding on the normal due date. This broadly means the tax unpaid on 31 January following the tax year (31 January 2015 for 2013/14).**

There are tables of maximum and minimum penalties (see below). **The maximum penalties are reduced for the type and quality of disclosure,** with higher reductions if the disclosure is unprompted. [paras 6 & 13 Sch 41 FA 2008]

2.2.3 Disclosure

The minimum penalties shown below presume that the maximum reductions for disclosure apply. In practice, however, the reductions given are up to the HMRC officer involved and could result in a higher penalty being payable. [para 13 Sch 41 FA 2008]

Making disclosure to HMRC includes: [para 12 (2) Sch 41 FA 2008]

- **Informing** HMRC of the failure
- Providing HMRC with reasonable **help in quantifying** the amount of tax unpaid
- Allowing HMRC **access to records** to check the amount of unpaid tax.

Disclosure is **unprompted** if at the time it is made the taxpayer had **no reason to believe that HMRC had or were about to discover the failure.**

The reduction in the penalty depends on the **quality of disclosure.** HMRC have indicated as a guide that they weight the elements of disclosure as **informing (30%), helping (40%) and giving access (30%).**

2.2.4 Territorial scope

Taxpayers who fail to notify HMRC of their liability and whose income and/or capital gains are linked to an 'offshore matter' face a penalty of up to 200% of the tax due. [paras 6(4) & 6A(3) Sch 41 FA 2008]

The level of the penalty is linked to the **tax transparency of the territory/country** in which the **income or gain** arises. Where it is **harder for HMRC to obtain information from another country, the penalties are higher.**

Countries and territories are divided into three categories: [para 21A Sch 24 FA 2007]

(a) **Category 1:** The **UK** and territories with **automatic exchange of information** on savings income with the UK (eg the EU, Canada and the USA)

(b) **Category 2:** Territories which **exchange information on request** with the UK and **least developed countries** (any country/ territory not in either of the other categories)

(c) **Category 3:** Territories which **do not exchange information** with the UK and territories whose **agreements with the UK do not allow exchange of information to the international standard** (eg Iran and Iraq)

Income tax and capital gains tax arising as a result of assets or activities in these territories can attract a **penalty of up to 100%, 150% or 200% respectively of the tax due** (see below). [para 6 Sch 10 FA 2010]

The current list of territories in each category is available on HMRC's website. [http://www.hmrc.gov.uk/offshorefunds/territories-category.htm]

2.2.5 Penalty rates

The minimum and maximum penalties are as follows: [paras 6 & 13 Sch 41 FA 2008]

Territory category	Behaviour	Maximum penalty	Minimum penalty with unprompted disclosure		Minimum penalty with prompted disclosure	
Category 1	Deliberate and concealed	100%	30%		50%	
	Deliberate but not concealed	70%	20%		35%	
			≥12m	<12m	≥12m	<12m
	Any other case	30%	10%	Nil	20%	10%
Category 2	Deliberate and concealed	150%	45%		75%	
	Deliberate but not concealed	105%	30%		52.5%	
			≥12m	<12m	≥12m	<12m
	Any other case	45%	15%	Nil	30%	15%
Category 3	Deliberate and concealed	200%	60%		100%	
	Deliberate but not concealed	140%	40%		70%	
			≥12m	<12m	≥12m	<12m
	Any other case	60%	20%	Nil	40%	20%

Where the failure to notify is not deliberate the penalty is reduced depending not just on the level of disclosure but also the amount of time that has elapsed since the tax first became unpaid. For example, if the individual makes unprompted disclosure to HMRC of a failure to notify chargeability of a UK source of income within 12 months of the tax due date, the penalty can be reduced to nil. If the disclosure is made 12 months or more after the tax due date the penalty can only be reduced to 10%.

Note that there is **no zero penalty for reasonable care** (as there is for penalties for errors on returns – see below), although the penalty may be reduced to 0% if the failure is rectified within 12 months through unprompted disclosure. The penalties may also be reduced at HMRC's discretion in 'special circumstances'. Inability to pay is not a 'special circumstance'. [para 14 Sch 41 FA 2008]

If tax related penalties are also imposed for late filing of the tax return or late payment of tax, the penalty for late notification is reduced correspondingly.

2.2.6 Reasonable excuse

There is no penalty if the taxpayer's failure is not classed as deliberate and he has a 'reasonable excuse' for his failure to notify taxable income. [para 20 Sch 41 FA 2008]

HMRC considers that the reasonable excuse must:

(a) Be an **unusual or unforeseeable event beyond the taxpayer's control**
(b) **Apply throughout the period** the taxpayer failed to comply, and
(c) The taxpayer must **notify HMRC as soon as possible after the reasonable excuse ends**.

Reasonable excuse **does not include**: [para 20(2) Sch 41 FA 2008]

- Having **insufficient money to pay** the penalty.

- **Placing reliance on another person** to act, unless the taxpayer can show that he took all reasonable steps to avoid the failure.

2.2.7 Appeals

Taxpayers have a right of appeal against penalty decisions to the First-tier Tribunal (see below), which may confirm, substitute or cancel the penalty. [paras 17 – 19 Sch 41 FA 2008]

3 Self assessment tax returns

3.1 Individual tax return (the SA100)

The **tax return (the SA100)** is an **eight page form, together with supplementary pages** for particular sources of income. HMRC sends taxpayers a return and the supplementary pages they need depending on their known sources of income, together with a Tax Return Guide and various notes relating to the supplementary pages.

Where a taxpayer filed their previous year's return electronically he may be sent a notice to file a return, rather than the official HMRC return form.

The return must include a **declaration that the return is correct and complete to the best of the signatory's knowledge and belief**, even where it has been prepared by someone else, for example a tax adviser. [s.8(2)]

HMRC has the power to **withdraw a notice to file a self assessment return on request by the taxpayer** and **cancel any late filing penalty** (see below) issued in connection with that return. [s.8B]

3.2 Short tax return

Certain individuals with simple tax affairs can submit a 'short tax return', which is four pages long with supplementary capital gains pages if required. The return cannot be self selected and cannot be ordered from HMRC's Orderline or downloaded online. HMRC **automatically issues the return to certain taxpayers**, who have relatively simple tax affairs, such as employees, pensioners, and landlords with small amounts of property income, based on information on the previous year's tax return.

The individual must have **only standard investment income**.

Tax does not have to be calculated on the form, although a simple 'rough guide' working sheet is available for the taxpayer's own information.

The short return can be submitted online in the same way as the SA100.

3.3 Three line accounts

Owners of small businesses, including landlords of property letting businesses, may include simplified 'three line' accounts when completing their tax return (ie income *less* expenses = net profit). The turnover of the business, or gross rents from property, must be less than £79,000 pa.

The taxpayer must keep records to support the tax return (see below) whether producing detailed or three line accounts.

> ### Exam focus point
>
> The limit of £79,000 (below which landlords need only submit three line accounts) is equivalent to the VAT threshold, which is given in the Association's Tax Tables. Find it now!

4 Filing tax returns

4.1 Filing deadlines

A self assessment return is usually issued in April following the tax year concerned. For example, HMRC will send out the 2013/14 return to taxpayers in April 2014.

Taxpayers and their advisers may either **file the return electronically or complete the return by hand.** The filing date for a tax return depends on how it is filed: [ss.8(1D) & 12AA(4)]

Type of return	Filing date
Paper return	Later of **31 October following the end of the tax year**, ie for 2013/14 this is 31 October 2014, and 3 months after date of issue (or 2 months if the taxpayer wishes HMRC to calculate his tax liability for him).
Electronic return	Later of **31 January following the end of the tax year**, ie for 2013/14 this is 31 January 2015, and 3 months after the date of issue.

> ### Exam focus point
>
> **Examiner's report – Personal Taxation**
>
> **November 2010 – Part I SFQ 12**
>
> Most were able to identify the filing dates, although many only stated one filing date for the first part. Many candidates did not state the year, or said January 2011 – as a general rule, dates must be given in full if full credit is to be awarded.
>
> **May 2011 – Part I SFQ 2**
>
> Whilst most candidates recognised that the late issuance of the tax return would delay the required date of submission for the paper tax return, there was confusion as to whether this delay was for 2 or 3 months.

4.2 Penalties for late filing

4.2.1 Late filing penalty

A single penalty regime applies across the taxes for the late filing of a return. [Sch 55 FA 2009]

The penalties for **late filing of an individual's self assessment return** are as follows: [paras 2 – 6 Sch 55 FA 2009]

Delay	Penalty
1 day late	**Fixed £100 penalty.** Applies even if no tax due or all tax paid.
3 months late	**£10 for each following day** – up to a 90 day maximum of £900 (in addition to the £100 fixed penalty)
6 months late	The **higher of £300 and 5% of the tax due** (in addition to above penalties)
12 months late	The **higher of £300 and** (in addition to above penalties): – **5% of the tax due** (where withholding of information was **not deliberate**), or – **70% × tax due** where withholding of information was **deliberate but *not* concealed**, or – **100% of tax due** where withholding of information was **deliberate and concealed**

Where the return is more than 12 months late the penalty can be reduced for disclosure, with higher reductions if the disclosure is unprompted, as follows:

Behaviour	Maximum penalty	Minimum penalty with unprompted disclosure	Minimum penalty with prompted disclosure
Deliberate and concealed	100%	30%	50%
Deliberate, not concealed	70%	20%	35%

The definition of what constitutes disclosure is the same as for the penalty for failure to notify chargeability (see above).

4.2.2 Offshore penalties

There are increased penalties where the return is at least 12 months late and involves an offshore matter related to a Category 2 or 3 country or territory (see above) and the late filing was deliberate.

The penalties for returns that are less than 12 months late and Category 1 penalties for returns which are more than 12 months late are the same as for returns involving only UK matters.

The Category 2 and 3 penalties for returns more than 12 months late are subject to a **£300 minimum**, and are as follows: [paras 6(3A), 6(4A) & 15(2) Sch 55 FA 2009]

Behaviour	Category 2			Category 3		
	Maximum	Minimum penalty with prompted disclosure	Minimum penalty with *un*prompted disclosure	Maximum	Minimum penalty with prompted disclosure	Minimum penalty with *un*prompted disclosure
Deliberate, not concealed	105%	52.5%	30%	140%	70%	40%
Deliberate and concealed	150%	75%	45%	200%	100%	60%

4.2.3 Reasonable excuse

There is no penalty if the taxpayer can show he has a 'reasonable excuse' for filing the return late. [para 23 Sch 55 FA 2009]

Reasonable excuse is defined in the same way as for the penalty for failure to notify chargeability (see above). According to **HMRC guidance**, 'reasonable excuse' is when some unusual or unforeseeable event beyond the taxpayer's control has prevented the return from being filed.

For example: [http://www.hmrc.gov.uk/online/excuse-missed-deadline.htm]

(a)   A failure in HMRC's own computer system
(b)   A computer failure just before or during the preparation of an online return
(c)   A serious illness has made the person responsible incapable of filing the return, or
(d)   Registering for HMRC Online Services but not receiving the activation code in time.

The taxpayer must have made a **reasonable effort to meet the deadline**, so he will **not** have a reasonable excuse where he:

(a)   Found the online system too complicated to follow
(b)   Was let down by an accountant
(c)   Forgot about the deadline
(d)   Did not try to re-submit the return on time once a problem with the IT system was put right, or
(e)   Registered for HMRC Online Services after the filing deadline.

The taxpayer should **keep records of any error messages** produced during an abortive attempt to file online, although this is not essential for a claim to be considered.

5 Payment of income tax and capital gains tax

5.1 Paying tax

In general, taxpayers make three payments of income tax and, where relevant, one payment of capital gains tax for each tax year. The pattern of payments is usually:

31 January in the tax year:	**1st payment on account of income tax**
31 July after the tax year:	**2nd payment on account of income tax**
31 January after the tax year:	**Final payment to settle the income tax liability for the year, and Payment of any CGT liability**

HMRC issues payslips/demand notes in a credit card type 'Statement of Account' format, but there is no statutory obligation for them to do so and the **onus is on the taxpayer to pay the correct amount of tax on the due date.**

Statements of account are normally issued shortly before a payment is due, when a payment is made, and at intervals so long as any tax remains outstanding. Copies of statements of account are normally only issued to agents if the client authorises all statements to be sent to the agent.

5.2 Payments on account

5.2.1 Relevant amount

Payments on account (POAs) are usually required where the taxpayer's tax (and Class 4 NICs but not Class 2 NICs or capital gains tax) due for the previous year exceeded the amount of income tax deducted at source (including PAYE deductions and tax credits on dividends). **This excess is known as 'the relevant amount'.**

The POAs are each equal to 50% of the relevant amount for the previous year, and are due by 31 January in the tax year and the following 31 July. [s.59A(2)]

POAs are not required if the relevant amount falls below £1,000 or if the relevant amount is less than 20% of the total liability. [s.59A(1)]

Example 1

Gordon is a self employed builder who paid tax for 2013/14 as follows:

		£
Total amount of income tax liability		9,200
This included:	Tax deducted on savings income	3,200
He also paid:	Class 4 NIC	2,206
	Class 2 NIC	138
	Capital gains tax	4,800

How much are the payments on account for 2014/15?

Exam focus point

Examiner's report – Personal Taxation

November 2008 – Part I SFQ 1

The letter was generally well answered albeit a small minority of candidates did not bother to present it as a letter. The most frequent omission was of an explanation as to the reasons why payments on account would be required for the 2008/09 year.

5.2.2 Claims to reduce payments on account

Where a taxpayer's liability in the year is expected to be lower than in the previous year (for example if he has sold a rental property) **he can claim to reduce his POAs:**

(a) **To a stated amount, or** [s.59A(4)]

(b) **To nil.** [s.59A(3)]

The claim must state the reason why the taxpayer believes his tax liability will be lower, or nil.

If the taxpayer's eventual liability is higher than that estimated he will have reduced the POA too far. Although the POA will not be adjusted, there will be an interest charge on the underpayment (see below).

There may be a penalty based on the difference between the expected and actual POAs if the claim was made fraudulently or negligently. This penalty is usually only charged if there are repeated excessive claims. [s.59A(6)]

If the current year's liability is likely to be higher than that of the preceding year, there is no requirement to increase the interim payments.

5.3 Payment of income tax and capital gains tax

5.3.1 Balancing payment

The balancing payment of any income tax due for a tax year (after deducting POAs and tax deducted at source), together with any capital gains tax liability for that year, is payable on the 31 January following the tax year. [s.59B(1), (2) & (4)]

Example 2

Giles had made payments on account for 2013/14 of £6,500 each on 31 January 2014 and 31 July 2014, based on his 2012/13 liability. He then calculates his total income tax liability for 2013/14 at £18,000 of which £2,750 had been deducted at source. In addition he calculates that his CGT liability for disposals in 2013/14 is £5,120.

What, and by when, is the final payment due for 2013/14?

5.3.1 Payment of CGT by instalments

As we saw earlier in this Text, if the **proceeds for a disposal are received in instalments**, the general rule is that the **whole of the gain remains chargeable up front** in the normal way. However, **if the proceeds are receivable in instalments over a period exceeding eighteen months, the taxpayer may elect for the payment of the CGT to be spread** over the *shorter* of: [s.280 TCGA 1992]

(a)   The **period** of instalments, and

(b)   **Eight years.**

In addition, there is an instalment option for CGT due on gifts which either do not qualify for gift relief (see earlier in this Text) or where **gift relief has been claimed but some part of the gain remains taxable, where the gifted assets are:** [s.281 TCGA 1992]

(a)   **Land**

(b)   **Shares or securities (quoted or unquoted) out of a controlling holding, or**

(c)   **Unquoted shares or securities.**

The person paying the tax can elect, in writing, to HMRC for the option to pay in **ten equal yearly instalments**. The first payment is payable on the **normal due date,** ie 31 January following the tax year.

Interest is normally chargeable on the outstanding balance. The rate of interest is given in the Association's Tax Tables.

The taxpayer may pay off the outstanding instalments (plus accrued interest) at any time. **The outstanding balance and accrued interest become immediately payable if the asset gifted is sold.**

Exam focus point

Examiner's report – Personal Taxation

November 2012 – Part I SFQ 12

Candidates were more aware of the ability to pay by instalments where the proceeds are being received in instalments than they were of the option to do so for gifts that do not qualify for gift relief. This generally hampered their ability to score heavily here.

5.4 Penalties for late payment

5.4.1 Penalties for late self assessment tax payments

There is a **standardised penalty regime for the late payment of tax**. It applies to all the main taxes including income tax and capital gains tax. [Sch 56 FA 2009]

The penalty for late payment of income tax or capital gains tax is as follows: [para 3 Sch 56 FA 2009]

Length of delay	Penalty
30 days (the penalty date)	5% of tax unpaid at that date
5 months after the penalty date	Further 5% of tax unpaid at that date
11 months after the penalty date	Further 5% of tax unpaid at that date

This gives a **maximum penalty of 15% × the unpaid tax.**

These penalties **do not apply to late payments on account of income tax.**

Example 3

Jennifer does not pay her balancing payment of tax for 2013/14 of £4,500 until 1 August 2015.

Calculate the late payment penalties.

Late payment penalties can be suspended where the taxpayer agrees a time to pay arrangement (where a tax debt is paid over time) with HMRC, unless they abuse the arrangement.

5.4.2 Reasonable excuse

There is no penalty if the taxpayer can show he has a 'reasonable excuse'. [para 16 Sch 56 FA 2009]

HMRC considers an excuse to be **'reasonable' where an unusual or unforeseeable event beyond the taxpayer's control has prevented him from paying by the due date**, for example, where a cheque is lost in the post or the taxpayer or a close relative suffers a serious illness.

5.5 Interest

5.5.1 Introduction

A single harmonised interest regime applies to most taxes including **income tax (including that paid via PAYE) and capital gains tax.** [ss.101–105, Sch 53 & 54 FA 2009, SI 2011/701]

There is **one rate of interest for late payments of tax and one for repayments of tax.**

5.5.2 Late payment interest

Late payment interest is charged on **any amount payable to HMRC, including any unpaid penalties** (see above) and **late payments on account** (see below), **between the late payment interest start date** (normally, the date on which the tax or penalty becomes due and payable) **and the date of payment.** [s.101(4) FA 2009]

Example 4

Calculate the late payment interest that Jennifer (Example 3) will have to pay.

Exam focus point

The rate of interest will be given in the Association's Tax Tables and it is this rate that you should use regardless of the actual rate currently applicable, if different. Also, make all calculations to the nearest month and pound unless told otherwise.

5.5.3 Interest on late payments on account

Late payment interest is payable if a taxpayer is **late paying his payments on account** (POAs), as outlined above. However, where the individual has **overpaid the POAs**, ie because his final liability is lower than that in the previous year, **late payment interest is only due in respect of 50% of the actual final liability.**

Illustration 1

Jess was late making payments on account of her 2013/14 liability. She paid £10,000 on 5 March 2014 and a further £10,000 on 26 August 2014.

Her tax return for 2013/14 showed a final liability of £17,000, so she overpaid her tax by £3,000 (ie £17,000 − (2 × £10,000)).

Late payment interest is due because Jess was late paying her POAs. However, it is only payable in respect of half of her final liability, ie on £8,500 for each POA.

BPP
LEARNING MEDIA

Interest therefore runs from 1 February 2014 to 4 March 2014 on the first late POA of £8,500, and from 1 August 2014 to 25 August 2014 on the second payment of account of £8,500. Repayment interest (see below) is due from HMRC in respect of the £3,000 overpayment.

5.5.4 Interest on reduced payments on account

Where a taxpayer makes a claim to reduce his payments on account and there is still a final payment to be made interest is charged as if each of the POAs had been the lower of:

(a)   The **reduced amount, plus 50% of the final balancing payment of income tax**, and

(b)   The amount which would have been payable had **no claim** for reduction been made.

Illustration 2

Herbert's payments on account for 2013/14 based on his income tax liability for 2012/13 were £4,500 each. However, when he submitted his 2012/13 income tax return in January 2014 he made a claim to reduce the payments on account for 2013/14 to £3,500 each. The first payment on account was made on 29 January 2014, and the second on 12 August 2014.

Herbert filed his 2013/14 tax return in December 2014. The return showed that his tax liabilities for 2013/14 (before deducting payments on account) were income tax £10,000 and capital gains tax £2,500. Herbert paid the balance of tax due of £5,500 on 19 February 2015.

Herbert has made an excessive claim to reduce his payments on account, and will therefore be charged interest on the reduction. The payments on account should have been £4,500 each based on the 2012/13 liability. This is lower than the reduced POA plus 50% of the final balancing payment of £5,000 (£3,500 + (50% × [£10,000 − £7,000])). Herbert will be liable to interest as follows:

- First payment on account

  −   on £3,500 − nil − paid on time
  −   on £1,000 between the due date of 31 January 2014 and payment date, ie 1 February 2014 to 18 February 2015 *(Note)*

- Second payment on account

  −   on £3,500 between the due date of 31 July 2014 and part-payment date, ie 1 August 2014 to 11 August 2014
  −   on £1,000 between the due date of 31 July 2014 and payment date, ie 1 August 2014 to 18 February 2015

- Balancing payment of income tax and capital gains tax

  −   on £3,500 between the due date of 31 January 2015 and payment date, ie 1 February 2015 to 18 February 2015

Note   Remember to exclude the actual due date and the date of payment from the calculation.

Exam focus point

Examiner's report – Personal Taxation

November 2012 – Part I SFQ 3

Probably one of the harder questions on the paper and usually poorly answered. Most did not appreciate that the payments on account had been underpaid by £2,000 each, rather than £3,000. Those that did, often calculated the interest on the £4,000 underpayment without reference to the fact that its two constituent £2,000s had been outstanding for different periods of time. Others double counted the calculation of interest on the late payments on account; once by reference to the payment on account due dates and once by reference to the balancing payment due date.

5.5.5 Repayment interest

HMRC pays repayment interest on overpayments of:

(a) **POAs**

(b) **Payments of income tax and capital gains tax**, including tax deducted at source or tax credits on dividends, and

(c) **Penalties**.

Interest is paid **between the repayment interest start date and the date of repayment.**

The repayment interest start date is the later of the date that the tax was paid to HMRC and the due date for payment of the tax, to the date the tax is repaid. [Para 2 Sch 54 FA 2009]

Tax is repaid when claimed, unless a greater payment of tax is due in the following 30 days, in which case it is **set off** against that payment.

Income tax deducted at source for a tax year and tax credits are **treated as if they were paid on 31 January following the tax year**.

6 Incorrect returns

6.1 Corrections and amendments

HMRC can amend a taxpayer's return to correct any obvious errors or mistakes or anything else in the return that HMRC has reason to believe is incorrect in the light of information available to it, within nine months of receiving the tax return. [s.9ZB]; [s.119 FA 2008]

The taxpayer can amend his tax return within 12 months of the 31 January filing deadline whether he has filed a **paper or online return** (ie by 31 January 2016 for the 2013/14 return). [s.9ZA]

6.2 Penalties for inaccurate returns or documents

6.2.1 Introduction

One penalty regime applies to all inaccurate returns in respect of all of the main taxes including income tax and capital gains tax returns. [Sch 24 FA 2007]

The regime applies to the **submission of inaccurate returns or documents and the failure to notify HMRC where an under assessment is made.**

6.2.2 Amount of the penalty

The amount of the penalty is a **percentage of the 'potential lost revenue'** (PLR) as a result of the inaccuracy or under assessment and **depends on the behaviour of the taxpayer** as follows:

Behaviour	Penalty
Mistake	No penalty
Careless (failure to take reasonable care)	30% of PLR
Deliberate understatement (but not concealed)	70% of PLR
Deliberate understatement with concealment	100% of PLR

The PLR is normally **the amount of tax lost.**

Like the penalties for failure to notify (see above) these standard penalties can be reduced if the taxpayer tells HMRC about the inaccuracy or under assessment or helps it to calculate or correct the error.

The amount of the **reduction depends on whether the disclosure is prompted**. An unprompted disclosure is where the taxpayer makes disclosure when he has no reason to believe that HMRC have or are about to discover the inaccuracy.

The **minimum and maximum** penalties are as follows: [Para 4 Sch 24 FA 2007]

Behaviour	Maximum penalty	Minimum penalty with unprompted disclosure	Minimum penalty with prompted disclosure
Mistake	No penalty		
Careless (failure to take reasonable care)	30% of PLR	0%	15%
Deliberate inaccuracy (but not concealed)	70% of PLR	20%	35%
Deliberate inaccuracy with concealment	100% of PLR	30%	50%

6.2.3 Offshore penalties

The above inaccuracy penalties are increased where the return involves an offshore matter related to a Category 2 or 3 country or territory (see above). The Category 1 penalties are the same as for returns involving only UK matters. [Sch 24 FA 2007]

The penalties, which can be **reduced for disclosure**, are: [Paras 4 & 10 Sch 24 FA 2007]

Behaviour	Category 2			Category 3		
	Maximum	Minimum penalty with prompted disclosure	Minimum penalty with unprompted disclosure	Maximum	Minimum penalty with prompted disclosure	Minimum penalty with unprompted disclosure
Careless	45%	22.5%	0%	60%	30%	0%
Deliberate, not concealed	105%	52.5%	30%	140%	70%	40%
Deliberate and concealed	150%	75%	45%	200%	100%	60%

6.2.4 Reasonable care

Where a taxpayer has taken reasonable care in completing a return and has taken reasonable steps to disclose any errors, no penalty will apply.

'Reasonable care' varies according to the person, their circumstances and their abilities.

HMRC expect taxpayers to make and **keep sufficient records** (see below) to provide a complete and accurate return and to **check the correct position** when they do not understand something.

If the taxpayer **does not promptly tell HMRC when they discover an error, HMRC will treat the errors as careless inaccuracies** even where the taxpayer took reasonable care.

Where the taxpayer uses an agent such as an accountant to complete a return, it **remains the taxpayer's responsibility to make sure that the return is correct.**

6.2.5 Appeals and suspensions

Where a penalty applies **HMRC must assess the penalty and notify the taxpayer**. This is treated in the same way as a tax assessment for the purposes of collection and enforcement, and may be appealed against.

A penalty for a careless inaccuracy may be suspended by HMRC for up to two years. The suspension must impose conditions on the tax payer which will assist him in avoiding such inaccuracies in the future. If the conditions are complied with, then the penalty is cancelled.

7 Keeping records

7.1 Introduction

A common framework for record keeping applies across the taxes, including income tax, capital gains tax and PAYE (along with corporation tax and VAT). [Sch 37 FA 2008]

One set of high level rules apply across the taxes but there are detailed rules for the individual taxes.

Taxpayers must keep all records used in making and delivering a correct tax return. These taxpayer records are crucial to HMRC's information powers described below.

HMRC can inspect 'in-year' records, ie *before* a return is submitted, if they believe it is reasonably required to check a tax position.

7.2 Which records must be kept?

Under the common framework the general rule is that taxpayers must keep **'information'** (rather than the underlying records themselves), that shows that they have prepared a **complete and correct tax return**.

The specific rules for income tax and capital gains tax are that individuals must keep **'adequate' business and accounting records**.

'Adequate' means keeping records to be sure that the right profit, loss, tax declaration or claim is made.

Taxpayers can usually keep copies of original documents except where the documents show domestic or foreign tax deducted or creditable. In this case the originals (eg dividend or interest certificates) must be kept.

7.3 Time limits for keeping records

The time period for keeping records depends on whether or not the taxpayer is in business. [s.12B] [IR booklet SA/RK BK1]

Records must be retained until the later of:

(a)   (i)   **5 years after 31 January following the tax year** (ie by 31 January 2020 for the 2013/14 return) **where the taxpayer is in business** (as a sole trader or partner or property letting), **otherwise**

        (ii)   **1 year after 31 January** following the tax year (ie by 31 January 2016 for the 2013/14 return), or

(b)   Provided notice to deliver a return was given before the date in (a):

        (i)   The time after which enquiries by HMRC into the return could no longer be started (see below), or
        (ii)   The date any such enquiries had been completed.

7.4 Record keeping penalties

The maximum (mitigable) penalty for each failure to keep and retain records is generally £3,000 per tax year. [s.12B(5)]

8 Taxpayer claims

8.1 Claims for relief

8.1.1 General principles

Generally any claims and elections that can be made in a tax return must be made in this way if HMRC issues a return. Claims for any relief, allowance or repayment of tax must be quantified at the time the claim is made. [s.42]

A claim may be made after the time limit for amending the tax return has expired.

BPP
LEARNING MEDIA

8.1.2 Time limits for taxpayer claims [Sch 39 FA 2008]

The **general time limit, where legislation does not state a specific date, is four years after the end of the tax year**. For example, for capital gains tax purposes the legislation specifies a time limit for making a claim for EIS deferral relief of the fifth anniversary of 31 January following the end of the tax year in which the EIS shares are issued, so this **overrides** the general time limit.

The legislation however does not specify a date for submitting a gift relief claim for CGT purposes and therefore the general time limit of four years after the end of the tax year applies.

> **Exam focus point**
>
> **Examiner's report – Personal Taxation**
>
> **November 2011 – Part I SFQ 6**
>
> Most candidates ... could not give the time limit for making any claim or election.

8.2 Claims for recovery of overpaid tax (overpayment relief)

A taxpayer may make a claim for a repayment of overpaid tax where: [Sch 1AB]

(a) An **amount of tax has been paid** which the **taxpayer believes was not due,** or
(b) An **assessment or determination has been raised** but the **taxpayer believes the tax is not due.**

Relief is also available for overpayment of **tax charged contrary to EU law.**

The claim must be made no later than **four years** after the end of the tax year to which the mistake relates.

The **taxpayer is responsible for determining the amount of their claim** and HMRC has the right to conduct an enquiry into the relevant period covered by the return, or to make either a discovery assessment or determination which may otherwise be out of date.

HMRC will **not allow a claim in certain circumstances,** which include the following: [Sch 1AB for IT & CGT].

(a) The amount of tax paid is excessive because:

(i) **Of a mistake in a claim, election or notice or a mistake in making or failing to make an election, claim or notice**

(ii) **Of a mistake in relation to certain capital allowances claims**

(iii) It was **calculated in accordance with practice generally prevailing** at the time

(b) The taxpayer ought previously to have been **aware of the mistake and to have made a claim within the time limit**

(c) The case has already been the **subject of a tribunal or court hearing**

(d) The taxpayer can seek relief by other steps under tax legislation.

9 HMRC's powers

9.1 Introduction

HMRC has one set of powers covering most of the taxes, including income tax and capital gains tax to ensure taxpayers comply with their obligations, pay the right amount of tax at the right time and claim the correct reliefs and allowances. [Sch 36 FA 2008]

HMRC also has powers to deal with **dishonest tax agents** who have been responsible for a loss of tax.

These powers allow HMRC to check taxpayers' affairs by:

- Asking taxpayers, tax agents and third parties for **information and documents**.
- **Visiting business premises** to inspect the premises, assets and records.

This enables HMRC to make cross-tax checks using one set of rules.

The Tax Tribunal deals with the exercise of the above powers and also taxpayer appeals. This Tribunal is made up of the First-tier Tribunal and Upper Tribunal (see further below).

9.2 Information powers

9.2.1 General provisions

HMRC usually informally requests information and documents from taxpayers in connection with their tax affairs. If, however, a taxpayer does not co-operate fully, **HMRC can use its statutory powers to request information and documents from taxpayers and even third parties via a written 'information notice'.**

9.2.2 Taxpayer notices [Para 1 Sch 36 FA 2008]

HMRC can issue a taxpayer notice for information and documents that are **'reasonably required' for the purpose of checking the taxpayer's tax position.**

A taxpayer notice may be issued either with or without the approval of the First-tier Tribunal (FTT). An authorised HMRC officer must agree before the request is referred to the FTT.

HMRC can request both statutory records and supplementary information, such as appointment diaries, notes of board meetings, correspondence and contracts.

The taxpayer (or third party – see below) must provide the information or document requested by the information notice within such period as is reasonably specified within the notice.

9.2.3 Third party notices [Para 2 Sch 36 FA 2008]

An information notice issued to a third party must usually be issued with either the agreement of the taxpayer or the approval of the FTT. [Sch 36 FA 2008]

An authorised HMRC officer must agree before the request is referred to the FTT.

The taxpayer to whom the notice relates must receive a summary of the reasons for the third party notice unless the Tribunal believes it would prejudice the assessment or collection of tax.

As above, **the request must be relevant to establishing the taxpayer's correct tax position.**

Tax advisers and auditors cannot be asked to provide information connected with their functions. For example, a tax adviser does not have to provide access to his working papers used in the preparation of the taxpayer's return.

In addition, HMRC cannot ask a tax adviser to provide communications between himself and either the taxpayer or his other advisers.

This 'professional privilege' does not apply in certain situations, for example, to explanatory material provided to a client in relation to a document already supplied to HMRC or where a tax agent has been found to have been engaged in dishonest conduct (see below).

9.2.4 Unknown-identity notices

In addition to the above HMRC also has the power to require *any person* **to provide information or documents** which are required to **check the tax position of a person(s) for which they do not hold full identity details** where HMRC believe **there is a serious loss of tax.** [Para 5 Sch 36 FA 2008]

HMRC can also issue an **'identity ascertainable notice'** where the **identity of the taxpayer(s) is not known but can be established by someone else** who has done business with that taxpayer, from information already held by HMRC.

HMRC does not have to suspect that there has been a serious loss of tax. The notice does not require the approval of the FTT, but may only request the name, last known address, and/or date of birth of the taxpayer(s). [para 5A Sch 36]

9.2.5 Data-holder notices [Sch 23 FA 2011]

HMRC may issue a data-holder notice to certain data-holders (for example, employers, banks and those processing payment card transactions) requiring them to provide 'relevant data', which may be general data or data relating to particular persons or matters. It may include personal data such as names and addresses of individuals.

HMRC may use this power for **general effective risk assessment** and also to **target non-compliant taxpayers**. Where this power overlaps with the general information powers detailed above, those **general powers take priority**.

9.2.6 Right of appeal

The recipient of an information notice has a right of appeal against the information notice unless the FTT has approved the issue of the notice.

There is no right of appeal if the information or documents relate to records the person must keep for tax purposes (statutory records).

Although approval of the FTT removes the right of appeal, the Tribunal may only approve the issue of a notice if the addressee has been advised that the information will be required and been given an opportunity to make representations to HMRC.

9.2.7 Restrictions on information powers

HMRC can only request information that is in the person's possession.

HMRC cannot request information that:

*   Relates to any pending **tax appeal**.
*   Constitutes **journalistic** material.
*   Is **legally privileged**.
*   Is **over six years old** (except with the approval of an authorised HMRC officer).
*   Relates to someone who **died over four years earlier**.

In addition, HMRC **cannot issue a notice** to check the taxpayer's tax position **if a return has already been made** for a period **unless**:

*   The return is the subject of an **ongoing self assessment enquiry**, (see below)
*   HMRC believes there has been a **loss of tax**, or
*   It relates to PAYE (as there is no enquiry framework for this).

9.2.8 Computer records

HMRC's powers to request and inspect documents explicitly include documents held on a computer or recorded electronically in any way. [s.114 FA 2008]

An 'authorised' person, who may be an HMRC officer or, in exceptional circumstances, a specialist from outside HMRC, can obtain access to a computer, and any other apparatus or material, which has been used in connection with a 'relevant document'.

Anyone obstructing HMRC in the exercise of its powers or failing to comply within a reasonable time may be charged a penalty of £300.

9.3 Inspection powers

9.3.1 Power to visit business premises

An authorised officer of HMRC can enter the business premises of a taxpayer whose liability is being checked, or of certain third parties, and inspect the premises, assets used in the business and business documents. The power does not extend to any part of the premises used solely as a dwelling. [Sch 36 FA 2008]

If an information notice has been issued, the documents required in that notice can be inspected at the same time.

The inspection must be reasonably required for the purposes of checking the taxpayer's tax position.

HMRC can inspect premises for the purpose of valuing them if this is necessary to check a person's income tax liability. HMRC can also inspect premises and any other property on the premises for the purpose of valuing, measuring or determining their character if necessary to check a person's CGT liability. The inspection must be agreed to by the occupier of the premises or the Tribunal.

HMRC can even exercise its powers before a return is received where, for example, it believes that a taxpayer:

- Did not notify chargeability to tax.
- Did not register for VAT if required.
- Is operating in the informal economy.

9.3.2 Carrying out inspections

HMRC will usually agree a time for the inspection with the taxpayer.

However, an authorised HMRC officer can carry out the inspection at 'any reasonable time' if either:

(a) **The taxpayer receives at least seven days' written notice**, or

(b) The inspection is carried out by, or with the approval of, an authorised HMRC officer. In this case, the HMRC officer carrying out the inspection **must provide a notice, in writing, to someone present at the premises (usually the occupier), or, if there is no one present, leave the notice in a prominent place on the premises**.

HMRC has issued Compliance Checks (CC) **factsheets** covering such unannounced visits, which are likely to be undertaken where, for example, there is a strong risk that the taxpayer would move the business or remove stock or other assets. [CC/FS4 & CC/FS5]

9.3.3 Right of appeal

There is no right of appeal against an inspection notice.

The occupier of the premises can refuse entry and prevent the inspection from being completed but may then be subject to penalties (see below).

9.4 Information power penalties

9.4.1 When can a penalty be charged?

A penalty may be charged for:

(1) **Failure to comply or obstruction**, or [para 39 Sch 36 FA 2008, para 30 Sch 23 FA 2011]
(2) **Providing inaccurate information and documents.** [para 40A Sch 36 FA 2008]

9.4.2 Failure to comply or obstruction

A penalty may be charged where a person: [para 39 Sch 36 FA 2008]

(a) **Fails to comply with an information notice**, or
(b) **Deliberately obstructs an inspection** that has been approved by the FTT.

Failing to comply includes concealing, destroying or otherwise disposing of documents required by an information notice.

If the document is *likely* to be the subject of an information notice, a six month time limit applies.

Concealing, destroying or otherwise disposing of documents may also be an indictable (ie criminal) offence.

9.4.3 Types of penalties

There are three types and amounts of penalty: [Sch 36 FA 2008 & Sch 23 FA 2011]

Type of penalty	Amount
Basic	£300
Daily	£60 per day
Tax-related	Based on tax

A basic penalty must be assessed before either a daily or tax-related penalty can be considered.

A daily penalty applies if the failure to comply or obstruction continues after the date the basic penalty is imposed.

A tax-related penalty may be charged, in addition to the basic penalty and any daily penalties, when HMRC believes that a significant amount of tax is at risk. The Upper Tribunal decides the amount based on the amount of tax at risk.

The above penalties **must be paid within a 30 day time limit.**

Where the failure to comply or obstruction relates to an identity unknown or data-holder notice and continues for **more than 30 days,** HMRC can apply to the Tribunal to **increase the amount of daily penalty from £60 to an amount not exceeding £1,000.**

9.4.4 Reasonable excuse

A person is not liable to a penalty if he can satisfy HMRC (or the FTT on appeal) that he has a reasonable excuse for:

- Failing to comply with an information notice, or
- Obstructing an inspection,

and the failure is remedied as soon as the excuse ends.

HMRC has indicated that daily penalties will not normally be assessed after the failure has been remedied.

Reasonable excuse does not usually include lack of money to pay the penalty.

9.4.5 Providing inaccurate information and documents

A penalty may be charged where: [para 40A Sch 36 FA 2008]

(a)   In complying with an information notice, a person **provides inaccurate information or produces an inaccurate document**, and

(b)   Either:

(i)   The inaccuracy is **careless** (failed to take reasonable care) or **deliberate,** or

(ii)   The person discovers the **inaccuracy some time later and fails to take reasonable steps to inform HMRC.**

The penalty may also be charged where a **person knows of the inaccuracy at the time** the information is provided, or the document is produced, but **does not inform HMRC at that time**.

The penalty is **£3,000 per inaccuracy.**

9.4.6 Appealing against a penalty

The taxpayer may appeal to the FTT against:

(a) The imposition of a penalty, and

(b) The amount of the penalty.

The appeal must be made to HMRC in writing, within 30 days of HMRC's issue of the original penalty notice.

The taxpayer *cannot*, however, appeal against a tax-based penalty for failure to comply or obstruction.

9.5 Criminal cash

HMRC Officers' have the power to **seize suspected criminal cash** under the Proceeds of Crime Act 2002 (POCA) and **exercise POCA search and seizure warrants.** [Sch 48 FA 2013]

9.6 Dishonest conduct of tax agents

This section is new

9.6.1 Overview

From 1 April 2013 HMRC has a number of new powers that it can use when it has evidence that a **tax agent** (ie an individual who, in the course of business, assists clients with their tax affairs) **has done something dishonest that leads to a loss of tax.** [Sch 38 FA 2012]

9.6.2 HMRC powers

HMRC can:

(a) Issue a **conduct notice** if it has determined that the agent has engaged in dishonest conduct. This sets out the evidence held by HMRC.

(b) Issue a **file access notice** (subject to prior approval by the FTT) to obtain the **working papers** of a tax agent where **either:**

    (i) **It has issued a conduct notice, or**

    (ii) The individual has been **convicted of a tax related offence involving fraud or dishonesty whilst he was a tax agent.**

(c) **Publish information about the tax agent**, including his name and address, **if a penalty for dishonest conduct** (see below) **exceeds £5,000.** This can include disclosing details of the dishonesty to a professional body of which the tax agent is a member.

9.6.3 Penalties

HMRC can issue a **civil penalty for dishonest conduct**. The minimum penalty is £5,000 (although this can be reduced in 'special circumstances') and can be as high as £50,000, depending on the tax agent's behaviour (ie extent of disclosure and assistance given to HMRC).

It can also impose a **penalty of £300** for failure to comply with a **file access notice**, with **additional daily penalties** of up to £60.

Interest is payable on **late paid penalties**.

9.6.4 Right of appeal

The tax agent may appeal, in writing within 30 days, **against both a conduct notice and any penalty imposed.**

He **may not, however, appeal against a file access notice**, although If HMRC has issued the notice to a third party (eg the taxpayer) because the working papers are no longer in the agent's possession, that **third party can appeal**.

9.7 Enquiries into returns

9.7.1 Overview

HMRC can conduct a compliance check into an individual's return. The term 'compliance check' is used to include **any kind of check using HMRC's information powers** set out above, **as well as formal enquiries.**

There are two main types of compliance check:

(a)   **Pre-return checks**, which are conducted **using the information powers set out above**, and

(b)   **Enquiries into returns**, claims or elections which have **already been submitted**. [s.9A]

In addition, HMRC may conduct a check **after a return has become final** (or where **no return has been submitted**) where they believe that an assessment or determination may need to be issued under the discovery provisions.

Examples of when a pre-return check may be carried out in practice include: [CH205320]

*   To assist with **clearances** or ruling requests
*   Where a previous check has identified **poor record-keeping**
*   To check that **computer systems** will produce the information needed to support a return
*   To find out about planning or **avoidance schemes**, and
*   Where **fraud** is suspected.

The rules relating to **enquiries into returns**, claims and elections are set out below.

Some returns are selected for an enquiry at **random**, others for a **particular reason**, for example, if HMRC believes that there has been an underpayment of tax due to the taxpayer's failure to comply with tax legislation.

Note that where a tax return has been submitted, HMRC can only issue a taxpayer notice in relation to that period where an enquiry is ongoing, or where HMRC has reason to believe that insufficient tax has been assessed for the period. [para 21 sch 36 FA 2008]

9.7.2 Raising the enquiry

Notice must be given by HMRC of the intention to conduct an enquiry by:

*   The first anniversary of the **actual filing date,** or

*   If the return is **filed late** or the **taxpayer amends the return** after filing it, the **quarter day** following the first anniversary of the actual submission date/ amendment filing date. The quarter days are 31 January, 30 April, 31 July and 31 October.

Where an enquiry was not raised within the limit which would have applied had no amendment been filed, it is restricted to matters contained in the amendment.

The officer does not have to have, or give, any reason for raising an enquiry. In particular the taxpayer will not be advised whether he has been selected at random for an audit.

9.7.3 During the enquiry

In the course of the enquiry:

(a)   **HMRC may issue a written 'information notice' (see above) to require the taxpayer to produce documents, accounts or any other information required. The taxpayer has the right to appeal to the FTT.** [Sch 36 FA 2008]

(b)   **HMRC may amend a self-assessment if it appears that insufficient tax has been charged** and an immediate amendment is necessary to prevent a loss of tax to the Crown. This might apply if, for example, there was a possibility that the taxpayer might emigrate, or bankruptcy proceedings be commenced. [s.9C]

(c)   Amendments may be made by the taxpayer whilst an enquiry is in progress, although they will not take effect until the end of the enquiry. The contents of the amendment may be taken into account in the enquiry.

(d)   **HMRC may postpone any repayment due as shown in the return until the enquiry is complete**. HMRC has discretion to make a provisional repayment but there is no facility to appeal if the repayment is withheld.

9.7.4 Completion of the enquiry

An enquiry is not complete until HMRC issues a closure notice. The notice must either state that the return needs no amendment, or must amend the return.

HMRC has only **one opportunity to raise an enquiry** and a tax return cannot be subject to an enquiry more than once. HMRC may, however, in limited circumstances, raise a **discovery assessment** if they are of the opinion that there has been a loss of tax (see below). [s.9A(3) & s.12AC(4)] [para 5(3) Sch 1A]

9.8 Determinations

HMRC may only conduct enquiries if a return has been submitted.

If a taxpayer has not submitted a return by the due filing date, HMRC may make a 'determination' (ie an estimate) of the amounts liable to income tax and capital gains tax and of the tax due. This determination is treated as if it were a self assessment. This enables the officer to seek payment of tax, including payments on account for the following year and to charge interest. [s.28C]

The determination must be made within the period ending **three years after the filing date, ie 31 January following the tax year,** so by 31 January 2018 for a determination raised in respect of the 2013/14 tax year.

The determination may be superseded by a self assessment made within the same period or, if later, within 12 months of the date of the determination.

Exam focus point

Examiner's report – Personal Taxation

May 2008 – Part I SFQ 8

Most candidates incorrectly thought that one could appeal a determination, albeit most also rightly thought that filing the return was the top priority. Less than half made it clear that the filing of the return would automatically supersede the determination, with many believing this would only be achieved through further negotiation with HMRC.

9.9 Discovery assessments

If HMRC discovers that profits have been left out of a return, that any self assessment has become insufficient, or that any relief given is excessive, a 'discovery' assessment may be raised to recover the tax lost. Conditions limit the circumstances in which a discovery assessment may be made. [s.29]

If the tax lost results from an error in the taxpayer's return but the return was made in accordance with prevailing practice at the time, no discovery assessment may be made.

A discovery assessment may only be raised where a return has been made if:

(a)   The omission is brought about either **carelessly or deliberately** by the taxpayer or his agent (eg tax adviser), or

(b)   **HMRC did not have information made available to him to make him aware of the loss of tax** at the time that enquiries into the return were completed.

Information is considered to be 'made available' to HMRC if it could be reasonably inferred by the officer or if it is contained in:

(i)   The return for the relevant tax year (or preceding two tax years),
(ii)   Any claim submitted for the relevant tax year (or preceding two tax years), or
(iii)   Accounts, statements or documents accompanying the return or claim or produced in the course of the enquiry.

Tax charged on a discovery assessment is due thirty days after the issue of the assessment. [s.59B(6)]

The time limits for raising a discovery assessment are as follows:

- **Ordinary** time limit   **4 years** from the end of the tax year
- Where the omission is **careless**   **6 years** from the end of the tax year
- Where the omission is **deliberate**   **20 years** from the end of the tax year.

10 Appeals system

10.1 Introduction

There are occasions when the taxpayer and HMRC may disagree, for example when HMRC make an amendment to a self assessment return after an enquiry or where HMRC raise a discovery assessment. In these circumstances the **taxpayer may appeal** against the amendment or discovery assessment.

All tax appeals are heard by the Tax Chamber of the independent Tribunals.

Most appeals are heard by the Tax Chamber of the FTT. The Upper Tribunal hears more complex tax cases and appeals against the decisions of the FTT. Appeals to the Upper Tribunal are only available on a point of law and with either the FTT's or Upper Tribunal's permission. There is no automatic right of appeal on a point of law.

Alternatively a taxpayer may either be offered or they may request an internal HMRC review. This does not affect the taxpayer's right to have the Tribunal hear the appeal after the conclusion of the review if they wish.

10.2 Internal reviews

An **internal review** is carried out by an **objective HMRC review officer not previously connected with the case**. This is a less costly and more effective way to resolve disputes informally, without the need for a Tribunal hearing. An appeal to Tribunal cannot be made until any review has ended. The taxpayer must either accept the review offer, or notify an appeal to the Tribunal, within 30 days of being offered the review, otherwise the appeal will be treated as settled.

HMRC must usually **carry out the review within 45 days**, or any longer time as agreed with the taxpayer. The review officer may decide to uphold, vary or withdraw decisions.

After the review conclusion is notified, the taxpayer has **30 days to appeal to the Tribunal**.

10.3 Tribunal hearings

If there is no internal review, or the taxpayer is unhappy with the result of an internal review, the case may be heard by the Tribunal.

It is allocated to one of four case 'tracks' depending on the complexity of the case. [para 23 SI 2009/273]

The **default track is the 'paper' case**, which is used for straightforward matters such as appeals against fixed filing penalties.

The Tribunal must **provide each party with a decision notice, within 28 days of their decision**, which states the Tribunal's decision and notifies the parties of any right of appeal. [para 35 SI 2009/273]

A decision of the **FTT may be appealed to the Upper Tribunal**. The party wishing to appeal must apply in writing to the Tribunal within 56 days of the Tribunal's decision. [para 39 SI 2009/273]

Decisions of the Upper Tribunal are binding on the Tribunals and any relevant public authorities, such as HMRC. A **decision of the Upper Tribunal may be appealed to the Court of Appeal**, and thereafter to the Supreme Court.

No costs will be awarded for standard or basic cases, except where either party behaves unreasonably. Costs will usually be awarded in complex cases unless the appellant opts out of the costs regime before the hearing. [para 10 SI 2009/273]

Chapter roundup

- Self assessment is the system under which taxpayers are required to complete returns and self assess their tax liabilities. Each return has working sheets to enable the taxpayer to calculate his own income tax and CGT liability. For electronic returns the taxpayer's tax liability is automatically calculated.

- An individual must advise HMRC within 6 months of the end of the tax year if he is chargeable to income tax or CGT and he has not already received a tax return.

- Tax returns are due on:
  - 31 October following the tax year for a paper return
  - 31 January following tax year for an electronic return.

- Late returns are subject to a penalty of £100, with additional daily penalties of £10 per day where the return is more than 3 months late. Tax geared penalties apply where the return is more than 6 months late.

- Income tax is due via payments on account on:
  - 31 January during the tax year
  - 31 July following the tax year.

  Payments on account are calculated as half of the previous year's income tax relevant amount.

- The balance of the income tax liability must be settled by 31 January following the tax year.

- Only one CGT payment is due on 31 January after the end of the tax year.

- Self assessment is enforced through a system of automatic penalties, based on the revenue lost and the behaviour of the taxpayer, with higher penalties where offshore tax evasion is involved, together with strict rules for interest on late paid tax.

- Penalties apply for failure to notify, late filing, late payment and if the return contains inaccuracies.

- Taxpayers have four years after the end of a tax year to claim available reliefs, unless the legislation states a specific date.

- HMRC has wide ranging powers to inspect a taxpayer's documents and premises.

- HMRC also has powers to deal with tax agents who have done something dishonest that leads to a loss of tax.

- Random enquiries are used to ensure that taxpayers are complying correctly with their obligations.

- Appeals are heard by the Tax Chamber of the First-tier Tribunal in the first instance. Appeals against decisions of the First-tier Tribunal are heard by the Finance and Tax Chamber of the Upper Tribunal.

- There is a right of appeal from the First-tier Tribunal to the Court of Appeal on a point of law, and thereafter, with leave, to the Supreme Court.

Quiz

1. When must an individual notify HMRC of a new source of income for 2013/14?

2. Brenda was issued with her 2013/14 tax return on 15 April 2014. By which date must Brenda submit the completed form?

3. John is self employed. For how long must he retain his 2013/14 business records?

4. Which taxes are included in an individual's payments on account?

5. An individual may reduce a payment on account to £nil. True or False?

6. Only CGT on gifts subject to gift relief qualify for CGT instalments. True or False?

7. Explain the penalties that HMRC can impose when they have evidence of dishonest conduct by a tax agent and the tax agent fails to comply with a request for information.

1.   By 5 October 2014.

2.   If Brenda submits the return online then it is due by 31 January 2015. If Brenda submits a paper return it must be submitted by 31 October 2014.

3.   Until 31 January 2020 (ie 5 years after 31 January 2015).

4.   Income tax and Class 4 NIC.

5.   True.

6.   False.

7.   HMRC can issue two penalties:

      (i)   For dishonest conduct, which can be anywhere between £5,000 and £50,000, and

      (ii)   For failure to comply with a file access notice. This is £300, with additional daily penalties of up to £60.

Solutions to chapter examples

Solution to Example 1

The relevant amount is:

	£
Income tax:	
Total income tax liability for 2013/14	9,200
Less: tax deducted for 2013/14	(3,200)
	6,000
Add: Class 4 NIC	2,206
	8,206

Payments on account for 2014/15:

		£
31 January 2015	× ½	£4,103
31 July 2015	As before	£4,103

There is no requirement to make payments on account of capital gains tax or Class 2 NIC.

Solution to Example 2

	£
Total income tax liability	18,000
Less: tax deducted at source	(2,750)
Relevant amount	15,250
Less: POAs for 2013/14 (2 × £6,500)	(13,000)
Balancing payment	2,250
CGT due	5,120

Total payment due on 31 January 2015 (excluding the first payment on account for 2014/15) £2,250 + £5,120 = £7,370

Solution to Example 3

Jennifer must pay a penalty of £225 (5% × £4,500) as the tax was not paid by 2 March 2015 (the penalty date, ie 30 days after 31 January 2015)

Note. A further 5% penalty of £225 would have been due if the tax had not been paid by 2 August 2015 (ie 5 months after the penalty date of 2 March 2015). The tax was paid on 1 August 2015 so no further penalty is due.

Solution to Example 4

Interest will run between the due date and the date of payment, ie 1 February 2015 until 31 July 2015 (6 months):

£4,500 × 3% × 6/12 = £67

Short Form Questions:

16.1 – 16.4 inclusive

Long Form Questions:

16.1	Interest payments
16.2	Radnor

Personal Taxation

Part D:
Other aspects of the syllabus

- discuss other aspects of the syllabus which includes accounts, law and professional responsibilities and ethics

Other aspects of the syllabus

1 Other examinable areas

As well as taxation, the **following areas may also feature** in the Personal Taxation paper:

(a)   **Law**
(b)   **Ethics**.

1.1 Law

You may already have studied law for the law E-Assessment, but certain key topics remain examinable on this paper.

These topics may be tested in a **Short Form Question or as part of a Long form Question**.

The following chapters in the ATT's manual 'Essential Law for Tax Practitioners' are examinable:

- Chapter 5 – Regulatory framework of the tax adviser (sections 1 – 10 only)
- **Chapter 8 – Working relationships and the law**
- **Chapter 18 – Introduction to property law**
- **Chapter 19 – Land law in England, Wales and Northern Ireland**
- **Chapter 20 – Dealings in land in England, Wales and Northern Ireland**

Ideally you should study all of the relevant chapters. However, the topics **highlighted in bold** are particularly relevant to core Personal Taxation topics and are also the chapters that have been examined in recent exams.

The following topics have been recently examined:

- **Working relationships and the law**: Employment written statements, terminating employment contracts, employees' duties, dismissal, statutory redundancy pay

- **Property law**: Exchange and completion, jointly owned property

- **Land law**: Legal estates and interests in land

Exam focus point

Examiner's report – Personal Taxation

November 2010 – Part II LFQ 2

Answers ... were disappointing and showed candidates continue to devote little time to the law aspect of the syllabus. Few candidates scored highly on what should have been an easy way to pick up marks.

1.2 Ethics

You may already have studied ethics for the ethics E-Assessment but **certain key ethics topics remain examinable** on this paper.

These topics may be tested in a **Short Form Question or as part of a Long form Question.**

The ATT's manual 'Professional Responsibilities and Ethics for Tax Practitioners' contains the professional rules and regulations that may be examined. However, note that you will not be examined on the contents of the chapters in the section of the manual concerned with Anti-money laundering. You will only be examined on money laundering issues to the extent they are covered in Chapter 5 of the ATT's manual 'Essential Law for Tax Practitioners' (see above).

In addition you may be examined on the content of the following publication, that is **available from the ATT's website** (http://www.att.org.uk/students/current/attcurrentstudentexaminations/ProfRules):

- Continuing Professional Development Regulations and Guidance 2011

The following have historically been popular examination topics:

- Disclosure
- Engagement letters
- Conflicts of interest
- Relevant communications

Exam focus point

The ATT's Law and Professional Responsibilities and Ethics manuals can be purchased by following the link on the ATT's website:

http://www.att.org.uk/students/current/attcurrentstudentexaminations/Law+Syllabus

You will also find much more valuable information on the ATT website, so take this opportunity to have a look at what is available as these publications are not available in the examination.

Now try the following questions:

Short Form Questions:

Q17.1 – Q17.15 inclusive

Personal Taxation

Question and Answer Bank

Short form questions

1.1 Mary, a single woman aged 67, has net income of £26,880. What are the total allowances available to Mary for 2013/14?

1.2 Darren, born 12 August 1940, is registered blind. His wife Edna was born on 15 January 1935. Calculate the maximum allowances that Darren may deduct from his net income in 2013/14.

1.3 Keith has a salary of £110,000 in 2013/14. This is his only income during the year. What is his personal allowance for 2013/14?

1.4 In 2013/14 James has a salary of £45,580 (PAYE £8,054). He makes a Gift Aid donation to the RNLI of £560.

What is his tax payable or repayable?

1.5 Joe is aged 90 and has net income of £32,800. He is married to Jean, who has no income. What allowances and tax reductions is Joe entitled to in 2013/14?

1.6 Andy receives a salary of £280,000 in 2013/14. During the year he won £1,500 on the lottery and paid qualifying interest of £100,000 on a loan to acquire close company shares. What is his tax liability?

1.7 Martin Keynes is aged 16 and is at school.

He has the following income in 2013/14:

£1,600 (net)   Interest from his Barclays bank account into which he pays his earnings from his newspaper round

£375 (net)   Interest from building society account set up in his name by his mother

How much interest is taxable on Martin for the year?

1.8 William was born on 6 March 1930 and is single. In the year ended 5 April 2014 he had income of £27,800 and paid £400 under Gift Aid to the NSPCC, a UK registered charity. What is William's personal allowance for 2013/14?

1.9 John is an unmarried student. In the year to 5 April 2014 he received the following:

	Gross £	Tax deducted £
Scholarship from a charity	1,935	–
Legacy from late grandfather	12,000	–
Earnings from employment	3,700	740
Building society interest	300	60

What is the maximum tax repayment he can claim?

1.10 Bert Harvey, born on 8 June 1948, has been married to his wife Betty, born on 18 June 1934, for many years. They have the following income in 2013/14:

		£
Bert	Earnings from employment	13,845
Betty	State pension	5,728
	Occupational pension	5,200

What is Bert's tax liability for 2013/14?

1.11 Pamela owns 1,000 £1 ordinary shares in Esher plc. The following dividends were declared:

8p per share for the year ended 31 March 2012, paid 1 June 2013
4p per share for the year ended 31 March 2013, paid 1 June 2014

What amount will Pamela enter into her tax computation for 2013/14?

1.12 Sharon received the following income in 2013/14:

	£
Bank deposit interest	2,100
Building society interest	1,800
UK dividends	8,550
	12,450

She has no other sources of income. What is the total amount of tax repayable to Sharon?

1.13 In 2013/14 Sandra has earnings from employment of £5,264. She also received bank interest of £3,800 and dividends of £34,000. What is her tax payable or repayable assuming she has suffered no income tax via PAYE?

1.14 Anita has earnings from employment of £125,000 (tax of £43,598 deducted via PAYE) in 2013/14. During the year she also received bank interest of £12,500 and dividends of £27,000. What is her tax payable?

1.15 Nicholas, a 79 year old retired journalist, received the following income during the year ended 5 April 2013:

	£
Taxable trade profits from freelance writing and lecturing	8,720
Net income distributed from his grandfather's discretionary trust	1,500

On 1 March 2014 Nicholas entered into a civil partnership with Paul, who is 66 years old and has net income of £5,000. Calculate Nicholas's tax payable/repayable for 2013/14.

1.16 Richard Key gifted some shares to his twin daughters, Donna and Dawn, age 17. Donna is married and presently working. Dawn is unmarried and at college. Each daughter received a dividend of £1,500 in 2013/14.

Explain who will be taxed on the dividend income received by Donna and Dawn.

1.17 Gilbert, aged 5, receives £75 each year in interest income from a deposit account set up for him as a gift from his father. If he has no other income how will this be taxed? Explain your answer.

1.18 Alan is a single man, born 7 January 1935. He has income from pensions of £50,000 in 2013/14 and makes the following payments:

(a) Mortgage interest of £5,040 on a loan of £56,000 taken out to purchase his main residence.

(b) Interest of £2,610 on a loan taken out to make a loan to a close company in which he owns 10% of the ordinary share capital.

(c) Maintenance payments to his first wife of £3,500 pa under a court order dated 1 July 1995.

Calculate Alan's tax liability for 2013/14.

2.1 Ian receives a salary of £27,040 and treasury stock interest of £20,000. Calculate Ian's tax liability for 2013/14.

2.2 Christopher has received the following amounts of interest on his NS&I products:

	Year ended 5 April 2014 £
Savings account	276
NS&I Certificates	125

He also received a tax repayment for 2012/13 to which HM Revenue & Customs added interest of £89.

Calculate Christopher's interest income for the year ended 5 April 2014?

2.3 Julian made a five year loan to Roch Ltd (unquoted debenture) and a five year loan to his next door neighbour, Bob. During 2013/14 he received interest on both of the loans.

Will the interest receipts be received gross or net? Explain your answer.

2.4 Lucy received the following income in 2013/14:

		£
1.	Lloyds Bank	
	Oxford Street branch	8,680
	Guernsey branch (paid gross)	640
2.	Interest on government stock issued in May 2008	5,000

What is her taxable income for 2013/14?

2.5 What is the maximum amount of cash and shares that an individual over the age of 18 can invest in an ISA in 2013/14?

2.6 What is the maximum amount that an individual under the age of 18 can invest in a Junior ISA in 2013/14?

2.7 What are the main income tax benefits of an ISA?

2.8 Bert, a single man, has taxable non savings income of £136,480 in 2013/14 (all earnings). He invests £120,000 of cash he inherited in qualifying Seed Enterprise Investment Scheme shares in November 2013. What is the tax reduction available to him?

2.9 Gemma has invested the following amounts in qualifying VCTs during 2013/14:

10 June 2013	VCT 1	£150,000
5 September 2013	VCT 2	£60,000

She receives dividends in 2013/14 as follows:

VCT 1	£3,000
VCT 2	£3,400

What amount of net dividends (if any) must be included in her taxable income? Explain your answer.

Exam focus point

Question 2.10 below is taken from the Pilot Paper for the Personal Taxation Certificate paper.

2.10 Simon is 14 and in full time education. During 2013/14 he received £5,500 (net) from a discretionary trust. He has no other source of income. Calculate Simon's tax position for 2013/14.

2.11 Belinda's grandmother died on 1 July 2013 leaving her entire estate to Belinda. The estate is still in administration so the executors made an interim payment of £5,000 to Belinda on 31 March 2014. The only estate income came from bank deposit investments. What income and tax figures will be reported on Belinda's R185 (Estate income) for 2013/14? Explain your answer.

2.12 In May 2013 Nicole bought a flat for her mother, Maureen, to live in. Nicole funded the purchase from a gift of £200,000 that she received from Maureen earlier that year. The annual rental value of the flat is £10,000. Maureen does not pay any rent or contribute towards the expenses of the property.

Calculate Maureen's pre-owned asset tax charge for 2013/14 assuming her taxable income for the year is £20,000.

2.13 Alison sells £12,000 4% Treasury Stock ex-interest on 15 June 2013. Interest is paid on the stock on 30 June and 31 December each year. How much interest is taxable on Alison in 2013/14?

2.14 Sylvia took out a life assurance single premium bond on 1 September 2009 for £20,000. She made the maximum withdrawal each year and encashed the policy on 30 November 2013, receiving £30,000. Her only other income in 2013/14 was her salary of £40,810 (tax deducted via PAYE of £6,274). Calculate Sylvia's tax payable.

2.15 Neil and Jenny have held a joint NatEast Bank account for many years. Jenny has only ever put £100 into the account. During 2013/14 interest received on the account amounted to £300. How much of the interest should be taxed on Jenny?

2.16 Edmund was born in May 1946. He holds 2,000 shares in Aslan plc. The company declared net dividends of £15 and £16 per share for the years ending 31 March 2013 and 31 March 2014 respectively. These dividends were paid on 26 June 2013 and 30 June 2014 respectively. In 2013/14 Edmund also received £75,000 from his employment, from which £20,600 of tax was deducted under PAYE. Calculate the income tax payable by Edmund for 2013/14.

2.17 In 2011 William gave his brother John £500,000 which John put towards the purchase of a £750,000 house. John emigrated in 2012 and, from 6 September 2013, William moved into the house and lived there rent-free. Full market rent for the occupation of this property would be £24,000 per annum. William is a higher rate taxpayer.

Calculate the tax charge that arises on William for 2013/14 and explain the election that he could make to avoid it.

2.18 Lisa, an additional rate taxpayer, owns 25% of the share capital of Phillips Ltd, a close company. On 6 April 2014 Phillips Ltd wrote off an outstanding interest-free loan of £30,000, which it had made to Lisa a few years previously. Lisa has a company car from Phillips Ltd, which, if she worked for the company, would give her a taxable benefit of £4,875 in 2013/14.

What are the tax implications of the above for Lisa?

3.1 Simon and his wife, Sarah, earn £54,500 and £52,000 pa respectively. In 2013/14 Sarah receives child benefit of £1,752. State who will suffer the child benefit charge and calculate the amount that must be included in his or her self assessment tax return.

3.2 Tanya earns an annual salary of £15,000. She is unable to work for five weeks due to illness. State whether Tanya is entitled to receive SSP and, if so, how much.

3.3 Annabel looks after a foster child, Jamie (age 13), throughout 2013/14. Her total foster care receipts for the year are £20,000. What is Annabel's 'qualifying amount' for qualifying care relief purposes for 2013/14?

Exam focus point

Questions 4.1 to 4.3 below are taken from the Pilot Paper for the Personal Taxation Certificate paper.

4.1 Ben owns a house which he lets out furnished to earn extra income.

In 2013/14 the property was let for the whole year at a rate of £1,500 per month (although he only received rental income of £16,500 as one month was paid late).

He incurred the following expenses in the year to 5 April 2014:

	£
Agent's fee	1,800
Mortgage interest	4,200
Water rates	120
Cost of building new porch	2,500
Insurance	500

Ben claims the wear and tear allowance.

Calculate Ben's taxable property income.

4.2 Harry owns a property which is let for ten weeks from 1 July 2013 at a rent of £160 per week. The tenants leave at the end of this period having paid only £1,300 of the total amount due. Harry writes off the outstanding debt.

The property is re-let to new tenants on 1 March 2014 for a rent of £400 per month payable in arrears. He received the first payment on 10 April.

He pays interest of £700 during the year ended 5 April 2014 on a loan to purchase the property.

What is his taxable property income for 2013/14?

4.3 John owns two properties:

Whitehouse – let at a rental of £4,000 per annum, payable quarterly in advance. The tenant was late in paying the last quarter's rent for the quarter to 5 April 2014 and John did not receive payment until 25 April 2014.

Blackhouse – let at a rent of £2,000 per annum payable quarterly in advance. Blackhouse was not let at all during 2012/13, however a tenant moved in on 30 June 2013.

What is John's taxable property income for 2013/14?

4.4 Henry owns a property which he lets for the first time on 1 July 2013 at a rent of £4,000 per annum payable monthly in advance.

The first tenants left without notice on 28 February 2014 and the property was re-let to new tenants on 4 April 2014 at a rent of £5,000 per annum payable yearly in advance.

Henry's allowable expenditure was £1,000 in the year. What is his taxable property income for 2013/14?

4.5 Polly lets out a furnished property for £8,000 per annum. She pays insurance of £300 per annum and water rates of £400 per annum. Polly claims the wear and tear allowance. What is the amount taxable as property income?

4.6 Brian rents out a room in his main residence for £5,000 per annum, allowable expenses relating to the rental were £600. What is Brian's taxable property income for 2013/14? Explain your answer.

4.7 State four of the conditions for a property to qualify as a furnished holiday let.

Exam focus point

Question 5.1 below is taken from the Pilot Paper for the Personal Taxation Certificate paper.

5.1 Daisy, a full time employee, was made redundant by her employer in June 2013. She received the following redundancy package:

	£
Statutory redundancy pay	3,800
Ex gratia cash payment	25,000
Market value of company car – ownership transferred to Daisy	12,000
Outplacement counselling	4,500

What amount, if any, will be taxable on Daisy?

5.2 Janet is a director of Dragon Ltd. The company accounts show the following remuneration:

Year ended	Salary	Bonus
	£	£
31 December 2013	9,000	2,400
31 December 2014	10,000	4,200

The bonus is paid on 28 February following the year end. The salary is paid evenly over the year.

What is the amount of Janet's taxable income for 2013/14?

5.3 Tina commenced employment with Harrison Electrics Ltd on 1 November 2012. She was paid a salary of £1,000 per month, paid on the last day of the month. From 1 January 2014 she was given the use of a new Ford Focus 1400cc which has a list price of £15,000 with all private petrol paid for by the company. The emission rate is 155g/km. What are her total earnings from Harrison Electrics Ltd for 2013/14?

5.4 In 2012 Whitegate plc bought a new 3 litre car which has a list price of £14,000 for the sole use of James, one of its directors. The emission rate is 178g/km. The company pays car expenses including all the petrol but James repays to the company a nominal £0.02 per mile for petrol consumed in private motoring. What is James's taxable benefit for 2013/14?

5.5 In 2013/14 Jim, a director of a wine importing company, is paid £10,000 per annum and is given the use of a new 2 litre car which has a list price of £16,000 and an emission rate of 180g/km, plus wine which cost the company £1,000. Jim's 20 year old student daughter, Jane, also works for the company on Saturdays, is paid £15 per day and has the use of a new 1,150cc car which has a list price of £12,000 and an emission rate of 92g/km. Jim uses £600 of the wine promoting the company's products. No private petrol is paid for by the company.

What are Jim's earnings for 2013/14?

5.6 Albert, who has been employed by Roberts Tools Ltd as a salesman for several years, earned a salary of £14,800 in 2013/14 and had the use of a 2 year old Ford Focus 1100, which has a list price of £12,000. The emission rate is 135g/km. No private diesel was paid for.

Albert is also given an expense allowance of £80 each month to cover incidental costs of travelling. At the end of the tax year, he calculated that, of this, £750 would be allowable for tax purposes.

What is the amount to be entered on Albert's form P11D in respect of benefits for 2013/14?

5.7 Grasshopper Ltd has a dispensation from HMRC in respect of travel and subsistence expenses directly reimbursed to its employees.

Mr Adams commenced employment with Grasshopper Ltd on 1 January 2014 and was paid £1,000 per month. His expenses were paid as:

(1) A round sum allowance of £100 per month payable on the 1st of the month, plus

(2) Reimbursement of specific travel and subsistence expenses of £250 up to 5 April 2014.

Calculate the amounts to be entered on the P11D for Mr Adams for 2013/14.

5.8 Sue earns £15,000 per annum working for Redbridge Ltd and uses the crèche provided by the company for her child. The cost to the employer is £3,000 per year.

Tara earns £52,000 working for Bluefield Ltd. Her employer begins paying her registered childminder's fees of £62 per week for the 52 weeks from 6 April 2013.

What amounts, if any, are taxable in respect of childcare for 2013/14?

5.9 Daphne is an employee of Surbiton Ltd. The company provided her with a credit card, and during the year paid the following amounts on her behalf:

	£
Annual fee	30
Daphne's private purchases	257
Interest charge for late payment	46
	333

What is Daphne's taxable benefit for 2013/14?

5.10 Joshua is an employee of Mumbles plc, earning £12,000 per annum. He received the following benefits in the year ended 5 April 2014:

	£
Work place parking (estimated value)	720
Childcare vouchers (weekly amount for 48 weeks)	65
Credit card expenditure: goods purchased for business use	272

What are Joshua's taxable benefits in 2013/14?

5.11 A company throws a staff party which cost £200 per head. What is the tax position for the employee?

5.12 Finlay, a chartered accountant, is the Finance Director of Globe Ltd, a company which is based in Derbyshire. He personally incurs the following expenses in 2013/14:

(1) Subscription to the Chartered Institute of Taxation of £280

(2) Subscription to local golf club of £250, as required by Globe Ltd in order to promote the firm's business contacts

(3) Subscription to the Naval Club in London of £200 in order to have somewhere to stay overnight when his duties necessitate an overnight stay in London.

What amount is he able to deduct from his employment income in 2013/14?

5.13 Bert earns £18,000 pa and lives in job related accommodation provided by his employer. The company pays £2,000 rent and £3,100 for household expenses in the year ended 5 April 2014. What are Bert's taxable earnings for 2013/14?

5.14 Paul was provided with two mobile phones costing £250 each and a laptop computer costing £5,000 by his employer on 6 April 2013. During 2013/14 he used his mobile phone 40% of the time for personal calls (the other was used by his daughter) and the laptop 60% of the time for non business purposes. What is Paul's taxable benefit for 2013/14?

5.15 John has a salary of £50,000 pa and has no other sources of income. He drives his own 1.5l engine car to work, which has CO_2 emissions of 149g/km, taking his 5 year old daughter to childcare on the way. John's employer has been paying the cost of the crèche, which is £200 per week for 46 weeks each year, since 1 June 2010. John is provided with a designated parking space at his employer's premises. This costs the employer £1,000 pa. Sometimes John has to drive to clients and his employer reimburses him for his business mileage at 60p per mile. In 2013/14 John did 5,000 business miles. Calculate John's earnings for 2013/14.

5.16 Ruth is an employee of Benson Ltd and earns a salary of £45,000 pa. Benson Ltd has loaned her £20,000 so she can redecorate her house. As at 5 April 2013 there was an outstanding balance of £15,000. On 5 January 2014 Ruth repaid a further £5,000. Ruth pays Benson Ltd interest at 3% pa on the loan. What is Ruth's taxable benefit for 2013/14?

5.17 Jason is an employee of Saranson Ltd. The company provide him with a house near their office. Saranson Ltd bought the house in 1995 at a cost of £80,000. Jason moved into the house in 2005 when its market value was £130,000. At 6 April 2013 the market value of the house was £250,000. The gross annual value is £5,000. Jason pays Saranson Ltd rent of £3,000 pa. Calculate Jason's taxable benefit for 2013/14.

5.18 Natalie is a receptionist at Hospitality Hotel. She was provided with the use of a dinner set by the hotel on 6 October 2012. Its market value at that date was £2,000. On 6 October 2013 the hotel agreed to sell the dinner set to Natalie for £1,000, its market value at that date was £1,500. Calculate the taxable benefit for 2013/14.

5.19 Judy is an employee of Markham Ltd. She earns £25,750 pa and is provided with a company owned flat. The flat cost the company £60,000 when it was bought in 1996. Judy moved into the flat in 2003 when its market value was £100,000. The annual value of the flat is £3,000. Markham Ltd also pays for Judy's heating and lighting bills, this costs the company £400 pa. Judy is also provided with furniture for use in her flat. The market value of the furniture was £2,500 in 2003. Calculate Judy's taxable benefit for 2013/14.

5.20 George was unexpectedly made redundant on 15 August 2013. His redundancy package was as follows:

	£
Payment in lieu of notice (provided for in his employment contract)	8,000
Ex gratia payment	40,000
Statutory redundancy pay	5,000

The £40,000 payment was not contractual and George did not expect it. How much of the package is taxable?

5.21 Alan receives a non-contractual termination payment of £51,000 from Duxton Ltd. He has spent 10 years out of his 30 years service with the company working abroad, his last 2 years of service being spent in the UK. How much of the termination payment will be exempt from income tax.

5.22 Charles Prosser is a company director and occupies a house owned by the company. The house was purchased in May 2006 for £400,000 and Charles moved in immediately. An extension was added in September 2013 at a cost of £30,000. The gross annual value of the house was £2,225. During 2013/14 Charles paid £2,725 as rent to the company.

Calculate the amount taxable on Charles for 2013/14 as a benefit in respect of the provision of accommodation.

5.23 Muriel receives the following benefits from her employment:

(i) A diesel Volvo XC90, registered in May 2010 and with a list price of £40,000.The CO_2 emissions are 194g/km. Fuel for private mileage is also provided.

(ii) A parking space is provided in a car-park close to the office; her employer pays £3,000 per annum to secure this space.

(iii) A loan of £200,000 on which she pays interest of 2%.

(iv) A mobile phone.

Calculate the amounts chargeable to income tax in respect of these benefits for 2013/14.

Exam focus point

Question 6.1 below is taken from the Pilot Paper for the Personal Taxation Certificate paper.

6.1 Ray was granted an Enterprise Management Incentive option in July 2010 to acquire 10,000 shares for £1.50 each in Ex Ltd, his employing company. The shares were worth £2 each at the date of grant. He exercised the option in July 2013 when the share price was £4.75.

Explain the income tax consequences of the grant and exercise, assuming all the conditions for a qualifying EMI option are met.

6.2 What is the maximum value of 'free shares' and 'partnership shares' that can be allocated to an employee per annum under a share incentive plan (SIP)?

6.3 George exercises his option over 10,000 shares which he received from an unapproved share option plan. The exercise price was £11.50 each and the shares were worth £15.00 each at the date of exercise. He is a higher rate taxpayer. What is the income tax payable on exercise?

6.4 Bruce signs an employee shareholder agreement with his employer on 1 December 2013. What amount is included in his employment income for 2013/14 assuming he receives 1,000 free shares on 1 December 2013 worth:

    (a)   £2,000

    (b)   £3,000

7.1 What are the classes of national insurance contributions (NICs) payable by (a) employees, and (b) self employed individuals, and on what are they based?

7.2 Explain what Class 1A NICs are based on and who pays the Class 1A liability.

7.3 Employees who are members of a final salary occupational pension scheme may contract out of the State Second Pension Scheme.

Explain the consequences for both the employer and the employee where the scheme is contracted out.

8.1 George has the following income:

	£
Employment income	28,000
Dividend income from shares	5,400

What is the maximum amount George can pay into his personal pension on which he is entitled to tax relief?

8.2 Norma is a housewife. She is 52 years old. Her only taxable income in 2013/14 is a dividend of £5,000.

Norma wants to take out a pension. Explain the maximum contribution that she can make for 2013/14 on which tax relief is available?

8.3 Daniel aged 30 is an employee of Smithson Ltd. His salary for 2013/14 is £52,000. The company does not have an occupational pension scheme so Daniel pays contributions into his personal pension.

In 2013/14 Daniel pays £5,000 into his pension. What is Daniel's higher rate tax liability for 2013/14?

8.4 Jeremy has earnings of £400,000 in 2013/14. He usually pays £8,000 into his personal pension each year. Advise him of the maximum contribution he can make to a personal pension in 2013/14 and obtain tax relief, and the tax consequences of contributing this amount.

8.5 Cindy plans to start drawing her pension in 2013/14. Her personal pension fund is worth £65,000. How much can Cindy take as a tax free lump sum?

8.6 Maxine has taxable earnings of £54,000 in 2013/14. Her employer deducts a contribution to the company's registered occupational pension scheme of £9,000 from these earnings before operating PAYE. She has no other taxable income.

Show Maxine's tax liability for 2013/14.

9.1 Wayne, age 34, is domiciled in America but has lived in London for 15 years. In 2013/14 he remits £10,000 (including overseas tax) of foreign dividends from a company resident in America and has a further £400,000 of foreign dividends which he does not remit. He is a higher rate taxpayer and has made a remittance basis claim. How much is his tax liability on his foreign dividends?

9.2 Egbert is UK resident. He worked in Germany many years ago and now receives a German pension of £10,000 each year. How much of the pension is taxable in 2013/14?

9.3 State the occasions when an individual may split the tax year.

9.4 Ernie, who is domiciled in Erehwon, has been resident in the UK for the last four tax years. He performs duties in respect of his employment with Emos Inc both within (£50,000) and wholly outside the UK (£20,000) in each tax year. He remits £10,000 of his earnings from his overseas duties to the UK.

How much of his earnings are taxable in the UK, assuming he claims to use the remittance basis in 2013/14 and

    (a)   Emos Inc is a US resident company?

    (b)   Emos Inc is a UK resident company?

9.5 The travelling costs of spouse and children who visit an employee working abroad do not give rise to a taxable benefit if paid by the employer. What length of service abroad must be undertaken to benefit from this treatment, and how many visits in a tax year are then allowed?

Exam focus point

Question 10.1 below is taken from the Pilot Paper for the Personal Taxation Certificate paper.

10.1 Jenny, a higher rate taxpayer, sold a painting on 15 May 2013 realising a chargeable gain of £18,000. Calculate Jenny's capital gains tax liability for 2013/14 assuming she had taxable income in the year of £28,870.

10.2 Justin made a disposal on 1 June 2013 realising a chargeable gain of £32,000. He made another disposal on 14 August 2013, realising a chargeable gain of £26,000. Calculate Justin's capital gains tax liability for 2013/14 assuming he had taxable income in the year of £26,470.

10.3 When can an individual use the remittance basis for his gains?

10.4 Which of the following assets are exempt for capital gains tax purposes?

- A diamond brooch
- A thoroughbred racehorse
- A lease with an unexpired term of 25 years
- A computer used in a business
- A limousine used by a car hire company.

10.5 In which of the following scenarios might a capital gains tax charge arise, and why? (Assume that the proceeds of the overseas disposals are not brought into the UK and ignore the effect of any double taxation agreements.)

(1) Sale of an overseas commercial property by a UK resident and domiciled individual.
(2) Sale of a UK residential property by an individual who is non-UK resident but UK domiciled.
(3) Sale of an overseas property by a UK resident but non-UK domiciled individual.

Exam focus point

Questions 11.1 and 11.2 below are taken from the Pilot Paper for the Personal Taxation Certificate paper.

11.1 David was left a painting in June 1991 on the death of his great aunt. Records showed she had purchased it in May 1987 for £7,200 and it was worth £11,200 on her death in 1991. David decided to sell the painting in May 2013 when it was worth £31,250. Calculate the chargeable gain on the sale of the painting.

11.2 Toby bought a plot of land in July 2003 for investment purposes for £18,000. In June 2013 a local developer offered him £125,000 for the plot. Toby decided to keep a quarter of the plot and sold the remaining site to the developer for £85,000. The plot that Toby retained was valued at £30,000. Calculate the chargeable gain arising in 2013/14.

11.3 Edwin has chargeable gains of £9,000 and allowable losses of £5,000 in 2013/14. He has allowable losses brought forward of £6,000. What are the allowable losses carried forward to 2014/15?

11.4 James has the following chargeable gains and losses arising from disposals of assets:

Tax year	2011/12	2012/13	2013/14
	£	£	£
Gains	2,000	4,000	13,800
Losses	(5,000)	(2,000)	(2,000)

All assets had been owned for many years. What is the maximum allowable loss carried forward to 2014/15?

11.5 Paul invites the following people to a celebration dinner:

(1) His wife
(2) His mother-in-law
(3) His business partner
(4) The ex-wife of his business partner
(5) His uncle
(6) His step-father
(7) His band manager

Who is connected with Paul for CGT purposes?

11.6 Callum bought a freehold shop for use in his business on 13 July 2005 for £120,000. On 12 March 2008, when the shop was worth £150,000, he transferred the shop to his wife, Grace, who also used the shop in her business. On 12 May 2013, Grace sold the shop for £170,000. What is Grace's chargeable gain on the shop?

11.7 James sold assets to the following individuals, creating chargeable gains and allowable losses as shown below:

	Date of sale	Chargeable gain/ (allowable loss) £
Charles, his brother	1 March 2013	10,000
	15 June 2013	(8,200)
	29 September 2014	14,000
Sarah, his sister	2 August 2013	21,500
	1 July 2014	8,000
Mr Smith (not connected with James)	22 December 2013	9,000

Which gain will the allowable loss be set off against? Explain your reasoning.

11.8 Julie owned a field which she purchased on 13 August 1989 for £8,000. On 10 September 2013, she sold a quarter of the field for development for £30,000. The remainder of the field was then worth £10,000. What is Julie's chargeable gain?

11.9 Mattheus made gains of £18,200 and losses of £7,000 in 2013/14. He has losses brought forward of £5,000.

Calculate the losses to carry forward to 2014/15.

11.10 Kidson purchased a plot of land on 1 January 1986 for £8,000. On 31 August 2013, he sold part of the land for £45,000 but declined an offer of £50,000 for the rest.

Calculate the taxable gain arising on the sale assuming this is the only capital transaction Kidson has in 2013/14.

11.11 Charles and Victoria had been married for many years but decided to separate amicably on 17 May 2013; neither party sought a divorce. On 12 October 2013 Victoria gave Charles a painting which was worth £40,000 and on 16 April 2014 she sold him a Sevres dinner service, which was valued at £15,000, for £10,000.

Explain how these disposals will be treated for capital gains tax purposes.

11.12 Peter owned a commercial property which he bought in February 1991 for £28,000. Peter sold the property on 5 December 2013 for £500,000, with £400,000 being receivable on completion and £100,000 in May 2014.

Calculate the chargeable gain for 2013/14.

Exam focus point

Question 12.1 below is taken from the Pilot Paper for the Personal Taxation Certificate paper.

12.1 Andrew bought 2,000 shares in X plc for £18,000 in August 2009 and a further 1,000 shares for £10,000 in September 2009. He sold 1,500 shares for £22,500 in January 2014. Calculate his chargeable gain.

12.2 Amber had the following transactions in the shares of Zingo Ltd:

		£
19.2.86	Purchased 2,000 shares, cost	10,000
20.9.93	Purchased 1,000 shares, cost	8,000
15.11.13	Sold 1,500 shares, proceeds	22,000

What is Amber's chargeable gain for 2013/14?

12.3 Mr Smith acquired 5,000 shares in S plc in April 1988 for £5,605. In July 2002 S plc made a bonus issue of one ordinary share for every five held. In December 2013 Mr Smith sold 3,500 of his shares for £6,250. What is the chargeable gain?

13.1 Lionel purchased a Victoria Cross medal in May 1996 for £3,000 and a vintage car in June 1988 for £4,000. He sold them both to a collector in May 2013 for £14,780 and £15,500 respectively.

What, if any, are his chargeable gains for 2013/14?

13.2 Giles purchased a picture in July 1994 for £4,500 and sold it in September 2013 for £7,500 before incurring £300 expenses of sale. What is Giles' chargeable gain?

13.3 Gail sold a painting for £90 in December 2013 which had cost £6,260 in January 1996. What is Gail's allowable loss for 2013/14?

13.4 On 1 April 1993 Mr Laycole acquired a painting on the death of his father at a probate value of £3,000. He sold the painting at auction for £7,200 on 30 October 2013 incurring costs of £350. Compute the chargeable gain.

13.5 In August 2013 Miranda, a sole trader whose business is ongoing, disposed of two assets on which capital allowances have been claimed.

	Purchase Price £	Disposal Proceeds £
Motor car	8,000	4,000
Machinery	5,500	7,500

Both assets were purchased in October 2008. Calculate Miranda's chargeable gain or allowable loss.

13.6 Adrienne acquired a 90 year lease on 31 March 1986 for £40,000. On 31 March 2014 she granted a sublease of 55 years for £30,000. The reversionary interest is valued at £82,500. What is Adrienne's chargeable gain?

13.7 Jerome acquired a freehold property for £30,000 in March 1994. In November 2013 he granted an 11 year lease for a premium of £10,000 at which time the reversionary interest was valued at £50,000. What is Jerome's chargeable gain?

14.1 Neil sold a house on 30 June 2013. He realised an £80,000 gain before taking account of any PPR relief. The house was originally purchased on 1 October 1986 and was occupied by Neil until 30 June 1989 at which date he purchased and moved into another residence, letting the original house until the date of sale.

What is his chargeable gain?

14.2 Robert owned a property with three storeys of equal value in Sheffield. He bought it on 30 June 1988 for £20,000. He used the top two storeys as his main residence. The ground floor was rented out to students. The ground floor has a separate access door. On 30 November 2013 Robert sold the whole property for £200,000. What is his chargeable gain?

14.3 Give two examples of periods of absence from a property which are deemed periods of occupation for the CGT principal private residence exemption.

Exam focus point

Question 15.1 below is taken from the Pilot Paper for the Personal Taxation Certificate paper.

15.1 Jeremy Brett, who had run a manufacturing business for many years, decided to reduce the size of the operation in 2013/14. He therefore gave one of the factories (which had always been used for his business) to his son John although John persuaded his father to accept £50,000 in return.

Jeremy had acquired the factory on 2 January 1986 for £42,000. It was worth £152,000 and standing at a gain of £110,000 when he transferred it to John in August 2013.

Calculate Jeremy's chargeable gain, if any, for 2013/14 and state the base cost for John, on the assumption that they claim gift relief.

15.2 On 1 May 2013 Arthur sold a business asset to his son, Hugo, for £12,000. At that time the market value of the asset was £22,000. Arthur had purchased the asset in July 1988 for £4,000.

Gift relief is claimed on the disposal. Who needs to make the claim and what is the deadline for the claim?

15.3 On 1 January 2014 Adam sold a business asset to his son, Bernard, for £12,000. At that time the market value of the asset was £22,000. Adam had purchased the asset in July 1988 for £4,000.

In 2015/16 Bernard permanently ceased to be resident in the UK. At the time he left the UK the asset had a market value of £25,000.

What chargeable gain arises as a result (assuming a joint claim for gift relief had been made in respect of the January 2014 disposal), on whom is this chargeable and in which tax year?

15.4 Robert bought an 80% holding in an unquoted trading company on 10 July 2007 for £160,000. He gave the holding to his daughter, Lauren, on 13 December 2013, when it was worth £300,000. At that date, the assets of the company were:

	£
Factory	300,000
Quoted investments	50,000
Net current assets	25,000
	375,000

What is the gain chargeable on Robert before the annual exempt amount, assuming they claim gift relief?

15.5 In July 2013 Phil sold an asset of his farming business to his daughter Shirley for £63,000 when its open market value was £95,000. Phil had bought the asset in May 1998 for £44,000. How much gift relief can be claimed by Phil and Shirley?

15.6 In March 2013 Keith Pringle purchased an antique tea set for £24,000. In September 2013 the teapot was broken and he received £4,000 from the insurance company as compensation in October 2013. The remaining tea set was valued at £16,000. Calculate the gain/loss arising.

15.7 Patrice makes a gain of £600,000 in July 2013 on the sale of a flat in Brighton (not her main residence). In November 2012 she had subscribed £800,000 for shares in a qualifying EIS company and makes the maximum possible claim for EIS deferral relief. In August 2014 Patrice emigrates to Switzerland.

What chargeable gains will arise in 2013/14 and/or 2014/15?

15.8 In 2002 John invested £50,000 to acquire a 10% shareholding in Silvanus Ltd. In July 2013 he sold all his shares in this company for £800,000. John has £150,000 of capital losses brought forward as at 6 April 2013 and made no other disposals in 2013/14.

What is the minimum investment John must make in qualifying EIS shares to reduce his gain on the disposal of the Silvanus Ltd shares to nil, assuming he wishes to use his capital losses?

15.9 Karina sells a painting on 12 June 2013 realising a gain of £45,000. She intends to reinvest the funds but is not sure in what type of asset. Briefly explain which reliefs are available to reduce Karina's CGT liability for 2013/14 if she reinvests the funds.

Exam focus point

Question 16.1 below is taken from the Pilot Paper for the Personal Taxation Certificate paper.

16.1 A landlord is allowed to submit a simplified return in respect of rental income provided the appropriate condition is satisfied. What is the condition and what needs to be recorded on the return?

16.2 Thomas Apple received his 2013/14 tax return on 19 May 2014. Outline Thomas's options for filing this tax return and paying the tax due.

16.3 John's income tax and CGT position for 2012/13 was as follows:

	£
Income tax liability	11,250
Tax deducted at source	(5,000)
	6,250
CGT liability	8,200
Payments on account made for 2012/13	(4,000)
	10,450

Calculate John's payments on account for 2013/14 stating the due dates.

16.4 Gareth filed his 2013/14 tax return on 15 December 2014. He deliberately omitted an amount of overseas interest income of £6,000 (gross) from a bank account in The Netherlands, that he was aware was taxable in the UK, from the return. Gareth is a higher rate taxpayer. The Netherlands is classified by HMRC as a Category 1 country.

Explain any penalties to which Gareth will be liable.

17.1 State which members are not required to hold professional indemnity insurance cover according to the ATT's PII Guidance and Regulations.

17.2 A prospective client has contacted you to take over from his existing adviser. He alleges that the previous adviser was incompetent and insists that you do not contact him. What should you do?

17.3 Sheila and Ken Walters, each a client of many years standing, have decided to divorce 'amicably'. They have effectively lived apart under the same roof for some time. Ken is only interested in his garden and Sheila has made the golf club her second home so they feel they should formally separate with an intention to divorce. They are both insistent that you should continue to act for them. What should you do?

17.4 What are a member's usual responsibilities in respect of due dates and interest on tax where a member undertakes tax compliance work for a client?

17.5 If a member is engaged in a fee dispute with a client he may call for arbitration from the ATT. True/ False.

17.6 Which type of fee arrangement is specifically considered within the regime for disclosure of tax avoidance schemes?

17.7 Robbie's firm is holding £20,000 of a client's money. How long can they hold the money before they should open a designated interest bearing client account?

17.8 What are the three ways in which land can be legally held?

17.9 What is the maximum number of legal owners of land?

17.10 In the case of registered land at what point does the beneficial interest pass from the seller to the buyer?

17.11 Sara has been unfairly dismissed. What orders may the employment tribunal make in her favour?

17.12 Property is anything that can be owned. Although the term is often used to refer to land, it is a much wider concept and includes all assets both tangible and intangible. Explain the difference in legal terms between ownership and possession of property.

17.13 An owner of land may agree to sell it in a number of different ways. Explain the four ways in which a sale of land may take place.

17.14 Personal property under English law can be divided into 'choses in action' and 'choses in possession'.

Explain what is meant by the underlined terms.

17.15 List six items that you would expect to see covered in a typical contract for consultancy services provided by an independent contractor.

1.1 Mr Daphnis

Mr Daphnis (born 7 June 1940) is married to Chloë (born 9 November 1934) and is registered blind.

Mr Daphnis' net income for 2013/14 was £27,280, made up of rental income (£17,280) and gross interest (£10,000). Chloë's only income is her pension of £4,500.

You are required to calculate Mr and Mrs Daphnis' allowances and tax reductions for 2013/14. Also give brief advice on how they could improve their joint tax position.

1.2 Mr Rich

Mr Rich earned £143,500 from his employment in 2013/14. He paid tax of £50,998 under PAYE.

He gave £12,000 (net) cash to Oxfam via Gift Aid in the year and paid £25,000 interest on a loan he had taken out in the previous year to purchase equipment for use in his employment.

You are required to calculate his tax payable/repayable.

1.3 Mr Poor

Mr Poor took early retirement in 2006 when he was 55. He now works part time. In 2013/14 his gross earnings were £7,385 (no tax deducted via PAYE). He received £900 in dividends and £1,900 of building society interest. He received interest on his Midwest Savings Bank account totalling £100.

You are required to calculate his tax payable/repayable.

1.4 Lauren

Lauren receives earnings from employment of £23,000 (£2,712 tax deducted via PAYE).

She also received the following investment income during 2013/14:

	£
UK bank interest	22,000
UK dividends	67,500
Payment from a discretionary trust	35,200

She makes monthly payments of £100 to charity under Gift Aid.

You are required to calculate Lauren's tax payable for 2013/14.

2.1 Fred

Fred (born 7 May 1934) is married to Wilma (born 6 September 1942). Fred received the following income in 2013/14:

	£
Rental income	17,200
Building society interest	4,400
UK Treasury Stock interest	290
UK company dividends	8,890

Wilma has no income.

You are required to calculate Fred's tax payable for 2013/14.

2.2 George and Mildred Roper

George Roper (aged 73) married Mildred (age 79) on 10 February 2014. Both have been married before. George pays his ex-wife Liz (age 79) £260 each month by way of maintenance after their divorce in 2000. Mildred's former husband Brian died in May 2008.

George's income for 2013/14 is as follows:

	£
Earnings from part time consultancy work (£312 income tax deducted via PAYE)	11,000
Pension from former employer (£720 income tax deducted via PAYE)	3,600
State pension (£110.15 per week)	5,728
UK Treasury stock interest	180
Rental income from holiday home	3,725
UK dividends received	3,375

George pays interest at 10% per annum on a loan which he had taken out to buy shares in Hi Tek Ltd. £10,000 of the loan is outstanding and he claims interest relief.

Mildred's income for 2013/14 is as follows:

	£
State pension (£110.15 per week)	5,728
Building society interest received	9,040
Distribution from discretionary trust	3,850
Interest from bank account in Guernsey (received gross)	2,071
Premium Bond winnings	400
UK dividends received	720

Mildred pays £500 each year to the NSPCC (a registered charity) under Gift Aid.

Calculate George and Mildred's tax payable/repayable for 2013/14.

2.3 Enterprise Investment Scheme

You are required to describe the income tax relief and capital gains tax exemption in respect of an investment in shares qualifying under the Enterprise Investment Scheme.

Your answer should cover the main points in brief outline only.

3.1 Jonty

Jonty, aged 38, is a married man whose wife has no income. The following information is relevant for the year ended 5 April 2014:

(1) His salary was £30,000 (including statutory sick pay of £173). Income tax deducted via PAYE was £4,112.

(2) His other income was:

	£
Building society interest received	80
Dividends received	63

(3) In March 2014 Jonty closed down his NS&I savings account which he had kept for many years. Interest of £142 was credited.

(4) He made a donation of £396 (net of basic rate tax) to Oxfam in May 2013 under Gift Aid.

(5) Jonty won £100 on the Grand National.

(6) He has two children aged 4 and 7, whom his wife looks after. He received working and child tax credits of £1,195.

You are required to compute the tax payable by/ repayable to Jonty for 2013/14.

3.2 Fiona

Fiona, who is 35, lives on her own. She has been running her own business for many years. Her taxable trading profits for 2013/14 are £32,000.

During 2013/14 she received the following investment income:

	£
UK dividends	10,000
Jersey bank interest (received gross)	4,300
Premium bond winnings	13,000

Throughout 2013/14 Fiona fosters a 7 year old girl, Lucy, and receives £18,000 for caring for her. She elects to use the simplified method for calculating her taxable foster care income.

On 31 March 2012 she borrowed £24,000 to invest in a 15% shareholding in a close company. She pays interest at 4% per annum. She repaid £10,000 of the loan when she received her Premium Bond winnings on 5 December 2013. She subscribed for £3,000 of shares in an EIS company with the remainder.

She received child benefit of £1,056 during 2013/14.

She pays an annual donation to charity of £1,600 under Gift Aid.

You are required to calculate Fiona's tax payable for 2013/14.

3.3 Jane Bradbury

Jane Bradbury is in her 30s. Her husband died in January last year leaving her to bring up their daughter, Poppy, now aged 4. Jane receives working and child tax credits totalling £4,115 and child benefit of £1,056 in the year.

Jane is a partner in a small firm making children's clothes. Her profit share for 2013/14 has been agreed at £8,079.

Jane pays interest of £3,800 each year on a loan she took out in 2003 to buy into the partnership.

Jane has an investment portfolio which generated dividends of £4,950 in 2013/14. Her only other income is bank interest received on a bank account of £200 and the widowed parent's allowance of £108.30 per week.

Calculate Jane's tax repayable for 2013/14.

4.1 Randall

Randall owns three unfurnished properties which are let on the following terms, all rents being payable quarterly in advance (on 31 March, 30 June, 30 September and 31 December). Randall is responsible for repairs on all properties; the rents on properties A and B are full rents. Property C is let to Randall's cousin at significantly below the market rate.

A   Let at £620 a year on a 20 year lease which commenced in 2003.

B   Let at £348 a year on a lease which expired on 30 September 2013, then empty until 31 December 2013 when let at £440 a year.

C   Let at £100 a year throughout the year.

Expenditure by Randall on these properties in the year was as follows:

	A £	B £	C £
Agent's commission	20		
Advertising for tenants		76	
Repairs: while let	142		119
while empty		255	

You are required to:

(1)   **Calculate the property income assessment for Randall for 2013/14.**

(2)   **Explain the income tax implications of receiving a premium on granting a lease.**

4.2 Corelli

Corelli, aged 41, owns three properties:

A 5 Arnhem Avenue
B 17 Blenheim Road
C 27 Cannae Road.

All are let out unfurnished at the market rate.

A This was let until 30 June 2013 at an annual rental of £1,200. On 30 September 2013, it was let out to a new tenant on a 10 year lease agreement. The annual rental is £800. The tenant paid a premium of £5,000 on 30 September 2013.

B This was let throughout 2013/14. The annual rental was £3,100. The rental due on 31 March 2014 was not received until 12 April 2014.

C This was let from 30 June 2013 at an annual rental of £600.

All the rents are payable quarterly in advance (on 31 March, 30 June, 30 September and 31 December) and are sufficient normally to cover the landlord's outgoings.

Properties A and B were acquired in 1984; property C was purchased on 15 April 2013.

Expenditure in connection with the properties was as follows:

		A	B	C
		£	£	£
Agent's commission	1 May 2013	25	35	10
	1 November 2013	25	35	10
Repairs (note)		–	100	1,800
Advertising for new tenants 10 July 2013		50	–	–

Note. The repairs in respect of property C are analysed as follows:

	£
Installation of new kitchen equipment	300
Retiling part of the roof after damage in May 2013	1,500
	1,800

Corelli's other income during 2013/14 was as follows:

	£
Dividends received	15,300
Salary (£1,402 deducted via PAYE)	16,450

(1) **You are required to compute Corelli's income tax payable for 2013/14.** (7 marks)

(2) **You are required to explain the difference between freehold and leasehold land.** (5 marks)

(Total = 12 marks)

4.3 Mary Taylor

Mary Taylor is aged 78 and a widow. Her husband died on 1 January 2009. She has owned a building for 15 years, which was let at an annual rental of £20,000 until 31 December 2013. With effect from 1 January 2014 the rent was increased to £25,000 per annum. Rent is paid quarterly in advance and all payments were received on time apart from the sum of £6,250, which was due on 1 April 2014 but not paid until 1 June 2014.

Mary incurred the following expenses in connection with the property in 2013/14:

	£
Repairs – re-tiling roof	6,500
Repairs – water damage due to burst pipe	3,800
Estate agent's letting fees	2,500
Interest on loan of £100,000 to purchase property	8,500
Accountant's fees	750

Mary lives in a large house and also lets rooms to students from the local college. For 2013/14 she received total rent of £5,250. She also incurred total expenses of £1,250 attributable to these lettings.

Mary has other income for 2013/14 from the following sources:

	£
Pension from husband's former employer (tax deducted £2,018)	19,531 gross
State pension	5,728 gross
UK company dividends	9,450 net
Income from non-discretionary trust fund (dividend income)	4,500 net

Mary has also made a gain of £25,000 from the maturity of a non-qualifying life assurance policy which she took out 20 years ago.

You are required to show your computation of the net amount of income tax payable by or repayable to Mary for 2013/14. **(15 marks)**

5.1 **Mr Thomas**

Mr Thomas is a director of a private company. His remuneration for 2013/14 was £30,000.

During the year ended 5 April 2014, the following benefits were provided to him:

(1)   Accommodation in a four bedroom house, owned by the company.

	£
Original cost 1997	80,000
Cost of extension 2001	25,000
Annual value	750

Mr Thomas moved in on 1 March 2006, at which time the house was valued at £134,375.

Expenses paid directly by the company 2013/14:	£
Council tax	1,400
Electricity	750
Gas	250
Telephone	350
Redecoration (internal)	700
Gardener	1,500

(2)   Interest-free loan for a non-qualifying purpose – first advance 6 June 2013

		£
6.6.13	advance	10,000
6.8.13	advance	5,000
6.12.13	repaid	7,500
6.2.14	advance	4,000
6.3.14	repaid	2,500

(3)   Cars   –   Mercedes, list price £21,500, purchased 1 June 2010. The emission rate is 130g/km.

                     –   1,600 cc Escape, list price £10,000, purchased 5 August 2013, used by Mrs Thomas. The emission rate is 91g/km.

         No petrol was provided for either vehicle.

You are required to calculate Mr Thomas's taxable benefits for 2013/14.

5.2 **Alf**

You have been consulted by Alf, one of the directors of your company, who has no shareholding in the company, concerning the taxability of earnings and benefits received. The following information is provided for the tax year 2013/14.

(1)   Alf's salary is £96,600 (tax deducted via PAYE of £28,462).

(2)   An expenses allowance of £2,500 for 2013/14 spent as follows:

	£
Business travelling	1,800
Entertainment:	
Overseas customers	400
Overseas suppliers	100
UK customers	200

(3) Benefits for the year were as follows:

    (i) The company purchased stereo equipment for Alf's personal use at a cost of £800. The company retained ownership of the equipment.

    (ii) Alf had exclusive use of a new 2.5 litre petrol engined car with a list price of £15,000. The emission rate is 160g/km. No petrol was provided for private motoring.

    (iii) Medical insurance was provided at a cost to the company of £300. Alf would have had to pay £450 to take out the insurance personally.

    (iv) Alf visited Saville Row for 5 tailored shirts, which were paid for by the company, on Alf's behalf at a cost of £400.

(4) Alf's other income for 2013/14 is as follows:

	£
Bank interest received	5,440
Dividends received	4,000

(5) He pays £1,600 each year to charity under Gift Aid.

You are required to calculate the tax payable by Alf for 2013/14, giving brief explanatory notes on the treatment of his benefits and expenses.

5.3 Mr Bjork

Mr Bjork is chairman and chief executive of Peepop Ltd.

He receives a salary of £46,000 per annum and during the income tax year 2013/14 he is provided with the following benefits:

(1) The use of a 2,100 cc petrol Jaguar motor car with a list price of £20,000 from 6 April 2013. The emission rate is 200g/km.

On 31 July 2013 he was involved in a serious road accident and the car was written off. He was charged with dangerous driving and the company met his legal costs of £2,000.

While he had use of the Jaguar, he contributed 50% of the cost of his private fuel.

When he resumed work on 1 October 2013, he was provided with a Mercedes car with a list price of £30,000 and the use of a chauffeur, who costs the company £23,250 per annum to employ. This car is used solely for business purposes. The emission rate is 170g/km.

(2) Throughout the year, his wife, who is not employed by the company, has been provided with the use of a 2 litre BMW car with a list price of £15,000 four years ago. The company meets all running costs and petrol bills. The emission rate is 220g/km.

(3) The use of video equipment which had been purchased by the company at a cost of £800.

(4) He is given a computer by Peepop Ltd on 6 October 2013, when it has a market value of £200. He has had use of that computer since 6 October 2011 when its market value was £3,000. His estimated personal use of the computer is 40%.

You are required to compute the total amount of benefits taxable on Mr Bjork for 2013/14.

5.4 HiTech Computers

Giles has worked for HiTech Computers plc for many years and he has recently been promoted to sales manager, receiving a £5,000 pay rise from 1 July 2013. His revised salary is £36,000 pa. He has continued to pay contributions into his registered occupational pension scheme of 5% of his salary and commission. He has received sales commission as follows:

Year ended 31 December 2012	£3,000 received 28 February 2013
Year ended 31 December 2013	£4,000 received 28 February 2014

As a result of his promotion, he has been provided with a flat in London, due to being required to spend increasing amounts of time in London. The company pays £5,000 annual rent on the property, which has an annual value of £2,400. He is required to contribute £100 per month towards this.

Giles still has an interest free loan from the company for the purchase of his private car. The amount outstanding was £15,000 on 6 April 2013 and £10,000 on 5 April 2014. He has a car parking space provided in London under the HiTech Computers plc building that costs the company £1,200 per annum.

Other benefits that Giles receives are as follows:

(1) Free medical insurance – the cost to the company is £385 per annum although if Giles had taken this out privately, he would have to pay £525 to cover both him and his wife.

(2) £100 per month payment towards the provision of crèche facilities for his child who attends a registered private nursery.

(3) A newspaper allowance of £20 per month.

You are required to calculate Giles's employment income for 2013/14, giving explanations of your treatment of the benefits.

5.5   **Grovelands**

Grovelands Ltd, an electrical company, was taken over in early 2013. Freddie, a senior executive in charge of business sales did not get along with new management and his employment was terminated on 31 December 2013. The company provided him with an *ex gratia* payment that was not provided for in his employment contract of £84,974, of which £72,487 was paid on 31 December 2013 and £12,487 in May 2014.

Freddie's salary from Grovelands Ltd for the year to 31 December 2013 had been £129,333. He subsequently took a part time consultancy post with another company for £8,400 per annum. The salary was to be paid in equal monthly instalments in arrears. This new job started on 1 February 2014.

Grovelands Ltd had allowed Freddie the use of a home entertainment system, which was worth £5,000 when loaned to him on 1 July 2012. On his departure from the company, Freddie bought the system (now worth £1,000) for £150.

Freddie's other income and expenses for the year 2013/14 were as follows:

	£
Benefits:	
Company car (2500 cc; list price in 2012 was £22,300; approved CO_2 emissions figure 194g/km).	
BUPA medical insurance cover (paid by Grovelands)	200
London Transport season ticket (reimbursed by Grovelands)	2,326
UK dividends – amount received	2,754
Bank interest received	1,386
Gift aid payment (net)	800

Freddie drove his company car on business for 1,200 miles (out of a total of 10,000 miles) during 2013/14. Grovelands Ltd paid directly for all the car's running expenses including petrol which amounted to £3,200 up to 31 December 2013, at which date the car was returned to the company.

(1) **You are required to compute Freddie's total income tax liability for 2013/14.**   **(15 marks)**

(2) **You are required to explain the meaning of summary dismissal and constructive dismissal.**   **(5 marks)**

(Total = 20 marks)

5.6   **Mr Morris**

Mr Morris, aged 41, joined William and Sons Limited in March 2011. He negotiated a package comprising a basic annual salary of £24,825, a two litre company car (list price £14,665; CO_2 emissions 167g/km) with all private petrol provided and also health insurance costing £340 paid on his behalf by the company.

Income tax of £3,077 was deducted from his salary via PAYE in 2013/14.

Mr Morris received the following amounts from his investments in 2013/14:

	£
Building society account interest	312
UK dividends	738

He also held a joint account with his wife at Burford Bank which had been credited with £256 worth of interest in 2013/14.

Mr Morris inherited a house in Devon from his father 15 years ago. This property (which is furnished) is let out by Mr Morris, who employs a letting agent to deal with the rental. The details for 2013/14 are as follows:

6.4.13 – 31.8.13 – Let to the Adams family
Gross rent per annum £8,000 payable quarterly in arrears

	£
Agent's fees	267
Repairs and maintenance	400
Gardener	100
Council tax (for 2013/14)	590
Water rates	85

1.10.13 – 5.4.14 – Let to the Potter family
Gross rent per annum £12,000 payable quarterly in arrears (Note)

Agent's fees	600
Repairs and maintenance (including £1,000 incurred in September 2013)	1,500
Gardener	200
Water rates	100
Cost and installation of new gas fire	435

Note. The rent due on 31 March was not actually paid until 15 April 2014.

Mr Morris claims the wear and tear allowance.

Mr Morris also pays £156 each year to Oxfam under the gift aid scheme (he does not intend to make an election to carry back the payment to 2012/13).

You are required to calculate Mr Morris's outstanding income tax payable for 2013/14. **(10 marks)**

6.1 **Sue**

Sue has been a director of Porchester Ltd for three years. Her salary in 2013/14 is £52,000.

In order to reward her performance to the company on 1 January 2014, she was granted 5,000 ordinary share options under an approved scheme to buy shares at £4.00 at any time in the next 10 years. The market value of the shares at January 2014 was £3.96. She is planning to buy the shares in 8 years time when she estimates that the share price will have risen to £10.00. She plans to sell them shortly afterwards (assume share price at date of sale = £10.40).

Sue has no other income in 2013/14.

You are required to:

(1) **Explain the income tax and capital gains tax consequences of the granting of the share options and the subsequent sale by Sue.**

(2) **Explain how your answer would change if the scheme was unapproved and the exercise price was £3.00, and calculate Sue's income tax liability for 2013/14.**

7.1 **Mr Howe**

Mr Howe recently started working for a new employer in December 2012. His employment package for 2013/14 is as follows:

Salary	£35,000
Company car (and petrol): CO_2 emissions 120g/km – list price of:	£9,500
Interest free loan to purchase an annual travel card	£1,472
Laptop (for wholly private use)	£1,449

You are required to write notes for an upcoming meeting with Mr Howe:

(1) **Calculating his employment income for 2013/14, and**
(2) **Explaining what National Insurance Contributions (NICs) are due and by whom they are payable.**

The following question is taken from the Pilot Paper for the Personal Taxation Certificate paper.

8.1 Mr Matthews

Mr Matthews, an architect, changed employers at the beginning of April 2013. He was sent a tax return form for the first time in respect of 2013/14. He has therefore approached the partner that you work for to help him with his tax affairs. Although it is already mid February 2015 he has just sent in his tax return, which he has started to complete himself, for review. He has calculated his total income as follows:

Source of income

	Total income £	Tax suffered £
Salary (from P60)	48,750	9,510
Medical insurance (from P11D)	375	
Allowance for business miles (own calculation)	111	
Parking in car park next to office (paid for by employer, figure from parking receipts retained and reimbursed)	720	
Building society interest received (from passbook)	320	80
Net income from Discretionary Trust (from R185 Statement of Income)	1,100	900
Total income	51,376	10,490

He has sent in his P60, P11D and the form R185 which agree with the above figures.

He has entered the following information on your firm's tax return questionnaire:

Date of birth: 1.10.1975

Business mileage

Drove 925 miles on business in 2013/14. Reimbursed by employer at 12p per mile

Subscriptions

Member of the Institute of Architects

Subscriptions paid by Mr Matthews: £285 paid 1 January 2013 and £295 paid 1 January 2014

Charitable donations

£10 per month paid to Dogs Trust
£15 per month paid to English Heritage

Can I get relief for these payment and if so how does it work?

Also – can you explain how a charity can benefit if I have overpaid tax?

Pension contributions

No pension provision at present

You are required to:

(1) **Review Mr Matthews' calculation of income and tax suffered and produce an amended version, explaining any changes that you have made.** (6 marks)

(2) **Produce notes for the partner to enable him to explain to Mr Matthews how he may be able to get relief for the charitable donations he has made and how the relief would be given.** (5 marks)

(3) **Calculate Mr Matthews' tax payable/repayable based on your calculation of total income giving relief for the charitable donations.** (3 marks)

(4) **Produce a statement outlining the tax rules concerning payments to a personal pension plan including how much Mr Matthews could contribute to a personal pension plan (based on his 2013/14 income), the tax saving that he would achieve and whether a claim can be made for relief against 2013/14 income.** (6 marks)

(Total = 20 marks)

8.2 Ed & Joan

Ed Tommy and Joan Ball both work for a design studio. They wish to start saving for their retirement and would like to make maximum contributions to a personal pension.

Ed is the managing director and his salary for 2013/14 is £140,000. Ed set up a personal pension scheme six years ago and made a contribution in that year but has not made any since. He would now like to make further contributions to this scheme.

Joan is an assistant designer and her salary for the year is £35,000. Neither Ed or Joan has any other income.

(1)   **Advise Ed and Joan of the maximum amount they can each contribute to a pension for 2012/13 and 2013/14.**

(2)   **Explain the method by which Ed and Joan will be given tax relief for their pension contributions and show their income tax liability assuming the maximum pension contributions are made.**

(3)   **Explain how they will be able to continue to contribute to their pensions if the design studio ceases trading on 5 April 2014 and they no longer have earnings.**

8.3   Dwaine Pipe

Dwaine is the sales director of a small central heating and plumbing company based in the Midlands. The company draws up accounts to 31 December each year.

Dwaine's salary (paid monthly) for the year ended 31 December 2013 was set at £40,000 per annum. This was raised to £44,000 at the Board meeting on 20 January 2014. Income tax deducted via PAYE in 2013/14 came to £12,350.

Dwaine also receives half yearly bonuses dependent on the performance of his sales team. These have been as follows:

Bonus period	Bonus	Awarded	Received
6 m/e 31.12.12	£3,000	31.3.13	30.4.13
6 m/e 30.6.13	£3,850	30.9.13	31.10.13
6 m/e 31.12.13	£4,250	31.3.14	30.4.14

In addition to his salary and bonus, Dwaine receives the following benefits:

1.   *Company cars*

Vauxhall Corsa, list price £10,629, first registered on 1 March 2008. He returned the car at the end of October 2013. The emission rate is 125g/km. He was required to pay £40 per month for the private use of the Vauxhall. All diesel for business use was paid by the company.

On 1 November 2013 he exchanged the Vauxhall for a brand new Audi A6, list price £18,500. A CD player was added at Dwaine's request at a cost of £400. The emission rate is 180g/km. Again the company paid for all petrol for business mileage.

Dwaine was involved in an accident on Christmas Day which left the Audi in the garage until 15 January 2014. He was provided with a replacement vehicle (another Audi) which he used until his own car was returned.

2.   *Mobile phone*

As Dwaine needs to be in contact with the office, he was provided with a mobile phone. The company reimbursed all Dwaine's calls at a cost of £2,400 in the year. Dwaine estimates that only 10% of these were for private reasons.

3.   *Interest free home loan*

The company lent Dwaine £75,000, interest free, on 1 June 2013 to buy his flat in Birmingham. Dwaine repaid £15,000 of the loan on 1 January 2014.

4.   *Nursery fees*

Dwaine's son Wayne started attending a local approved nursery on 6 April 2013, for which the company has agreed to meet the costs. These amounted to £45 per week (for 46 weeks) in 2013/14.

5.   *Personal pension*

The company does not have an occupational pension scheme and has therefore agreed to make contributions into Dwaine's personal pension plan. Dwaine makes payments of £150 per month – the company add an extra £100 per month.

6. *Central heating system*

Dwaine's new flat came without central heating. The company provided the materials free of charge and Dwaine fitted the system himself. The materials cost the company £800 and usually retail at £1,200 to customers.

7. *Staff suggestion scheme*

Dwaine won second prize in the scheme being a crate of champagne costing £150. His suggestion will save the company around £3,000 in costs.

8. *Round sum allowance*

Dwaine is given a general allowance of £1,000 each year. In 2013/14 he spent this as follows:

	£
Hotel bills while away on business	710
Entertaining customers	160
	870

He was unable to account for the remainder.

His other income for the year was as follows:

Interest on ISA account	£1,000
Interest received on Building Society account (joint with his wife)	£20,000
Premium bond winnings	£120

Dwaine also made a donation to Oxfam of £400 under Gift Aid.

You are required to calculate the income tax payable/(repayable) by Dwaine for the year ended 5 April 2014.

9.1 **Ricardo Garcia**

Ricardo Garcia is resident and domiciled in Spain.

He has recently married a British woman and will be coming to live permanently in London when he retires; he has advised you that he will continue to return to Spain for holidays.

He has a large pension from the Spanish company that he used to work for, which he will need to bring into the UK for living expenses. He will keep his Spanish bank account and his large portfolio of Spanish investments.

The house which he presently owns in Spain will be rented out.

Mr Garcia has requested that you write to him explaining the basis of taxation in the UK on his worldwide income. He does not require any calculations at this stage.

You are required to draft a letter to Mr Garcia as requested.

9.2 **Paul Thomson**

Paul was born in Australia but has lived in the UK for many years since his parents emigrated here when he was a child. Paul regards the UK as his permanent home and does not intend to return to Australia. He holds a British passport.

For the past five years Paul has been employed in the UK but on 6 June 2013 started a secondment to the Kampala office for a period of 18 months.

He will need to return to the UK so that he can report back to the UK company. He will make two visits, each one three days long. He will receive remuneration from the UK company of £1,100 in total for these visits. His salary from the UK company prior to his secondment was £2,000 per month.

For the duration of his secondment Paul is paid £3,000 per month (gross) by the Kampala company for his duties for them.

You are required to calculate Paul's UK taxable income for 2013/14 assuming:

(1) Paul is allowed to split the tax year for 2013/14, or
(2) Paul is treated as remaining UK resident for 2013/14.

Ignore double tax relief.

10.1 Peter Jones

Peter Jones' income and chargeable gains for 2013/14 were as follows:

	£
Building society interest received	4,800
Dividends received	800
Rental income	6,624
Chargeable gain on disposal on 23 October 2013 (before annual exempt amount)	38,000

You are required to:

(1) Calculate the income tax repayment due to Peter Jones for 2013/14.

(2) Calculate the capital gains tax due for 2013/14.

10.2 Simon James

Simon James writes to you on 3 March 2014 on various matters, including the following in relation to capital gains tax:

'I recently read an article in the financial columns of a newspaper which explained the meaning of residence and domicile. Unfortunately, that article did not consider the relevance of these concepts in determining taxation liabilities. I am particularly concerned with the capital gains tax implications and I should be grateful if you would explain the significance of those terms in relation to that tax.'

You are required to write a letter explaining the relevance of residence and domicile in determining an individual's liability to capital gains tax.

11.1 Dorrit

Dorrit makes the following disposals of chargeable assets during 2013/14:

Date		Proceeds £	Original cost £
(1)	15 May 2013	115,000	32,000
(2)	31 July 2013	45,000	62,000
(3)	24 October 2013	47,000	16,000

Dorritt has employment income of £50,000 and UK property income of £3,000.

You are required to calculate Dorrit's capital gains tax liability for 2013/14.

11.2 Harbottle

The following information relates to your clients Fred and Iris Harbottle, both aged 30, who have been married for five years.

Fred is employed full time by a firm of chartered accountants at a salary of £40,000.

Iris is not currently working as she is staying at home to look after their two young children, aged 4 and 6. She leaves them with registered childminders one afternoon a week for which she pays £20 a week.

They have each inherited a portfolio of investments, details of which are as follows:

Fred has approximately £100,000 invested in shares currently yielding £7,000 gross dividend income.

Iris has approximately £30,000 invested in shares which yields dividends of £1,200 (gross).

They intend to make disposals of their investments during January 2014 resulting in chargeable gains of £11,500 for Fred and £2,500 for Iris.

They also have a National Savings & Investments Savings Account in joint names which yields £2,000 each year.

You are required to:

(1) Calculate the income tax and capital gains tax liabilities of the couple for 2013/14, and   (6 marks)

(2) State what planning action the couple may take in order to reduce their 2013/14 income tax and capital gains tax liabilities.   (4 marks)

(Total = 10 marks)

12.1 Julie Green

You are currently preparing the tax return of Julie Green, who runs her own marketing company. You have completed all of her return apart from the capital gains tax pages. As well as selling a painting that she had been left by her great aunt for proceeds of £25,000 (chargeable gain £12,000), she had a number of transactions in respect of her holding of Target plc shares.

The gains in respect of the Target plc shares have been calculated by your firm's new capital gains software, but as part of the review process you are required to check the calculations.

Julie Green's file records the following transactions:

Date	Event	Cost/proceeds £
1 June 1996	Purchase 50 shares	1,000
18 September 1999	Purchase 50 shares	3,800
21 May 2000	Purchase 100 shares	9,300
10 December 2000	Bonus issue 1:2	N/A
15 January 2005	Purchase 100 shares	8,200
29 June 2013	Sale 75 shares	10,150

From her tax return questionnaire you establish that on 16 August 2013 she sold another 75 shares for £8,500.

You are required to calculate the gains arising in 2013/14 in respect of the Target plc shares, producing a complete working sheet to place on the file.

12.2 Mr Jones

Mr Jones purchased 5,000 shares in XYZ plc in August 1985 for £6,250. He subsequently carried out the following transactions.

Date	Number of shares bought/(sold)	Cost (proceeds) £
September 1985	2,000	3,000
November 1988	5,000	9,500
October 1990	(3,000)	(6,500)
May 2004	1,000	3,000
July 2013	(7,000)	(31,500)

The company has 100,000 shares in issue.

You are required to calculate the chargeable gains for Mr Jones for 2013/14.

12.3 Richard Price

Richard Price works for PB plc, a large UK quoted trading company. He has acquired shares in PB plc via a company share option plan in recent years as follows:

Date	Shares Acquired	Cost £
15.3.93	2,000	2,000
17.12.99	4,000	10,000

In May 2002 there was a 1:5 rights issue at £5 per share which Richard took up in full.

On 4 October 2013, Richard sold 1,800 shares at £7.50 each.

Calculate the chargeable gain on the disposal.

12.4 Eric James

On 3 March 2014 Eric James sold 2,000 ordinary shares (4% shareholding) in Toucan Play plc for £9,100. These shares had been acquired as a result of a takeover on 4 June 2003 of Parrot Games plc in which Eric had held 1,000 shares. These had been acquired in January 2002 for £4,000.

The terms of the takeover were 2 ordinary shares and 4 preference shares in Toucan Play plc for every share held in Parrot Games plc. Immediately following the takeover the ordinary shares and preference shares in Toucan Play plc were valued at £4.20 and £2 respectively.

You are required to calculate the chargeable gain arising from the above transaction.

13.1 Doug

Doug sold the following items on 1 August 2013:

(1) A Ming vase bought in January 1987 for £2,000. The sales proceeds were £8,000.

(2) A Leonardo cartoon bought in March 1987 for £7,200 and sold for £5,500.

(3) A lathe bought for use in his business in March 1988 which cost £4,300. The sales proceeds were £9,500. Doug had claimed capital allowances on this asset.

You are required to calculate Doug's taxable gain for 2013/14 assuming he made no other disposals in the year.

13.2 Mr Cole

Mr Cole made the following disposals in 2013/14:

(1) On 2 June 2013 he sold his 1952 vintage Ford motor car for £7,200. He had bought the car in June 2008 for £3,600 and had incurred restoration costs of £500.

(2) On 2 September 2013 he sold 5 acres of land out of a 40 acre plot for £38,000. He had acquired the whole plot (for investment purposes) for £32,000 in July 1992. The value of the remaining 35 acres was £82,000 in September 2013.

(3) On 1 November 2013 he sold an antique chest for £7,000. He had bought this in June 2002 for £4,000.

(4) On 3 December 2013 he sold a painting for £11,500, incurring costs of sale of £150. He had been left the painting by his grandfather who had paid £2,000 for it in June 1988. It was worth £4,700 when his grandfather died in August 1992.

(5) On 15 January 2014 he sold a vase for £900. He had paid £7,500 for this in August 2000 believing it to be a Shelley vase but in fact it was a reproduction.

You are required to calculate the capital gains tax payable by Mr Cole for 2013/14 assuming he has taxable income of £29,010 in the year.   **(10 marks)**

13.3 CGT Leases

(1) Joe acquired an 80 year lease on a property for £38,000 on 29 July 1987. He assigned the lease on 29 July 2013 for £79,000.

(2) As (1) except that it was a 57 year lease when it was acquired.

(3) Harold acquired the freehold of a property for £25,000 on 1 May 1994. On 1 October 2013 he granted a 60 year lease on the premises for a premium of £30,000, the value of the reversion being £7,500.

(4) As (3) except that the lease granted was a 20 year lease, the premium received £20,000 and the value of the reversion £17,000.

You are required to calculate the chargeable gains arising in (1) to (4) above.

The following question is taken from the Pilot Paper for the Personal Taxation Certificate paper.

14.1 Owning two homes

Your managing partner has asked you to write an article to be published on your firm's website. There have been a number of queries submitted recently concerning the capital gains tax implications of owning two homes and she feels that this would be a good topic to have an article on.

She has supplied you with a case study of a typical family to refer to in the article.

Case Study

Family	Mr and Mrs Hammond; two children aged 4 and 2.		
	Current family home:	Bought 15 August 2001	
		Cost	£150,000
	Occupied throughout period of ownership by Mr and Mrs Hammond		
	To be sold May 2013	Proceeds	£560,000
New acquisitions May 2013	House in country	Cost	£400,000
	Flat in town	Cost	£175,000
Plans	Mr Hammond to reside in flat in town Monday night – Thursday night; weekends in country house		
	Mrs Hammond to reside in country house.		
	Flat in town either:		

(a)   To be sold after five years when Mr Hammond will live full time in country, or

(b)   To be let after five years and sold five years later.

House to be family home until children leave home.

You are required to draft an article:

(1)   **Explaining the key capital gains tax implications arising from the above, broken down in to sections as follows:**

  (i)   **The capital gains tax implications of selling the current family home.**   **(2 marks)**

  (ii)   **The capital gains tax implications for Mr and Mrs Hammond of residing in two homes and any action that they should consider.**   **(5 marks)**

  (iii)   **The advice that you would give Mr and Mrs Hammond based on their circumstances and the resulting capital gains tax consequences of the flat either being sold after five years or being sold after ten years, having been let for five years.**   **(7 marks)**

  (iv)   **The capital gains tax consequences of the sale of the house in 20 years.**   **(1 mark)**

(2)   **Answering a frequent question from couples – what is the difference between owning our house as joint tenants or owning it as tenants in common?**   **(5 marks)**

You should assume that the facts of the case study will be reproduced on the website.

(Total = 20 marks)

14.2 Peter Stamp

On 2 May 1986 Peter Stamp, a retired solicitor, bought a private dwelling house for £70,000, which he sold for £270,000 under a contract dated 3 July 2013. The house was situated in grounds of one half of a hectare.

He lived in this house as his only residence until 1 February 1990. It was then let for residential purposes until 1 December 1999. From that date until the date of sale the property was unoccupied.

You are required to compute the chargeable gain arising on the sale of the house.

14.3 Mr Richman

White Cottage
Plumsted
Yorkshire

2 May 2014

Dear Mr Jones,

I have recently (on 4 April 2014) sold a house, 'Red Bricks', for £370,000. The house was originally purchased on 6 April 1986 for £90,000 and was used as my principal residence until 5 April 1991. From 6 April 1991 until 5 April 1998 the house was empty while I was working abroad. I am an architect and have always been treated as self employed from when I started to practise in 1976.

On my return to the UK in April 1998 I moved back into the house. In April 1999 the house was converted (at a cost of £20,000) to a flat upstairs (which I used as my residence) and offices downstairs from which I ran my practice. I moved out of the flat at Red Bricks on 5 October 2011 and the flat was empty until the whole property was sold on 4 April 2014. The flat occupied exactly half of the property and I believe this has been agreed with HM Revenue & Customs. I continued to use the offices for my practice until shortly before the sale and now rent business premises.

I should be grateful if you would write to me setting out how any capital gains tax liability will be calculated, taking into account any reliefs due and when the tax will be payable. I made no other disposals in 2013/14.

Yours sincerely

A Richman

You are required to draft a letter as requested.

15.1 Fran and Anna

Fran sold a factory worth £500,000 to her friend Anna for £100,000 on 1 June 2013 and moved her business to new premises. Fran had bought the factory on 1 January 1996 for £75,000. On 1 July 2015 Anna sold the factory for £520,000.

Both Fran and Anna have elected for gift relief to apply and have used the factory for the purposes of their respective sole trades.

You are required to calculate the chargeable gains for Fran and Anna. Assume that 2013/14 tax rates and legislation continue to apply throughout.

15.2 Joe Bloggs

Joe Bloggs had the following transactions in December 2013:

(1)   He sold his flat for £700,000, which he had purchased in July 1985 for £200,000. He has always used his spare bedroom, which is approximately one quarter of the total floor space, as an office and property expenses have always been apportioned accordingly.

(2)   Joe sold unquoted trading company shares to his daughter for £375,000. The shares had recently been valued at £450,000. The company had no investments. He had purchased the shares for £75,000 in September 1990.

You are required to calculate the amount subject to capital gains tax for 2013/14 on the above disposals assuming all available reliefs are claimed.

15.3 P J Laval

P J Laval had the following transactions in assets during the year 2013/14:

(1)   Sold his house, 'Chez Nous', for £99,000 on 14 May 2013, having bought this for £37,000 on 6 April 1985, incurring expenditure of £2,000 on an extension on 6 May 1986. The house has never been used as his only or main residence.

(2)   Sold 1,400 shares in Vic plc, a quoted company, for £8,710 on 18 July 2013 having purchased 1,400 shares on 10 February 1986 at a cost of £3,500.

There was a bonus issue of 1:4 on 10 March 1987.

(3) On 31 March 2014, PJ gave his entire holding of shares in Lavaling Ltd, his personal trading company, to his son. If he had sold his shares on that date to a third party he would have realised a capital gain of £80,000. At that date, the company's assets consisted of:

	Book value at 31.3.14 £	Market value at 31.3.14 £
Freehold property	20,000	130,000
Quoted securities	8,000	30,000
Stocks	70,000	70,000
Debtors	35,000	35,000
Cash and bank balances	21,000	21,000
	154,000	286,000

PJ has never worked for the company.

You are required to:

(1) **Compute the amount of capital gains tax payable by PJ Laval for the 2013/14 tax year, assuming he claims all available reliefs and has taxable income of £24,510.** **(13 marks)**

(2) **Briefly describe the three ways in which land can be legally held: freehold, leasehold, and common hold.** **(5 marks)**

(Total = 18 marks)

15.4 Simon

You have received the following memorandum from a partner in your firm:

'To: Frances Ackland
From: Simon Evans
Date: 3 November 2013
Subject: Deferral of gains

I have just disposed of some shares in Blue Ltd, an unquoted company. I need some advice on how I can postpone paying tax on the gain arising from this sale. I remember reading something in the Tax Department's newsletter a while ago about a special relief to enable me to do this. Can you give me some details?

You should know that I acquired the Blue Ltd shares in September 1991 as a gift from my father. He had originally acquired them in 1986 and we elected to defer the gain arising. You will find the details in my personal tax affairs file. I sold the Blue shares for £200,000 on 30 October 2013. I have no other assets for CGT purposes and no other spare cash other than the proceeds of the Blue shares.

I would like to use some of the proceeds of the sale to invest in a house in France, probably about £100,000. My wife and I intend to move to France in the next couple of years to restore the house. I am currently an additional rate taxpayer.'

You ascertain that the deferred gain on the Blue shares was £15,000 and that they were worth £65,000 in September 1991.

You are required to write a memorandum in reply. **(10 marks)**

15.5 Emily

Emily made the following disposals in 2013/14:

(1) *Factory*

Acquired 1 July 2006 for £150,000. Emily let out the factory rent free to her partnership business. The factory was sold for £225,000 on 10 July 2013 as the partnership required bigger premises.

(2) *Painting*

This had been acquired by Emily's husband Arthur on 1 March 1999 for £50,000. Arthur had given the painting to Emily on 1 July 2004 when it was worth £60,000. Emily sold the painting for £73,000 on 2 May 2013.

(3) *Vase*

Emily had acquired this asset on 10 August 1991 for £46,000. She sold it on 1 December 2013 for £19,000.

(4)   Emily sold 2,000 shares in Goodinv Ltd (an unquoted trading company) to her sister for £10,000 on 1 February 2014. She had acquired the 1% shareholding for £4,000 in May 2001 and they were worth £80,000 on 1 February 2014.

You are required to calculate Emily's CGT liability for 2013/14 assuming she claims all available reliefs and had taxable income for the year of £24,010.

15.6   Peter

Peter made the following disposals in 2013/14:

(a)   He purchased a building for £200,000 on 1 January 1986 which he let commercially as offices. On 10 April 2013 he sold the building for £600,000.

(b)   He held 20,000 shares (1% shareholding) in Forum Follies plc which he purchased in May 1989 for £50,000. In March 2014, Exciting Enterprises plc acquired all the share capital of Forum Follies plc. Under the terms of the takeover for every two shares previously held in Forum Follies plc shareholders received three ordinary shares in Exciting Enterprises plc plus £1 cash. Immediately after the takeover the ordinary shares in Exciting Enterprises plc were quoted at £3 each.

(c)   Peter purchased shares in Dassau plc, a quoted company, as follows.

	No of shares	Cost £
December 1987	1,000	2,000
April 1990 1 for 2 rights issue		£2 per share

In November 2013 he sold 1,200 shares for £9,500.

Peter had capital losses brought forward from 2012/13 of £6,400.

You are required to calculate the CGT payable by Peter for 2013/14, assuming his taxable income in the year was £29,510, and state the due date for payment.

15.7   Sarah Stone

Sarah had the following transactions in 2013/14:

12 April 2013

She sold all her shares in Peterson Ltd for £150,000. Sarah has never worked for the company. She had acquired the shares as follows:

Date	No	Cost £	Notes
1/3/89	50,000	25,000	Probate value from father
1/8/02	5,000	10,000	Purchased
1/10/03	1:5 rights issue	£3 per share	

15 June 2013

She sold an antique brooch which she had purchased in September 1997 for £5,800. She received £8,000 after selling costs of £250.

19 September 2013

She sold her stamp collection for £3,100. She had purchased it for £7,000 in June 1990.

21 January 2014

She sold a house which she had bought as an investment property in January 1986 for £28,000. She added a loft bedroom at a cost of £10,000 in February 1987. She sold it for £75,000.

Sarah had capital losses brought forward of £15,000.

Calculate Sarah's CGT payable assuming her taxable income for the year was £31,010.

16.1 Interest payments

(1) Hugh's self assessment of income tax due for 2012/13 was £20,000 and Hugh made the following payments on account in respect of the 2013/14 year:

Date of payment	Amount
	£
2 March 2014	10,000
2 September 2014	2,500

Hugh determined that his self assessment of income tax due for 2013/14 was £22,000 and paid the balance of tax due on 31 January 2015.

Calculate the interest due on each payment on account and the balancing payment for 2013/14.

(2) Assume that Hugh's self assessment of income tax due for 2013/14 was £18,000 (instead of the £22,000 in (1)) and that the balancing payment was made on 31 January 2015.

Calculate the final interest due on each payment on account and the balancing payment, if any, for 2013/14. **(10 marks)**

16.2 Radnor

Radnor had a self assessment income tax liability, in respect of 2012/13, of £10,000.

On 11 November 2013 he claims to reduce the payments on account for 2013/14 to £3,000 each, in the belief that his profits will suffer because of the loss of a major customer.

He makes payments on account of £3,000 each on 31 March 2014 and 30 September 2014.

On submission of his self assessment return for 2013/14 he has a self assessment income tax liability in respect of his business profits of £7,500. Any additional tax due was paid on 31 January 2015.

You are required to:

(1) **Calculate the late payment interest due assuming that Radnor's claim to reduce the payments on account was innocently wrong.**

(2) **What penalty could be charged if HMRC discovered that his claim to reduce the payments on account was made fraudulently?** **(10 marks)**

1.1 Allowances

	£
PA (born between 6 April 1938 and 5 April 1948)	10,500
Less: restriction (W)	(390)
	10,110

(W) Restriction = ½ £(26,880 – 26,100) = £390

1.2

	£
PA (born between 6 April 1938 and 5 April 1948)	10,500
Blind person's allowance	2,160
	12,660

The married couple's allowance (MCA) does not reduce net income. It is a tax reduction, ie a deduction from the tax liability. The MCA would be available as at least one of the couple was born before 6 April 1935.

1.3

	£
PA (basic)	9,440
Less: restriction (W)	(5,000)
Restricted PA	4,440

(W) Restriction = ½ £(110,000 – 100,000) = £5,000

1.4

	£
Earnings/ net income	45,580
Less: PA	(9,440)
Taxable income	36,140
£	
32,010 × 20%	6,402
700 × 20% (W)	140
3,430 × 40%	1,372
Tax liability	7,914
Less tax suffered: PAYE	(8,054)
Tax repayable	(140)

Working

Basic rate band extended by £700 (£560 × 100/80)

1.5

	£
PA (born before 6 April 1938)	10,660
Less: Restriction: ½ × £(32,800 – 26,100) = £3,350 restricted to £1,220	(1,220)
Reduced to level of basic PA	9,440
MCA – tax reduction	7,915
Less: excess restriction £(3,350 – 1,220)	(2,130)
	5,785
@ 10%	579

1.6

	£
Earnings/ net income (note)	280,000
Less: Deductible payment:	
Loan interest (W)	(70,000)
	210,000
Less: PA (> £118,880)	(NIL)
Taxable income	210,000
£	
32,010 × 20%	6,402
117,990 × 40%	47,196
60,000 × 45%	27,000
Tax liability	80,598

Note. Lottery winnings are exempt.

Working – cap on tax relief

Maximum relief for loan interest paid of £100,000 is higher of:

(a)   £50,000
(b)   25% × £280,000 = £70,000, ie £70,000

1.7   £2,000 (£1,600 × 100/80)

The interest from the building society account will be assessed on his mother as income > £100 gross.

1.8

	£
PA (born before 6 April 1938)	10,660
Less: ½ £(27,800 – 500 – 26,100)	(600)
	10,060

The allowance is restricted where adjusted net income exceeds £26,100. Adjusted net income is net income reduced by the gross amount of Gift Aid donations (ie £400 × 100/80 = £500).

1.9

	£
Earnings	3,700
Interest income	300
Net income	4,000
Less: PA	(9,440)
Taxable income	–
IT repayable:	
Earnings – PAYE	740
Interest – 20% tax credit	60
	800

Scholarship received by a full-time student is not taxable. Legacy (ie inheritance) is a capital receipt and not taxable as income.

1.10

	£
Bert	
Net income	13,845
PA (born after 5 April 1948)	(9,440)
Taxable income	4,405
Tax	
£4,405 × 20%	881
Less: tax reduction – MCA	
£7,915 × 10%	(792)
Tax liability	89

Bert receives the MCA as his wife was born before 6 April 1935

1.11 $1,000 \times 8p = £80 \times 100/90 = \underline{£89}$

Dividends are taxed on the receipts basis and come with a notional 10% tax credit.

1.12

	Savings income £	Dividend income £
BDI (£2,100 × 100/80)	2,625	
BSI (£1,800 × 100/80)	2,250	
Dividends (£8,550 × 100/90)		9,500
Net income	4,875	9,500
PA	(4,875)	(4,565)
Taxable income	–	4,935
Tax @ 10%		493
Tax credit on dividends (£4,935 @ 10% – **taxable** dividend)		(493)
Tax due		Nil
Less tax deducted at source on interest (£4,875 @ 20%)		(975)
Tax repayable		(975)

Note. Tax credits on dividends are offset first to maximise the relief available. Remember that the dividend tax credit cannot give rise to a refund of tax.

1.13

	Non savings £	Savings £	Dividends £
Employment income	5,264		
Bank interest £3,800 × $\dfrac{100}{80}$		4,750	
Dividend £34,000 × $\dfrac{100}{90}$			37,778
Net income	5,264	4,750	37,778
Less: PA	(5,264)	(4,176)	
Taxable income	–	574	37,778

Tax	£574 @ 10% (savings)		57
	£31,436 @ 10% (dividends)		3,144
	£6,342 @ 32½% £(37,778 – 31,436) (dividends)		2,061
Tax liability			5,262
Less:	Dividend credit 10% × £37,778		(3,778)
	Tax on interest 20% × £4,750		(950)
Tax payable			534

1.14

	Non savings £	Savings £	Dividends £
Employment income	125,000		
Bank interest £12,500 × $\frac{100}{80}$		15,625	
Dividend £27,000 × $\frac{100}{90}$			30,000
Net income	125,000	15,625	30,000
Less: PA (income > £118,880)	(NIL)		
Taxable income	125,000	15,625	30,000

Tax	£32,010 @ 20 % (non savings)	6,402
	£92,990 @ 40% £(125,000 – 32,010) (non savings)	37,196
	£15,625 @ 40% (savings)	6,250
	£ 9,375 @ 32½% £(150,000 – 125,000 – 15,625) (dividends)	3,047
	£20,625 @ 37½% £(30,000 – 9,375) (dividends)	7,734
Tax liability		60,629
Less:	Dividend credit 10% × £30,000	(3,000)
	PAYE	(43,598)
	Tax on interest 20% × £15,625	(3,125)
Tax payable		10,906

1.15

	£
Trade profits	8,720
Discretionary trust income (£1,500 × 100/55)	2,727
	11,447
Less: PA (born before 6 April 1938)	(10,660)
Taxable income	787
Tax @ 20%	157
Less: MCA (£7,915 × 2/12 × 10%)	(132)
Tax liability	25
Less: tax deducted (£2,727 × 45%)	(1,227)
Repayable	(1,202)

Income from a discretionary trust comes with a 45% tax credit. MCA is given to the partner with the higher income and in the year of a civil partnership (or marriage) is reduced by the number of complete tax months prior to the date of the partnership.

1.16   Income of minor unmarried children (ie Dawn) is taxed in the hands of the parent if it derives from a parental settlement and exceeds £100 (gross) in the tax year. Therefore, Richard is taxed on Dawn's income. As Donna is married, the dividend is treated as her own income.

1.17   Investment income of a child arising out of a gift by his parent is aggregated with the income of that parent. However where the income does not exceed £100 (gross) pa it is treated as the income of the child.

Therefore, this income would be taxed on Gilbert and would be covered by his personal allowance.

1.18   Alan – 2013/14

		£
Income		50,000
Less:	Deductible payment:	
	Loan interest	(2,610)
		47,390
Less:	PA (basic – as net income significantly > £26,100)	(9,440)
Taxable income		37,950

Tax thereon:

	£
£32,010 @ 20%	6,402
£5,940 @ 40%	2,376
	8,778
Less: Maintenance payment (Max £3,040 × 10%)	(304)
Tax liability	8,474

There is no relief for mortgage interest payments for an individual's residence.

2.1

	Non savings £	Savings £
Employment income	27,040	
Treasury stock interest (received gross)		20,000
Less: PA	(9,440)	
Taxable income	17,600	20,000
Tax:		
£17,600 @ 20%		3,520
£14,410 @ 20% (£32,010 – £17,600) (savings)		2,882
£5,590 @ 40% (£20,000 – £14,410)		2,236
£37,600		8,638

Note that 'tax liability' is **before** deducting tax suffered at source.

2.2

	£
NS&I savings a/c (received gross)	276
Interest income	276

Interest on NS&I Savings Certificates and HMRC repayment interest are tax free.

2.3   Interest from loans made by an individual to an individual are received gross.

Interest paid by a company to an individual in respect of an unquoted debenture is paid under deduction of 20% income tax.

2.4

	£
UK bank interest (£8,680 × 100/80)	10,850
Guernsey interest	640
Interest on government stock (paid gross)	5,000
Net income	16,490
Less: PA	(9,440)
Taxable income	7,050

2.5   Maximum overall investment – £11,520
Maximum cash investment – £5,760

2.6   Maximum investment – £3,720

Note. An individual between 16 and 18 can also invest the maximum in a regular cash ISA. This does not affect the Junior ISA limit.

2.7   There is no income tax on interest or dividends received on investments within an ISA.

2.8 Tax on taxable income

	£	£
32,010 × 20%		6,402
104,470 × 40%		41,788
		48,190
Less: SEIS income tax reduction: £100,000 (max) × 50% (restricted)		(50,000)
Tax liability		0

It is not possible to have a tax reduction in excess of the tax on taxable income.

Bert can, however, claim to carry back the remaining relief of £1,810 (£50,000 − £48,190) against his 2012/13 income tax liability.

2.9 The first £200,000 worth of VCT investments made in a tax year will give rise to tax free dividends.

Taxable net dividends (excess over £200,000)

$$\frac{10,000}{60,000} \times £3,400 = \underline{£567}$$

2.10

	£
Trust income (£5,500 × 100/55)	10,000
Less: PA	(9,440)
	560
Income tax:	
£560 @ 20%	112
Tax deducted:	
Trust: £10,000 @ 45%	(4,500)
Tax repayable	(4,388)

2.11 Interim payments from an estate in administration are taxable in the year of receipt. Payments are treated as being paid out of non savings first, then savings, then dividends and come with the appropriate tax credit for the type of income.

Belinda's grandmother's estate only has savings income, so the payment will be treated as coming from savings income and must be grossed up at 100/80. The amounts reported on the R185 will be:

	Net income	Tax credit
	£	£
Estate income (from savings) £5,000 × 20/80	5,000	1,250

2.12 There is a pre-owned asset tax (POAT) charge on Maureen as the property was purchased using money that she had previously gifted. The POAT charge is based on the annual rental value of the property.

Income tax charge (within the basic rate band): £10,000 × 20% = £2,000

2.13 Alison sells the stock on 15 June 2013 'ex interest', which means that she (rather than the buyer) receives the next interest payment due on 30 June 2013. She will obtain relief for the days that she did not own the stock.

		£
30.6.13	Interest: 4% × £12,000 × ½	240
	Less: accrued income relief (15.6.13 − 30.6.13)	
	$£240 \times \dfrac{\frac{1}{2}}{6}$	(20)
		220

2.14

	Non savings £	Savings £
Employment income	40,810	
Life assurance premium bond (W1)		14,000
Less: PA	(9,440)	
Taxable income	31,370	14,000
Tax:		
£31,370 @ 20%		6,274
£ 640 @ 20% (£32,010 – £31,370) (savings)		128
£13,360 @ 40% (£14,000 – £640)		5,344
£45,370		11,746
Less: top slicing relief (W2)		(384)
Less: tax suffered		
PAYE		(6,274)
Life assurance premium bond: £14,000 × 20%		(2,800)
Tax payable		2,288

Workings

(1)   *Life assurance premium bond*

Policy held for 4 complete years:

	£
Proceeds on encashment	30,000
Add: withdrawals within 5% limit: 4 × 5% × £20,000	4,000
	34,000
Less: initial premium	(20,000)
Overall profit	14,000

(2)   *Top slicing relief*

The profit is taxed as the top slice of income, so £13,360 (£31,370 + £14,000 – £32,010) is taxed at the higher rate. Top slicing applies.

Number of complete years = 4. One slice = £14,000/4 = £3,500

	£
Total income: £31,370 + £3,500	34,870
Less: basic rate band	(32,010)
Slice taxed at higher rate	2,860
Total taxed at higher rate £2,860 × 4	11,440
∴ Amount taxed at basic rate £(13,360 – 11,440)	1,920
(ie £1,920 @ 20%)	384

Check:

	£
Tax liability in respect of the policy	
Tax on slice: £2,860 @ 20% (40% – 20% credit)	572
Tax due: £572 × 4 years	2,288
Tax calculated: £(128 + 5,344 – 384 – 2,800)	2,288

2.15 $\frac{1}{2} \times £300 \times \frac{100}{80} = £188$

As it is a joint bank account they are each entitled to half of the interest, regardless on the amount of capital contributed by each of them.

2.16   Income tax calculation

	Non savings £	Dividends £
Employment income	75,000	
Dividends (£15 × 2,000 × 100/90)		33,333
	75,000	33,333
Personal allowance (W)	(5,274)	
	69,726	33,333

Tax thereon:

	£
32,010 @ 20%	6,402
37,716 @ 40%	15,086
33,333 @ 32$\frac{1}{2}$%	10,833
103,059	32,321
Less: Tax credit on dividends	(3,333)
Tax deducted via PAYE	(20,600)
Tax payable	8,388

Working – Personal allowance

	£	£
PA (only basic PA available due to level of income)		9,440
Total net income	108,333	
Less: limit	(100,000)	
Excess	8,333	
Restricted by excess × ½		(4,166)
Available PA		5,274

2.17   The pre-owned asset legislation would apply.

The formula to calculate the chargeable amount is R × DV/V where R is the rental value of the land, DV is such part of the land's value as can be reasonably attributed to the consideration provided by William and V is the value of the land.

As William contributed £500,000 towards the acquisition of a £750,000 house, DV/V = $^{500}/_{750}$ = 0.66666

Chargeable amount = 0.66666 × £24,000 × $^{7}/_{12}$ = £9,333

Tax charge £9,333 × 40% (higher rate taxpayer) = £3,733

William could elect for the £500,000 he gifted to be treated as a gift with reservation of benefit for IHT purposes.

2.18.   Lisa is treated as receiving a dividend in respect of both the write off of the interest free loan and the company car benefit. As she is an additional rate taxpayer she will pay tax at 37.5% and receive a 10% tax credit as follows:

	£
Loan write off: £30,000 × 100/90 = £33,333 @ 37.5%	12,500
Car benefit: £4,875 × 100/90 = £5,417 @ 37.5%	2,031
Less dividend tax credit: £(33,333 + 5,417) @ 10%	(3,875)
Taxable	10,656

Note. If the interest free loan had been outstanding for any part of 2013/14 Lisa would also have been treated as receiving a dividend in respect of the benefit of the interest free loan.

3.1   As both Simon and Sarah earn over £50,000, the higher earner suffers the child benefit charge, ie Simon, even though Sarah actually receives the child benefit.

The amount that he must include in his self assessment tax return is:

	£
Income	54,500
Less: threshold	(50,000)
Excess	4,500
÷ £100	45
Charge: 1% × £1,752 × £45	788

3.2 As Tanya earns more than £109 per week she is entitled to receive SSP of £86.70 per week.

The total SPP due is £433.50 (5 × £86.70).

3.3 Qualifying amount:

	£
Fixed amount	10,000
Amount per child:	
≥ 11: 52 weeks × £250	13,000
Total 'qualifying amount'	23,000

4.1

	£
Gross rents (£1,500 × 12) (accruals basis)	18,000
Less: Agent's fees	(1,800)
Interest	(4,200)
Water rates	(120)
Insurance	(500)
Wear and tear allowance (£(18,000 – 120) × 10%)	(1,788)
Property income	9,592

The cost of building the new porch is capital expenditure and cannot be deducted for income tax purposes.

4.2

	£
Rent receivable (10 × £160) + £400	2,000
Less: Bad debt £(1,600 – 1,300)	(300)
Interest	(700)
Property income	1,000

4.3

	£
Whitehouse: Rent accrued in the year	4,000
Blackhouse: (9/12 × £2,000)	1,500
Property income	5,500

No bad debt relief as payment was actually received.

4.4

	£
Rents receivable (£4,000 × 8/12)	2,667
Expenses paid	(1,000)
Property income	1,667

Note. The rent receivable from the new tenants will begin to be assessed in 2014/15 (we can ignore the two days falling into 2013/14).

4.5

	£
Income	8,000
Less: insurance	(300)
water rates	(400)
wear and tear allowance: 10% × £(8,000 – 400)	(760)
Property income	6,540

4.6 Brian should elect to assess rents received over £4,250, ie £750 (£5,000 – £4,250) under the 'rent a room' scheme, otherwise property income of £4,400 (£5,000 – £600) would be assessable.

Note. No further deduction is available for expenses where 'rent a room' relief applies.

4.7   Four from:
- Available for letting for 210 days a year
- Actually let for 105 days in a year
- Not more than 155 days in a year are periods of longer term occupation (ie let to same tenant for more than 31 continuous days).
- Situated in the UK or any other EEA state
- Furnished
- Let with a view to a profit

5.1

	£
Statutory redundancy pay	3,800
Ex gratia cash payment	25,000
Value of car	12,000
Outplacement counselling (exempt)	–
	40,800
Less: exemption	(30,000)
Taxable	10,800

5.2   Salary:

	£	£
9/12 × £9,000	6,750	
3/12 × £10,000	2,500	9,250
Bonus received in 2013/14 (28.2.14)		2,400
		11,650

5.3

	£
Salary (5 × £1,000)	5,000
Car benefit (£15,000 × 23% × 3/12)*	862
Fuel benefit (£21,100 × 23% × 3/12)*	1,213
	7,075

$$* \frac{(155-95)}{5} = 12\%$$

Percentage: 11% + 12% = 23%

5.4

	£
Car (£14,000 × 27%)*	3,780
Petrol (£21,100 × 27%)	5,697
	9,477

There is no reduction in the taxable benefit for contributions made by an employee towards the cost of private petrol. Only made for full refunds (in which case the benefit would be nil).

$$* \frac{175-95}{5} = 16\%$$ (round down the emissions so it is divisible by 5)

11% + 16% = 27%

5.5   Earnings:

	£
Salary	10,000
Car (£16,000 × 28%)*	4,480
Second car (£12,000 × 10%)**	1,200
Cost of wine	1,000
Earnings	16,680
Less: expenses	(600)
	16,080

The second car is assessed on Jim because his daughter receives it by virtue of *his* employment, not hers (would you expect a company car if you just worked on Saturdays?)

* $\dfrac{180-95}{5} = 17\% + 11\% = 28\%$

** emissions are between 76 and 94g/km so percentage is 10%

5.6 Form P11D:

	£
Car (£12,000 × 22%)*	2,640
Expenses allowances (12 × £80)	960
	3,600

The amount spent by Albert on allowable expenses would be claimed separately by him on his tax return. The company must report the full allowance.

* $\dfrac{135-95}{5} = 8\% + 14\% = 22\%$ (*Note.* For cars running on diesel, there is a 3% supplement, ie 11% + 3%)

5.7

	£
Round sum allowance (£100 × 4) (not covered by dispensation)	400
Specific reimbursement – covered by dispensation	–
	400

A dispensation means that the item covered by it does not have to be reported on the P11D.

5.8 Sue: Nil (no taxable benefit for onsite work place nursery).
Tara: £1,768 (£(62 – 28) × 52 weeks)

Tara is a higher rate taxpayer (earning £52,000 per annum). As she joined the company's childcare scheme after 6 April 2011 only £28 per week of vouchers are tax free.

5.9 Private purchases £257 only. She will only ever be taxable on the goods/services bought with the card.

5.10 £480 (48 × (£65 – £55)) – as Joshua is a basic rate taxpayer, the first £55 per week of childcare vouchers is exempt (ie a tax free benefit). Both workplace parking and business use of a company credit card are tax free benefits.

5.11 An annual staff party becomes a taxable benefit to employees if it cost the employer > £150 per head. Where the cost exceeds £150 per head the full amount becomes taxable.

Each employee here has a £200 benefit.

5.12

	£
Professional subscriptions allowed	280
Subscription for accommodation allowable	200
	480

Golf club subscription disallowed as it is not incurred wholly, exclusively and necessarily in the performance of his duties.

5.13

	£
Salary	18,000
Accommodation – not taxable as job related	–
Household expenses £3,100	
limited to 10% × £18,000	1,800
Earnings	19,800

5.14

	£	£
Mobile phone for employee – not taxable	–	
Mobile phone for family member: 20% × £250	50	
		50
Laptop – 20% × £5,000	1,000	
Less: 40% business use	(400)	600
		650

Note. If private use of laptop had been merely incidental there would be no taxable benefit.

5.15

	£	£
Salary		50,000
Benefits: Crèche		
(£(200 – 55) × 46) (Note)	6,670	
Parking space	–	
Business miles		
(5,000 × 60p)	3,000	
Less: authorised mileage rates (5,000 × 45p)	(2,250)	
		7,420
Earnings		57,420

Note. As John's employer began paying for the childcare costs before 6 April 2011 he is entitled to £55 per week tax free, even though he is a higher rate taxpayer.

5.16

	£
Average method: $\frac{15,000 + 10,000}{2}$ × 4% (official rate of interest)	500
Less: interest paid: 5/4/13 – 5/1/14: £15,000 × 3% × 9/12	(338)
6/1/14 – 5/4/14: £10,000 × 3% × 3/12	(75)
	87
Strict basis:	
5/4/13 – 5/1/14: £15,000 × (4% – 3%) × 9/12	112
6/1/14 – 5/4/14: £10,000 × (4% – 3%) × 3/12	25
	137

Ruth can use the average basis but HMRC may elect to use the strict basis if they wish.

5.17

	£
Gross annual value	5,000
less rent paid by Jason	(3,000)
	2,000
Additional charge (use MV as moved in > 6 yrs after purchase)	
£(130,000 – 75,000) × 4% (official rate of interest)	2,200
	4,200

5.18 Assessable benefit on sale of dinner set is the greater of:

	£
(a)	
Market value at acquisition	1,500
less price paid	(1,000)
	500
(b) Original market value	2,000
less assessed in respect of use (2012/13)	
$^{6}/_{12}$ × 20% × £2,000	(200)
less assessed in respect of use (2013/14) $^{6}/_{12}$ × 20% × £2,000	(200)
less price paid	(1,000)
	600

∴ Benefit is £600 plus benefit for use in 2013/14 of £200 = £800

5.19

		£
Flat:	Annual value	3,000
	Household expenses	400
	Furniture (20% × £2,500)	500
		3,900

Note. There is no additional charge for the accommodation as the original cost was less than £75,000.

5.20

	£	£
Payment in lieu of notice (taxable in full)		8,000
Ex gratia payment (£30,000 exemption applies)	40,000	
Statutory redundancy pay (£30,000 exemption applies)	5,000	
	45,000	
Less: Exemption	(30,000)	15,000
Taxable		23,000

5.21

	£	£
Ex gratia (ie non contractual) payment	51,000	
Less: Exemption	(30,000)	30,000
Taxable	21,000	
Less: foreign service exemption (not 'substantial')		
$\frac{10}{30} \times £21,000$	(7,000)	7,000
Taxable	14,000	
Total exemption		37,000

5.22

	£
Annual value	2,225
Less: rent paid	(2,225)
	NIL
£(400,000 – 75,000) × 4% (official rate of interest)	13,000
Less: balance of rent paid (£2,725 – 2,225)	(500)
Net benefit	12,500

The calculation is based on expenditure incurred by the company *before* the tax year in question.

5.23 Car

	%
Base percentage	11
Add for emissions 190 (rounded down) – 95 = 95 ÷ 5	19
Add for diesel	3
Applicable percentage	33

Assessable benefit 33% × £40,000 = £13,200

Fuel 33% × £21,100= £6,963

Parking space – Tax free benefit

Loan – benefit assessed = £200,000 × (4% – 2%) = £4,000

Mobile phone – NIL

6.1 There are no income tax consequences at the date of grant.

When the option was exercised there would not normally be an income tax charge. However, as the option was granted at a discount there is an income tax charge at the date of exercise. The amount of the discount at the date of grant is charged to income tax, giving chargeable employment income of £5,000 (10,000 × (£2.00 − £1.50)).

Note that the amount of the discount is taxed as this is lower than the difference between the market value of the shares at the date of exercise and the exercise price ie £32,500 (10,000 × (£4.75 − £1.50))

6.2 'Free shares' are the shares an employer can give to an employee – maximum £3,000 per annum.

'Partnership shares' are the shares the employee is allowed to purchase from pre-tax salary to be held in the plan – maximum is the lower of £1,500 and 10% of salary per annum.

6.3 *Unapproved share option gain:*

	£
MV at date of exercise: 10,000 × £15	150,000
Exercise price: 10,000 × £11.50	(115,000)
Option gain	35,000
Income tax @ 40%	14,000

6.4 As Bruce has employee shareholder status, he can receive shares worth £2,000 or more and deduct £2,000 from the market value of the shares when calculating his employment income. The amount included as employment income is:

(a)

	£
MV of shares	2,000
Less: Deemed amount	(2,000)
Employment income	Nil

(b)

	£
MV of shares	3,000
Less: Deemed amount	(2,000)
Employment income	1,000

7.1 Employees pay Class 1 primary NICs based on their earnings from employment, which includes cash payments such as salary and expenses and also income from certain share schemes.

Self employed individuals pay Class 2 NIC based on their accounts profit and Class 4 NIC based on their taxable profits.

7.2 Class 1A NICs are based on taxable benefits paid to P11D employees (ie directors and employees paid £8,500+). Only the employer pays Class 1A NICs.

7.3 Contracting out of the State Second Pension Scheme

Where the employee 'contracts out' they will only be entitled to the basic pension from the State and will obtain their additional pension from the employer's scheme.

Both the employee and employer are entitled to a rebate between the lower earnings limit and the earnings threshold.

The employee pays a reduced rate of Class 1 NIC of 10.6% on earnings between the primary earnings threshold and the upper accruals point.

The employer also pays a reduced rate of 10.4% on earnings between the secondary earnings threshold and the upper accruals point.

Above the upper accruals point, the standard NIC rates apply, ie the employee pays 12% up to the upper earnings limit and 2% thereafter. The employer pays 13.8% above the upper accruals point.

8.1 Higher of: (i)   100% × earnings ie £28,000
             (ii)   £3,600

ie £28,000 (*Note.* Dividends are not relevant earnings for pension contribution purposes)

8.2 Norma has no relevant earnings. She may make a maximum contribution of £3,600 (gross) into a personal pension.

8.3

	£
Employment income	52,000
less PA	(9,440)
Taxable income	42,560
BRB extended to £32,010 + (£5,000 × $\frac{100}{80}$)	(38,260)
	4,300
Tax @ 40%	1,720

8.4 Jeremy can pay up to £400,000 into a pension in the year and obtain tax relief. He would pay 80% directly to the pension scheme (£320,000) and the fund would reclaim the 20% (£80,000) from HMRC. He would obtain tax relief at higher rates by extending his basic rate and higher rate bands, by the amount of the gross contributions of £400,000, to £432,010 and £550,000 respectively.

He has made contributions of £10,000 (£8,000 × 100/80) in each of the previous three years, so his annual allowance for 2013/14, including unused amounts carried forward, is £170,000 (current year of £50,000 plus £40,000 carried forward from the three previous years).

Since he would be paying more than this into his pension, he will have to pay an annual allowance income tax charge on the excess of £230,000 (£400,000 – £170,000).

The excess contributions are treated as his top slice of income. He has taxable income of £390,560 (£400,000 – £9,440) (full personal allowance available as net adjusted income is £nil (ie £400,000 – £400,000)).

Jeremy has £41,450 (£432,010 – £390,560) of his basic rate band remaining and £117,990 of his higher rate band remaining. The annual allowance tax charge is therefore:

	£
£41,450 × 20%	8,290
£117,990 × 40%	47,196
£70,560 × 45%	31,752
£230,000	
Annual allowance charge	87,238

8.5 Maximum tax free lump sum: 25% × £65,000 = £16,250

8.6

	£
Employment income	54,000
Less occupational pension contribution	(9,000)
Net income	45,000
Less PA	(9,440)
Taxable income	35,560

Tax

	£
£32,010 × 20%	6,402
£3,550 × 40%	1,420
35,560	7,822

9.1 As Wayne is taxable on the remittance basis the dividends will be treated as non savings income, rather than dividend income. He will pay tax at 40% (and not the dividend rate of 32.5%) as he is a higher rate taxpayer.

(£10,000 × 100/90) @ 40%   £4,444

In addition, as he has been UK resident for at least 12 out of the last 14 tax years and is over the age of 18, Wayne will be subject to the higher additional £50,000 remittance basis income tax charge. So, his total tax liability will be £54,444.

Notes

(1) Wayne will not receive a personal allowance as he has made a remittance basis claim.

(2) Even though remitted dividends are taxed as non savings income, they must still be grossed up by 100/90 in Wayne's income tax computation (and the 10% credit is available to reduce his tax liability).

9.2 As Egbert is UK resident he is taxable on his worldwide income on an arising basis. However, only 90% of foreign pensions are taxable on the arising basis so he will be taxed on £9,000 (90% × £10,000).

9.3 An individual can split the tax year if he:

(1) Leaves the UK part-way through the tax year and either:

    (i)   He or his spouse starts to work full-time overseas or
    (ii)   He ceases to have a home in the UK

(2) Comes to the UK part-way through the tax year and either:

    (i)   He starts to have his only home in the UK, or
    (ii)   He starts full-time employment in the UK, or
    (iii) he ceases (or his spouse ceases) working full-time abroad, or
    (iv) He starts to have a home in the UK.

9.4 Ernie is resident but not domiciled in the UK. As he has been resident for the last four years he can only use the remittance basis in respect of his foreign earnings if they are 'chargeable overseas earnings', ie they are in respect of wholly overseas duties for an overseas employer.

(a) The conditions appear to have been satisfied for his earnings to be treated as 'chargeable overseas earnings' as he has an overseas employer. The amount taxable in the UK is:

	£
UK duties (arising)	50,000
Foreign duties (remitted)	10,000
Taxable in UK	60,000

The additional remittance basis charge does not apply as he has only been UK resident for the last four tax years.

(b) As his employer is not an overseas employer, his earnings do not fall within the definition of 'chargeable overseas earnings', so his entire earnings, ie £70,000, are taxable in the UK.

9.5 Length of service 60 days; 2 visits per person.

Note. The employee can claim a deduction for the costs to offset the employment benefit. If the employee pays for the travelling then it is *not* an allowable deduction.

10.1

	£
Chargeable gain	18,000
Less: annual exempt amount	(10,900)
	7,100
£3,140 @ 18% (£32,010 – £28,870)	565
£3,960 @ 28% (£7,100 – £3,140)	1,109
Total CGT	1,674

10.2

	£
Chargeable gain (£32,000 + £26,000)	58,000
Less: annual exempt amount	(10,900)
Taxable gain	47,100
£5,540 @ 18% (£32,010 – £26,470)	997
£41,560 @ 28% £(47,100 – 5,540)	11,637
Total CGT	12,634

10.3 An individual can use the remittance basis if he is resident but not domiciled in the UK.

10.4 A racehorse, as wasting chattels are exempt from CGT.

The limousine, as cars are exempt from CGT.

10.5 (1) Yes – UK resident and domiciled individual is chargeable on gains on worldwide assets as they arise.

(2) No – Individuals who are not UK resident are not subject to CGT on disposals of asset located in the UK, unless used by a branch or agency in the course of a UK trade.

(3) Yes – However UK resident but non-UK domiciled individuals may be able to use the remittance basis either automatically or by making a claim, in which case they are only charged on the gains realised on the disposal of overseas assets to the extent that the gain is remitted to the UK.

11.1

	£
Sale proceeds	31,250
Less cost (probate value)	(11,200)
Chargeable gain	20,050

11.2

	£
Sale proceeds	85,000
Less: cost $\dfrac{85,000}{85,000+30,000} \times £18,000$	(13,304)
Chargeable gain	71,696

11.3

	£
Gains	9,000
Current year losses (must be set against current year gains)	(5,000)
	4,000
AEA	(10,900)
	–
Losses c/f (*Note.* Losses b/f reduce chargeable gains to AEA level only)	6,000

11.4

	2011/12 £	2012/13 £	2013/14 £
Gains	2,000	4,000	13,800
Losses	(5,000)	(2,000)	(2,000)
	(3,000)	2,000	11,800
c/f	3,000		(900) c/f £2,100
			10,900

Note. Losses b/f reduce gains down to AEA level only.

11.5 The persons connected (for CGT purposes) to Paul are his:
- Wife
- Mother-in-law
- Business partner
- Step-father

11.6

	£
Proceeds	170,000
Less: cost	(120,000)
Gain	50,000

Note. Transfer between spouses is on no gain/no loss basis, so Grace's base cost is £120,000.

11.7   As losses from a sale to a connected person can only be set against gains to the same connected person, the loss of £8,200 will be carried forward and set against the gain of £14,000 arising on the sale to Charles on 29 September 2014.

Note. Carry back of the loss is not allowed.

11.8

	£
Proceeds	30,000
Less: cost	
$\dfrac{30,000}{30,000+10,000} \times £8,000$	(6,000)
Chargeable gain	24,000

11.9

	£
Gains	18,200
Losses	(7,000)
	11,200
Losses b/f £(11,200 – 10,900)	(300)
	10,900
Less: annual exempt amount	(10,900)
Taxable gain	Nil

Losses c/f (5,000 – 300) = £4,700

11.10

	£
Proceeds	45,000
Cost £8,000 × $\dfrac{45,000}{45,000+50,000}$	(3,789)
Chargeable gain	41,211
Less: AEA	(10,900)
Taxable gain	30,311

Note. No claim is available for a 'small part' disposal as proceeds > £20,000 and > 20% of MV of land.

11.11 *Painting*

- No gain/no loss as a disposal between spouses
- Treatment applies until after the end of the year of separation

Dinner service

- Gain/loss may arise as this is a disposal between connected persons; proceeds taken as £15,000, being the market value.
- Spouses remain connected until decree absolute (ie until divorce is finalised).

11.12 *Calculation*

	£
Proceeds	500,000
Cost	(28,000)
Gain	472,000

All the proceeds must be taxed up front even though they are not all received in December 2013.

12.1 *Gain:*

	£
Proceeds	22,500
Cost (W)	(14,000)
Chargeable gain	8,500

Working – Share pool

	No of shares	Cost £
Purchase Aug 2009	2,000	18,000
Purchase Sept 2009	1,000	10,000
	3,000	28,000
Sale Jan 2014	(1,500)	(14,000)
c/f	1,500	14,000

12.2 *Gain:*

	£
Proceeds	22,000
Cost (W)	(9,000)
Chargeable gain	13,000

Working – Share pool

	No of shares	Cost £
Purchase 19.2.86	2,000	10,000
Purchase 20.9.93	1,000	8,000
	3,000	18,000
Sale 15.11.13	(1,500)	(9,000)
c/f	1,500	9,000

12.3 *Gain:*

	£
Proceeds	6,250
Cost (W)	(3,270)
Chargeable gain	2,980

Working – Share pool

	No of shares	Cost £
Purchase April 88	5,000	5,605
Bonus issue (1 for 5)	1,000	–
	6,000	5,605
Sale Dec 2013	(3,500)	(3,270)
c/f	2,500	2,335

13.1

		£
Victoria Cross:	Proceeds	14,780
	Less: cost	(3,000)
		11,780

Chargeable gain not to exceed 5/3 × £(14,780 – 6,000) = £14,633

∴ Gain =	11,780

Vintage car: Exempt

Note. Medals are only exempt if awarded for bravery or inherited.

13.2

	£
Proceeds	7,500
Selling costs	(300)
	7,200
Less: cost	(4,500)
Gain	2,700

Chargeable gain not to exceed 5/3 × £(7,500 – 6,000) = £2,500

So, gain is £2,500.

13.3

	Cost £
Gross proceeds (deemed)	6,000
Cost	(6,260)
Allowable loss	(260)

13.4

	£
Gross proceeds	7,200
Less: Incidental costs	(350)
	6,850
Less: Acquisition cost (probate value)	(3,000)
Chargeable gain	3,850
Limited to 5/3 × £(7,200 − 6,000)	2,000

13.5

Motor car: exempt

Machinery:

	£
Proceeds	7,500
Less: cost	(5,500)
	2,000

Restrict to 5/3 × £(7,500 − 6,000) = £2,500

Chargeable gain = £2,000

Note. There is never a capital loss on an item on which capital allowances have been claimed, as a balancing allowance would be given instead through the capital allowances computation.

13.6

Grant of long lease:

	£
Proceeds	30,000
Less cost	
£40,000 × $\dfrac{30,000}{30,000+82,500}$	(10,667)
	19,333

13.7

	£
Grant of short lease:	
Proceeds (capital element of premium) (W)	2,000
Cost £30,000 × $\dfrac{2,000}{10,000+50,000}$	(1,000)
Chargeable gain	1,000

Working

	£
Premium	10,000
Less: property income: £10,000 × $\dfrac{50-(11-1)}{50}$	(8,000)
Capital element	2,000

14.1

	£
Gain	80,000
PPR relief: $\frac{69}{321} \times £80,000$	(17,196)
Gain attributable to letting	62,804
Less: letting relief	
Lowest of (i) £40,000	
(ii) PPR relief: £17,196	
(iii) Letting gain ($\frac{252}{321} \times £80,000 = £62,804$)	(17,196)
Chargeable gain	45,608

Working

	Occupation	Non-Occupation (Let)	Total
1.10.86 – 30.6.89	33		33
1.7.89 – 30.6.10		252	252
1.7.10 – 30.6.13 (last 3 years)	36		36
	69	252	321

14.2

	£
Proceeds	200,000
Less: cost	(20,000)
	180,000
Less PPR exemption £180,000 × 2/3	(120,000)
Chargeable gain	60,000

Note. As the students occupy separate self-contained accommodation, the ground floor is treated as a separate residence, the gain on which is fully chargeable to CGT.

14.3 Any **two** of:

(a) Any period employed outside the UK
(b) Periods of up to four years working elsewhere in the UK if he or his spouse/civil partner is employed, or elsewhere in the UK *or* overseas if either is self employed
(c) Up to three years for any reason
(d) The last 3 years of ownership where the property has been the principal private residence at some time.

Note. (a) – (c) must be preceded and followed by a period of actual occupation.

15.1

	£
Jeremy's chargeable gain (sale at below market value)	
Actual proceeds	50,000
Less cost	(42,000)
Gain chargeable now	8,000

Note. The balance of the gain, £102,000 (ie £110,000 – £8,000), is deferred

	£
Base cost for John	
MV in August 2013	152,000
Less deferred gain (see above)	(102,000)
	50,000

15.2 The claim must be made jointly by Arthur and Hugo. The claim must be submitted before 5 April 2018 (ie 4 years after the end of the tax year of the gift).

15.3

	£
Deemed proceeds (MV)	22,000
Less: Cost	(4,000)
Gain before gift relief	18,000
Chargeable on Adam (sale at below market value)	
£(12,000 − 4,000)	(8,000)
Deferred by gift relief	10,000

The deferred gain (£10,000) is taxed on Bernard in the year he becomes non-resident (ie 2015/16).

15.4

	£
Proceeds (MV)	300,000
Less: cost	(160,000)
Gain	140,000
Gift relief (CBA/CA)	
$\dfrac{300,000}{300,000+50,000} \times £140,000$	(120,000)
Chargeable gain	20,000

15.5 *Sale at below market value*

	£
MV	95,000
Cost	(44,000)
Gain	51,000
Chargeable now £(63,000 − 44,000)	(19,000)
Gain eligible for gift relief	32,000

15.6

	£
Proceeds	4,000
Less cost: £24,000 × $\dfrac{4,000}{4,000+16,000}$	(4,800)
Loss	(800)

15.7 *2013/14*

Patrice can claim to defer the entire gain (there is no upper limit for EIS deferral relief and the amount spent on EIS shares exceeds the gain).

	£
Gain	600,000
Less EIS deferral relief	(600,000)
Chargeable gain	−

2014/15

As Patrice emigrates (ie becomes non-UK resident) within three years, the chargeable gain of £600,000 will crystallise.

15.8 Gain on sale of Silvanus Ltd shares:

	£
Proceeds	800,000
Cost	(50,000)
Gain before EIS relief	750,000

Therefore, John's minimum EIS investment (and claim for EIS deferral relief) will be:

£(750,000 − 150,000 − 10,900) = £589,100

15.9 There are two reliefs available to Karina in 2013/14:

(1) *EIS deferral relief*

If Karina subscribes for shares in a qualifying EIS company she can defer the gain on the painting. When she sells the EIS shares, the gain on those shares will be exempt if she has held them for at least three years and the deferred gain on the painting will become chargeable at that date.

(2) *SEIS reinvestment relief*

If Kate subscribes for shares in a qualifying SEIS company before the end of the 2013/14 tax year, she will receive a 50% CGT exemption, based on the amount she spends on investing in the shares. So, if she reinvests £45,000, £22,500 of the gain will be exempt. If, however, she invests £90,000, the full £45,000 will be exempt. Note that the exemption is capped at £50,000 as the maximum SEIS investment is £100,000.

When she sells the SEIS shares in the future any gain will be exempt if she has held them for at least three years.

16.1 Landlords can submit simplified returns for rental income when the total annual gross income from property is under £79,000 (the VAT threshold).

They need only record three amounts:

- Gross property income
- Total allowable expenses
- Net income

16.2 If Thomas files online the return must be filed and the tax due paid by 31 January 2015. If he submits a paper return he must file by 31 October 2014. Any tax due should be paid by 31 January 2015.

16.3 POAs for 2013/14

	£
Income tax liability 2012/13	11,250
Less: tax deducted at source	(5,000)
Relevant amount	6,250

POAs of £3,125 are due on 31 January 2014 and 31 July 2014. Any balancing payment is due 31 January 2015.

16.4 Gareth filed an incorrect tax return. The tax lost as a result of the inaccuracy is £6,000 × 40% = £2,400.

The inaccuracy involves an overseas source of income. However as the overseas source of income is from a Category 1 country the increased offshore penalties do not apply.

Gareth's action was deliberate but not concealed (he has not made arrangements to conceal it for example by submitting false evidence in support of the incorrect figure). He is therefore liable to a maximum penalty of 70% × £2,400 = £1,680. This may be reduced depending on whether Gareth makes a prompted or unprompted disclosure of the omission to HMRC and the quality of Gareth's cooperation with HMRC in correcting the error.

17.1 The following members are not required to hold professional indemnity insurance for their work:

- Members who receive an honorarium of less than £1,000 in total per annum in their personal capacity, and

- Members who carry out *pro bono* work in their personal capacity.

Note. Ensure that you are referring to the latest version (January 2013 version) of the PII Guidance and Regulations.

17.2 If the client's permission is not received, the prospective adviser should normally not accept the appointment, unless satisfied that circumstances exist that make it appropriate to override the normal rule. It would require exceptional circumstances to justify acceptance of the appointment and such cases are likely to be rare. It would be advisable to document at that time the facts, circumstances and justification.

17.3 Quite possibly an amicable divorce settlement can be reached. As long as both clients agree, you may act provided that there is adequate disclosure of all relevant facts to both parties and provided that no preference is shown in advising one against the other and that you are satisfied that the circumstances of the conflict can be managed. In practice this may be difficult but there may be sufficient 'mutuality of interest' between the parties to allow this course to be followed. In this situation, where applicable, both clients should be advised to consider seeking independent advice on whether it is appropriate for you to act for both parties.

17.4 Where a member undertakes tax compliance work for a client this will normally include responsibility for keeping the client informed of the amount of tax due for payment, the due date for payment and drawing the client's attention to the fact that interest accrues from that date.

17.5 False. The ATT will not arbitrate between a member and his client upon the amount of a disputed fee.

17.6 Contingent fees may be considered to be a premium fee under the Tax Avoidance Disclosure regime. A member should be aware of the requirements of the Tax Avoidance Disclosure regime and the consequences of applying such fees.

17.7 Where money of any one client in excess of £10,000 is held by the firm for more than 30 days, it is recommended that the money should be paid into a separate interest-bearing bank account designated as that of the client.

17.8 Land can be held either (i) freehold, or (ii) leasehold. Commonhold is not a separate legal estate but is a freehold estate in commonhold land.

17.9 The maximum number of legal owners of land is four.

17.10 The beneficial interest in registered land passes from seller to buyer when contracts are exchanged.

17.11 An employment tribunal can make an order for reinstatement, re-engagement or awards of basic and/or compensatory compensation.

17.12 In legal terms, ownership is the most extensive possessory right conferred by the law. Ownership is the right of exclusive use and enjoyment of property. Owners can do with their property what they wish, eg use it, sell it, give it away or use it as security for a loan.

Possession is the exercise (or power of exercising) physical control over property.

17.13 Unconditional sale – the contract is not subject to any conditions.
Conditional sale – the contract is subject to an event occurring, eg grant of planning permission.
By option – the contract can be triggered by the service of a notice.
By pre-emption – if the seller wants to sell he must first offer it to the person who has the pre-emption right.

17.14 Personal property is divided into choses in action (intangible property such as debts, shares, negotiable instruments and all forms of intellectual property) and choses in possession (tangible property of which the owner has actual enjoyment, for example leasehold land and buildings, and personal chattels such as furniture and machinery).

17.15 Any six from:

- Names of client and consultant
- Commencement date of contract
- Description of services
- Fees
- Expenses
- Confidentiality
- Non-exclusivity
- Termination

1.1 Mr Daphnis

	£
Allowances:	
Personal allowance (born between 6 April 1938 and 5 April 1948)	10,500
Restricted : ½ × (27,280 – 26,100)	(590)
PA	9,910
Blind person's allowance	2,160
Tax reductions:	
Married couple's allowance (born before 6 April 1935, based on age of older spouse) (relief restricted to 10%)	7,915

Mrs Daphnis

PA (born before 6 April 1938)	10,660

Some of this is being wasted as Mrs Daphnis has income of only £4,500.

Mr Daphnis's personal allowance has been restricted due to high net income. In order to maximise the benefit of the allowance the interest generating bank account could be held in joint names, leading to a 50:50 split of interest for tax purposes.

The revised position would be:

	Mr £	Mrs £
Current net income	27,280	4,500
(Less) / plus 50% interest	(5,000)	5,000
Revised net income	22,280	9,500

There is now no need to restrict Mr Daphnis' personal allowance and Mrs Daphnis wastes a smaller amount (£10,660 – £9,500) of her personal allowance.

1.2 Mr Rich

INCOME TAX COMPUTATION 2013/14

	Non savings income £
Employment income	143,500
Less: Qualifying loan interest (below £50,000 minimum cap)	(25,000)
	118,500
Less: PA (W1)	(7,690)
Taxable income	110,810
£	
32,010 @ 20%	6,402
15,000 @ 20% (W2)	3,000
63,800 @ 40%	25,520
Tax liability	34,922
Tax suffered at source (PAYE)	(50,998)
Tax repayable	(16,076)

Workings

(1) *Personal allowance*

	£	£
Basic PA		9,440
Total income	118,500	
Less: Gift Aid (W2)	(15,000)	
Less: limit	(100,000)	
	3,500	
÷ 2		(1,750)
Restricted PA		7,690

(2) Basic rate band extended (and total income reduced for personal allowances purposes (W1)) by gross donation, ie £15,000 (£12,000 × 100/80).

1.3 Mr Poor

INCOME TAX COMPUTATION 2013/14

		Non savings income £	Savings income £	Dividend income £
Employment income		7,385		
Dividends received	$(£900 \times \frac{100}{90})$			1,000
Building society interest	$(£1,900 \times \frac{100}{80})$		2,375	
Bank deposit interest	$(£100 \times \frac{100}{80})$		125	
Net income		7,385	2,500	1,000
Less: PA		(7,385)	(2,055)	
Taxable income		nil	445	1,000

Tax:	£
£445 @ 10%	44
£1,000 @ 10%	100
Tax liability	144
Less: notional credit on dividends	(100)
	44
Less: Tax suffered at source	
Interest (£2,500 @ 20%)	(500)
Tax repayable	(456)

Notes

- The personal allowance is set off against non savings income first, then against savings income.
- The tax credit on the dividends is deducted before other tax credits to maximise the repayment.

1.4 Lauren

	Non savings income £	Savings income £	Dividend income £
Employment income	23,000		
Bank interest (£22,000 × 100/80)		27,500	
UK dividends (£67,500 × 100/90)			75,000
Discretionary trust income £35,200 × 100/55	64,000		
Total income	87,000	27,500	75,000
Less: personal allowance (income > £118,880)	(NIL)		
Taxable income	87,000	27,500	75,000

		£
Tax		
£32,010 @ 20%		6,402
£1,500 @ 20% (W)		300
£53,490 @ 40% £(87,000 – 32,010 – 1,500)		21,396
£27,500 @ 40%		11,000
£37,000 @ 32½% £(151,500 – 87,000 – 27,500)		12,025
£38,000 @ 37½ % £(75,000 – 37,000)		14,250
Tax liability		65,373
Less:	Tax credit on dividends	(7,500)
	Tax paid on bank interest £27,500 × 20%	(5,500)
	Tax paid on discretionary trust income £64,000 × 45%	(28,800)
	PAYE	(2,712)
Tax due		20,861

Working

Basic and higher rate band extended by gross Gift Aid donation of £1,500 (£(100 × 12) × 100/80)

Note. The difference between the basic and higher rate band is always £117,990.

2.1   **Fred**

	Non savings income £	Savings income £	Dividend income £	
Property income	17,200			
Interest (£4,400 × 100/80)		5,500		
Gilt (treasury stock) interest (received gross)		290		
Dividends (£8,890 × 100/90)			9,878	
Net income	17,200	5,790	9,878	Total = £32,868
Less: PA (W)	(9,440)			
Taxable income	7,760	5,790	9,878	

		£
Tax	£13,550 @ 20%	2,710
	£9,878 @ 10%	988
		3,698
	Less: Married couples' allowance (W)	(575)
	Tax liability	3,123
	Less: Tax deducted:	
	Dividends	(988)
	Interest	(1,100)
	Tax payable	1,035

Working

	£
PA (born before 6 April 1938)	10,660
Less: ½ £(32,868 – 26,100) = £3,384	
Max 'restriction' £(10,660 – 9,440)	(1,220)
Allowance given, ie basic PA	9,440
Unused restriction (£3,384 – 1,220)	2,164
MCA	7,915
Less: unused restriction	(2,164)
	5,751

Tax reduction @ 10% = £575

2.2 George and Mildred Roper

GEORGE ROPER
TAX COMPUTATION 2013/14

	Non savings income £	Savings income £	Dividend income £	
Employment income	11,000			
Pension income	3,600			
State pension	5,728			
Rental income	3,725			
Gilt interest		180		
UK dividends (£3,375 × 100/90)			3,750	
Total income	24,053	180	3,750	
Less: interest relief (£10,000 × 10%)	(1,000)			
Net income	23,053	180	3,750	Total = £26,983
Less: PA (W1)	(10,059)			
Taxable income	12,994	180	3,750	

		£
Tax	£(12,994 + 180) @ 20% (Note)	2,635
	£3,750 @ 10%	375
		3,010
Less:	Tax reductions:	
	Maintenance relief (W2)	(304)
	MCA (W1)	(132)
Tax liability		2,574
Less:	tax deducted:	
	Tax on dividends	(375)
	PAYE £(312 + 720)	(1,032)
Tax payable		1,167

Note. As non savings income exceeds £2,790 the 10% starting rate band is not available for the savings income.

Workings

		£
1	Personal allowance:	
	PAA (born between 6 April 1938 and 5 April 1948)	10,500
	Less: ½ (£26,983 – £26,100)	(441)
	Allowance given	10,059
	Married Couples' Allowance:	
	MCA (as Mildred born before 6 April 1935)	7,915
	Tax reduction @ 10% × 2/12 (as 10 full tax months before the wedding) =	132

Note. MCA given to George as his net income is higher than Mildred's.

		£
2	Maintenance payment £260 × 12	3,120
	Relief restricted to	3,040
	Tax reduction @ 10%	304

Note. Maintenance payments allowable as Liz was born before 6 April 1935 (ie aged 79).

MILDRED ROPER
TAX COMPUTATION 2013/14

	Non savings income £	Savings income £	Dividend income £	
State pension	5,728			
Building society interest (£9,040 × 100/80)		11,300		
Discretionary trust (£3,850 × 100/55)	7,000			
Guernsey bank interest (received gross)		2,071		
Dividends (£720 × 100/90)			800	
Net income	12,728	13,371	800	Total = £26,899
Less: PA (W1)	(10,573)			
Taxable income	2,155	13,371	800	

	£
Tax: £2,155 @ 20% (non savings)	431
£635 @ 10% (2,790 – 2,155) (savings within starting rate band)	63
£12,736 (13,371 – 635) @ 20%	2,547
£800 @ 10%	80
Tax liability	3,121
Less: Tax deducted:	
Dividends	(80)
Interest (£11,300 × 20%)	(2,260)
Trust income: £7,000 × 45%	(3,150)
Tax repayable	(2,369)

Note. Premium Bond winnings are exempt from income tax.

Workings

1   *Personal allowance*

	£
PA (born before 6 April 1938)	10,660
Less: ½ £(26,274 – 26,100) (W2)	(87)
PAA given	10,573

2   *Adjusted net income*

	£
Actual net income	26,899
Less: gross donation to charity (£500 × 100/80)	(625)
Adjusted net income for age allowance purposes	26,274

Note. Do not need to extend the basic rate band as Mildred is not a higher rate taxpayer.

2.3   Enterprise Investment Scheme

The EIS is intended to encourage investment in the ordinary shares of unquoted companies. When a qualifying individual subscribes for eligible shares in a qualifying company, the amount subscribed qualifies for tax relief equal to 30% of the investment. The tax relief is given as a tax reduction in the income tax computation.

A *qualifying individual* is one who is not connected with the company at any time in the period from two years before the issue (or from incorporation if later) to three years after the issue. An individual is connected with the company if his shareholding exceeds 30%, if he is a partner of the company or if he is an employee or a non-qualifying director of the company.

A *qualifying director* is one who does not receive payment from the company apart from reasonable remuneration.

Eligible shares are generally newly issued ordinary shares. However, preference shares can also qualify so long as the amount and timing of the payment of dividends does not depend on a decision by the company, investor, or anyone else and the dividends are not cumulative (ie the right to receive the dividends does not roll forward to future periods).

A *qualifying company* is (broadly) an unquoted trading company. Certain trades are excluded. The company must be unquoted when the shares are issued.

The maximum total investment that can qualify in a tax year is £1,000,000 per individual.

Generally speaking, relief is given on an actual basis: a 2013/14 investment will attract relief against 2013/14 tax. However, a taxpayer can claim to carry back his EIS investments to the previous tax year.

If an individual disposes of shares (or receives value from the company, for example by taking a loan from the company) within three years of their issue, the tax reduction obtained may be wholly or partly withdrawn.

If the shares are given away or sold otherwise than at arm's length within the three years, all of the tax reduction is withdrawn.

On an arm's length sale or a receipt of value within the three years, the tax reduction to be withdrawn is:

$$\text{Consideration obtained} \times \frac{\text{Tax reduction obtained on issue}}{\text{Issue price of shares}}$$

However, the withdrawal cannot exceed the tax reduction originally obtained (which may have been less than 30% of the issue price, for example because the individual did not have enough tax to reduce.

A transfer of shares between spouses/partners in a civil partnership does not give rise to a withdrawal of the tax reduction. The reduction obtained remains associated with the shares, and if the recipient partner disposes of the shares outside the marriage/partnership within three years of their issue, it is withdrawn by an assessment on the recipient partner.

The death of a shareholder is not treated as a disposal.

If shares are disposed of after three years from issue, the following consequences ensue.

(a)   The tax reduction is not withdrawn (although earlier partial withdrawals stand).

(b)   If there is a gain for CGT purposes and EIS relief has not already been wholly withdrawn, the gain is exempt.

On a disposal before or after the expiry of the three year period, any loss for CGT purposes is restricted by reducing the issue price (but not so as to create a gain). The reduction is the tax reduction obtained and not withdrawn.

When shares issued under the EIS are sold at arm's length at a loss at any time (within or outside the first three years), and the EIS relief is not wholly withdrawn, the loss may be relieved in the same way as a trading loss.

Tutorial note. The above detail can be found in ss.156–257 ITA 2007.

3.1   **Jonty**
INCOME TAX COMPUTATION 2013/14

	Non savings income £	Savings income £	Dividend income £
Employment income	30,000		
Building society interest £(80 × $\frac{100}{80}$)		100	
Dividends £(63 × $\frac{100}{90}$)			70
NS&I interest		142	
Net income	30,000	242	70
Less: PA	(9,440)		
Taxable income	20,560	242	70

Tax:

	£	£
20,560 @ 20% (W)		4,112
242 @ 20%		48
70 @ 10%		7
Tax liability		4,167
Less: notional credit on dividend		(7)
Less: tax suffered at source £(20 + 4,112)		(4,132)
Tax repayable		28

Workings

If Jonty was a higher rate taxpayer his basic rate band would be extended by the gross donation, ie £495 (£396 × 100/80). However, he is a basic rate taxpayer so his basic rate band is not affected.

Note. Betting income, and the WTC and CTC are not taxable.

3.2 **Fiona**

	Non savings income £	Savings income £	Dividend income £
Trade profits	32,000		
UK dividends (£10,000 × 100/90)			11,111
Jersey bank interest (received gross)		4,300	
Total income	32,000	4,300	11,111
Less: interest relief (W1)	(827)		
Net income	31,173	4,300	11,111
Less: personal allowance	(9,440)		
Taxable income	21,733	4,300	11,111

	£
Tax	
£(21,733 + 4,300) @ 20%	5,207
£5,977 @ 10% £(32,010 – 21,733 – 4,300)	598
£2,000 @ 10% (W2)	200
£3,134 @ 32½% £(11,111 – 5,977 – 2,000)	1,019
	7,024
Less: EIS relief (£3,000 @ 30%)	(900)
Tax liability	6,124
Less: tax deducted on dividends	(1,111)
Tax due	5,013

Workings

1 Loan interest relief

	£
£24,000 × 4% × 8/12	640
£14,000 × 4% × 4/12	187
	827

2 Basic rate band extension:

Gross gift aid donation £1,600 × 100/80 = £2,000

Notes

(1) Premium Bond winnings are tax free.

(2) Foster care income of £18,000 is tax free as it falls within the qualifying amount of £20,400 (£10,000 flat rate plus £200 per week as Lucy is under the age of 11) for qualifying care relief purposes.

(3) The loan interest qualifies as a deductible payment (s.392 ITA 2007).

(4) A 30% tax reduction is available on subscription for shares in a qualifying EIS company (up to a maximum subscription of £1,000,000).

(5)   Child benefit is not taxable income. There would be no high income child benefit tax charge as adjusted net income is below £50,000.

3.3   Jane Bradbury

	Non savings income £	Savings income £	Dividend income £
Trade profits	8,079		
Bank interest (£200 × 100/80)		250	
Dividends (£4,950 × 100/90)			5,500
WPA (£108.30 × 52)	5,632		
Less: Deductible payments:			
Interest relief (Note 1)	(3,800)		
Net income	9,911	250	5,500
Less: personal allowance	(9,440)		
Taxable income	471	250	5,500

		£
Tax	£471 @ 20%	94
	£250 @ 10% (within starting rate band)	25
	£5,500 @ 10%	550
Less:	Tax credits:	
	Dividends (£5,500 × 10%)	(550)
	Interest (£250 × 20%)	(50)
Tax payable		69

Notes

(1)   The interest on the loan to purchase an interest in a partnership is deductible (s.388 ITA 2007) and is clearly not subject to the cap on income tax reliefs as it is below £50,000.

(2)   WTC, CTC and child benefit are not taxable. There is no high income child benefit charge as adjusted net income is below £50,000.

4.1   Randall

(1)

		Property	
	A £	B £	C £
Rent	620	284 (W)	100
Agent's commission	(20)		
Advertising for tenants		(76)	
Repairs (Note)	(142)	(255)	(100)
Profit/(loss)	458	(47)	Nil

	£
Profit on A	458
Less loss on B	(47)
Property income assessment	411

Working

	£
April – Sept ($\frac{6}{12}$ × £348)	174
Dec – March ($\frac{3}{12}$ × £440)	110
	284

Note. The repair expense incurred on Property C cannot be deducted in full as the property is let at an uncommercial rent.

(2) When a premium or similar consideration is received on the *grant* (that is, by a landlord to a tenant) of a short lease (50 years or less), part of the premium is treated as rent so is taxed as property income in the year of grant.

A formula is used to identify the amount of the premium that is taxable as property income:

$$P \times \frac{50-Y}{50}$$ where Y = number of years on the lease minus 1 year

4.2 Corelli

TAX COMPUTATION 2013/14

(1)

	Non savings income £	Dividend income £
Employment income	16,450	
Dividends (£15,300 × $\frac{100}{90}$)		17,000
Property income (W)	6,560	
Net income	23,010	17,000
Less: PA	(9,440)	
Taxable income	13,570	17,000

		£
Tax:	£13,570 @ 20%	2,714
	£17,000 @ 10%	1,700
Tax liability		4,414
Less: notional credit on dividend		(1,700)
Less: PAYE		(1,402)
Tax payable		1,312

Working

Property income:

	A £	B £	C £
Income (3/12 × £1,200 + 6/12 × £800)	700		
		3,100	
(9/12 × £600)			450
Expenditure:			
Agent's commission:			
1.5.13	(25)	(35)	(10)
1.11.13	(25)	(35)	(10)
Repairs	–	(100)	(1,500)
Advertising	(50)	–	–
	600	2,930	(1,070)
Net rents			2,460

Note. Installation of new kitchen equipment is a capital *not* a revenue expense.

Lease premium:

	£
£5,000 × $\frac{(50-(10-1))}{50}$	4,100

Total property income: £2,460 + £4,100 = £6,560

(2) Freehold is an absolute interest in land, which allows the freeholder to do as he wishes (subject to general law, eg planning) with his land.

Leasehold is a qualified interest in land, which is limited in time. The lease normally contains a range of covenants binding on the tenant and his successors and the lease may be forfeitable if these conditions are not complied with.

4.3 **Mary Taylor**

Income tax computation 2013/14

	Non savings	Savings income (policy gain)	Dividends
	£	£	£
Earned income			
Pension	19,531		
State pension	5,728		
Unearned Income			
Dividend income (£9,450 × $^{100}/_{90}$)			10,500
Trust income (£4,500 × $^{100}/_{90}$)			5,000
Property income (W1)	200		
Life assurance gain		25,000	
Net income	25,459	25,000	15,500
PA (reduced to basic PA as income well in excess of £26,100)	(9,440)		
Taxable income	16,019	25,000	15,500

Tax liability			
Non savings income	16,019 @ 20%		3,204
Dividend income	15,500 @ 10%		1,550
Life assurance gain	491 @ 20%		98
Life assurance gain	24,509 @ 40%		9,804
	56,519		14,656
Less: top slicing relief (W2)			(1,862)
			12,794

Less: tax deducted:
– Pension	2,018	
– Dividends £(1,050 + 500)	1,550	
– Life assurance gain (£25,000 × 20%)	5,000	(8,568)
Income tax payable		4,226

Workings

W1   *Property income*

Property 1

	£	£
Rental income $^9/_{12}$ × £20,000		15,000
$^3/_{12}$ × £25,000		6,250
		21,250
Less: Repairs £(6,500 + 3,800)	10,300	
Agent's fees	2,500	
Loan interest	8,500	
Accountancy	750	
		(22,050)
Loss		(800)

Property 2

(i)   Normal assessment

	£
Rental income	5,250
Less: expenses	(1,250)
	4,000

(ii)   Rent-a-room election (to be made by 31 January 2016)

	£
Rental income	5,250
Less exemption	(4,250)
	1,000

Hence the election would be made, therefore property income = £1,000 – £800 = £200

W2   *Top slicing relief*

	£	£
Additional tax on gain above basic rate band £24,509 @ 20%		4,902
Less: Tax on slice		
Annual equivalent: £25,000 ÷ 20 years	1,250	
Less: remaining BR band	(491)	
Slice chargeable at higher rate	759	
Additional tax (ie at [40% – 20%]) on slice £759 @ 20%	152	
£152 × 20 years		(3,040)
Top slicing relief		1,862

5.1   **Mr Thomas**

TAXABLE BENEFITS – 2013/14

	£
Accommodation (W1)	3,125
Related expenses (W1)	4,950
Loan interest (W2)	317
Car 1 (W3)	3,870
Car 2 (W3)	667
Taxable benefits	12,929

Workings

1   Accommodation

	£
Annual value	750
Additional charge: 4% (official rate of interest) × £(134,375 − 75,000)	2,375
	3,125

Mr Thomas occupied the property for the first time more than 6 years after it was purchased in 1997, therefore the additional charge is based on the market value of the property when first occupied, not on cost plus alterations carried out prior to occupation.

Related expenses

	£
Household bills – electricity, gas, telephone £(750 + 250 + 350)	1,350
Council tax	1,400
Redecoration	700
Gardener	1,500
	4,950

2   *Cheap taxable loan*

Average basis: $\dfrac{(10,000 + 9,000)}{2} \times \dfrac{10}{12} \times 4\%$ (official rate of interest) = £317

		£
Strict basis:	£10,000 × 2/12 × 4%	67
	£15,000 × 4/12 × 4%	200
	£7,500 × 2/12 × 4%	50
	£11,500 × 1/12 × 4%	38
	£9,000 × 1/12 × 4%	30
		385

HMRC may insist on the strict basis, although in practice the difference is likely to be considered insignificant.

3   *Cars*

Mercedes: £21,500 × 18% $\left(\left(\dfrac{130 - 95}{5}\right) = 7 + 11 = 18\%\right)$ = £3,870

Escape: £10,000 × 10% (emissions between 76 and 94g/km) × 8/12 = £667

5.2 **Alf**

	Non savings income £	Savings income £	Dividend income £
Employment income (W1)	101,760		
Interest (£5,440 × 100/80)		6,800	
Dividends (£4,000 × 100/90)			4,444
Less: personal allowance (W2)	(3,938)		
Taxable income	97,822	6,800	4,444

	£
Tax: £32,010 @ 20%	6,402
£ 2,000 @ 20% (W3)	400
£63,812 @ 40%	25,525
£ 6,800 @ 40%	2,720
£ 4,444 @ 32½%	1,444
Tax liability	36,491
Less: Tax credits:	
Dividends £(4,444 × 10%)	(444)
PAYE	(28,462)
Interest £(6,800 × 20%)	(1,360)
Tax payable	6,225

Workings

1   Employment income

	£	£
Salary		96,600
Expenses allowance:		
Gross allowance (Note 1)	2,500	
Less business travel	(1,800)	
		700
		97,300
Benefits:		
Stereo equipment £(800 × 20%) (Note 2)	160	
Car £(15,000 × 24%) (Note 3)	3,600	
Medical insurance (Note 4)	300	
Clothing (Note 4)	400	
		4,460
Taxable employment income		101,760

Notes

(1)   The expenses allowance is taxable, but Alf can claim the cost of business travel as an allowable deduction. Entertainment of clients is not deductible as this would not have been deductible for his employer.

(2)   The annual value of the stereo equipment subject to tax is 20% of its cost.

(3)   The emission percentage is ([160 – 95g] ÷ 5) + 11% = 24%.

(4)   The taxable value of the medical insurance and clothing is the cost to the company of providing the benefits.

2   Personal allowance restriction

	£	£
Basic PA		9,440
Total income £(101,760 + 6,800 + 4,444)	113,004	
Less: gift aid (W3)	(2,000)	
Less: limit	(100,000)	
	11,004	
÷ 2		(5,502)
Restricted PA		3,938

3   Basic rate band extended (and income reduced for personal allowance purposes (W2)) by gross Gift Aid donation: £1,600 × 100/80 = £2,000

5.3   Mr Bjork

TAXABLE BENEFITS

		£
Jaguar:	car (£20,000 × 32% × $^4/_{12}$) (W1)	2,133
	petrol (£21,100 × 32% × $^4/_{12}$) (W1)	2,251
Mercedes:	no private use (all business use)	
BMW:	car (£15,000 × 35%) (W2)	5,250
	petrol (£21,100 × 35%) (W2)	7,385
Legal costs		2,000
Use of video equipment £800 × 20%		160
Use of computer £3,000 × 20% × 40% × 6/12 (significant private use)		120
Gift of computer (W3)		2,520
Total benefits		21,819

Workings

1   $\left(\dfrac{200-95}{5}\right) = 21\% + 11\% = 32\%$

2   $\left(\dfrac{220-95}{5}\right) = 25\% + 11\% = 36\%$ (35% cap)

3   Computer – taxable benefit is the higher of:

			£	£
(i)	MV			200
(ii)	MV when first provided		3,000	
	Less: amounts assessed:			
	2013/14 (see above)		(120)	
	2012/13 £3,000 × 20% × 40%		(240)	
	2011/12 £3,000 × 20% × 40% × 6/12		(120)	
				2,520

ie £2,520

5.4   HiTech Computers

EMPLOYMENT INCOME FOR 2013/14

	£	£
Salary:		
April – June ($^3/_{12}$ × £31,000)	7,750	
July – March ($^9/_{12}$ × £36,000)	27,000	
		34,750
Commission – paid in year		4,000
		38,750
Accommodation (from date of promotion):		
Higher of (i) Rent paid £5,000 × $^9/_{12}$ = £3,750	3,750	
(ii) Annual value £2,400 × $^9/_{12}$ = £1,800		
Less contribution (£100 × 9 months)	(900)	
		2,850
Loan interest $\dfrac{15,000+10,000}{2}$ × 4% (official rate of interest)		500
Car parking space (not taxable as near to place of work)		–
Medical insurance (cost to employer)		385
Crèche facilities (note)		–
Newspaper allowance £20 × 12		240
		42,725
Less: pension contribution (see later in the Text) (5% × £38,750)		(1,938)
Employment income		40,787

Note. Whether Giles joined the employer's childcare scheme either before or after April 2011 the £100 monthly payment (approximately £25 per week) should not be taxable as, if he joined before 6 April 2011, up to £55 per week is automatically exempt, and if he joined on or after that, up to £28 per week is exempt as he is a higher rate taxpayer (based on a basic earnings assessment).

5.5 Grovelands

(1) INCOME TAX LIABILITY 2013/14

	Non savings Income £	Savings Income £	Dividend Income £
Employment income – Grovelands (W1)	155,877		
Employment income – new post (2/12 × £8,400)	1,400		
Bank interest (£1,386 × $\frac{100}{80}$)		1,732	
Dividends (£2,754 × $\frac{100}{90}$)	_____	_____	3,060
Total income	157,277	1,732	3,060
Less: PA (income > £118,880)	(NIL)	_____	_____
TAXABLE INCOME	157,277	1,732	3,060

TAX PAYABLE

	£
Non savings (excluding compensation) £113,390 (W1) + £1,400 = £114,790	
£32,010 @ 20%	6,402
£1,000 @ 20% (W4)	200
£81,780 @ 40%	32,712
Savings £1,732	
£1,732 @ 40%	693
Dividends £3,060	
£3,060 @ 32.5%	994
Compensation £42,487	
£31,418 @ 40% £(151,000 – 114,790 – 1,732 – 3,060)	12,567
£11,069 @ 45% £(42,487 – 31,418)	4,981
INCOME TAX LIABILITY	58,549

Workings

(1)   *Employment income – Grovelands Ltd*

	£	£
Salary (£129,333 × 9/12)		97,000
Benefits:		
Motor car (£22,300 × 30% * × 9/12)	5,017	
Car fuel (£21,100 × 30% × 9/12)	4,747	
BUPA	200	
Season ticket	2,326	
Entertainment system (W2)	4,100	
		16,390
		113,390
Termination payment (W3)	72,487	
Less: Exempt under *s.403 ITEPA 2003*	(30,000)	
		42,487
		155,877

* The car and fuel benefit percentage is: ([194 – 95] ÷ 5) + 11% = 30% (round down).

(2) *Entertainment system*

	£	£
6.04.13 – 31.12.13		
£5,000 @ 20% × 9/12 =		750
Transfer higher of		
(i) MV @ transfer	1,000	
Or		
(ii) MV when 1st available	5,000	
Less		
– assessed 2012/13		
£5,000 @ 20% × 9/12	(750)	
– assessed 2013/14 (above)	(750)	
	3,500	3,500
Less: price paid		(150)
		4,100

(3) *Termination payment*

The compensation for loss of office payment is assessed on a receipts basis and not by reference to the year in which the employment ceased.

Termination payments are treated as the top slice of income when calculating income tax.

(4) *Gift aid payment*

Gross donation: £800 × 100/80 = £1,000.

Higher rate relief is obtained by extending the basic and higher rate bands by this gross donation to £33,010 and £151,000 respectively.

(2) Summary dismissal occurs where an employer dismisses an employee without notice or without waiting for a fixed term contract to expire. Provided that the employee has committed an act of gross misconduct, the employer incurs no liability for breach of conduct. The employee is only entitled to receive contractual salary and benefits up to the date of termination of the employment.

Constructive dismissal arises where an employee resigns as a result of the employer breaching some essential term of the employment contract without the employee's consent. The employer in this case is liable for breach of contract.

Marking scheme

		Marks	
(1)	Employment income – new post	½	
	Bank interest	1	
	Dividends	1	
	Personal allowance	½	
	Tax calculation	3	
	Grovelands employment income:		
	– Salary	½	
	– Car	1½	
	– Fuel	1	
	– BUPA	½	
	– Season ticket	½	
	– Entertainment system	2½	
	– Termination payment and £30,000 exemption	1½	
	Gift aid	1	
			15
(2)	Summary dismissal – definition	1	
	– no breach	1	
	– employee entitlement	1	
	Constructive dismissal – definition	1	
	– breach	1	
			5
	Total		20

5.6 Mr Morris

MR MORRIS – INCOME TAX PAYABLE FOR 2013/14

	Non savings Income £	Savings Income £	Dividend Income £
Employment income (W1)	34,106		
Building society interest ($£312 \times \frac{100}{80}$)		390	
Bank interest ($£256 \times 1/2 \times \frac{100}{80}$)		160	
Dividends ($£738 \times \frac{100}{90}$)			820
Property income (W2)	4,635		
Total income	38,741	550	820
Less: PA	(9,440)		
TAXABLE INCOME	29,301	550	820

TAX LIABILITY

	£	£
£29,301 @ 20%		5,860
£550 @ 20%		110
£820 @ 10%		82
INCOME TAX LIABILITY		6,052
Less: UK dividends	82	
BSI	78	
Bank interest	32	
PAYE	3,077	
		(3,269)
INCOME TAX PAYABLE		2,783

Note. As Mr Morris is a basic rate taxpayer no further relief is due for the charitable donation which does not impact on the tax calculation.

Workings

1 *Employment income*

	£
Salary	24,825
Car (£14,665 × 25%)*	3,666
Fuel (£21,100 × 25%)*	5,275
Health insurance	340
	34,106

* The car and fuel benefit percentage is: ([167 − 95g] ÷ 5) + 11% = 25% (rounded down).

2 *Property income*

	£	£
Gross rental income (5/12 × £8,000 + 6/12 × £12,000)		9,333
Less:		
Agent's fees £(267 + 600)	867	
Repairs £(400 + 1,500)	1,900	
Gardener £(100 + 200)	300	
Council tax	590	
Water rates £(85 + 100)	185	
Wear and tear allowance (£(9,333 − 590 − 185) @ 10%)	856	(4,698)
		4,635

The cost of the new gas fire is capital expenditure and cannot be deducted for income tax purposes.

Marking scheme

	Marks
Building society interest	½
Bank interest	½
Dividends	½
Personal allowance	½
Tax calculation	1
Tax credits	1
Salary	½
Car	1
Fuel	1
Health insurance	½
Rent	1
Expenses	1½
Wear and tear allowance	1
Max	10

6.1 **Sue**

(1) If the scheme is approved there are no tax consequences on the grant or exercise of the options where the share are issued at not less than the market value on the date the options were granted and the option is exercised after 3 but before 10 years of the date the options were granted.

When Sue comes to sell the shares she will have a chargeable gain as follows (covered in the Capital Gains Tax (CGT) section of the Text):

	£
Sale proceeds = 5,000 × £10.40	52,000
Cost = 5,000 × £4.00	(20,000)
Gain	32,000

(2)   If the scheme is unapproved an income tax charge will arise on the exercise of the option as follows:

	£
Market value at date of exercise	10.00
Less exercise price	(3.00)
	7.00 per share
Employment income (£7.00 × 5,000 shares)	£35,000

Sale of shares (CGT covered later in the Text)

	£
Sale proceeds	52,000
Cost = MV at date of exercise (5,000 × £10)	(50,000)
Gain	2,000

Income tax liability 2013/14

	£
Employment income (£52,000 + £35,000)	87,000
Less: PA	(9,440)
Taxable income	77,560
Tax:	
£32,010 @ 20%	6,402
£45,550 @ 40%	18,220
Income tax liability	24,622

Tutorial note

In general terms, there is little difference between an approved and an unapproved scheme if the shares are exercised and then immediately sold. The approved scheme gives rise to a capital gain. The unapproved scheme results in an employment income charge but a much smaller capital gain.

However, most taxpayers would rather have profits taxed under the approved scheme rules (ie making their profit chargeable to CGT rather than income tax) as the CGT annual exempt amount of £10,900 is available and the rate of CGT is 28% compared to 40% for a taxpayer paying income tax at the higher rate, or 45% at the additional rate.

You should revisit this question after you have covered the Capital Gains Tax section of this Study Text.

7.1   **Mr Howe**

Notes for meeting with Mr Howe:

(1)   *Employment income*

	£
Salary	35,000
Company car benefit: £9,500 × 16% (W)	1,520
Fuel benefit: £21,100 × 16% (W)	3,376
Interest free loan – exempt as < £5,000	–
Laptop: £1,449 × 20%	290
Employment income	40,186

Working

Car benefit percentage:

$$* \frac{(120-95)}{5} = 5\% + 11\% = 16\%$$

(2)   *NIC*

Both Mr Howe and his employer must pay Class 1 NIC on his 'earnings', ie his salary of £35,000.

Only Mr Howe's employer has to pay Class 1A NIC on his taxable benefits:

	£
Car benefit	1,520
Fuel benefit	3,376
Laptop	290
Total liable to Class 1A NIC	5,186

No Class 1A NICs are due on the interest free loan as it is an exempt benefit for income tax purposes.

8.1 Mr Matthews

(1) REVIEW OF CALCULATION OF TAXABLE INCOME

	Total income £	Tax suffered £
Earned income		
Salary	48,750	9,510
Medical insurance	375	
Car parking space (Note 1)	–	
Less:		
Deduction for business mileage (Note 2)	(305)	
Subscriptions (Note 3)	(295)	
	48,525	
Unearned income		
Bank interest (Note 4)	400	80
Trust income (Note 5)	2,000	900
Net income	50,925	10,490

Notes

(1) Provision of a car parking space at or near the place of work is an exempt benefit and therefore the reimbursement of the parking expenses does not form part of taxable income.

(2) Payments received for business mileage are not taxable provided they do not exceed HMRC's Authorised Mileage Rates. Where an employee is reimbursed for business mileage at a rate less than the authorised rates then a claim can be made for the shortfall as a deduction from income.

	£
Amount due under authorised rates (925 × 45p)	416
Amount actually received (925 × 12p)	(111)
Amount to claim	305

(3) Payments of a subscription to an approved HMRC body that relates to the individual's employment is allowable as a deduction from employment income under s.344 ITEPA 2003. Relief is given for the amount paid in the tax year.

(4) The gross amount of the building society interest must be included in the computation of income. The tax deducted is £80, which means £320 is the net amount and gross income of £400 must be included. Tax of 20% of the gross income is deducted at source from building society interest.

(5) The gross amount of the discretionary trust income must be included in the computation of income. The tax deducted is £900, which means £1,100 is the net amount and gross income of £2,000 must be included. Discretionary trust income comes with a tax credit of 45%.

(2) Tax relief is available for donations made to charities if Gift Aid is claimed. The gift is deemed to be made net of basic rate tax, which the charity can claim from HMRC. If the donor is a higher or additional rate taxpayer, higher or additional rate tax relief is obtained by extending the basic or higher rate band respectively by the gross amount of the payment.

For example, Mr Matthews donates £120 per tax year to the Dogs Trust. Mr Matthews' basic rate band will be extended by £150 (£120 × 100/80) which means a further £150 of income will be taxed at the basic rate of tax rather than the higher rate. If he was an additional rate taxpayer, his higher rate band would also be extended by this same amount.

The above relief is available provided that the donor makes a Gift Aid declaration, which must contain the name and address of the donor, the name of the charity and a statement that the donor has paid sufficient income or capital gains tax to cover the basic tax relief due to the charity in respect of the gift.

In addition, the donor must not receive any significant benefit from the charity as a result of the gift – although an exception to this rules applies if the benefit is simply free entry to a charity's properties.

(3)   CALCULATION OF TAX PAYABLE/(REPAYABLE)

	£
Net income	50,925
Less: Personal allowance	(9,440)
Taxable income	41,485
£32,010 @ 20%	6,402
£375 (W) @ 20%	75
£9,100 @ 40%	3,640
Tax liability	10,117
Less tax deducted at source	(10,490)
Tax repayable	(373)

Working

	£
Donation to Dogs Trust (£10 × 12)	120
Donation to English Heritage (£15 × 12)	180
	300
Extension to basic rate band (£300 × 100/80)	£375

(4)   Contributions to a personal pension plan are made net of basic rate income tax.

If the taxpayer is a higher rate taxpayer higher rate tax relief is obtained by extending the basic rate band by the gross amount of the payment. The higher rate band is also extended by this same amount if the taxpayer is an additional rate taxpayer.

The maximum gross allowable contribution is based on the higher of:

(i)   £3,600 and
(ii)   100% × the taxpayer's relevant earnings.

Relevant earnings consist of his employment income (including benefits) less allowable expenses ie:

	£
Salary	48,750
Medical insurance	375
Car parking space	–
Less:	
Deduction for business mileage	(305)
Subscription	(295)
Relevant earnings	48,525

Mr Matthews can therefore contribute up to £48,525 and obtain tax relief. This is within the annual allowance so no annual allowance charge would apply. However, it is unlikely he would wish to contribute this entire amount to a pension and should choose an amount that will leave him with sufficient income to maintain his current lifestyle.

For example if he chose to contribute, say, £6,500 (gross), this would result in a tax saving of £1,300, as a further £6,500 of income would be taxed at 20% rather than 40%. He would pay £5,200 (£6,500 × 80%) into the fund and HMRC would transfer £1,300 (£6,500 × 20%) into the pension fund.

Pension contributions must be paid in the current pension input period so it is not possible for Mr Matthews to claim relief against his 2013/14 income, as it is now mid February 2015.

Marking scheme

<table>
<tr><td></td><td></td><td></td><td>Marks</td></tr>
<tr><td>(1)</td><td>Insurance</td><td>½</td><td></td></tr>
<tr><td></td><td>Car space</td><td>1</td><td></td></tr>
<tr><td></td><td>Business mileage</td><td>2</td><td></td></tr>
<tr><td></td><td>Subscriptions</td><td>1</td><td></td></tr>
<tr><td></td><td>Interest</td><td>1</td><td></td></tr>
<tr><td></td><td>Trust income</td><td>½</td><td></td></tr>
<tr><td></td><td></td><td></td><td>6</td></tr>
<tr><td>(2)</td><td>Paid net of basic rate tax</td><td>1</td><td></td></tr>
<tr><td></td><td>Basic and higher rate bands extended</td><td>1</td><td></td></tr>
<tr><td></td><td>Illustration</td><td>1</td><td></td></tr>
<tr><td></td><td>Declaration</td><td>1</td><td></td></tr>
<tr><td></td><td>No benefits</td><td>1</td><td></td></tr>
<tr><td></td><td></td><td></td><td>5</td></tr>
<tr><td>(3)</td><td>Personal allowance</td><td>½</td><td></td></tr>
<tr><td></td><td>Tax calculation</td><td>1</td><td></td></tr>
<tr><td></td><td>Tax credit</td><td>½</td><td></td></tr>
<tr><td></td><td>Donations</td><td>1</td><td></td></tr>
<tr><td></td><td></td><td></td><td>3</td></tr>
<tr><td>(4)</td><td>Payment net of basic rate tax</td><td>½</td><td></td></tr>
<tr><td></td><td>Extension of basic and higher rate bands</td><td>1</td><td></td></tr>
<tr><td></td><td>Maximum contribution</td><td>2</td><td></td></tr>
<tr><td></td><td>Relevant earnings</td><td>1</td><td></td></tr>
<tr><td></td><td>Apply to Mr Matthews</td><td>2</td><td></td></tr>
<tr><td></td><td>Relevant tax year</td><td>1</td><td></td></tr>
<tr><td></td><td>Maximum</td><td></td><td>6</td></tr>
<tr><td></td><td></td><td></td><td>20</td></tr>
</table>

8.2 Ed & Joan

(1) *Maximum contributions*

Ed and Joan can contribute any amount to their pension regardless of the level of their earnings. However tax relief will only be given for contributions up to their earnings for the tax year. In addition, a tax charge will apply if the contributions exceed the available annual allowance.

Ed can contribute a maximum of £140,000 and receive tax relief on his contributions. His annual allowance is £200,000 (£50,000 for the current year and each of the three previous years as he has been a member of a pension scheme but has not made contributions for the last three years), so there will be no annual allowance charge if he contributes the full amount.

Joan can contribute £35,000 and receive tax relief on the contributions. This is also within the annual allowance so no charge would apply.

They cannot obtain relief for 2012/13 as contributions must be made in the current pension input period.

(2) *Tax relief*

Basic rate tax relief is given through the pension holder paying contributions net of 20% basic rate tax. This means that they pay only 80% of the gross payment into the pension. HMRC pays the extra 20% on their behalf to the pension provider.

Ed will pay £112,000 (£140,000 × 80%) and Joan will pay £28,000 (£35,000 × 80%).

In addition Ed will be entitled to higher rate relief. This is given by extending the basic rate band for the year by the amount of the gross contribution.

Joan's tax liability

	£
Employment income	35,000
Personal allowance	(9,440)
Taxable income	25,560

Tax liability	
£25,560 @ 20%	5,112

Note. As Joan is a basic rate taxpayer the pension contribution does not affect her income tax computation.

Ed's tax liability

	£
Employment income	140,000
Personal allowance (Note)	(9,440)
Taxable income	130,560

Tax liability:	
£130,560 at 20% (Note)	26,112

Note. Higher rate tax relief will be given by extending Ed's basic rate tax band for 2013/14 to £172,010 (£32,010 + £140,000). As net earnings, as adjusted for gross personal pension contributions, are below £118,880 there is no restriction to the personal allowance.

(3) *No earnings*

There is no need for an individual to have earnings to be able to make contributions to a personal pension. A contribution of up to £3,600 gross per tax year may be made into a pension regardless of the level of earnings.

8.3 Dwaine Pipe

INCOME TAX COMPUTATION 2013/14

	Non savings income £	Savings income £
Employment income (W1)	56,387	
Interest on ISA		Exempt
BS interest £$(20,000 \times \frac{100}{80}) \times 50\%$		12,500
Premium bond winnings		Exempt
Net income	56,387	12,500
Less: Personal allowance	(9,440)	–
Taxable income	46,947	12,500

Tax thereon:	£
£32,010 @ 20%	6,402
£2,750 @ 20% (W7)	550
£24,687 @ 40%	9,875
Tax liability	16,827
Less: tax deducted:	
PAYE	(12,350)
Interest (£12,500 @ 20%)	(2,500)
Tax payable	1,977

Workings

1 *Earnings*

	£
Salary	
(£40,000 × $^9/_{12}$)	30,000
(£44,000 × $^3/_{12}$)	11,000
	41,000
Bonuses (Note 1)	
Awarded 30.9.13	3,850
Awarded 31.3.14	4,250
	49,100
Company cars:	
Vauxhall (W2 + W3)	960
Audi (W4 + W5)	2,205
	52,265
Mobile phone	Exempt
Interest free loan (W6)	2,250
Nursery fees £17 × 46 (Note 2)	782
Pension contributions by employer	Exempt
Central heating (cost to employer)	800
Staff suggestion scheme	Exempt
Round sum allowance	1,000
	57,097
Less: allowable expenses	
Hotel bills	(710)
Total	56,387

2 *Vauxhall*

	£
£10,629 @ 20% × 7/12 (W3)	1,240
Less employee contributions (7 × £40)	(280)
Car benefit	960

No fuel benefit as no private diesel provided.

3 $\left(\dfrac{125-95}{5}\right)$ = 6% + 14% (diesel) = 20%

4 *Audi*

(£18,500 + £400) @ 28% × 5/12 = £2,205

No reduction of benefit for time car in garage as unavailable for < 30 consecutive days.

No fuel benefit as no private petrol provided.

5 $\left(\dfrac{180-95}{5}\right)$ = 17% + 11% = 28%

6 *Interest-free loan*

Average

$\dfrac{75,000 + 60,000}{2}$ × 10/12 × 4% (official rate of interest) = £2,250

	£
Strict basis	
£75,000 × 7/12 × 4%	1,750
£60,000 × 3/12 × 4%	600
	2,350

HMRC may elect for strict basis; unlikely in practice.

7   *Basic rate band extension*

Personal pension contributions

	£	£
Paid: £150 × 12	1,800	
$\times \dfrac{100}{80}$		2,250
Gift Aid		
$£400 \times \dfrac{100}{80}$		500
Basic rate band extended by:		2,750

Notes

(1)   Bonus becomes taxable in the year in which a director is *entitled* to the payment (even if this is before actual receipt).

(2)   As Dwaine is a higher rate taxpayer only the first £28 per week of childcare costs paid by employer for approved childcare are tax-free. He therefore has a benefit of £17 per week (ie £45 – £28).

9.1   **Ricardo Garcia**

Our address

Your address

Date

Dear Mr Garcia

UK taxation on moving to this country

Thank you for your recent letter informing me of your proposed move. I set out below the main points of UK taxation on income which would be relevant to you.

Domicile and residence

The tax treatment of individuals in the UK depends on two concepts – domicile and residence.

'Domicile' is a person's 'permanent home country'. It is normally a 'domicile of origin', being the domicile normally of one's father, and so you are presumably domiciled in Spain at present. However, it can be changed to a 'domicile of choice'. This is not done merely by the act of emigrating: it requires very positive cutting off of ties in the previous domicile, to show that there is no intention to return.

If you were unwilling to cut such ties, you would retain your domicile in Spain. In fact, this may be to your advantage, as foreign domiciled individuals can be taxed more favourably in respect of their foreign income than UK domiciled individuals in certain circumstances.

A number of tests are used to determine and individual's residency status, including the number of days you spend in the UK in a tax year. If you come here to live permanently you will be treated as resident in the UK from the date you arrive. This is the main factor that affects your UK tax position.

Remittance basis of taxation

As a foreign domiciled individual, you can make a claim to have your overseas sources of income taxed only if remitted to (ie brought into) the UK. This will initially at least have a cash flow advantage as you are only taxed when you bring the income into the UK. However there are certain disadvantages depending on the type of income remitted. These are explained where appropriate below.

This remittance basis applies automatically to foreign income in certain circumstances, for example if you have little or no unremitted foreign income. However, based on the information provided (ie your large sums of overseas income that you do not plan to bring into the UK) you do not appear to qualify for the automatic remittance basis.

Allowances

Normally, as an EEA resident, you are entitled to a personal allowance deducted from your income. However, if you claim to be taxed on the remittance basis, you will lose your entitlement to personal allowances. You would not lose your allowances if the remittance basis applied automatically.

Income

From the details given, you appear to have three main sources of income:

(1)   *The pension*

On the basis that you retain your foreign domicile and claim for the remittance basis to apply, the pension income will be taxable only when remitted to (ie brought into) the UK. However, if you do not make a claim, or become UK domiciled, only 90% of the income from your Spanish pension will be taxable in the UK.

As it appears that you are planning to bring all of the pension income into the UK, you may decide not to make the claim for the remittance basis so that you are only taxed on 90% of the income. In this case, the income will be taxed at 20%, 40% and possibly 45% depending on your level of income.

(2)   *Investment income*

Assuming the pension income takes you over the basic rate threshold, without a claim for the remittance basis your Spanish bank interest will be taxable at 40% and any dividend income from your portfolio will be taxable at 32.5% on an arising basis. The rates increase to 45% and 37.5% respectively if your taxable income exceeds £150,000.

If you make a claim for the remittance basis to apply you will only be taxable when you bring the funds into the UK. However, if and when it is remitted, it will be taxed as non savings income, so even the dividends will be taxed at 40% (or 45%).

This will need to be weighed against the position for your pension income before deciding whether or not to make the remittance basis claim.

(3)   *The rent*

Your foreign rental income is taxable in the UK on an arising basis at 40% (assuming you are a higher rate taxpayer, 45% if you are an additional rate taxpayer) unless you make the remittance basis claim, in which case you will only be taxed on the amounts remitted to the UK. If rent does not cover expenses, there may be nothing to remit, so there will be no tax. Expenses of letting are deductible in arriving at the taxable amount.

Impact of long-term residence

Once you have been resident in the UK for at least seven tax years, from year eight you will need to pay an additional annual £30,000 tax charge if you claim the remittance basis. Once you reach that stage, however, you can make a decision each tax year whether it is more beneficial to claim the remittance basis (and pay the £30,000 tax charge) or to be taxed on worldwide income and gains for that year on an arising basis.

Once you have been resident for at least 12 tax years, from year 13 the additional charge increases to £50,000.

Remittance planning

Assuming you retain your foreign domicile and would like to make a claim for the remittance basis to apply to your overseas income, I would advise you to have these amounts paid into a bank account in Spain separate from your savings. You can then spend that money when you visit Spain and not be charged to UK tax on it. If you bring across money from a different bank account (ie your previous savings) it cannot be taxed as it does not represent income arising while resident in the UK.

Note, however, that there will be a remittance if, for example, assets are purchased in Spain with your untaxed foreign funds and then brought into the UK or if you take out a loan in Spain, bring the money to the UK, and use the Spanish income and gains to pay off the loan, you are held to have remitted the income and gains to the UK.

Conclusion

I hope that the above comments are of use to you. If you wish to discuss these or any other matters further, please do not hesitate to contact me. I suggest that we have a meeting when you next come to the UK so that we can discuss your taxation affairs in more detail.

I look forward to meeting you.

Yours sincerely

A Adviser

9.2 Paul Thomson

(1) **2013/14**

If Paul is allowed to split the tax year he will be treated as non-resident for his period overseas, and he will only be taxed on his UK income:

	£
Earnings – UK duties only (£2,000 × 2 months) + £1,100	<u>5,100</u>

(2) If Paul is treated as remaining UK resident throughout 2013/14 he will be taxable on his worldwide income in 2013/14:

	£
Earnings – overseas duties 6.6.13 – 5.4.14 (£3,000 × 10)	30,000
– UK duties	5,100
	35,100

10.1 Peter Jones

(1) INCOME TAX REPAYMENT – 2013/14

	Non savings income £	Savings income £	Dividend income £
Building society interest × 100/80		6,000	
Dividends × 100/90			889
Rental income	6,624		
Net income	6,624	6,000	889
Less: personal allowance	(6,624)	(2,816)	
Taxable income	–	3,184	889
Tax:			
Savings income: £2,790 × 10%		279	
£394 × 20%		79	
Dividend income: £889 × 10%		89	
Tax liability		447	
Less: tax deducted at source:			
Credit on dividend			
(cannot give rise to refund)		(89)	
Building society interest			
£6,000 × 20%		(1,200)	
Repayment due		(842)	

Note. Remaining basic rate band is £27,937 (£32,010 – £3,184 – £889).

(2) CAPITAL GAINS TAX – 2013/14

	£
Chargeable gains	38,000
Less: annual exempt amount	(10,900)
Taxable gain	27,100
Tax:	
£27,100 @ 18% (all within remaining basic rate band)	4,878

10.2 Simon James

Our address

Your address

10 March 2014

Dear Mr James

Relevance of residence and domicile

Thank you for your letter of 3 March in which you refer to certain capital gains tax matters.

I assume you are aware of the meaning of these terms and are concerned with just the capital gains tax implications.

In order to be liable to UK capital gains tax on gains arising in a tax year the person to whom the gain accrues must be resident in the UK at some time in the tax year.

If you cease to be UK resident and have been resident for four out of the last seven tax years, you remain within the scope of UK capital gains tax unless your absence covers at least five years. If you return within five years, any gains made during the period of non residence are taxable in the year of return if the assets were acquired prior to leaving the UK.

Individuals who become UK resident or lose their UK residence part way through a tax year may be able to split that year into taxable and non-taxable parts in certain circumstances, for example, if you leave the UK to take up full-time employment abroad, so long as the number of days you spend in the UK fall below a certain level.

Domicile status is of importance where gains are realised on overseas assets. A UK resident person domiciled in the UK is liable on gains arising on his assets wherever located. A UK resident person with a non UK domicile can make a claim to be only chargeable on overseas gains on a remittance basis, ie when the gains are remitted to the UK. The remittance basis can also apply automatically in certain circumstances, for example if you have little or no unremitted overseas income.

This does not, however, make gains realised prior to becoming resident, chargeable. If a foreign domiciled person wishes to bring funds into the UK it is advisable that he does not remit from sources which are chargeable to capital gains tax (or income tax) on a remittance basis. Thus proceeds giving rise to gains on a remittance basis should be paid into a separate overseas bank account and remittances to the UK should be made from past savings held in another account.

It should be noted that if an individual has been UK resident for seven out of the preceding nine tax years, he will be subject to an additional annual £30,000 tax charge if that individual claims to be taxed on the remittance basis in year eight. This charge increases to £50,000 when he has been resident for at least 12 out of the previous 14 tax years. It is therefore necessary to consider each tax year whether it is in fact advantageous to claim the remittance basis in respect of overseas income and gains.

If a non-UK domiciled individual makes a claim to use the remittance basis, he can only set losses on overseas assets against chargeable gains if he makes an irrevocable overseas capital losses election in the first year that he makes the remittance basis claim. This will allow the total of his overseas and UK losses to be set against remitted foreign gains of that tax year, then unremitted foreign gains and finally against any UK gains.

If you require any further clarification on this matter please do not hesitate to contact me.

Yours sincerely

A Adviser

11.1 Dorrit

	£
Disposal 1 £(115,000 – 32,000)	83,000
Disposal 3 £(47,000 – 16,000)	31,000
Less: Loss on disposal 2 £(45,000 – 62,000)	(17,000)
Chargeable gain	97,000
Less: Annual exempt amount	(10,900)
Taxable gain	86,100
CGT @ 28% (no basic rate band left)	24,108

11.2 Harbottle

(1) 2013/14 INCOME TAX LIABILITIES

(i) Fred

	Non savings income £	Savings income £	Dividend income £
Employment income	40,000		
NS&I interest (½ share)		1,000	
Dividends			7,000
Total income	40,000	1,000	7,000
Less: PA	(9,440)		
Taxable income	30,560	1,000	7,000

Tax liability

	£	£
30,560 @ 20%		6,112
1,000 @ 20% (savings)		200
450 @ 10% (dividends)		45
32,010		
6,550 @ 32½% (dividends)		2,129
38,560		8,486

(ii) Iris

	Savings income £	Dividend income £
NS&I interest (½ share)	1,000	
Dividends		1,200
Total income	1,000	1,200
Less: PA	(1,000)	(1,200)
Taxable income	Nil	Nil
Income tax liability		Nil

2013/14 capital gains tax liabilities

(i) Fred

	£
Gains	11,500
Less: Annual exempt amount	(10,900)
	600
Capital gains tax at 28% (no basic rate band left)	168

(ii) Iris

	£
Gains	2,500
Less: Annual exempt amount	(10,900)
	NIL
Capital gains tax	NIL

Summary

	Fred £	Iris £	Total £
Income tax liability	8,486	NIL	8,486
Capital gains tax liability	168	NIL	168
	8,654	NIL	8,654

(2)   PLANNING ACTION

Currently, as the computations in (1) above show, Iris is not fully using her personal allowance of £9,440 nor her capital gains tax exempt amount of £10,900. The following action should be taken:

(i)   Ensure that Iris fully uses her 2013/14 personal allowance by the transfer of investments from Fred and/or the transfer of the NS&I account from joint names into her sole name. The effect of this would be to increase Iris's income and decrease Fred's income. To achieve the desired effect there must be an outright gift so that Iris is beneficially entitled; Fred must no longer participate in the income from the investments gifted.

(ii)   The value of assets transferred into Iris's name must be at least sufficient to yield £7,240 additional income (£9,440 – £2,200).

This would also reduce Fred's savings and/or dividend income by £7,240, saving tax at the higher rate on £6,550 and basic rate tax on income of £690 in 2013/14.

(iii) Fred and Iris should also make their maximum investment in an ISA – they could invest up to £11,520 each per annum in an ISA shares account. The dividends received on these shares will be exempt from tax.

(iv)   Assuming the couple continue to realise capital gains of £14,000 each tax year, the gains should be shared such that each spouse may take advantage of their £10,900 annual exempt amount.

Investments may be transferred between spouses at no gain/no loss and this should be done before disposal of assets to third parties.

Marking scheme

				Marks
(1)	Fred	–	income	1
		–	PA	½
		–	tax calculation	1½
	Iris	–	income	1
		–	PA	½
	Fred	–	AEA	½
		–	CGT	½
	Iris	–	AEA	½
				6
(2)	Use Iris's PA and AEA			1
	Transfer of investments			½
	Outright gift			½
	Value of income transferred			1
	ISA			½
	Sharing of gains			½
	No gain/no loss transfer			1
	Max			4
				10

12.1 Julie Green

Gain

	£
Disposal 29.6.13	
Proceeds	10,150
Cost (W)	(4,181)
Chargeable gain	5,969
Disposal 16.8.13	
Proceeds	8,500
Cost (W)	(4,181)
Chargeable gain	4,319
Total chargeable gains	10,288

Working – Share pool

	No of shares	Cost £
Purchase 1.6.96	50	1,000
Purchase 18.9.99	50	3,800
Purchase 21.5.00	100	9,300
	200	14,100
Bonus issue (1 for 2)	100	–
Purchase 15.1.05	100	8,200
	400	22,300
Sale 29.6.13	(75)	(4,181)
	325	18,119
Sale 16.8.13	(75)	(4,181)
c/f	250	13,938

12.2 Mr Jones

Gain

	£
Proceeds	31,500
Cost (W)	(11,943)
Chargeable gain	19,557

Working – Share pool

	No of shares	Cost £
Purchase Aug 1985	5,000	6,250
Purchase Sept 1985	2,000	3,000
Purchase Nov 1988	5,000	9,500
	12,000	18,750
Sale Oct 1990	(3,000)	(4,688)
	9,000	14,062
Purchase May 2004	1,000	3,000
	10,000	17,062
Sale July 2013	(7,000)	(11,943)
c/f	3,000	5,119

12.3 Richard Price

	£
Gain	
Proceeds (1,800 × £7.50)	13,500
Cost (W)	(4,500)
Chargeable gain	9,000

Working – Share pool	No. of shares	Cost
		£
Purchase 15.3.93	2,000	2,000
Purchase 17.12.99	4,000	10,000
	6,000	12,000
RI (1 for 5)	1,200	6,000
	7,200	18,000
Sale 4.10.13	(1,800)	(4,500)
c/f	5,400	13,500

12.4 Eric James

Sale of shares in Toucan Play plc

	£
Proceeds	9,100
Less: Cost (W)	(2,049)
Chargeable gain	7,051

Working

	£
2,000 Ordinary shares (2,000 × £4.20)	8,400
4,000 Preference shares (4,000 × £2)	8,000
Total consideration received on takeover:	16,400
Allowable cost of shares sold:	
$\dfrac{8,400}{16,400} \times £4,000$	2,049

13.1 Doug

	£
Summary	
Gains (W1 and W3)	8,533
Less: current year loss (W2)	(1,200)
	7,333
Less: AEA	(10,900)
Taxable gain	–

Workings

		£
1	Ming vase:	
	Proceeds	8,000
	Allowable cost	(2,000)
		6,000
	Gain cannot exceed 5/3 × £(8,000 – 6,000) = £3,333	
	∴ Chargeable gain	3,333
2	Leonardo cartoon:	£
	Proceeds (deemed)	6,000
	Allowable cost	(7,200)
	Allowable loss	(1,200)
3	Lathe:	£
	Proceeds	9,500
	Allowable cost	(4,300)
		5,200

Restrict to $\dfrac{5}{3} \times £(9,500 - 6,000) = £5,833$ ∴ restriction does not apply.

13.2 Mr Cole

Summary	£
Car	–
Land	27,867
Chest	1,667
Painting	6,650
	36,184
Less: current year loss	(1,500)
Net chargeable gains	34,684
Less: Annual exempt amount	(10,900)
Taxable gain	23,784

CGT payable:	£
£3,000 @ 18% £(32,010 – 29,010) (remaining basic rate band)	540
£20,784 @ 28% £(23,784 – 3,000)	5,820
Total CGT	6,360

Workings

(1) *Vintage car*

Disposal of a motor vehicle is exempt for CGT purposes.

(2)

Land	£
Sale proceeds	38,000

$$\text{Less:} \quad \text{Cost} \times \frac{A}{A+B}$$

$$£32,000 \times \frac{38,000}{38,000 + 82,000} \qquad (10,133)$$

	£
Chargeable gain	27,867

(3) *Antique chest*

	£
Sale proceeds	7,000
Less: Cost	(4,000)
	3,000
Compared to	
$5/3 \times (7,000 - 6,000) =$	1,667
Lower gain taken	

(4) *Painting*

	£
Proceeds	11,500
Less: Costs of sale	(150)
	11,350
Less: Probate value	(4,700)
Chargeable gain	6,650
Compared to	
$5/3 \times (11,500 - 6,000) =$	9,167
Lower gain taken	

(5) *Vase*

	£
Deemed proceeds	6,000
Less: Cost	(7,500)
Loss	(1,500)

Marking scheme

Summary:	Marks
Gains	½
Loss offset	1
AEA	1
CGT calculation	1
Car exempt	1
Part disposal apportionment	1
Antique chest	2
Painting	1½
Vase	1
Total	10

13.3 CGT Leases

(1) Assignment of long lease

	£
Proceeds	79,000
Cost	(38,000)
	41,000

(2) Assignment of short lease

	£
Proceeds	79,000
Cost: $£38,000 \times \dfrac{88.371}{100.000} \quad \dfrac{\% \text{ for } 31 \text{ years}}{\% \text{ for } 57 \text{ years}}$	(33,581)
Chargeable gain	45,419

(3) Grant of long lease – CGT part disposal

	£
Proceeds	30,000
Cost: $£25,000 \times \dfrac{30,000}{30,000+7,500}$	(20,000)
Chargeable gain	10,000

(4) Grant of short lease out of freehold

	£
Proceeds: capital element of premium (W)	7,600
Cost: $£25,000 \times \dfrac{7,600}{20,000+17,000}$	(5,135)
Chargeable gain	2,465

Working

	£
Premium	20,000
Less: property income: $£20,000 \times \dfrac{50-(20-1)}{50}$	(12,400)
Capital element	7,600

14.1 Owning two homes

A Tale of Two Properties!

(1) It is becoming increasingly common for a family to have not one but two homes that are occupied as residences. The purpose of this article is to set out the key capital gains tax implications of such a situation, using the case study of Mr and Mrs Hammond.

(i) On the sale of the current family home there will be no capital gains tax implications and the capital gains tax pages of the tax return do not need to be completed. This is due to the valuable relief known as principal private residence (PPR) relief which ensures that the sale of a property which has been the taxpayer's only or main residence is exempt from capital gains tax ie no gain chargeable (and no loss allowable).

(ii) However, where a taxpayer owns two properties, even if he actually resides in both, PPR relief can only apply to one property. It is worth noting at this point that a husband and wife living together such as Mr and Mrs Hammond can only have one PPR between them, ie it is not possible for the flat to be Mr Hammonds' PPR and for the house to be Mrs Hammond's.

Instead, Mr and Mrs Hammond should elect which of the house and flat they wish to have treated as their main residence for the purposes of PPR relief. The election should be made within two years of residing in the two properties, in this case by May 2015. If you do not make an election, HMRC will make the decision for you based on the facts.

Mr and Mrs Hammond do have a right to vary the election by a further written notice which can take effect for any period starting not more than two years before the date of the second notice.

(iii) In this situation I would advise Mr and Mrs Hammond to elect for the flat to be treated as their main residence.

Although the country house is likely to be the property that has the largest gain on sale, we must also take into account their long term plans. Whilst the house is likely to be owned for the next 20 years, the flat is likely to be sold within five years and therefore a gain will arise on this property first.

If the election is made for the flat to be treated as the main residence, and it is sold after five years, any gains will be exempt from capital gains tax.

If the flat is let out after five years, it will cease to be the couple's main residence. However, as it has been their main residence at some point during their period of ownership, then on the subsequent sale of the property not only will the gain relating to the five years of residence be exempt, but also the gain relating to the last three years of ownership. The gain relating to the remaining two years of ownership is also likely to be completely exempt due to an additional relief known as letting relief.

This applies where a property which has been the taxpayer's main residence is then let out – the gain relating to this period is exempt up to the lower of:

– The gain already exempt under the PPR relief rules
– The gain relating to the let period
– £40,000

(iv) Finally, on the sale of the country house, the gain relating to the period when the flat was the main residence will be chargeable to capital gains tax, but the balance of the gain will be covered by the PPR relief rules

(2) On a related point, I am often asked by couples – what is the difference between owning a property as joint tenants or tenants in common.

Under joint tenancy, the husband and wife own the property but each holds 100% of the property. If the husband and wife (as co-owners) wish to sell the property they must both agree to do so. It also means that on the death of one of the spouses, the ownership of the entire property is vested automatically in the surviving spouse.

However, as tenants in common each owner owns a share of the whole property, eg Jane owns 60% and Paul owns 40% of the whole house, not a particular area which represents a percentage of the building.

Each owner can dispose of their interest to whomever they want and do not need to seek the other owner's agreement.

On death the property passes according to the terms of the deceased's will (or under the rules of intestacy).

Marking scheme

				Marks
(1)	(i)	No CGT on sale of home	½	
		PPR relief	½	
		Explanation	<u>1</u>	
				2
	(ii)	One property eligible for PPR	1	
		Husband and wife – one PPR	1	
		Election	1	
		Time limit	1	
		May 2015	½	
		Consequence of no election	½	
		Varying election	<u>1</u>	
		Maximum		5
	(iii)	Elect for flat	½	
		Bigger gain on country house	½	
		Flat sold earlier	1	
		Effect of election	1	
		Effect of letting	1	
		5 years' exemption	½	
		Last 3 years exempt	1	
		Letting relief	1	
		Amount of letting relief	<u>1</u>	
		Maximum		7
	(iv)	Part chargeable/part exempt	<u>1</u>	
				1
(2)		Joint tenancy:		
		Each has interest in 100% of property	1	
		Joint decision to sell	½	
		Treatment on death	1	
		Tenants in common:		
		Each has % share	1	
		No consent needed to sell	½	
		Position on death	<u>1</u>	
				<u>5</u>
		Total		<u>20</u>

14.2 **Peter Stamp**

Computation of chargeable gain on sale of house

Period	Explanation	Occupation or deemed occupation (months)	Non occupation (months)
2.5.86 – 1.2.90	Actual occupation	45	
2.2.90 – 1.12.99	Letting		118
2.12.99 – 3.7.10	Absence		127
4.7.10 – 3.7.13	Last three years deemed occupation	<u>36</u>	<u> </u>
		<u>81</u>	<u>245</u>

Total ownership period = 326 months

	£
Proceeds	270,000
Less: cost	(70,000)
Gain before PPR relief	200,000
Less: Exemption for main residence $\dfrac{81}{326} \times £200,000$	(49,693)
	150,307

Less: letting exemption: lowest of
£49,693 (gain exempted by private residence relief)
£72,393 (chargeable gain attributable to letting) (W)
£40,000 (maximum relief available for lettings)

	£
Less: letting exemption	(40,000)
Chargeable gain	110,307

Working

Gain in let period: $\dfrac{118}{326} \times £200,000 = £72,393$

14.3 Mr Richman

Our address

Your address

7 May 2014

Dear Mr Richman

SALE OF 'RED BRICKS'

Thank you for your letter of 2 May regarding the sale of your property 'Red Bricks'. As requested I have set out below how the capital gains tax liability will be calculated, taking into account all possible reliefs.

Principal private residence exemption

On the sale of a property which has at some time been used as your principal private residence (PPR) some of the gain arising will be exempt from capital gains tax.

The amount of this exemption is calculated as:

$$\text{Total gains} \times \frac{\text{Period of occupation as PPR}}{\text{Period of ownership}}$$

In addition to any actual periods of occupation you are allowed to include certain deemed periods of occupation, whilst you were absent from the property.

Deemed periods of occupation

The following can be included as periods of occupation:

(1) The last three years of ownership, since the property has at some time been used as your PPR, and

(2) Four years of your period of absence whilst working abroad, since you used the property as your PPR both before and after the absence, and there was no other exempt residence during your period abroad (see below as regards the restriction due to use as offices), and

(3) Up to three years for any reason whatsoever.

You will therefore see, from the appendix attached, that you are deemed to have occupied the house as your principal residence for 22 of the 28 years of ownership.

Business use

During the period whilst part of the house was used exclusively as offices, the gain attributable to that part of the property will not be exempt as you are not occupying it as your PPR.

The last three years of ownership of both parts of the house will qualify as deemed occupation as you had occupied the whole of the property as a private residence at some point beforehand.

Capital gains tax payable

Accordingly, I calculate that a gain of £55,714 (see appendix) will arise after all reliefs of which £10,900 is covered by your annual exempt amount. The rate at which the balance will be taxed depends on the level of your taxable income in the year. Gains falling within the basic rate band of £32,010 are chargeable at 18%, while gains in excess of this amount are chargeable at 28%.

Assuming your taxable income fully uses the basic rate band, tax of £12,548 will be payable on 31 January 2015. If you have part of your basic rate band left the tax liability will be lower as part of the gain will be taxed at 18%. If you would like me to calculate the exact amount due please let me have details of your income during the year.

I trust the above answers your query, but if you require any further assistance please do not hesitate to contact me.

Yours sincerely

A. Jones

Appendix

1. *Calculation of chargeable gain*

	£
Proceeds	370,000
Less: cost	(90,000)
Enhancement expenditure	(20,000)
Gain before PPR relief	260,000
Less: PPR relief (£260,000 × 22/28)	(204,286)
Chargeable gain	55,714

2. *PPR exemption*

	Occupation	Non-occupation	Total
6.4.86 – 5.4.91 (actual)	5		5
6.4.91 – 5.4.98			
(deemed 4 years)	4	–	4
(3 years for any reason)	3	–	3
6.4.98 – 5.4.99 (occupation)	1	–	1
6.4.99 – 5.4.11			
(12 years joint use)	6	6	12
6.4.11 – 4.4.14			
(final 3 years deemed occupation)	3		3
	22	6	28

15.1 Fran and Anna

(1) *Fran's gain:*

	£
Proceeds (MV) June 2013	500,000
Allowable cost	(75,000)
	425,000
Excess of actual consideration over cost: £100,000 – £75,000	(25,000)
Gain deferred	400,000
Gain chargeable in 2013/14	25,000

(2) *Anna's gain:*

	£	£
Proceeds July 2015		520,000
Cost (MV)	500,000	
Less: gain deferred (from part 1)	(400,000)	
Base cost		(100,000)
Chargeable gain in 2015/16		420,000

15.2 Joe Bloggs

MR BLOGGS – CHARGEABLE GAINS 2013/14

	£
Chargeable gains (W1 + W2)	425,000
Less: annual exempt amount	(10,900)
Taxable gain	414,100

Workings

1 *Sale of flat*

	£
Sale proceeds	700,000
Less: cost	(200,000)
	500,000
Less: PPR relief (75% × £500,000)	(375,000)
	125,000

2 *Sale of shares:*

	£
Proceeds (market value)	450,000
Less: cost	(75,000)
	375,000

Part of the gain of £375,000 may be subject to a gift relief claim under s.165 TCGA 1992:

	£	£
Gain before relief		375,000
Less: *Excess actual proceeds:*		
Actual proceeds	375,000	
Less: cost	(75,000)	
Gain chargeable now		(300,000)
Gain eligible for gift relief		75,000
Gain taxed now		300,000

15.3 P J Laval

(1) CAPITAL GAINS TAX PAYABLE 2013/14

	£
House (W1)	60,000
Vic plc shares (W2)	5,910
Lavaling Ltd (W3)	15,000
Total gains	80,910
Less: Annual exempt amount	(10,900)
	70,010
Tax	
£7,500 @ 18% (£32,010 – £24,510)	1,350
£62,510 @ 28% (£70,010 – £7,500)	17,503
Total CGT	18,853

Workings

(W1) House 'Chez Nous' – 14 May 2013

	£	£
Proceeds		99,000
Less:		
Cost	37,000	
Enhancement	2,000	
		(39,000)
Chargeable gain		60,000

(W2)   Vic plc shares – 18 July 2013

Gain

	£
Proceeds	8,710
Cost (W)	(2,800)
Chargeable gain	5,910

Working – Share pool

	No. of shares	Cost
		£
Purchase 10.2.86	1,400	3,500
Bonus issue (1 for 4)	350	–
	1,750	3,500
Sale 18.7.13	(1,400)	(2,800)
c/f	350	700

(W3)   Lavaling Ltd shares – 31 March 2014

At the time of disposal, the market value of Lavaling Ltd's chargeable assets were:

	£
Chargeable business assets	
Freehold property	130,000
Other chargeable assets	
Quoted securities	30,000
	160,000

The proportion of the gain of £80,000 which is eligible for gift relief is found by applying the fraction:

$$\frac{\text{Market value of chargeable business assets}}{\text{Market value of chargeable assets}} = \frac{130,000}{160,000}$$

$$£80,000 \times \frac{130,000}{160,000} = £65,000$$

	£
Overall gain	80,000
Less: Gift relief	(65,000)
Chargeable gain	15,000

(2)   Freehold is an absolute interest in land. Subject to general law the freeholder can do as he wishes with the land.

A leasehold interest is qualified. The term is limited in time and the lease normally contains a range of covenants that are binding on the tenant.

Commonhold property is not a separate legal estate but is a freehold estate in commonhold land. It must originally be freehold. Individual parts (commonhold units) are held by the unit holders. Each unit holder is a member of the commonhold association which owns and manages the common parts of the property.

Marking scheme

		Marks
(1)	**CGT summary:**	
	Gains	1
	AEA	1
	Tax @ 18% on gains within BRB	1
	Tax @ 28% on gains above BRB	1
	House 'Chez Nous'	
	Enhancement expenditure	1
	Gain calculation	1
	Vic plc shares	
	Purchase	1
	Bonus issue	1
	Disposal from pool	1
	Gain calculation	1
	Lavaling Ltd shares	
	Identify CAs and CBAs	1
	CBA/CA fraction	1
	Proportion of gain eligible for gift relief	1
	Chargeable gain	1
	Max	13
(2)	Freehold – absolute interest	1
	Can do as wish with	1
	Leasehold – qualified interest	1
	Limited in time	½
	Limited by covenants	½
	Commonhold – not a separate legal estate	1
	Originally freehold	1
	Ownership	1
	Management association	1
	Max	5
	Total	18

15.4 Simon

To: Simon Evans
From: Frances Ackland
Date: 5 November 2013
Subject: Deferral of gains

Thank you for your memorandum of 3 November.

First of all, I have calculated that the gain on the disposal of the Blue Ltd shares is £150,000 (see Appendix).

Enterprise Investment Scheme

The relief you may have read about is Enterprise Investment Scheme deferral relief. Briefly, you can obtain the relief if you subscribe for new fully paid up ordinary shares in an unlisted trading company provided it is not carrying on certain non qualifying trades such as farming or property development. The acquisition must be made within one year before your disposal (but I presume this is not the case here) and three years after the disposal (ie by 29 October 2016). At the time of the acquisition, you must be resident in the United Kingdom. You must make the claim by the fifth anniversary of 31 January following the end of the tax year in which the EIS shares are issued (ie by 31 January 2020 if the EIS shares are issued in 2013/14). However, you may wish to make a claim sooner in order to avoid having to pay tax on the gain.

In order to defer the gain of £150,000 you would need to invest at least an amount equal to this gain. However, since you wish to invest about £100,000 of the proceeds in the French house, this leaves you only £100,000 to invest in the shares, so only £100,000 of the gain can be deferred. The remainder of the gain of £50,000 would remain chargeable to CGT. From this an annual exempt amount of £10,900 is deducted, leaving £39,100 chargeable to tax. As you are an additional rate taxpayer the tax rate is 28%, which would result in a liability of £10,948.

Any gains deferred would usually become chargeable when you sell the EIS shares. However, if you become not resident broadly within three years of the acquisition of the shares, the gain you have deferred will be treated as becoming chargeable immediately before this time. This is obviously a danger since you wish to move to France.

Seed Enterprise Investment Scheme

One other relief you may be interested in is Seed Enterprise Investment Scheme Reinvestment relief. This is similar to EIS deferral relief except that you are entitled to a CGT exemption of 50% of the amount that you spend on subscribing for new SEIS shares, rather than merely a deferral.

The maximum exemption available is £50,000 if you purchase shares worth £100,000 (the maximum allowable investment), which fits in perfectly with your requirements, but the balance of the gain would remain chargeable and cannot be deferred under the EIS scheme (above) as both reliefs cannot be claimed in respect of the same expenditure.

SEIS reinvestment relief is generally only available for disposals and reinvestments taking place in the 2013/14 tax year, so you would need to subscribe for such shares before 6 April 2014. However, it is possible to make the investment in the following year (2014/15) and make a claim to treat them as having been acquired in the previous year if necessary.

Note that your investment would be in smaller, early stage companies starting genuine new ventures so would be riskier than EIS investments or investments in quoted companies.

Please let me know if you require any further details.

Appendix

	£	£
Proceeds		200,000
Less: cost	65,000	
less: held over gain	(15,000)	(50,000)
Gain before relief		150,000

15.5   Emily

Computation of taxable gains:

	£
Factory (W1)	75,000
Painting (W2)	23,000
Shares (W4)	6,000
Less: current year loss relief (W3)	(27,000)
Net chargeable gains	77,000
Less: annual exempt amount	(10,900)
Taxable gains	66,100

CGT:

	£
£8,000 @ 18% (£32,010 – £24,010)	1,440
£58,100 @ 28% (£66,100 – £8,000)	16,268
Total CGT	17,708

Workings

1   *Factory*

	£
Proceeds	225,000
Less: cost	(150,000)
Chargeable gain	75,000

2   *Painting*

Transfer to Emily on 1 July 2004 on no gain/no loss basis

Sale by Emily

	£
	£
Proceeds	73,000
Less: cost (= cost to Arthur)	(50,000)
Chargeable gain	23,000

3   *Vase*

	£
	£
Proceeds	19,000
Less: cost	(46,000)
Loss	(27,000)

4   *Shares*

The sale of unquoted shares at below market value qualifies for gift relief:

	£
	£
Proceeds (MV) February 2014	80,000
Less: cost	(4,000)
	76,000
Excess of actual proceeds over cost (ie real profit): £10,000 – £4,000	(6,000)
Gain deferred	70,000
Gain chargeable in February 2014	6,000

15.6 **Peter**

Summary of gains:

	£
	£
Building (W1)	400,000
Forum Follies plc (W2)	5,000
Dassau plc (W3)	7,100
	412,100
Less: losses b/f	(6,400)
Chargeable gains	405,700
Less: annual exempt amount	(10,900)
Taxable gain	394,800

	£
	£
£2,500 @ 18% (£32,010 – £29,510)	450
£392,300 @ 28% (£394,800 – £2,500)	109,844
Total CGT	110,294
CGT due 31.1.15	

Workings

1   *Building*

	£
	£
Proceeds	600,000
Less: cost	(200,000)
Chargeable gain	400,000

2   *Takeover of Forum Follies plc*

A gain only arises on the date of the takeover in respect of the cash element:

	£
	£
Cash received (W)	10,000
Cost (W)	(5,000)
Chargeable gain	5,000

Working – Analysis of takeover consideration

Takeover package	Market value £	Original cost £
Shares: $\dfrac{20,000}{2} \times 3 \times £3.00$	90,000	45,000
Cash: $\dfrac{20,000}{2} \times £1$	10,000	5,000
Total	100,000	50,000

3   *Dassau plc shares*

(i)   *Gain*

	£
Proceeds	9,500
Less cost (W)	(2,400)
Chargeable gain	7,100

Working – Share pool

	No of shares	Cost £
Purchase: Dec 1987	1,000	2,000
Rights issue (1 for 2 @ £2)	500	1,000
	1,500	3,000
Disposal: Nov 2013	(1,200)	(2,400)
c/f	300	600

15.7   Sarah Stone

	£
Summary	
Peterson Ltd (W1)	82,000
Antique brooch (W2)	2,200
House (W4)	37,000
Stamp collection (W3)	(1,000)
	120,200
Less: capital losses b/f	(15,000)
Net chargeable gain	105,200
Less: annual exempt amount	(10,900)
Taxable gain	94,300
£1,000 @ 18% (£32,010 – £31,010)	180
£93,300 @ 28% (£94,300 – £1,000)	26,124
Total CGT	26,304

Workings

1   *Peterson Ltd shares*

     Gain

		£
Proceeds		150,000
Less: cost (W)		(68,000)
Chargeable gain		82,000

     Working – Share pool

	No of shares	Cost
		£
Acquisition 1.3.89	50,000	25,000
Purchase 1.8.02	5,000	10,000
	55,000	35,000
Rights issue (1 for 5 @ £3)	11,000	33,000
	66,000	68,000
Sale: 12 April 2013	(66,000)	(68,000)
	–	–

2   *Antique brooch (15.6.13)*

	£
Net proceeds (£8,250 – £250)	8,000
Less: cost	(5,800)
Chargeable gain	2,200

     Limited to: $^5/_3 \times (8,250 - 6,000) = £3,750$ (does not apply)

3   *Stamp collection (19.9.13)*

	£
Proceeds (deemed as a chattel sold for < £6,000)	6,000 (replace actual proceeds)
Less: cost	7,000
Allowable loss	(1,000)

4   *House (21.1.14)*

	£	£
Proceeds		75,000
Less: Cost	28,000	
Enhancement	10,000	
		(38,000)
Chargeable gain		37,000

16.1 Interest payments

(1)   *Payments on account for 2013/14 are based on the actual liability for 2012/13*

		£
Due	31 January 2014 (ie half of the 2012/13 self assessment)	10,000
	31 July 2014	10,000

The balancing payment for 2013/14 is due on 31 January following the end of the tax year:

		£
Due	31 January 2015	2,000

The payments actually made were as follows:

		£
Paid	2 March 2014	10,000
	2 September 2014	2,500
	31 January 2015	9,500
		22,000

Interest on late payment runs from the due date for payment until the actual date for payment as follows:

Due date	Paid	Amount	Months overdue	Interest rate	Interest due
		£		%	£
31 January 2014	2 March 2014	10,000	1	3	25
31 July 2014	2 September 2014	2,500	1	3	6
31 July 2014	31 January 2015	7,500	6	3	112
		20,000			143

(2) The due dates are:

	Due		Amount
			£
Payments on account	31 January 2014		10,000
	31 July 2014		10,000
Balancing payment	31 January 2015		NIL

Interest due is as follows:

Due date	Amount due	Paid	Amount paid	Amount charged	Months overdue	Interest rate	Interest due
	£		£	£		%	£
31 January 2014 (N1)	9,000	2/3/14	10,000	9,000	1	3	22
31 July 2014	9,000	2/9/14	2,500	2,500	1	3	6
31 July 2014	Nil	31/1/15	5,500	6,500(N2)	6	3	97
	18,000		18,000				125

Notes.

(1) Originally £10,000 was due (50% × 2012/13 self assessment of £20,000). However late payment interest under Para 2 Sch 53 FA 2009 is only charged on a POA of £9,000, ie 50% of the final liability.

(2) Interest is charged on the amount underpaid, ie £9,000 – £2,500.

16.2 Radnor

(1) Interest on late payment of tax

	Due date	Tax originally due	Amended tax	Interest rate	Date of payment	Tax overdue	Months overdue	Interest payable
		£	£	%		£		£
(1)	31 January 2014	5,000	3,000	3	31 March 2014	3,000	2	15
(2)	31 July 2014	5,000	3,000	3	30 September 2014	3,000	2	15
(3)	31 January 2015	–	1,500	3	31 January 2015	–		

There will also be interest on the £1,500 – £750 of which should have been paid on 31 January 2014 and £750 on 31 July 2014:

	Due date	Tax originally due	Amended tax	Interest rate	Date of payment	Tax overdue	Months overdue	Interest payable
		£	£	%		£		£
(4)	31 January 2014	–	750	3	31 January 2015	750	12	22
(5)	31 July 2014	–	750	3	31 January 2015	750	6	11

(2) Penalty on an incorrect claim to reduce payments on account

The maximum penalty is the difference between the amount that would have been paid, but for the fraudulent claim, and the amount of payments on account actually made.

	£
Tax actually due 2013/14	7,500
Tax paid – reduced payments on account	(6,000)
Penalty (maximum)	1,500

Personal Taxation

Index

BPP
LEARNING MEDIA

REVIEW FORM

Name: _____   Address: _____

_____

How have you used this Text?
(Tick one box only)

☐ Home study (book only)

☐ On a course_____

☐ Other _____

Why did you decide to purchase this Text?
(Tick one box only)

☐ Have used BPP Learning Media Texts in the past

☐ Recommendation by friend/colleague

☐ Recommendation by a lecturer

☐ Saw advertising

☐ Other _____

During the past six months do you recall seeing/receiving either of the following?
(Tick as many boxes as are relevant)

☐ Our advertisement in *Tax Adviser*

☐ Our Publishing Catalogue

Which (if any) aspects of our advertising do you think are useful?
(Tick as many boxes as are relevant)

☐ Prices and publication dates of new editions

☐ Information on Text content

☐ Facility to order books off-the-page

☐ None of the above

Your ratings, comments and suggestions would be appreciated on the following areas of this Text.

	Very useful	Useful	Not useful
Introductory section	☐	☐	☐
Quality of explanations	☐	☐	☐
Examples	☐	☐	☐
Chapter roundups	☐	☐	☐
Exam focus points / Examiner's reports	☐	☐	☐
Legislative references	☐	☐	☐
Question bank	☐	☐	☐
Answer bank	☐	☐	☐
Index	☐	☐	☐

	Excellent	Good	Adequate	Poor
Overall opinion of this Text	☐	☐	☐	☐

Do you intend to continue using BPP Learning Media Products?   ☐ Yes   ☐ No

Please note any further comments and suggestions/errors on the reverse of this page. The BPP Learning Media publishing manager of this edition can be e-mailed at: ambercottrell@bpp.com

Please return to: Amber Cottrell, Tax Publishing Manager, BPP Learning Media Ltd, FREEPOST, London, W12 8AA.

REVIEW FORM (continued)

TELL US WHAT YOU THINK

Please note any further comments and suggestions/errors below.